DATE DUE

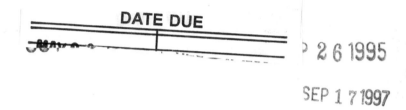

LOVE, Janis

★

LOVE, Janis

★

Laura Joplin

VILLARD BOOKS
NEW YORK
1992

Library of Congress Cataloging-in-Publication Data

Joplin, Laura.
   Love, Janis / Laura Joplin.—1st ed.
      p.   cm.
   Includes index.
   ISBN 0-679-41605-6
   1. Joplin, Janis. 2. Singers—United States—Biography. 3. Rock
musicians—United States—Biography. I. Title
ML420.J77J6   1992
782.42166'092—dc20   92-53652
[B]

Design by Robert Bull Design

Manufactured in the United States of America

9 8 7 6 5 4 3 2
First edition

This book is dedicated to Janis Joplin,
and to all those who loved her.

CONTENTS

★

CHAPTER ONE October 1970   3

CHAPTER TWO Our Ancestors   11

CHAPTER THREE Janis's Childhood   21

CHAPTER FOUR Adolescence   45

CHAPTER FIVE College and the Venice Beat Scene   73

CHAPTER SIX Austin, Texas   91

CHAPTER SEVEN The San Francisco Beat Scene   115

CHAPTER EIGHT Home Again   131

CHAPTER NINE The San Francisco Hippie Movement   145

CHAPTER TEN Success with Big Brother   171

CHAPTER ELEVEN After the Monterey Pop Festival   199

CHAPTER TWELVE Breaking Up with Big Brother   217

CHAPTER THIRTEEN The Band from Beyond   243

CHAPTER FOURTEEN Rest, Romance, and Regroup   267

CHAPTER FIFTEEN Full Tilt Triumph   285

★

CHAPTER SIXTEEN The Memorial Celebration   313

Acknowledgments and Sources   329

Index   337

LOVE, Janis

★

OCTOBER 1970

★

What good can drinking do?
What good can drinking do?
I drink all night,
But the next day I still feel blue

—Janis Joplin, "What Good Can Drinking Do?"

*I*N THE FALL of 1970 I was living a graduate student's bohemian life in a roomy Victorian apartment in a seedy neighborhood in south Dallas, Texas. Sunday afternoon, October 4, 1970, I spent quietly at home. I made myself a cup of tea and stepped from the kitchen to walk through the dining room. Pouring through the large window, the brilliant afternoon sunshine soaked my body.

I paused as thoughts fleetingly passed through my mind until I was grabbed by an overwhelming desire to speak with my sister. I hesitated, thinking of the trouble I would have if she didn't answer the telephone—the difficulty of trying to prove to whoever picked up the phone that I was really Janis Joplin's sister. Then the hesitation vanished. Walking toward the telephone, I was thrilled by that unique bond I had with my older and more daring sister.

I had last seen Janis during the middle of August 1970. Our relationship had a special constancy that went beyond time apart and dissimilar lives. We didn't always agree and sometimes shared heated words about our differences, but that would drop away each time we met. In August we had talked about sex, romance, marriage, careers, cars, houses, clothes, our hometown, her fame, and our family. When we parted, we had planned to get together in California at Christmas, when I had time off from graduate school.

By the time I walked across the yellowed oak floor to the telephone beside my bed in the living room, the compulsion to call had evaporated. I felt no reason even to try. But the thought would come back to me that night. Why hadn't I called? I went to bed early, readying myself for a busy class schedule the next day. I was fast asleep, relaxed under the quilts, when the telephone rang.

"Janis is dead," my father's tense voice stated simply. It was one o'clock early Monday morning. The startling words seemed unreal. I pulled myself from sleep just enough to answer, "No." He repeated, "Janis is dead." I shook my head as though trying to throw the unwanted words out, repeating insistently, "No." Shock slammed into my heart and hardened it like ice crystals. Janis was dead.

My roommate appeared from her bedroom, knowing something was wrong. "Janis is dead," I repeated to her. She disappeared and reappeared with two aspirins and a glass of water. "What are these for?" I asked. "Take them," she urged, trying to give me the kind of comfort an American knew best. I downed them, knowing I hadn't the vaguest idea of how to stop the ache. I cried myself into a troubled sleep, wondering, Why didn't I call her this afternoon?

The next day my parents telephoned, saying they were going to Los Angeles to settle Janis's affairs. My brother, Michael, and I did not go, as our parents wanted to keep us away from the cameras and press attention. Crowds of people had gathered outside the Landmark Hotel, where she lay, as word slowly spread among her friends. Police stretched out the official yellow KEEP OUT ribbons and the crowd milled and shivered in confusion, frustration, grief, and shock.

Mother's sister, Barbara Irwin, lived in Los Angeles, and she helped my parents with the necessary arrangements. They met Janis's attorney, Robert Gordon, whose elegance and firmness both comforted and frustrated them. From Bob they learned the details of Janis's death and about the stipulation in her will that her body be cremated and her ashes scattered off the California coast near Marin. My parents were anguished. Not only had they lost their firstborn daughter, but they couldn't even take her home for a proper burial.

Before he left Texas, my father had told me that they weren't sure of the cause of Janis's death. It might be a drug overdose, but it could also be that she passed out, fell, and suffocated in the shag carpet. When they got to California, they neglected to call me, they were so consumed by their duties there. I wandered around Dallas in a vacuum of facts, hearing the litany on the radio and the gossip of the partially informed in the halls of Southern Methodist University's classroom buildings.

I became furious at those faceless rock-and-roll people who had considered themselves Janis's friends. How could they let her do heroin? Everyone was doing drugs, including me, but heroin was different! She should have known better! They should have stopped her! Didn't anyone care enough to intervene? I chastised myself for not having been a better sister and knowing about the heroin. Why didn't someone do something? Most of all I blamed her role as the Queen of Rock and Roll, that lofty perch from which no mortal woman could hear caution or wisdom.

The coroner's report was soon final, and the verdict was an overdose of heroin. She had only been using for a few weeks, taking it as a late-night relaxer every third day or so, after a hard day recording a new album for Columbia Records.

My parents wrangled with Bob Gordon, and he fretted with the press, the police, and the coroner to ensure a quiet ceremony for the family to pay their last respects. In a funeral chapel they said good-bye to Janis while my brother and I both sat in confused isolation in separate Texas towns.

Nothing showed the weaknesses in our family quite like the way we handled Janis's death. We had no funeral to attend as a family. There was no grave for a later pilgrimage. There was no wake full of loved ones who could share our affection and our loss. We cried alone.

It would never be enough to say simply that I loved Janis. She meant much more to me than that. When I was born, Janis was six years old. She took me under her wing as soon as I was able to hobble after her. On the wall of the bedroom we shared, Mother hung pictures of two girls giggling and telling stories to each other. That is how I remember my early years, intertwined with my constant companion and interpreter of the world, my elder sister. She helped me with everything and took me everywhere. In turn, I idolized her.

★

With six years' difference in age, our daily experiences were often inexplicable to one another. I started grade school when she went on to junior high. I started junior high when she was entering college. I started college when she became the hippie rock-and-roll queen. So our relationship was never based on sharing the same challenges in life. Our alliance was something more basic, a fundamental trust that continued through all changing circumstances. We talked straight to the core. We shared images, fantasies, and feelings that were like secret rooms that others might not even know existed.

My parents called and I got the final details. It was finished, in some ways. In other ways my experience had hardly begun. Several weeks after Janis died, Bob Gordon called. "Would you like to come to the party? Janis left twenty-five hundred dollars in her will to throw a party for her friends after her death." Janis had been taken by the idea of partying after a friend died. She told writer Michael Thomas, "Chocolate George [so nicknamed because he had a passion for chocolate milk], one of the Angels, got killed, and they threw a free thing in the park. We got lots of beer, and they got the Dead and us [Big Brother]. It was just a beautiful thing, all the hippies and Angels were just stoned out of their heads . . . you couldn't imagine a better funeral. It was the greatest party in the world." When Bob asked me to come to Janis's party, I didn't delay in saying, "Yes, I'll come." I never hesitated in going. I had to see what it was like out there and who those people were. I needed to touch her house and her things, and find bits of her life that I hadn't known from my vantage in Texas.

Janis's house was half-empty when I arrived October 25, as she had left her possessions to her friends. Many had already come by to claim an Oriental rug, a carved cherry cabinet, and other special items. Bob gallantly explained that he figured sisters were friends too, and that if I saw anything I wanted to keep, I should tell him. The furniture was already promised, her roommate Lyndall Erb explained. So I searched among the remaining trivia. I found my keepsake, a silver-plated cigarette lighter I had given Janis for her birthday. It had embossed roses around its oval belly. It was heavy in my hand, and the weight felt good. Lyndall said it was broken, as though, Who would want that? I didn't even smoke. I didn't need the fire, just the warmth of the connection. A gift from me to Janis, and now from Janis to me.

Janis's California crew didn't know what to do with me, but

they did put me up in her house. Lyndall Erb had moved into Janis's bedroom after she died. Lyndall went through the pretense of offering to move out so I could stay there. I declined, saying the bed in the living room was fine for me.

Arriving at the party at the Lion's Share in San Anselmo on October 26, I sat amid people trying to force themselves to be jovial, but they naturally turned to quiet conversations about who was doing what. Someone next to me eagerly pointed out the tie-dyed satin sheet that hung behind a pick-up band of friends playing onstage. They crowed that a recent lover of Janis's had torn that big hole in it while in the midst of passion because he had kept his cowboy boots on. Several people pushed renowned tattoo artist Lyle Tuttle to take his shirt off and show me his tattooed torso. He and I agreed that we didn't think it necessary.

Someone offered me a brownie, and I was eager for some food, having eaten little at dinner. Only later did he mention that they were hashish brownies. The air was getting thick inside my head, and I beat a hasty retreat on the arms of Bob Gordon and John Cooke, Janis's lanky and amiable road manager, an Easterner who had refashioned himself in Western garb. I reached the sidewalk and the cool night air just in time to throw up on John Cooke's left boot. I thought it couldn't get much worse!

The coup de grâce was waking from my drug-induced slumber to feel Seth Morgan, a ruggedly handsome man who had been introduced to me as Janis's fiancé, trying to slide into the bed in which I was sleeping in the living room. A woman wrapped in blankets on the floor nearby stopped him, saying, "Janis's sister is there. Come over here." So he crawled in beside her, trying to reject her enticing caresses, but finally relenting. Janis's supposed fiancé made love to her close girl-friend on the night of Janis's wake.

I spent a mere three days in San Francisco, but I had been to Janis's home, and I had met her friends and then some. I was ready to go back to Texas and my own life. I thought my grieving was over. I thought I was returning to the routine of life, friends, and work that made up my life in Texas. But I had barely graced the first stage of grief—shock. I still had to live through the ravages of sorrow, guilt, anger, regret, and fear.

My family took years to share our grief over Janis's death. A door had closed the day she died, and no matter how hard Michael and I tried, we hardly ever got our parents to open it again. Pop's agony over losing his daughter turned visible as arthritis spread to every joint in his body. He lived out his sorrow, always worried that his support of Janis's nontraditional inclinations had contributed to her death. When Michael and I showed signs of asocial behavior, he was quick to warn against it, obviously worried about where it would lead us.

Mom locked her feelings in an internal closet that held all the warm memories of an adored firstborn child and worries over a daughter's transgressions. She was never as gentle, soft, or loving again after Janis died. It was almost as if she believed that acknowledging her colossal grief would knock her to the ground, and she would never rise again. Instead, she tended Janis's fans like a gardener cared for her flowers. Until Mom's eyesight failed, every fan who wrote the family a letter after Janis died received a heartfelt response. She worked to give them the guidance that they requested. She wanted to answer their complaints about the world's mistreatment of them. She wrote to one woman:

How do I cope with the memories? Simply by remembering with joy the happy times and the many, many times of laughter we had with all our children. These far outweigh the lesser times and problems.

How do I cope with remembering the problems? Trying to do so without bitterness, knowing my children were loaned to me for 16–18 years; they were not my possessions. Each child growing up and becoming self-sufficient must untie the maternal/paternal umbilical cord. Gradually in adult lives, our young people begin to relate to us as people, and we can relate to them as other, completely separate individuals.

How do I cope with bitterness? I just give it up, without reservation and without looking back wondering "if this" or "if that." . . . To fail to do so will result in a warped perspective which twists upon itself. It is not easy; I try and keep on trying.

How do I cope with the anguish of losing a daughter? Simply by being grateful for the times with her and the riches it did bring . . . and NEVER, NEVER forgetting.

How do I ever forgive? It takes working at. It MUST be done. After all, I am NOT the judge of any person, either evil or good. The religious thesis in prayer is: Forgive MY sins as I forgive others. That being so, I must do it.

My own grief settled into my life like a cat settling into a sun-warmed spot on a rug, except its claws were always extended to cause piercing pain if ever I loosened my stiff control of my life. I carried it around for eighteen years, until one day it burst out as anger. I kicked boxes of files around my office, files that contained the legal papers that defined my obligation to Janis's career. I grabbed every artifact of hers that lay around my house and boxed them up and shipped them to my brother. I made him come get her Porsche, which I had stored in my garage. I was desperately trying to be free of something. Finally I broke down and sobbed. Grief jolted my body, bringing old memories to mind like slides of a personal travelogue. It felt so bloody good, I sought out every last kernel of hiding sorrow and threw it away, forever. Finally I understood that I had held on to my grief because it seemed like the last thing I had of her; it had been my silent resistance to accepting her death. It was an absurd emotional overreaction, but afterward when I walked down the hall, I seemed to float. I was giddy. I was free.

That specter haunted me no more. I didn't know what other masks there were to be torn away, but having tossed aside this one, I was unafraid of the others. I found myself strangely drawn to a better understanding of Janis.

I listened to these words that my sister spoke, reflecting an idea from our common upbringing: "Don't compromise yourself, it's all you got." I knew that my search for Janis was about the truth. I could not be content with anything less than a full understanding of her life, her choices, and her times.

Janis said, "Let yourself go and you'll be more than you've ever thought of being." Free of my grief, I was free to love her again. I released my assumptions about Janis, willing to let her life tell me what it could.

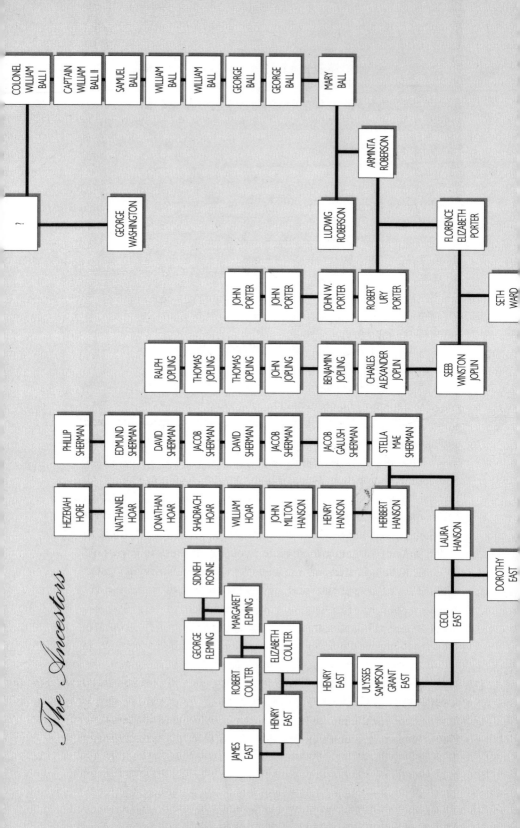

The Ancestors

COLONEL WILLIAM BALL I

CAPTAIN WILLIAM BALL II

SAMUEL BALL

WILLIAM BALL

WILLIAM BALL

GEORGE BALL

GEORGE BALL

MARY BALL

?

GEORGE WASHINGTON

ARMINTA ROBERSON

LUDWIG ROBERSON

FLORENCE ELIZABETH PORTER

JOHN PORTER

JOHN PORTER

JOHN W. PORTER

ROBERT URY PORTER

SETH WARD

RALPH JOPLING

THOMAS JOPLING

THOMAS JOPLING

JOHN JOPLING

BENJAMIN JOPLING

CHARLES ALEXANDER JOPLIN

SEEB WINSTON JOPLIN

PHILIP SHERMAN

EDMUND SHERMAN

DAVID SHERMAN

JACOB SHERMAN

DAVID SHERMAN

JACOB SHERMAN

JACOB GALUSH SHERMAN

STELLA MAE SHERMAN

HEZEKIAH HOAR

NATHANIEL HOAR

JONATHAN HOAR

SHADRACH HOAR

WILLIAM HOAR

JOHN MILTON HANSON

HENRY HANSON

HERBERT HANSON

LAURA HANSON

SIDNEH ROSINE

MARGARET FLEMING

GEORGE FLEMING

ELIZABETH COULTER

ROBERT COULTER

HENRY EAST

ULYSSES SAMPSON GRANT EAST

CECIL EAST

DOROTHY EAST

JAMES EAST

HENRY EAST

CHAPTER TWO

OUR ANCESTORS

★

When I'm sitting round late in the evening, child
Wondering why, why, why did I ever leave
Well, I went out searching for something, baby
I left it behind now, babe, now I see

—Janis Joplin, "Catch Me, Daddy"

HE NAMES THAT I know from my father's side
of the family are Joplin (or Jopling), Porter, and Ball. My
mother's family name was East, with Hanson (formerly
Hoar, and before that, Hore), Sherman, Coulter, Fleming, and Rosine
also related.

The first of my ancestors to reach the American shores were
fishermen from the Hore family who ventured the rough Atlantic to
harvest the rich waters off Nova Scotia. There, twenty-five-year-old
Hezekiah Hore was stung by the salt spray of opportunity. He lusted
for the miles of unused farmland, dense forests, and thriving game. He
was the second son in a second marriage. Besides a fishing fleet, the
family owned rich land leases from the days of Henry VIII's confisca-
tion of the Catholic Church's property. None would be his because he
was not the eldest son. In 1633, twelve years after the *Mayflower* first
landed, Hezekiah Hore sailed on the ship *Recovery* to a new life in the
Massachusetts Bay colony.

Hore joined a group of cousins and neighbors in founding the
town of Taunton, Massachusetts. He settled among people generally

★

considered to be Puritans, but from the first, nonbelievers were a sizable minority. These other Pilgrims celebrated life in colorful clothes and with hearty laughter. Hezekiah prospered as a farmer and business-man. Like his peers, he sought to break away from the tyranny of the Church of England, the English government, and an economic system that kept each man slotted into the station of life in which he was born.

Conflicting religious sects disrupted the otherwise tranquil coex-istence of the colonists. Each group was an uncompromising defender of its own views. Puritans, Baptists, Separatists, and Quakers argued heatedly. At the height of the tyranny of oppression in the Plymouth colony, ships carrying Quakers could be fined and the Quakers whipped and imprisoned. Several were hanged.

Roger Williams set many hearts on fire because of his cries for religious tolerance and respect for the Indians. His accusations in-fluenced the life of another of my ancestors in the Bay colony, Phillip Sherman, Williams's son-in-law. "No man has the right to force an-other to join any church!" Williams complained. "There should be no state religion in the new land." He especially infuriated settlers with his defiant support of Indian rights. He lived among them, learned their language, and charged, "No Englishman should take the land of the Indians without permission and payment." His troublemaking views so threatened the Plymouth colony, they evicted him and his followers. Phillip Sherman left with this group of more liberal colonists to form the colony of Rhode Island. The remaining Bible-reading settlers cap-tured the surviving Indians and sold them into slavery in the West Indies.

Reacting to their parent's zeal, the children of the first settlers ushered in a new era of caution and stability. William Ball, one of my father's ancestors, moved from Chesapeake Bay to Virginia, where he built his Georgian-style mansion, Millenbeck. He would be the grand-father of George Washington.

Phillip Sherman became a Quaker, a farmer, and a speaker at meetings. John Porter and Thomas Jopling were farmers in Virginia. All were caught up in the "Great Awakening," a time of religious fervor and discovery of an inner self in the early 1700s. This group cast off their parents' views that mere living could bring satisfaction. They wanted the "New Light" to shine from within, so that all would know the glory and euphoria of a spiritual rebirth. They hit the roads and founded new communes, denounced slavery, and converted Indians while revitalizing their churches.

Frontier wars also consumed their energy. During the seven years (1755-63) of the French and Indian War, thousands of settlers lost their lives. A young Swedish woman who was my mother's first American ancestor, Sidneh Rosine Brown, felt the brunt of the abominable violence of the racial and territorial clashes. It was night when a knock came at the door. "Who keeps house?" the English voice asked. Her young husband opened the door and his surprised body was pierced through by Indian lances. Sidneh's two-year-old baby's head was smashed against the door frame. The house and barn, with livestock inside, were burned as the band of six Indians and one Frenchman dressed as an Indian danced and whooped in the smoky night air. Sidneh was forced to march with them to Canada and gave birth to a son along the way. The Indians gave this new life their ceremonial christening in an ice-cold stream. Sidneh won the approval of her captors when she refused to eat her share of the last edible thing that they carried, a leather pouch that had held rifle shot. She was eventually sold to the French in Canada for $5.30 and stayed with the governor to recuperate before she was traded back to the English settlements.

Sidneh returned to Virginia, where she married George Fleming, a recent emigrant to the New World. A man of great girth and guts, his ship had foundered on rocks three miles from the coast with no lifeboats on board. Throwing his belongings and his gold overboard, George Fleming had lashed himself to his wooden trunk and floated to land on an incoming tide. Settling down, George and Sidneh made a comfortable life for themselves buying convict labor contracts.

The smaller wars eventually erupted into the major conflict of the times, the American Revolution. John Porter enlisted in 1776 as a sergeant. Shadrach Hoar became a corporal. One from Virginia and one from Massachusetts, they fought in the same campaign to stop the British in their northern assault on the colonies. This, the Saratoga campaign, was a decisive and skillful battle, which succeeded due to the skill and daring of the commander, Benedict Arnold, a man history recalls for his later traitorous acts.

★

Jacob Sherman defied his Quaker upbringing to shoulder a rifle and march into the fray in Boston. He fought in a battle that became known as Bunker Hill. In his "Crisis" paper of December 23, 1776, Thomas Paine described the day: "These are the times that try men's souls. The summer soldier and the sunshine patriot will, in this crisis, shrink from the service of their country; but he that stands it now deserves the love and thanks of man and woman."

Far from receiving the gratitude of his loved ones for his efforts, Jacob Sherman was disowned by his parents for violating the Quaker belief in nonviolence. His efforts helped found a country but tore apart a family. He was the last of the Quakers in our family.

The next generation of family members brought all of my family groups westward. Benjamin Jopling was a scrawny Scotsman with the large, rough hands of a man used to hard work. In 1826 Jopling joined the Methodist Church during one of its tent revivals and his life changed abruptly. The Methodist Church was the first to publicly disclaim slavery. The Methodist-Episcopal Church split off in 1844 as a proslavery movement, and Benjamin went with them. They were a true people's church, with no paid missionaries. The spirit moved members to pass the word along by traveling in community groups to new territories and founding new churches.

This inner force compelled Benjamin Jopling to uproot his family from their relatives and head for the frontier in northeastern Alabama. White men had recently found gold on lands owned by the Cherokees. No amount of diplomatic wrangling could keep the federal government from finding a way to force the Cherokees from their land. Benjamin became an established community member until urged on by the signs of TEXAS OR BUST on wagons passing through. He finally settled near Fort Worth, where he farmed and helped to build the fort that gave the settlement its name. Along the way he was married four times, had twenty-two children, and outlived all of his wives.

John Milton Hanson took a northern route in his westward journey from Massachusetts. His father, William Hoar, had changed the family name to Hanson. With his new bride, Lauretta, John first tried the life in New York and then Ohio until they settled Henry County, Iowa, thirty miles from the Mississippi River. In exchange for the team of horses that had hauled them to Iowa, they received raw land.

14

Ten years later, the ever-alluring call of a better future obliged John Hanson to chase his dreams in the California Gold Rush. He left his wife and eight children, taking his eldest son with him. His wife soon died and the children were placed with neighbors and relatives until, six years later, John returned home to resume his role as householder. He was a man of marked intelligence, had wide respect within the community, and lived to a ripe old age.

In Virginia, John W. Porter married the daughter of a Baptist preacher. The young couple planned their future from stories in letters from John's brother, Beverly Porter, who lived in the distant world of Texas, then a Mexican territory. John's wife was a tough pioneer woman, stout of body and strong of heart, whose inner convictions and faith in her husband carried her across the frontier. In 1833, husband and wife, two children, and a handful of slaves set off from Nashville on a flatboat bound for New Orleans. Porter had loaded the boat with pork and stoves as trade goods, which he bartered for sailboat passage to the Texas port of Velasco. There they found brother Beverly Porter dying in the cholera epidemic of 1833. Undaunted, John and his group made salt from seawater to afford the purchase of oxen and wagons to begin their inland journey. They dogged the twists and turns of the Brazos River until they reached a rolling, hilly area that was lush with deep green grass and dotted with pines. There Porter claimed his homestead as allowed by treaty. He called it Porter's Prairie, and fashioned crude log cabins for himself and his slave families.

John W. Porter's son, Robert Ury Porter (my father's great-grandfather), shared the gift of making a fortune with many in his generation. After his father's death, he managed his mother's interests. He bred cattle and cultivated the raw land with grains and fruits. He had his slaves cut and mill lumber from the farm and the East Texas woodlands. They built the first two-story house in Burleson County, a white clapboard affair modeled after the gracious Southern home. It had broad verandas front and back, with the upper porches for sleeping during the muggy Texas summer nights. There was a central hall with rooms on either side and a detached kitchen to keep the all-too-common kitchen fires from spreading.

Robert got married and took his young bride to New York to buy furniture for their new home: oak four-poster beds, highboys and lowboys, rugs, and a parlor piano. He built the first Methodist Church

★

and the first school building in the county. During the Civil War, Robert served as a purchasing agent for the Confederacy. The success of his group's connection to Mexico enabled the South to maintain its forces much longer than it could have if it had relied solely on Southern supplies.

Robert's brother joined Terry's Texas Rangers, the scourge of the Northern armies. This group was known for its daring and pluck, though by the end of the war two-thirds had lost their lives. They rode thoroughbred mounts and time after time defeated the Yankees, who paled in comparison to the cunning Comanches, whom the Texans had fought at home.

On the other side of the Civil War fought the Hansons. Henry W. Hanson (my mother's great-grandfather) enlisted as a volunteer in the Fourth Iowa Cavalry when he was eighteen. He served as an orderly in a General Roberts's headquarters. His awe of the service was such that he wore his uniform often years after the conflict had ended.

His generation of progressives was attuned to serving society, and Henry joined the Masonic Lodge and the Grand Army of the Republic, which was devoted to the active work of relief. At birth he had been named merely Henry, but as an adult, with his respect for the pomp of institutional life, he felt the need for a middle name, so he gave himself the initial *W.*

The next generation continued the westward migration, with Mother's family stopping in Nebraska. Ulysses Sampson Grant East, my mother's grandfather, was an Illinois boy born to patriotic parents during the Civil War. Grant, as he was called, caught the fever of the Oklahoma land rush in which several of his relatives participated, but he took a more northerly route. A soft-spoken but autocratic man, Grant ended up farming in the southeastern corner of the state, in an area the Pawnee Indians had recently been forced to vacate.

Grant's neighbor was a fellow recently relocated from Iowa, Herbert Hanson. Herbert had lost his job as a mail carrier in Iowa and couldn't farm because of a baseball injury to his leg. His father told him, "Go to Nebraska, Herbert. Any man who can lift a hammer can earn a good living there." Since Herbert's family had sometimes been reduced to eating potatoes for lunch and potato water for dinner, they needed a change. In Nebraska he prospered, eventually owning both a plumbing store and a secondhand furniture store.

Herbert was active in the Republican party. If you wanted something done in the little farming community of Clay Center, Nebraska, you were told, "Go see Herbert Hanson. He can make it happen." In fact, he was so politically and socially active that his wife, Stella Mae Sherman Hanson, was left alone to raise their eight children. She resented his absences and became fretful, often writing her children (when they were grown) sentences that started with, "I am grieving so about . . ."

W.E.B. Du Bois began the first movement asserting equal rights for blacks while my Porter ancestors were forced to deal with their ownership of slaves. Family myth says Robert Porter called his slaves together and said, "Those of you who want to leave may. I will take care of any of you who wish to stay." To his credit, he did help buy land and mules for one of these families. He taught his children that slavery was wrong. He could accept defeat and change.

My grandmother Florence Porter Joplin started life in the protected Southern tradition, which soon gave way to the economic realities of the late 1800s. Born to a father who was sixty-two years of age, she suffered from his declining ability to farm the land. While visiting a cousin in Big Springs, Texas, she helped entertain by baking fresh breakfast rolls for a group of cowboys who came calling on Sundays. She soon wed the shy ranch foreman, Seeb Joplin.

Seeb had been raised near Lubbock, Texas, as the eldest of eleven children. Seeb's father, Charles Alexander Joplin (who had dropped the *g* in Jopling), helped found the local Methodist Church and served as a county commissioner. He helped lay out streets, design municipal buildings, and plan social charities. Charles was a man of humor and industry, but he did not put much faith in education for his children. Rather, he felt they should shoulder much of the burden of the farm work. Seeb was a markedly intelligent boy, but got little more than a sixth-grade education. His training on the land would have stood him well in earlier eras, but he came of age when all the land available for homesteading was gone.

Seeb flirted with the romance of new frontiers when he drove a herd of cattle from the ranch he managed to Billings, Montana. With his brother, he ventured on a narrow-gauge railway to Dawson, Alaska. He was offered eight hundred dollars to winter over just to keep one cow alive, but he shied from the snowbound climate and returned to

★

Texas. He and Florence raised their two children on a large ranch they managed outside Tahoka, Texas. Women's suffrage may have been voted into law in 1920, but real emancipation for my families came in reduced numbers of children. Florence Porter Joplin grew up in a family of sixteen. She had only two children. That was liberation! My father, Seth Ward Joplin, was born in 1910, the second and last child of Seeb and Florence.

"Ask the madam," is how Seeb dealt with many questions his two children asked him. It was a sign of the formality that governed their household, even in its remote spot on the West Texas plains. Grandmother Joplin taught her children to respect people because of their merits. She had learned a lesson during the Reconstruction days of riots, race-related killings of blacks and whites, and the Republicans in state government forcing real estate taxes so high that the prewar owners would be forced to sell their land. The lesson was how to lay low, and she passed it on.

One of the frequent stock-market panics caught the ranch's owner in its tumultuous slide and forced the sale of the land Seeb managed. For a time he was the sheriff of the town of Tahoka, but his personality was too gentle. Seeb finally found his niche managing the stockyards in Amarillo, Texas. Florence helped by running a boarding-house for the men who worked for Seeb. Her cooking was so good that men sought jobs with Seeb for that reason alone. Florence learned to drive an automobile solely so that she could attend cooking classes.

In Nebraska, my mother's parents, Cecil East and Laura Hanson, met and married in the farming community of Clay Center. They were still caught in the fever of land ownership and moved along with the East clan to western Oklahoma. They traded Nebraska farms for Oklahoma ranches. Cecil's temperament suited the independence and roughness of a rancher's life. His little herd thrived and he was committed to developing the local community. His wife, however, pined for her family in Clay Center and broached the subject so often that her husband finally relented. With two toddling children they returned to the Hanson family routine of Sunday dinners and singing around the piano.

Cecil was an ambitious man. He roamed the countryside looking for livestock to buy and trade to supplement his basic farming income. Laura tended an acre-sized kitchen garden, canning and storing in the root cellar enough food for the family to eat throughout the year. They both worked long and hard, but Cecil put all his money into high-profit hogs who contracted a disease and had to be put to death. They were devastated because losing the hogs cost them the farm. Laura took the children to live with her parents. Cecil moved to Amarillo to find work and a way to support his family. He soon succeeded, selling what a farmer knew best: real estate.

The East family moved to Amarillo during my mother's senior year in high school. Mom saw her mother lose her integral place in the family economy when her father began earning wages instead of sharing the farm work with his wife. The new roles forced upon Cecil and Laura were not kindly accepted by either. They, in turn, blamed each other for the unwanted patterns of their new lives. They shouted at each other, tormenting their four children with their arguing. Cecil began to have affairs, hunting for the solace his wife could not give him. He also began to drink occasionally, a clear affront to Laura's increasingly strict religious views.

All of my grandparents began life on a rural frontier, but their children became city dwellers. The structures that had defined life since the founding of the country—the Bible, the family, and personal reputation—were beginning to lose their pivotal power. From one generation to the next, seemingly outdated ideas, guideposts, attitudes, and ambitions were cast aside with the changing look each new group of adolescents saw in their future.

Authors William Strauss and Neil Howe, in their book *Generations,* describe the process as a predictable cyclical set of stages. In twenty-year increments, our society focuses and refocuses its energy. The culture moves through a concentration on spiritual experiences and personal growth into a period of recommitment to civic groups that work diligently solving cultural crises. Strauss and Howe describe American culture as oscillating between two pivotal poles: "SECULAR CRISES, when society focuses on reordering the outer world of institutions and public behavior; and SPIRITUAL AWAKENINGS, when society focuses on changing the inner world of values and private behavior."

The ambitions and expectations of any one person are thus defined by the times in which they were born and raised. Their cohorts, born during the same twenty-year time period, share a unique set of historical experiences as well as "society-wide attitudes toward families, schooling, sex roles, religion, crime, careers, and personal risk," explain Strauss and Howe. "At various moments in history, Americans have chosen to be more protective of children, or more generous to old people, or more tolerant of unconventional young adults. Then, after a while, the mood has swung the other way. Each time this happened, the social environment changed differently from each cohort-group. . . . Trees planted in the same year contain rings that indicate when they all met with a cold winter, wet spring, or dry summer. Cohort-groups are like trees in this respect. They carry within them a unique signature of history's bygone moments."

My ancestors were born, lived, and died as part of generational groups that were formed and limited by the historical events and attitudes of their day. They in turn exhibited like characteristics, causing and reacting to other historical events that formed the life experiences of a generational group that followed them. The story of my ancestors' lives is the saga of American pioneers, exploring and sometimes conquering what was seen as the frontier of their day. Whether it was spiritual growth, homesteading land, or founding institutions that promised answers to then urgent questions, my family members committed their lives to the task. They bequeathed their faith in a better future along with the energy and talents needed to move the society one more step along the evolutionary path.

CHAPTER THREE

JANIS'S CHILDHOOD

★

I ain't quite ready for walking
I ain't quite ready for walking
And what will you do with your life
Life just a-dangling?

—Janis Joplin, "Move Over"

FOLKS CALLED MY mother the "Lily Pons of Texas," a compliment for her ability to sing like the great operatic soprano. Dorothy East's voice was pure, clear, and powerful, bringing the Broadway show tunes she favored to vivid life on the Texas plains. She also kicked up her heels with the jazzy songs of Cole Porter. She sang at any opportunity, which in Amarillo meant church, weddings, and the Kiwanis Club. Whenever she sang, her father's face beamed, his eyes watering. Her mother retained her dour personality, seldom even cracking a smile.

The high point of Mom's high school career was singing lead in a citywide stage production. Because it was an important charity event, the organizers hired a Broadway director to give the show extra polish. Everyone talked about good things happening for this talented young woman. The director of the show pulled Mother aside, saying, "If you want a job in New York I can get you one, but I don't recommend it. I've gotten to know you during this show and those people just aren't your kind of folks." She took his advice and did not go to New York. Instead she won a college scholarship in a singing contest. She followed the urging of her church pastor and applied to Texas Christian University in Fort Worth, Texas.

In 1932, in the midst of the Great Depression, my mother packed the only two dresses she owned and proceeded to college, ready to seize her future. Instead of inevitable triumph, she hit against the limitations of a single voice teacher who taught only opera. Broke and disenchanted after one year of school, Mom returned to Amarillo to work.

This was the 1930s. The flapper was hip and Dorothy was a liberated woman. Along with her peers she scandalized her parents by cutting off her long hair in a "bob" style. She chose figure-skimming dresses, heels, and jaunty hats—in styles that her future father-in-law, Seeb Joplin, would call "go-to-hell" hats. She smoked cigarettes, for the shock value. Smoking was quite a parental affront in those days. Cigarettes were illegal in fourteen states and legislation was pending in twenty-eight other states. Young women—such as Edna St. Vincent Millay—were expelled from college for smoking.

Mom began helping out at an Amarillo radio station, KGNC. Her local reputation as a free spirit was made when, frantically trying to figure out why the music wasn't being broadcast, she screamed, "I can't figure the damn thing out!" only to discover that her expletive had traveled to every house and farm within a hundred miles.

A blind date at Christmas brought my parents together. Pop was on break from engineering studies and ready for a good time. Dorothy loved to dance, so she brought him to her favorite spot until she realized he felt uncomfortable in that loud and boisterous scene. Away from the noise, their talk soon turned to areas they both favored: literature and the world of ideas.

Dorothy had often escaped the hostility in her house by spending hours reading Dostoyevsky and Tolstoy in the local library. Seth was interested in American literature. The first money my father earned as a boy went to buy *The Complete Works of Mark Twain* and *The Complete Works of Edgar Allan Poe*. As their relationship grew through letters, Pop wrote, "Don't tell me what you are doing. Tell me what you are thinking."

Seth was a strikingly handsome guy with a square jaw and a wry grin. He was said to have the bluest eyes in high school. He was a flirt who regularly won the "slow races"—a challenge to creep around the school in your car on tires stuffed with rags while talking to the girls. (They used rags in their tires because rubber for new tires had been scarce since World War I.) Seth liked to wear suits with a fedora, which he kept carefully cocked on the side of his head.

He was painfully shy at times, and used to spending a lot of time alone. His parents' home had housed the boarders Seeb hired for running the stockyards. Florence didn't like the influence of the rough men on her kids, so she boarded her daughter in town to go to school. My father was given his own one-room cabin out back.

Lack of money forced Seth to quit college one semester shy of a degree. Though he was intellectually curious and an avid reader, school bored him. He was more a playboy, known to make bathtub gin during the last days of Prohibition in order to enliven college parties. He lived a risqué life, smoking marijuana, which was legal but not widely available. Back in Amarillo in an era of 25 percent unemployment, he spent time with his girl and worked at the only job he could find, as a gas-station attendant.

Dorothy got a temporary job filling in for a vacationing credit clerk at the local Wards store. She spent the two weeks showing her boss that he should want her to keep the job rather than take the vacationing girl back. She achieved her goal and was eventually made head of the department.

Dorothy and Seth spent hours together, often visiting at the Joplins' house. They enjoyed the gentleness and lively conversation of his parents. Dorothy felt accepted and enjoyed escaping the ongoing arguments that hung in the air at the East home. In a moment of candor, Dorothy's father, Cecil, confided in Seth, "My wife and I used to talk and share things, but now it's so hard for her to hear, it seems we never talk about anything." Laura had worn a hearing aid since childhood. At this time in her life, she often preferred to turn it off rather than listen to what people told her. Her primary commitment was the church.

Cecil was a religious man as well, but his views of life had changed with age. He was known to have a drink of alcohol, an act his wife felt was the devil's work. Cecil even drank with Seth, once getting him drunk and then laughing when the young man threw up on the porch outside.

When the tension at the East home erupted, Laura would scribble a note and place it on the bureau. Then she would take her bags and try to hitchhike back to Nebraska, but Cecil always found her and brought her home.

The poor relationship of the Easts made Mother take a silent vow: "I will never argue with my husband. I will always make things work." She chose in Seth a man who was gentle, kind, and sensitive. Seth selected Dorothy because she was strong like his mother but more exciting and challenging in a way that fit the craziness of the times.

Around 1935, Seth's best friend in college recommended him for a job at the Texas Company, later Texaco, in Port Arthur, Texas. It was more than six hundred miles away, but it was a real job and a chance to start a new life. Seth jumped at it, and Dorothy quit her job to follow. Her boss at Wards called to see if doubling her salary would keep her in Amarillo, but it just made her angry. "If I'm worth twice the salary now, then you've been cheating me" was her retort. She quickly found work in the credit department at Sears.

Four years after Seth and Dorothy met, they finally could afford to marry. On October 20, 1936, Dorothy East and Seth Joplin were wed. There was no gathering of family and hours of celebration. It was a simple ceremony with two friends, due to their distance from family and the strain of the times.

Port Arthur was the refinery capital of the world. It was only twenty miles away from the largest oil strike to date, at Spindletop in Beaumont. Petroleum was king of the times, the source of many new fortunes and a restructuring of the economic landscape. Seth and Dorothy could see their lives in a future of spewing oil that meant a steady income. Texas led all other states in oil production, and Port Arthur was in the center of the excitement.

The town of Port Arthur was founded by a visionary developer, Arthur Stilwell. He chose its site with the help of voices in his dreams that he called fairies. He placed it on the edge of beautiful freshwater Lake Sabine, only twenty miles from the Gulf of Mexico. Stilwell designed the town with broad boulevards, grand avenues, and expensive homes along the lakeshore. He used Dutch development money and expertise to dredge a canal linking the town to the Gulf of Mexico. The city became the first inland oceangoing port for the refineries. Port Arthur was destined, they said, to be the shipping port for the entire Texas petroleum industry.

Then Stilwell came under financial siege from John "Bet-a-Million" Gates, who wrested control of the city's development. He made his fortune selling barbed wire throughout the Western states, forming a company that later became U.S. Steel. Gates sold the picturesque lakeshore to neighboring cities that wanted the right to continue the intracoastal canal to their communities. The town mansions no longer had vistas of white-capped waves and sailboats bobbing in the steady breeze. Instead, they overlooked oceangoing tankers creeping eerily and slowly through the canal.

Dorothy and Seth began life under FDR's New Deal, but war rumblings in Europe clouded their sense of the future. In 1936 Germany occupied the Rhineland and Japan invaded China.

Seth worked at the only Texaco plant that made containers for petroleum, cans that traveled around the globe. As war came, Seth's packaging plant grew ever more vital. He was called to join the army three times, but was always deferred because of the importance of his job to the war effort.

With the inevitable collapse of the East marriage, Laura and her youngest daughter, Mimi, came to live with Seth and Dorothy. It became the opportunity for my parents to buy their first house, a two-bedroom brick bungalow on the edge of town. Money was tight, so that when Seth went to Sears to buy a push lawnmower, he used time payments to afford its eight-dollar price.

Surrounded by uncertainty, fear, and never-ending work, Dorothy and Seth celebrated life. They were frequently found across the Sabine River in Vinton, Louisiana, a town that specialized in offering freely flowing liquor and good dance music to a Texas crowd. Clicking her heels and snapping her fingers, Dorothy sometimes danced on the tops of tables. Seth sometimes wondered if he would ever be able to contain her.

One day, Seth came home from work and whispered to Dorothy, "Let's do something for posterity!" West Texas morals held that it was okay to drink and carry on before a person settled down. With Dorothy's pregnancy, the revelry abruptly ended.

Janis Lyn Joplin was born at nine-thirty A.M. on January 19, 1943. That morning, when labor started, Dorothy told her husband to go to work. "Women have been having babies for centuries. I'll be fine." Afterward she confided softly, "The next time I have a baby, I

★

want you with me." Janis weighed only five and a half pounds at birth and was three weeks early. But by eight months of age she was a thriving twenty pounds. With World War II raging, it was an awfully optimistic bet on the future to bring life into the world.

Seth sent his wife a touchingly humorous note marking Janis's birth (the content can be understood only when one considers his work in a manufacturing plant):

> I wish to tender my congratulations on the anniversary of your successful completion of your production quota for the nine months ending January 19, 1943.
>
> I realize that you passed through a period of inflation such as you had never before known—yet, in spite of this, you met your goal by your supreme effort during the early hours of January 19, a good three weeks ahead of schedule.

Janis was the first child in either of our parents' families born in a city and not on a farm. She was the first to have much cultural exposure beyond the radio or church. She also changed the lives of her parents immediately. Living with her extended family afforded Janis extra love and attention. By her third birthday, the United States had dropped the A-bomb on Hiroshima, the war was ending, and everyone's life was changing. Dorothy's mother and sister moved on to other homes, and the Joplin routine became more settled.

Pop was the wage earner and had the final word on most big decisions. The other 90 percent of the choices were left to Mother. She was clearly in charge of the home and the children. Dorothy quit her job and devoted herself to mothering young Janis. She took her to the Bible-thumping First Christian Church for church school, which Mother eventually taught. Mother had spent hours as a child sewing elaborate clothes for her dolls, and now she did even more for her beautiful young daughter. Janis had pretty organdy dresses with ruffles, skirts and blouses trimmed in ribbon and lace, and cute sailor outfits for play clothes.

Pop was used to formality in the relationships within his family. He wanted to be called by the respectful term "Father," so he taught his daughter to say "Mother" instead of "Mom." Mother was a more informal person, and so she didn't push her daughter to say "Father." Instead, Janis naturally took to calling him "Daddy."

Though the days were spent with mother and daughter together, the afternoons marked Seth's return from work. Each evening Janis waited for her dad on the front porch. As soon as he arrived, they would hug, sit on the steps, and talk. One day Mother happened to overhear Seth telling Janis about his experience in college making bathtub gin. "Is that the proper topic for a conversation with a child?" she asked him later. Pop refused to argue the point; instead, he quit spending the evening time visiting with Janis on the front step. Janis was crushed and never knew why.

Mother bought Janis an old upright piano and taught her daughter how to play. She and Janis sat on the piano bench together, with Janis singing the simple nursery songs Dorothy taught her. Janis often lay in bed at night singing those songs, over and over, to put herself to sleep.

Janis practiced her scales regularly, with the typical errors and frustrations. Pop hated the intrusion of the raucous noise on his peaceful evenings. He loved piano, but he wanted the tunes of Chopin played by Rubenstein. He complained, and Dorothy agreed to sell the piano to avoid the potential argument in the house.

Pop also wanted the piano sold because having it around was emotionally painful for his wife. Mom had recently had an operation to remove her thyroid gland. Something happened to her vocal chords in surgery and her voice was changed forever. She would never be able to command pure tones and full volume for singing, though her speaking voice was fine.

Before Janis was six years old, Mom had two miscarriages. The loss of those babies made Janis even more special to her parents. Finally, in 1949, Dorothy gave birth to a second child, Laura Lee. With my birth, our parents decided to move to a larger home. They located a nice three-bedroom house on a quiet street across from a large pasture on the outskirts of town. The neighborhood was called Griffing Park. Kids were everywhere. The streets were laid out like spokes on a wheel, and the hub was a proud new elementary school, Tyrrell Public School. Four years later, our brother, Michael Ross, was born.

The Griffing area owed its unique character to an experimental farm started on the site in 1896. It had been part of the town's initial promotion, a method of demonstrating the soil's fertility. The operators displayed potatoes, beans, peas, figs, oranges, lemons and limes, citrons, and pomegranates. Eucalyptus, camphor, pecan, and palm trees flourished among oleander bushes and roses.

Our new house at 3130 Lombardy Drive was a redwood frame home that the contractor had painted white. My father cursed the unnecessary paint on the redwood every summer he lived in the house because it meant he had to spend most of his vacation scraping and painting the house's exterior. Like most homes in the area, which was only four feet above sea level, it was built on brick piers about one and a half feet high. Port Arthur was subject to torrential storms and regular rising water.

Our parents planted white gardenias outside the living room and azaleas outside the bedrooms. Purple wisteria grew on stubby treelike bushes, draping abundant and aromatic blossoms like clusters of delicate grapes. A mimosa tree cast its brilliant, feathery pink-tipped blossoms in the spring, followed by a dense layering of brown seedpods that we kids split open. Two conical evergreens marked the front corners of the lot, with a live oak given a prominent position in the middle of the front yard. Mother lined the drive with a changing display of annual flowers and Pop planted a large vegetable garden bordered with day lilies in the backyard. A pecan and two chinaberry trees completed the landscaping.

Our parents were industrious, strapped for cash but creative. Our living room was set off by a rectangular panel over the couch. It was just a part of the wall that was painted a different color than the surrounding area. Over the years it was framed by wood and decorated with various trivets and brass plates. It had originally been created by a lack of money to buy sufficient paint to cover the whole wall. When there was an uncovered spot, they just called it art. Slowly it became a fixture and also a lesson. What seemed to be a problem was turned into an advantage.

Janis was a bright, precocious child with a winning smile and a manner about her that charmed people. She had a full face, small, twinkling blue eyes, a broad forehead that Mother always said showed her intellect, and fine, silky blond hair that had a soft curl in it. For special occasions Mother fixed it in ringlets pulled and draped to the side. Otherwise, it was bobbed and left to its own tousled ways. People might have found her features plain if a buoyant spirit and zest for life hadn't overshadowed her looks. She was a child who liked people. She always made strangers welcome. Her sensitivity to others showed in a considerate willingness to go out of her way to include others in play.

Janis displayed an independence that pleased her parents when it showed her creativity and originality. At other times they gritted their teeth and were shocked by her blatant displays of disobedience and challenges to their authority. She excelled in the typical young child's love of testing limits, whether at work or play. When she and her father played dominoes outside in the warm evening air, they would sit, he in a sleeveless undershirt and an old pair of suit pants and she in a playsuit, laying out the dominoes on a wooden stool he had made. When dark descended and the mosquitoes came out in force, they would hurry inside. One night after they had packed everything up and dashed toward the kitchen, Janis dropped the dominoes on the steps. Pop asked her to pick them up before they went inside. She clenched her jaw and defied his request. They sat amid droning and biting insects for a full two hours before she complied.

In 1946 Benjamin Spock published *The Common Sense Book of Baby and Child Care.* It became Dorothy's ready resource. Spock said, "Trust your instincts and don't be afraid to love your baby. Relax, cuddling is as important as cleanliness." Parenting prior to Spock had been Victorian. Babies were kept on schedule and there was inflexible family discipline. With Spock, people saw children less as an extra pair of hands for farm work and more as the point of marriage itself.

As psychology started to make inroads into the average person's mind, mothers began to see their efforts as essential to the child's development. Mom spent her efforts stimulating our minds and creative juices while teaching us the social rules. Pop set the final limits on acceptable behavior. He was in charge of the ultimate discipline in the household. If Janis disagreed with Mother's limits, she often created some sort of scene to force Pop to ask, "What's going on?" He was otherwise not willing to enter the fray. Most of the time he would support Mother, but not always. When it came time for reinforcing limits, Pop was the one stuck with the job. He did on occasion spank his children, but it often seemed to us that his soul ached more with each swat than our behinds ever did.

As Janis grew older she began to play with the local gang of kids. We lived in a true neighborhood, with a large group of playmates of all ages within hailing distance. The climate in Port Arthur is temperate, with winters generally no colder than 40 degrees. We could play outside almost all year long. All day in the summers and on weekends, and most afternoons and evenings after school, a roaming mass of enthusiasm poked around the neighborhood, creating games and exploring the world.

The windows were open most of the year, and at night, when the house noises had died down, you could lie in bed and listen to the neighborhood sounds. Janis and I slept together when I was young and talked in whispers as we lay. Off in the distance were the staccato voices of neighbors in their houses. A mother called a child to bed, kids argued with their siblings, or a married couple discussed the day. Few secrets were possible in those circumstances, so we learned to accept our neighbors as they were.

Janis was sometimes a leader in organizing things, being one of the older kids. She often vied for power with the more powerful boy next door, Roger Pryor. He was a tall, muscular, quick-witted guy with bright eyes and sandy-blond, curly hair. He spent hours at our house because he doted on the attention our father gave to him. Janis resented their times together and so competed with Roger. She would challenge him in little ways, and when the game permitted, try to wrestle him to the ground and gleefully sit on him. Pop made them each a pair of stilts and instituted the great stilt race, a series of spontaneous challenges around the house or to the tallow trees and back.

Pop enthralled all the kids because he was an engineer-tinkerer who invented and made playground equipment for our backyard. Who cares about swings when you have a homemade Giant Stride? We spent hours holding on to rings attached to ropes at the tips of a large X balanced in the middle atop a tall pole. We would run in a circle, swinging ourselves out when we got enough momentum.

It was so like Pop, making wonderful toys that we used to the max, only to find that we had turned his ideas into ingenious ways of hurting ourselves. The Giant Stride was taken down after the older kids got too good at swinging us younger kids out at a 90-degree angle. We couldn't keep holding on, and sailed through the pecan tree, landing with bruises and tears. One of the neighbors even broke his arm. What was it about fun that was dangerous? Pop wanted to go beyond what he had been taught was the safe, reasonable way to live. But when he broke out of those limits, something always told him he had gone too far.

The same thing happened with a seesaw he built that had a pivot in the center that allowed you to go around in a circle at the same time you were going up and down. That meant you could clobber a younger child who strayed in the path of your fast-moving arc. It was grand, until it was dismantled.

He put up a tightrope between the pecan tree and one of the chinaberry trees. It was a taut steel cable about six inches off the ground that allowed us to fantasize about participating in high-wire acts. Pop would often come home from work and sit in the backyard and laugh and talk with the kids while he drank a beer.

Sometimes we put on neighborhood plays, draping sheets on the clothesline to form two sides and the back of a stage. Janis was especially adept at impromptu planning and acting. Another game we liked, Annie Over, was played only at our house. It was a game of blind catch, with one person throwing a ball over the roof of a house to a player on the other side. If the other person caught it, then he or she could run around and try to tag the person who had thrown it. When I got old enough to demand to play but was too young to throw, my gallant sister made up a new category of team player, a cheater. Each side was allowed one cheater who would lie on the grass and peek under the house to see if the other person had caught the ball and was running or had missed the ball and let it bounce. There were certain advantages to houses standing on brick piers.

Michael was ten years younger than Janis and four years younger than I. We liked to play with him as if he were a living doll. We would take him into Mom's closet and dress him up, then trot him out for everyone's laughter, including his own.

We had an attic fan to cool the house off from the sweltering summer heat and humidity. For us kids, it was powerful, magical, and fun. It was placed in the hallway off the living room that led to two of the bedrooms. We often played by pulling the thick cotton rope that opened the plywood covering the attic opening and feeling the sudden

★

forceful rush of cool air. We were Marilyn Monroes with flying hair, holding our rippling clothes and laughing uproariously.

Pop was especially ingenious at getting the gang of kids to help with the chores. Like Tom Sawyer trying to get the fence painted, he invited everyone over to help wax the oak floors. He cleaned out the living room and dining room and spread the floor with wax. Then he took any number of dirty bare feet and strapped clean towels on them. Off he would send us to skate and play bumper cars on the glasslike surface the new wax created. We never had so much fun.

Sometimes we took the lesson of creativity too far. Once we took a dead boa constrictor from a neighbor boy's snake collection. We tied a rope around its neck and put it in the ditch that ran beside the road in front of our house. We stretched the rope across the road and hid in the tall grass on the other side. Then we spied an approaching car and carefully pulled the rope to simulate the snake coming out of the grass and crossing the road. "EEEEIIIIIII!" the poor woman screamed, her tires burning so much rubber as she braked that we gasped for oxygen. We realized this act was beyond redemption, so we dragged the snake off, doused it with gasoline, and burned it.

We spent a lot of time cooking at our house. Pop had been raised in a boardinghouse, with his mother making fresh desserts every day. He wanted the same service in his own home, much to Mother's frustration. At least our grandmother had trained him to be an excellent baker. We liked his apple, cherry, or lemon meringue pies, chocolate or any other cake, sugar and peanut butter cookies, and Russian tea cakes. The last required pecans, and in Port Arthur that meant the kids were kept busy shelling the harvest from the local trees.

Pop wasn't as schooled a cook as Mom. Once he made a white sheet cake and was trying a new kind of burned-sugar frosting. When he brought the cake to the table, he found the frosting so thick, gooey, and tough that he couldn't cut through it. Instead, we peeled the frosting off the whole cake and began to pull it like taffy.

We ate American Southern food: roast beef, chicken, stew, ham hocks and pinto beans, vegetable soup, corn bread, and lots of vegetables. We kept an aluminum pot on the kitchen stove that had the word GREASE embossed on it and a lid with a painted red lemon-drop-shaped handle. It held the flavoring that made dishes taste yummy: bacon grease! That and Tabasco sauce were our primary flavorings.

Mom tried to broaden our horizons with new recipes such as chicken curry and chow mein. We ate them up. She was a good cook. She prided herself on using Sophia Loren's recipe to make spaghetti sauce from scratch. Biscuits were her specialty, and we could never get enough of them for dousing with honey after a meal.

Our parents tried to be sensitive to our dislikes when planning a menu. Once they changed brands of mayonnaise, from expensive Hellman's to cheaper Miracle Whip. I couldn't stand it and protested vehemently. Dad said, "Oh, you can't tell the difference. You're just complaining." Janis spoke up for me and suggested a blind taste test. They prepared samples of the two brands in the kitchen and brought them to me in the dining room. It was easy to tell the difference, and so the folks bought Hellman's for me from then on.

Mother presided over the holiday events. She baked cookies and annually made a turkey for Thanksgiving and a ham for Christmas. Each dinner had sweet potatoes, acorn squash, biscuits, dressing, and more. We always had a tree for Christmas, decorated with lights, tinsel, colored balls, and a few special ornaments—little carved wooden angels blowing trumpets, a plastic snowman, and a red metal Santa. One year, Pop took us kids for a drive on Christmas Eve to see the lights around town. When we returned, Mother was sewing, but Santa had sneaked in and placed presents under the tree. I couldn't believe my mother was so dense as to have Santa in the house and not see him! Janis shook her head at my childish gullibility, but she didn't say a word about it.

Most Christmases we shared modest gifts. There was always one nice present for each child, plus an extra two or three smaller ones. Some years when money was tight they struggled to provide that. For our gifts to others, Mother took us to Woolworth's downtown. She would hand us each a few bills and send us into the store to make our selections. She would sit out front and wait until we were through.

Due to our semitropical climate, we had to endure the annual storm season, which fostered family togetherness as we made the most of the theatrics of Mother Nature. The storms came on suddenly. First, the sky darkened and the winds came up. If it wasn't raining, we kids climbed up as high as we could in the tallow tree and rocked as the wind shook the tree. We screamed with excitement. Eventually we were hustled inside under indignant parental warnings that we were in

★

danger. But we didn't care. Then the real fury of the storm blackened the sky, and the house shuddered in the wind while the rain beat like tom-toms on all sides. By then we were huddled around a candle in the living room. Often we played games, the parental method of handling childhood stress. A favorite was musical chairs, fun at any time but more fun in the dark when you couldn't really see the chairs you were trying to claim.

In 1948, Janis experienced her first snow and made a snowman. About ten years later it snowed again. I was stuck in bed with the mumps and couldn't get outside to play in the first snow of my life. I really put up a fuss with Mother, but she wouldn't budge. My sister and brother made a snowman outside my window so that I could see it. Then Janis innocently came in to visit me. Checking to be sure Mom wasn't looking, she said, "Laura, look at the snowball. Feel it." I sucked in my breath and cried, "Oh, thanks." I was a bit disappointed in snow. It wasn't light and fluffy but cold and icy. I hid it under my pillow until it started to melt. Mother saw the problem and said, "That was nice of your sister. Let me put it in the freezer until you're well."

Our home might have been in Port Arthur, Texas, but we felt we were citizens of the world. Weekly, Pop brought us to the only building in town with tall Roman columns atop an expansive stairway—the public library. As a family we walked each short step, which made me feel the climb was ceremonial in nature, as though we were approaching the altar of a Mayan temple. We came to believe firmly in the unquestionable value of the knowledge stored within books.

Our frequent sojourns to the library were also cause to bring up a parental pet peeve. Our folks had moved into a Southern society but did not favor the local dialect. They did everything they could to teach us to talk properly. Mother particularly harped on the word *window* because too many locals said it as "winder." My father's favorite was the word *library*. We had a tendency to call it "libary," leaving out the first *r*. He would respond, "Now, I've had blueberries and strawberries, but I don't think I've ever had a liberry." We would laugh and say, "Okay, okay." We learned their lessons so well, the kids at school sometimes yelled derisively at us, "Yankee! Yankee!"

I grew up thinking that anything I needed to know could be found in the library. Other children reached full family recognition as adults through a Bar Mitzvah or a church ceremony. In our family, we gained respect according to the books we read. I grew a foot the day I finally convinced Pop, after much pleading and demanding, that I could read an adult book. My primary criterion was a visual one: The book had to have a plastic dust jacket, because children's books never did. As we descended the steps from the library, slowly and ceremoniously, I held up my plastic-covered book so that all people ascending could see that the world had to reckon with a new mind.

Books were more than ideas for us. They were alive. We read, learned, and shared thoughts with all the authors represented by the rows and rows of books in the library. The opinions that mattered—the printed ones—backed us in discussions we had in school. Since books were published in New York and Chicago, we believed those were the places where the best thinkers dwelled. Someday, perhaps, we would live among the people we then knew only on paper.

Reading and ideas defined our family life. No one hesitated to broach any topic during the dinner-table conversation, and our parents expected each child to contribute to discussions. Personal thought on a subject was paramount for Mom and Pop. They asked, "What do you think, Janis?" "How about you, Laura?" Then they listened seriously to our replies. In this way they taught us about personal integrity. If you could state your opinion and back it up, then you should stick to it. That didn't mean they wouldn't try to argue you out of things they didn't like, but they would respect your right to your view.

Janis was well schooled in questions by our father. If he had been a meditating man, his mantra would have been "Who am I?" He always looked beyond the moment. I remember the rains in Port Arthur. It seemed to shower every other day, but Pop never took it for granted. He would call to us, "Hey you kids, come here." Then we would all step out on the porch and squeeze together on the top step. He would coach us, "Take a deep breath and savor all the new smells the rain has released." We would stand there absorbing the odors as the rain rolled off the porch roof and splattered on the cement, throwing cool drops high on our legs. It is so easy to get caught in the routine of life. Pop made us stop and realize the preciousness in each moment. We would sometimes ponder where the rain had come from. Had it recently been in Borneo or Chicago? Did families stand in other places wondering about us?

Pop was a mystical spirit who never lost his awe of life itself.

★

It was almost as if God had placed his soul here on earth before he had finished explaining the upcoming experience. Pop said he should have been a monk because he savored contemplation so much. I joked with him a few years before he died, asking, "How could you have been a monk, since you don't believe in God?" He just laughed that caught-off-guard chuckle, and said, "Yes, that could present a problem." We decided that monks spend their lives hunting for God, and that surely defined him if anything did.

He looked for the mental wrinkles in everything he saw. He would turn a boring trip to the post office into an exciting adventure. He would tell us to study the faces on the wanted-men posters, then he would drive us around town to hunt for them. Michael loved Pop's trick to entertain bored children on automobile trips. Pop explained the rules of his game, saying, "Pick a license plate on any car you see and memorize it. As we drive along, I want you to find another one just like it!" It was a Zen koan: If you can see your way beyond the puzzle, then you've solved it.

While Pop brought us life's imponderables to savor, Mother laid out possibilities like a three-course meal. She never talked about limits, only about our goals and how we might reach them. The only boundaries she saw in life were found in the structure of society and its institutions. She felt that a clever person could work around those confines. Everything was merely a matter of planning and seizing the chances that came along.

Our lives were filled with the blossoming of opportunity. Income was up over 200 percent since the end of the war, and people used the extra money to provide for their children the things that they had lacked growing up. We were a generation of indulged young ones.

Mom was quick to follow up on an interest expressed by her children, especially if it was artistic in nature. Janis's innate drawing talents gave Mother the perfect opportunity to rise to the occasion. She bought beautiful full-color books of the masterpieces of art that hung in all the museums of the world. If we couldn't get to culture, then she would bring it to us. Mom also arranged private art lessons for Janis with the best teacher in town. Janis drew constantly. Roger Pryor, the handsome and confident boy next door, watched Janis spend hours sketching the horse that his family staked in the neighborhood. Janis told him, "Horses are particularly hard to draw because the distance from the neck to the head is different than from the neck to the tail." She worked at it until she got it right. Then she was pleased.

Mom believed that it took only a little extra effort to turn something good into something excellent. She explained that wanting to give her kids choices came from her early life. Even in her seventies she complained half-bitterly about being given plain oatmeal for breakfast for eighteen years. She let her kids choose their breakfast, and much of the rest of their lives as well.

Mother was the best teacher I've ever known. Her gift was based on that trait all inspiring teachers have—a genuine faith in the ability of those she taught. She thought being human was about learning; therefore, it wasn't a foreign process—it was as natural as breathing in and out. She believed that people only needed opportunity.

Learning from Mom was an everyday experience, a manner of interacting as our paths crossed in the house. We sang a lot, as kids do, just aimless tunes thrown into the air for the sheer fun of doing it. Mom often stopped what we were doing for an impromptu lesson. "When you sing, stand up straight and provide support from here"— she would poke my diaphragm. "That's better, can you hear it?" she would ask. "Enunciate, enunciate. Put the endings on your words. Your audience can't understand you otherwise." Sometimes we looked at each other and laughed, waving at the nonexistent audience we were supposed to be entertaining. Then Mom would pick up the laundry and be off about her business.

There was a lot of hard work and practice in our household as well. Mom cajoled, negotiated, stimulated, and oftentimes laid down the law about homework, music practice, or any kind of effort that was instructive in nature.

She bought most of the toys for us and had very clear ideas about what was acceptable. We never got toys that did something on their own; they were always raw materials that stimulated the imagination of the user. We had to provide the spark that made the experience fun. Mom provided ample supplies of blocks, Lincoln Logs, Tinkertoys, cards, pick-up sticks, dolls, farm animals, books, colors, paints, and

★

paper. She would throw in good board games such as Clue and Monopoly.

Making the commonplace more interesting was a motto both of our parents believed in. Once Pop brought home boxes of old stationery that the plant was throwing out. We promptly set about folding squadrons of airplanes, which we stationed on every inch of floor space in the house. The final erupting battle was a blinding, howling smash of pink, green, yellow, and white bombers and fighters soaring through the house. During the development of the paper-airplane game, Mom was making dinner and supporting our ideas for strategy as they developed. Pop would help find new styles of airplane folding.

Mom monitored our lives constantly, seeing oversight as her primary parental role. She interjected herself in two ways into our development. First, she praised us unceasingly. Mother always found a positive remark to make about whatever our endeavors. Hastily thrown-together projects got the comments they deserved—a selective word about some noteworthy possibility she saw. Otherwise, she would provide her second method of involvement: suggestions. Our childish energies might be scattered among ten compelling projects at once, or the intricacies of our social life as we grew older, but Mom's statements always called us to focus. "Here, let me show you," Mother would say. Often she prefaced it with, "When I was your age my grandmother taught me to sew. She wouldn't let me just put clothes together. She made me learn French sewing, where the edges of the seams are rolled and whipped under. We designed our clothes and made our own patterns. We made dresses as fine as any found in New York. That's where I learned that hard work pays off." Then she would turn the story to our task at hand, saying, "You can see that happen for you in your work, if you just slow down and practice until you get it right." We hated our unknown great-grandmother. The problem was, Mom was right. There was nothing worse than mustering the resentful bravado to defy her gentle teachings, only to see that our way was wrong.

Mom's love of greatness might have been interpreted as ambitious zeal had her natural aggressiveness not been tempered by maternal forgiveness and support. We might have even thought she was too hard on us if her efforts hadn't had the full support of our father. In one pout against having to redo a project, I sought his support. He was relaxed in his evening retreat, reading while sitting in his brown leather armchair in his bedroom. He confided in me that he knew firsthand that follow-through was important—he had almost flunked out of college because of his lack of it. I sucked in my breath. My heroic image of my father had been sullied. In one horrendous moment I saw the embodied statue of George Washington crumble into pieces of worthless marble, leaving only a man.

In this way I realized that inspired hard work was the *only* way to succeed. It wasn't that my mother or father demanded so much from me, but that the world expected it. Nothing was ever complete. It could always be made better. At times it was maddening, because no matter how much we did, there was always more to do.

Mother explained her attitude toward learning in a characteristic quote from an irrefutable source, Abraham Lincoln: "You cannot strengthen the weak by weakening the strong. . . . You cannot build character and courage by taking away man's initiative and independence. You cannot help men permanently by doing for them what they could and should do for themselves." It was always hard to argue with Mom when she brought up things like that.

Janis entered junior high with a trail of schoolwork that was respectable but not spectacular; it appears that school wasn't challenging enough to inspire her best efforts. She was a quick, intelligent girl whose report cards had always shown she was "making acceptable progress" in most areas. In a few areas she was "Commendable." By the fourth grade a few areas had been checked as "Needs improvement." She didn't always practice good sportsmanship, or keep her work or the room clean.

Her junior high report cards were another matter. They showed a girl increasingly at odds with her teachers. She wasn't satisfied with the routine of education. Janis asked questions like "Why do people have hair on their toes?" She began to get unsatisfactory marks in work habits and citizenship because she talked too much and didn't get all of her work done on time. Only some teachers found her a problem, and it wasn't a matter of the teachers not liking Janis. The woman who favored Janis the most also gave her the worst marks in following directions, getting work done, and respecting the rights of others, i.e., talking out of turn.

Janis was taught to try for excellence at home, but she was

★

criticized by teachers who wanted her to be quiet and follow directions at school. She was more inquisitive and energetic than the school program allowed. Janis was given a different female role model than most young Southern girls. Her mother was strong, independent, intelligent, ambitious, and assertive. Janis wasn't raised to see women as passive or behind-the-scenes. Our mother had lived on a farm where a woman's work was equal to a man's, even if it was different. There was little room in a farmer's marriage for the pedestal that women were placed on in the Eastern cities. Our mother didn't have to rip off her corset to find her power. It came naturally. It grew from her experience on the farm and was hardened by the problems her parents had.

Mother married a man who liked her for her strength and never tried to own her. It never occurred to them to raise daughters whose primary goals would be female attractiveness or compliance. They focused on what they believed were the important qualities in life—character, intelligence, and talent.

Janis maintained a proper social standing through junior high. She and Mom sewed her first evening dress, a pink net affair to which she received a matching pink evening bag for Christmas. She joined the Junior Reading Circle for Culture, which was her introduction to reading and criticizing good literature outside of the family environs. Her journalism teacher, Miss Robyn, asked Janis to join her Tri Hi Y club, which she did. Janis hosted a gathering at our house, a night of Italian street café life. She covered card tables in red-checked cloths and spent weeks melting candle wax on wine bottles to give the proper atmosphere.

Janis participated in Glee Club throughout junior high. In the ninth grade she sang a solo at the Christmas pageant, her first public singing beyond church. Due to quirks about enrollment dates in kindergarten, Janis was the member of a class in which many kids were up to eighteen months older than she was. In the ninth grade, that was an embarrassing difference because she wasn't as physically developed as many. She weighed less than one hundred pounds and hadn't passed through puberty. Many of the other girls were amply endowed and loved to show off their newfound femininity in low-cut dresses and flouncing full skirts. Luckily her best friend, Karleen Bennett, was close to her age and exactly her size. At least she wasn't alone.

With parental help, Janis began to perfect their primary passion in life: bridge. We had been taught the rudiments of the game as soon as we were able to sit atop two 3-inch-thick Century dictionaries and be at table-top height. Then we learned to deal, count cards, and bid according to the basic rules. Our folks showed unimaginable patience in letting us play a hand, supporting our feeble strategy and including us as equals in the game. By junior high, Janis was taking special bridge lessons, playing with our parents and their friends, and inviting her friends over for a game.

Jack Smith was Janis's ninth-grade boyfriend, a tall, handsome fellow with a marked intelligence and politeness about him that guided his own passion for knowledge. Jack gave Janis a necklace with her initial on it, a style that was all the rage in junior high. He splurged and got her a five-dollar one, because his feelings went far beyond the normal one-dollar variety. Jack said Janis often called him a big cry, and it was only years later that she explained what that meant. A cry was a sob and a sob was an S.O.B., and she would never say that word back then.

Jack and Janis read *Ivanhoe* in school. The story inspired her. The gallant, wounded knight Ivanhoe was rescued from his enemies and nursed back to health by a young Jewess and her father. Returning to his true love, Ivanhoe had to leave her to joust for the life of the Jewess. Treacherous nobles accused the Jewess of witchery because of her ability to heal Ivanhoe. Similarly, Janis often looked to Jack to rescue her. Her expectations for men were now clear. She merely sought a knight of the Round Table, a man who belonged in Camelot.

Janis arrived at Jack's door one day wanting to see the movie *The Ten Commandments*. Neither of them had money, so they resorted to counting out the pennies in Jack's money jar. They arrived at the box-office window laden with copper coins. Janis stood politely aside as Jack tried to explain his embarrassing predicament to the ticket lady, who recounted the coins. "I lost a bet with a friend," Jack mumbled. Janis stepped over and jokingly poked him, saying half-seriously, "You shouldn't lie, especially about a movie about God."

Janis, Jack, and Karleen Bennett began to get interested in that other compulsion of adolescence: sex. They traded much-read copies of *Peyton Place* and *Splendor in the Grass*, with the best parts dog-eared and

★

indexed. "Be sure to read page 89," they wrote in notes among themselves.

Janis's ninth-grade birthday party was a neighborhood scavenger hunt. She graduated from her Arthur Murray dance class. Along with the entire family, she watched the Miss America pageant and pondered what it would be like to be Miss Texas. We discussed the styles of dress worn by the contestants and planned a new one for Janis.

Though Janis was developing some problems in school, she also had supportive experiences there as well. Miss Dorothy Robyn taught her ninth-grade journalism class and was the head of the journalism club. Janis excelled in both. She illustrated *The Driftwood,* the school literary magazine. The art she drew consisted of stylish stick figures and thin-line sketches illustrating the stories and experiences. She had the ability to capture emotion in quick strokes. In her scrapbook, Janis pasted a Journalism Award Certificate given her for the work, writing beside it, "Miss Robyn walks up in the middle of class and casually says, 'Oh, I thought you might like to see this.' I nearly fell out of my chair I was so excited."

Janis wrote a story for *The Driftwood* titled "The Most Unusual Prayer":

> My family includes one brother, one sister, one father, one mother and me. We take turns saying the blessing at dinner each night.
>
> My sister Laura says it one night. I say it the next. Michael, my little brother, has been listening to us for two years.
>
> About three months ago Laura said the blessing: "Thank you, God, for the birds and the flowers and the things we play with. Thank you, God, for the lovely nights and the lovely days. Amen."
>
> After she had finished, we all heard a weird chant from Mike's end of the table: "Birds, flafers (flowers), 'tatoes, peas, water, bubber (butter), plate." It was Michael saying the blessing.
>
> Since then Michael has been joining in on all the blessings. The other night when we decided it was Mike's turn to say the blessing, he proceeded with a short but inclusive "Thank you for ebeything. Goodbye."

Journalism class was Janis's favorite, in spite of getting poor citizenship marks from Miss Robyn. She couldn't corral her enthusiasm sufficiently to accept the structure of the class. She talked, gossiped, and doodled. Her best friends were in the class with her—Karleen, Jack Smith, and others. Janis sometimes led others through the door marked DO NOT ENTER in the journalism room. It went up a narrow staircase to the dome on top of the building. From there you could see the city spread out before you.

While Janis worked on *The Driftwood,* I began to write a neighborhood newspaper. I always emulated Janis whenever I could. I wrote on such timely topics of interest to an eight-year-old as "Where the Wind Comes From." I asked anyone who would talk to me, and decided that perhaps the huge fans in the field across the street by the Baptist Church had something to do with it.

Janis liked to manipulate the home scene whenever possible, and my copying her was one of her tools. She would say, "I won't love you if you don't do what I say." So I would. Once she got in a huff and screamed, "I'm going to run away," and stomped her feet around the house. I yelled, "I'm going with you." I asked my father what you did when you ran away, and he said you got a bamboo pole, which we had, and tied all your things in an old red bandana and hung it on the end of the pole. So I ran around the house getting ready before Janis said, "Laura, I wasn't serious."

Art was becoming a way Janis interacted with the world. It provided entrées and a sense of identity and specialness. In 1957 she approached the librarian during one of the frequent family library visits. "Do you need any volunteers around here?" "Absolutely," was the reply. That summer, Janis worked doing posters for the library bulletin boards. The *Port Arthur News* took a photo of her in front of her illustration of the Scarecrow of Oz. The headline read, LIBRARY JOB BRINGS OUT TEENAGER'S VERSATILITY. They quoted her: "It gives me a chance to practice art and at the same time to do something worthwhile for the community."

Port Arthur could be a very proper place, offering a clear idea of what young ladies should be like. Janis was well on her way down the accepted path for young ingenues, but with increasing age came increasing awareness. The pristine image of the town contrasted with Port Arthur as a port city, with wide-open prostitution and gambling blatantly advertised on the sides of buildings. None of it, of course, was discussed in polite society. Headlines calling the town SIN CITY spiced

★

newspapers around the country as a new district attorney vowed to clean it up.

In Janis's seventh-grade year, 1954, the Supreme Court had banned school segregation. We all held our breath in the highly segregated South to see what would come of this grand chess game in the North. We lived a racially isolated childhood. The blacks in town, at least 40 percent of the population, lived "on the other side of the tracks." They kept in their place and we in ours. The few times our family ever went to the ocean to enjoy the beach, about twice a summer, we had to drive through the black part of town. It didn't take a genius to see the smaller, tattered homes, raggedly clothed children, and general state of inequality.

Our parents were frank about it. "Society's treatment of the Negro is wrong, but you can't do anything about it. You'll only get hurt if you try." There wasn't much opportunity to do anything anyway, beyond trying to smile and be kind to a black person on the street, if they would look at you. Still, discussions were in all the newspapers and magazines. Our parents subscribed to *Time,* and we were all expected to read it cover to cover. Like the rest of the country, Janis was influenced by the rumbling racial challenges.

Added to that was Janis's ill-fated job as salesclerk in a toy store. She was elated when she came running to us, gushing that she had the job. A Christmas salesgirl! She took it seriously, and asked Mom for tips about helping customers choose the right toy in the right price range. Then her boss told her to mark up one group of toys. That was no problem, until the next day. She came home with an aching sense of dishonesty. "They had me mark the same toys back down, and put a sale sign up! It's dishonest," she said. It seemed as though everywhere she looked, she saw social hypocrisy. People she used to respect were no longer admirable. The emperor had no clothes.

Janis did the only thing a bright, determined, idealistic girl could do. She went searching. She simply turned her head away from the prescribed path to face the layers of life that society had told her were not the proper ones for a young lady. She didn't make a clean break just yet. She was merely curious. With simplistic reasoning, she decided that if the good people weren't all good, then perhaps the supposedly bad people weren't all bad. She was off to see for herself.

CHAPTER FOUR

ADOLESCENCE

★

Well I know that you got things to do and places to be
And I guess I'll have to find the thing and place for me
I may wind up in the street a-sleeping 'neath a tree
Still I guess you know I've gotta go

—Powell St. John, "Bye Bye Baby"

SEEKING NEW HORIZONS, Janis joined the summer program of the Port Arthur Little Theater just after the ninth grade. She spent most of her efforts painting scenery for the productions, and also ushered on the evenings of the performances. *Sunday Costs Five Pesos* was the only stage play in which Janis had a role. She played an ingenue, appropriate casting for that time in her life.

The Little Theater program was run by the mother of Grant Lyons, a student one year ahead of Janis. The Lyonses were Eastern folk who had come to Port Arthur for work in the refineries. They aspired to a broader cultural experience than was readily available in provincial Port Arthur.

Grant ran with a group of intellectuals who were united by their disdain for the level of mental sophistication of their classmates and the town in general. The Little Theater enabled them to identify with the greater artistic world. The workshops were also a great place to meet girls. The daily activities in the program brought together a large group of adolescents who began to hold parties and hang out together. The

★

core group was Grant's nucleus of friends—Dave Moriaty, Adrian Haston, Jim Langdon, and Randy Tennant. There was no leader; they were all equally powerful in their own right.

Dave was a slender fellow with thick, wavy hair and large, piercing eyes. He saved money from mowing lawns and raising bees to buy a seventeen-foot sloop, which gave him instant social status, something he made much use of in his headlong pursuit of girls. He was intent on becoming a scientist, building rockets with Randy Tennant in his spare time. Randy Tennant was a twinkle-eyed, slender-built fellow, a scientist with an artistic bent. Grant was the athlete, later becoming an all-district linebacker and an all-state baseball player. He was a hunk with sandy hair who had a passion for folk music. Dave, Grant, and Randy were members of the Latin club and the theatrical club, and served in various functions on the school newspaper. Jim Langdon was a shorter, stockier guy with large blue eyes that sat on his face in such a way as to give him a lovable Basset hound look that the girls craved. He was an incredible flirt, and girls fretted continuously over becoming his steady. His passions included playing trombone in the school band as well as local dance bands. Adrian Haston was a tall, slender, dark-haired fellow who had droopy eyelids that matched his slow-talking voice and gentle demeanor. He was exceedingly kind and intelligent. He played in the band and loved music. The year before Janis met them, several of guys had been active in student government and received meritorious citations. Whatever they did, they did together.

They steered the socializing in the Little Theater group to their own ends, taking great delight in mocking anyone brazen enough to admit they believed in anything good. Adolescent cynicism was their modus operandi.

The Little Theater group did what most adolescents did in Port Arthur and other small towns: They piled in a car, drove to an out-of-the-way spot, sat, and talked. They liked Sarah Jane Road, a dead-end track on the back of the Atlantic-Richfield refinery that was lined with tall sweet gum trees from which hung aimless masses of gray Spanish moss. That road stimulated talk of death because it was rumored that a woman named Sarah Jane had hanged herself from one of the trees. "I wonder if Sarah's in heaven looking at us right now?" Janis would say. "Heaven? What makes you think there is even a God, girl? Religion is just sugar coating for pea-brained idiots incapable of coming to terms with their own mortality." Jim Langdon could always command the discussions with his deep, booming voice and an ability to speak with authority, no matter what the topic. Janis argued with him, "How can you not believe in God? You must!" They all laughed and mocked her naïveté.

That was it! People questioned God. Her ninth-grade experiences let her see that society wasn't living by the morals it tried to foist on its youth. In the summer Janis realized that the groovy people didn't even believe in God, the Ten Commandments, and hell. Discovering the hypocrisy of society and the possibility that God wasn't guiding things after all freed her from adopting the status quo. If the supposedly "good" people weren't really good, and if God wasn't there to follow, then she could make decisions about her behavior on her own terms. She was free to look around the world with her newly awakened vision, taking in all walks of life. Perhaps the supposedly "bad" wasn't so at all, especially if the protectors of local social codes were breaking them whenever they could get away with it.

As the summer ended and Janis got ready to launch her high school career, Mother rose to the occasion. She wanted to provide a nice home for Janis so that she would feel proud to bring her friends over. To Mom that meant buying new furniture. We'd had the same old maple-framed furniture from Sears that the folks had purchased when they moved into the house. Mother became intent on modernizing.

The forefront of the architecture and art of the time was the modern movement, which threw away with brazen abandon the gargoyles of ancient history and exposed the beauty of the simplicity of structure underneath. Mother loved it. She fancied herself on the forefront of design. We drove to Fingers furniture store in Houston and picked up new living-room and dining-room sets. Mom chose a heavy-duty brown nubby-tweed stuffed couch. It was flanked by two end tables made of blond ash that had slender, triangular-shaped legs and a glass-covered storage area. On them sat a matched pair of brown aluminum conical lamps trimmed with a swirl of bright brass and topped by a narrow strip of a lamp shade. The dining-room set matched the end tables, blond wood with brown-tweed seat covers. On the windows she hung long-wearing fiberglass curtains.

The summer of 1957 and on into her first year in high school, Janis wore lots of makeup, straight skirts and white shirts, bobby sox and loafers, and had softly curled hair. Her sophomore year was marked by her embarrassment with her undeveloped body. She was still up to a year and a half younger than many of the girls in her class, and her relative physical immaturity became increasingly important to her. Her body was slow to change. She remarked later about why she was unhappy in school: " 'Cause I didn't have tits at age fourteen." She spoke in a derisively humorous tone, but there was truth in there too. When she entered the tenth grade, she was still very slender and had just begun to develop hips and soft breasts.

Regrettably, Janis's face blossomed in a never-ending series of painful bright red pimples, the worst brand a girl could have. Such magazines as *Seventeen* explained that pimples were caused by drinking Cokes, eating French fries and chocolate, and poor face-washing practices. She denied herself all such pleasures and scrubbed endlessly, but still the glaring dots appeared. Mother took her to a dermatologist, who continued the charges. "Pimples are your fault!" he seemed to say. "Keep your hands off your face." Then he pricked her face and squeezed the skin in an attempt to clear them up. He tried to burn the big ones with selective applications of dry ice, but nothing seemed to work. No one realized then that pimples are caused by bacteria and hormones and could be treated with antibiotics. When nothing worked, Janis got furious at the doctor and angry at her predicament.

Adolescence is a time of searching and trying on roles. Until age fourteen or so, childhood develops in predictable patterns. When puberty kicks in, all bets are off. For most girls, puberty is a high-pressure experience characterized by mood swings and irrational emotional outbursts. For some girls, the intensity of the changes is even greater. For Janis it was wrenching.

The question each young person asks is, "Who am I?" It is generally paired with, "Who do I want to be?" Janis had already been well schooled in the importance of these essential questions of life by our parents. In her sophomore year she was consumed by the overwhelming need to answer them. She was intelligent and inquisitive.

She didn't just look at the options set before her by society; she surveyed the world.

Janis was surprised and then overwhelmed by a perceived inability to attain the social ideal. She had always had a strong ego and a proud sense of herself, but in high school she began questioning. She thought she had "pig" eyes, incapable of ever being one of the long-lashed lovelies so brilliantly photographed in glamour magazines. She hated her name and her initials. Unlike her classmate Arlene Elster, whose initials were ACE, Janis said, "JLJ, it spells nothing!" She bit her nails, which further embarrassed her. She tried putting a red rinse on her hair, thinking it would change her look, but all she saw in the mirror was Janis with reddish hair. She went to the toniest salon in town and had Mr. Allen give her a new do, but it didn't change her social standing.

Janis looked around school and saw the hierarchy of social groups. At the top were those in class government; next came the athletes, the cheerleaders, the kids with great personalities whom everyone liked, and finally a giant mess of others of indistinguishable quality. She clearly felt among the last group, while her ego felt she deserved to be in the top tier.

"The main goal of high school was to *not* be different," said Kristen Bowen, classmate and family friend. "Clubs were *the* thing." In January 1958, Janis joined the Future Teachers of America. She pasted her candle and card, with red, white, and blue ribbons on it, in her scrapbook. She was active in Tri Hi Y, making centerpieces for dinners and decorating for dances. She made posters for candidates in school elections, hosted poster parties, and was known to place a fifty-cent bet on the outcome of an election.

Turning to an alternative "in" group, Janis and Karleen began to hang out with the Vitalis-coiffed toughs who could be called the "Fonzies" of their day. They formed car clubs and wore black leather jackets with names embroidered on the back, such as "Nighthawks" or "Highway Prowlers." For a while, Janis dyed her hair orange like the tough girls who hung in the car clubs. Janis loved one of the guys, Rooney Paul. He was not a joiner in school activities. He lived alone with his mother and had gone to work at an early age. When Janis met him, he worked at the drive-in. Rooney was a skinny six feet tall. He hung out at a run-down café across the street from the school called the Bucket, and nicknamed "the Bloody Bucket." He was very good-looking in a sexy fashion. He had thick, long hair that swept back in a duck tail with just the right amount of loft in the front. His thick lips begged girls to kiss them. Janis and Rooney Paul dated for a while, but not long enough to be true steadies. Still, the relationship they formed continued throughout high school.

Karleen Bennett was still Janis's best friend. Arlene Elster was also close to Karleen, so the three gathered at Karleen's house frequently. Arlene lived only a few blocks from Karleen. They discovered that the keys to Karleen's mother's car fit Arlene's mother's car, so Karleen and Janis would walk the few blocks to Arlene's, then they would drive the car to Karleen's house just for the thrill of taking it. When Arlene was ready to go home, she would back the car home so that no mileage would register on the odometer. They spent a lot of time sitting by the swimming pool at the country club and flirting with the lifeguards.

Once they decided to roam the city as photographers. Camera in hand, they headed to the canal to walk across the drawbridge to Pleasure Pier. A statue of some notable town father caught their attention, and they posed and reposed each other clambering on it. This social affront insulted the sensitivities of a proper family out with their young children. Their scornful glances further heightened the thrill of the adventure.

Janis often asked Karleen how to do things, and she was easily led. Out in the car in winter at a drive-in restaurant, Karleen was smoking a cigarette. Janis saw the exhaled breath and said, "I can't believe you can hold that much air." Karleen smirked, not telling Janis that the breath she saw was merely frost in the frigid air.

Janis had an early curfew on school nights, whose violation would mean grounding. Once, realizing she would be late, she asked Karleen, "What's the absolutely quickest way to get to my house from here?" Karleen suggested a route and Janis was off, driving Pop's work car home. Later that night Janis returned to Karleen's, mournfully relating a story of running a stop sign and broadsiding a car. "You didn't tell me I had to stop at the stop signs!" she accused. Luckily no one was hurt, but it was a bad accident and grieved everyone involved.

Pop took special pride in his autos, not that we had any distinctive models to crow about. He kept them in good running condition, clean and waxed. He bought used cars, choosing models he read about and ones his engineer's eye decided were in good shape. In addition to his affection for the cars themselves, he demanded a weighty sense of responsibility from others. He was more than a little upset about Janis's irresponsibility in running the stop sign. It was the biggest problem any of his kids had ever caused and he seethed in astonishment, yelling in a voice we seldom heard, "How could you be so dumb? Someone could have been hurt!" Janis was crushed, embarrassed, frustrated, and upset that she had failed so miserably. It was just another sign that she didn't measure up to the standards of the world. She was grounded and spent the time moping around the house in an emotional climate that was hostile and resolute. Our parents realized that their strictness on time limits was part of the cause of the accident. They tried to ease up and put time in proper perspective to safety.

In tenth grade, Janis took social studies, English, plane geometry, biology, gym, and Latin. She received A's and B's and a few C's for grades. "I have enjoyed having her in class," was the comment written by one of her teachers. "Janis is an excellent student and thinker." However, she continued to receive poor marks for her behavior in class. "N's [needs improvement] will become X's [unsatisfactory] unless talking is stopped." This trend continued throughout high school.

The Port Arthur schools were excellent. They paid higher salaries than those of most towns in Texas. Fifty-seven thousand people lived in the town, which was the center of the world's largest oil-refining district. Many of the wealthiest oil companies had their newest and biggest refineries in the area. The companies invested in the school system as a way to train top-quality workers for the local plants.

On April 28, 1958, the United States conducted atomic tests on the Eniwetok Atoll in the Marshall Islands. A sense of potential annihilation hung in the air, a terrifying reality for those who were willing to look. It figured in all decisions in hidden, subtle, subconscious ways.

In her sophomore year, Janis worked on the yearbook staff, along with several of the guys from the Little Theater group. They were slowly emerging as the most important group she had met. They introduced her to a new horizon, one that had grabbed their minds and lives. In 1957, Jack Kerouac published *On the Road,* the first mind-blowing saga of another way of life. It chronicled the "Beat" generation, precursors of the beatniks. Janis's gang saw Kerouac's character Dean Moriarty as a fanciful, modern-day outlaw. Kerouac used the term "white nigger."

The Beats reduced life to its essentials in order to feel alive again. They romanticized poverty and those living in that divine state of grace, most notably the black male jazz musician. They looked for leadership in his balance between humility and freedom. The Beats dressed to show their contempt for society and its values. They smoked grass, drank excessively, and talked in rambling stream-of-consciousness lingo that only the converted could understand. Their works challenged the naïve readers in Texas with the implied question, "Are you hip?"

Some say the term *beat* referred to a deadbeat, or being beat up. Kerouac thought it was from the word *beatific,* to walk to the beat of an inner, soul-guided music. The gang in Texas was desperately trying to break out of the mindless routine they felt society trying to force upon them. They yearned to be part of the *real* world, and they knew that wherever it was, it wasn't in Port Arthur. The Beats offered awareness about the *whole* world, not just the parts that proper society wanted to tell kids about. To Janis, they seemed to promise answers to the questions of existence that so dominated her life.

Many Beat affectations showed up in teen movies, led by *Rebel Without a Cause* with James Dean in 1955. The film displayed a hero who was forced to rebel against the constraints of society, guided by a higher moral imperative. On the big screen he complained, "My parents don't understand me." He mocked the square world with an insolent attitude and a new uniform: blue jeans. The Hollywood image machines had discovered the huge adolescent audience. For the first time they geared programs especially for teens, a group that had been used to listening to the same things that their parents did.

The Beats became the guideposts for the intellectual gang that formed out of the Little Theater summer workshops. Janis wrote a note in Karleen's yearbook:

To a good ole egg. I've tried in vain to analyze you but I can't so I figured—what the hell (heck), stay confused. I wish I could figure you out. Who do you like now—Mickey, Dennis, Jim or David? I hope I will get to know and understand you better next year. Remember me always, SEZ Janis.

P.S. Remember—I AM A VIRGIN!

During the summer between Janis's tenth and eleventh grades, she again participated in the Little Theater workshops. It was the same group of people, only she was older and more capable of handling herself. The Little Theater group was the one place where she felt comfortable and fully accepted. The social leaders of the workshop remained the boys—Dave, Jim, Adrian, Randy, and Grant.

This group of five guys didn't admit women into its inner circle, but kept them on the periphery, as girlfriends or dates. In Janis's sophomore year, she had occasionally dated guys in the group. She went to a DeMolay fraternal society installation dance with Roger Iverson, an occasional group member. She'd had a date with Dave Moriaty to go sailing. But she wasn't anyone's girlfriend.

When Janis wanted something she went for it full force. If she wasn't invited initially to go to some event the guys were attending, Janis wheedled herself an invitation. She took it upon herself to call one of them and ask, "What's going on? I'm ready to do something." Slowly she became a steady member in her own right. She was a girl, she wasn't anyone's girlfriend, and she was a member of the gang. "Janis was self-assured and assertive enough to make friends with five guys who were handfuls themselves," said Adrian.

Her hormones had finally kicked in to give her the physical maturity she so craved. She expected Lana Turner hourglass curves. Instead, her body defied her desire to retain her eighteen-inch waist. Her torso thickened and her hips headed toward the staunchness of a yeoman farmer's wife, but her bosom developed only a gentle curve. She was never heavy in high school, but she lost the lithe grace of a young fawn and held a soft roll of baby fat just below her belly button that thwarted her desire to have a flat stomach.

Adopting the Beat attitude in her life, Janis caustically derided

★

those who identified themselves by their superficial physical beauty. Someone who was pretty or popular had to prove she also had intellect before Janis would stoop to socialize with her. Several girls passed the test, though, and Janis was quite friendly with some of the most popular girls in school.

To some of her classmates, she appeared sullen and belligerent. Mother kept trying to help her fit in by making or buying her nice clothes, most of which Janis refused to wear. Some of the loudest arguments during Janis's high school days were over clothes. She screamed indignantly when our maid washed the Keds that she had labored to get to just the right degree of dirty!

Since the schoolboard wouldn't accept girls in pants, Janis wore black or purple leotards while her classmates were still marching in step with bobby sox and loafers. She wore her skirts right above the knee when most of the others placed their hems right below it. When the Barbie fashion dolls were introduced in 1959, Janis had a wardrobe no Barbie would be caught wearing. Janis was becoming a beatnik.

Janis and her friends took what little they knew of Kerouac's characters' life-style of snubbing society and blended it with a righteous attitude regarding their own flagrant behavior. They weren't outcasts; they were rebels!

In July 1958, *Time* magazine wrote an article about Jerry Lee Lewis and his child bride. The following issue contained several letters to the editor deriding Lewis's supposedly lax morals and poor character as representative of the "youth of today." "This letter writer is crazy!" Janis stomped around the house, fuming at the unjust charges against her generation. "Then write your own letter to the editor and tell them your views," was Mother's reply. Janis did write a supportive letter and received a reply, thanking her for writing and saying that many others like her had written upholding the quality of the youth of today. She was proud of the letter and kept it in her scrapbook.

Time, our family staple weekly reading, wrote about the Beats in 1957. We also watched Steve Allen's television talk show, and on one program Steve televised the hip new art form of free-form jazz, with Allen playing piano behind Jack Kerouac reading his writing.

Janis set herself apart at a time when people didn't want to be different. Her classmates were just discovering mass movements. Their generation gelled around the new sound of rock and roll, led by Bill Haley and the Comets, who jumped onto the scene in 1954 with "Rock Around the Clock," which was used in the movie *Blackboard Jungle*. A host of others soon followed—Elvis Presley, Buddy Holly, the Big Bopper, and more. The radio was the vehicle of liberation for teenagers, allowing them to talk directly to each other. Rock music was especially suited to the radio because it didn't need a big band or a large ballroom.

Rock in those days was never listening music but always dancing music. It required audience participation. Elvis swung his hips and made the jitterbug erotic, and it was called bop. The Twist and other popular dances drew more people to the new sound.

Rock and roll owed its roots to folk music, black rhythm and blues, and country and western. Many blacks felt that they were being ripped off as the white kids took their songs and made large fortunes recording them. But the white kids were also finding a way to address and include blacks and the black experience in their segregated lives. Janis and her friends were more interested in the root music of rock than in the Elvis style of rock and roll.

The large black minority in Port Arthur was blocked into a community in the oldest part of town, a downtown area bordered by Houston Avenue. The only blacks we saw regularly were domestics. In spite of that, we were well aware of the nightlife that was the mainstay of Houston Avenue, a sign of other qualities of life. The fact that it was forbidden made it even more intriguing. The blacks were only one of many defined cultural groups in our town. The area was a "melting pot of workers, Catholic Southern Louisiana Cajuns, Protestant East Texas rednecks, and a few East Coast managers," explained Jim Langdon. The international port, with its oceangoing vessels, attracted many nationalities—Dutch, Irish, Italian, Mexican, German, Syrian, French, and more. The abundant heritages made it that much more difficult for us to see African-Americans as anything other than just another group, with its own stories and traditions.

Racial integration was beginning to get national attention. On September 4, 1957, Arkansas governor Orval Faubus used the state militia to block black students who were trying to attend Central High School. The upshot was that President Eisenhower ordered U.S. Army

★

troops to escort nine black students to class. In September 1958, Governor Faubus closed four schools in defiance of the Supreme Court. It wasn't until June 1959 that the federal court said that the Arkansas law allowing the school closures was unconstitutional and that blacks were allowed to enroll. In August 1959, 250 demonstrators assembled near Central High School in Arkansas to protest integration.

Port Arthur was solidly segregated, but the times sparked some tentative cross-race interaction. There was a black-versus-white tackle football game every Sunday afternoon in a field close to the borderline of the communities. "It was never angry or racist, it was just football, black against white," explained Jack Smith.

Despite such intermingling, there were segregated waiting rooms for professional offices that served both races. The hospital had a separate black wing. Signs saying WHITES ONLY graced the water fountains.

Our parents were quiet rebels who recognized the authority of the larger society. The best they did was to pay a fair wage to the cleaning women who worked for us and give them our cast-off furniture when we bought new.

Race relations figured prominently in the Beat literature that Janis read with her gang. They adopted Kerouac's ideals of the poor black man's higher morality. Janis's social studies class was taught by Miss Vickers, a stout dowager true to the schoolmarm cliché, including all traits that an excellent teacher should have. Miss Vickers liked to bring current events to class and one day raised the issue of race and the court decisions. One by one the students emphasized the value of segregation and their denial of any validity to the black claims. Janis and Karleen exchanged looks and Janis stood up. "Society's treatment of the black person is wrong! They are people like you and me." She expressed her heartfelt belief in equality and was greeted by derisive yelling in class. Karleen slumped in her seat, too intimidated to rise to her best friend's defense. After class and down the hall they heckled her, "Nigger lover! Nigger lover!" Janis cringed in righteous indignation.

She went through much the same process when she dared question the value of unions. Our father was in management and she often heard tales of the arguments in the plants. The choice between union and management allegiance often drew the line in friendships. The local unions were big, powerful, and inclined to violent strikes. To Janis, it was a matter of what was right. How could you discover what was right until you could talk about everything, including whether the union viewpoint was fair and accurate. To many people, union support meant blanket support—right or wrong. Janis was in the minority side in our blue-collar town.

"Janis and I adopted a tough attitude to the world to survive," Jim Langdon explained. "Port Arthur was hostile. It was outrageous that people so much stupider than me were going to push me around. I wouldn't stand for being victimized by the Neanderthals of the world. Being tough worked. I got through." Janis assumed a way of walking, a certain body posture, and a style of cussing designed to get people to leave her alone. A few classmates took to following her around school, begging her to say a cussword. They went off laughing when their taunts finally succeeded in her striking out with a verbal retort.

She began to develop a deliberate image to use in confrontations at school. She went to Karleen's house and sat in the middle of the bed, practicing a special laugh. She cackled and listened to the effect. "Was it loud enough, Karleen? Was it irritating enough?"

By daring to rebel against the social code of conformity, Janis and her friends made themselves easy targets for the normal adolescent barbs. The guys got as much flak as Janis did, but the barbs stung her more deeply than they did her friends. They embedded themselves in a way that made them hard for her to release, then or years later.

Society's resistance to what was obviously the right thing to do—racially integrate—further heightened Janis and her intellectual pals' views of the backward nature of their hometown. They began to see themselves as victims of an ignorant world. The national racial conflict with its local echoes spurred them to pursue the other side of life. It was almost as if some people in society were ready, waiting for someone to shove the racial issue to the forefront. Janis's gang responded to the call.

The routine at home—Pop working and Mother caring for the kids—changed radically in Janis's junior year. Grandmother Laura East needed nursing care and our mother had to find some extra money to help pay for it. Mom enrolled in a typing course at the local business college to hone her skills before she started to apply for jobs. She was so obviously competent that before the semester ended, the school hired her to teach the course! She took on the job of training young ladies to be secretaries, guiding them from adolescence to their first paying jobs. At the same time, Janis was systematically breaking the local social codes, almost as though ticking them off a list. The contrast made Janis's defiance even more uncomfortable at home.

Our parents liked her interest in pursuing a subject whether it was a school assignment or not. Once she got the idea of making beer in the bathtub. "You're not old enough to drink, dear," they said to her enthusiastic plans. "I know. I don't care. I just want to make it," she replied. She amassed the materials and worked on fermenting the mash, but something went wrong and the goo soured horribly. She carted the failed brew out to the backyard and buried it. Although our father often mentioned his fond memories of making bathtub gin, no one seemed to make the connection with Janis's beer efforts. Perhaps in her own fumbling fashion she had been trying to succeed in his eyes.

Janis's junior and senior years were marked by periods of peace broken by instances of outrageous behavior that led to confusion, panic, and yelling at home. "She just changed totally, overnight," Mom said with a sigh. "A complete turnabout from her former self, and I didn't know what to do. I didn't understand it." Perhaps Janis was one of the minority of girls who have a severe problem with the hormonal imbalances and physical changes of puberty. Perhaps she was just too intelligent and had too strong a sense of righteousness to accept the myriad compromises that life asks of us. She was incapable of drifting through life. Once she began challenging cultural values and standing for truth, she crossed an invisible line that could never be retraced. Rebellion took on a value and meaning of its own. Each challenge or request that she stop a behavior resulted in a firm attachment to the activity. Resistance brought equal resistance and a heightened escalation of the problem.

Janis's searching left an ocean-sized wake of chaos in the house. I was emotionally terrorized by the flying discord, and did the only thing an eleven-year-old could do—I hunted for a higher authority. I started going to church and prayed for everyone.

In retrospect, Janis's behavior was not so terribly shocking. Most of the time she just hung out with her pals and talked. They congregated at Jim Langdon's house because his father worked nights and his mother was willing to make herself scarce. "We just had fun, good clean fun," Adrian Haston said. The group gathered in the evenings or on the weekends and searched for something interesting to do. Sometimes they went to the beach, like everyone else, to build campfires and have picnics. Occasionally they stopped at the abandoned lighthouse and snooped around and talked. In flat, marshy Port Arthur, there were few high spots to catch the eye, but two available ones were the water towers and the Rainbow Bridge. The gang climbed them both, often, to sit and look at the world below. They held a goal of climbing every water tower in the area at least once.

The group had its own version of the drag. While other kids cruised a four-to-five block strip of town, gawking at each other, this gang took to the highway. They carved a groove in the triangle from Port Arthur to Beaumont to Orange and back. They spent half their lives in cars. They would stop at a diner along the way for some java, soak up the working-class ambiance, and continue their intense discussions. They talked about movies like *Picnic,* in which the female hero leaves everything for a man who loves her for qualities other than her beauty. They were typically paranoid about being spotted by their parents in some unapproved activity. "Canoe racks" was a signal for Dave to duck down in the seat because a car with canoe racks, like the one his father had, was approaching. It was always good for a rise, whether or not the car-top carriers were visible. Most discussions concerned the evils in the world, the hypocritical social structure, the banality of the school, the boring town, and prudish sexual values.

Janis started reading *Mad* magazine with the guys. She laughed at Alfred E. Neuman, whose cartoon antics poked fun at the world of adults and presented a sense of a national underculture that held a satirical view of life. *Mad* cartoons mocked middle-class America, television, the suburbs, and anything else that smacked of accepted values. For a while Jack Smith and Tary Owens put out a high school humor magazine, giving the young commentators a place to voice their opinions.

They devoured the poetry of Lawrence Ferlinghetti, the owner of the famed City Lights Pocket Book Shop in San Francisco, who gave new writers a start in the business. He wrote titles that caught their fancy, such as *A Coney Island of the Mind.* They jumped on the wild new works of Allen Ginsberg, whose initial poetry style, modeled on William Blake and Walt Whitman, had given way to performance poetry, introduced by his notorious poem "Howl." They read Irving Stone's *Lust for Life,* the fictionalized biography of Vincent van Gogh, a man driven to create art. They were drawn to D. H. Lawrence's *Lady Chatterly's Lover* when it was banned as obscene by the U.S. postmaster general. Janis and Karleen read Leon Uris's *Battle Cry,* James Jones's *From Here to Eternity,* and Mickey Spillane's detective novels. They sometimes chose books according to the number of cusswords in them. Pop often took the girls to the library with him. He went through a ritual of reviewing what they picked out. He would take the book and look at the title, and if he didn't know it, he'd sit it on his open palm. He told them his secret method of determining the quality of a piece: "If a book is heavy, they used good paper and it's probably a good book."

The gang also dwelled on girls and sex. This was primarily a guys' group that a girl had chosen to invade on their terms. Whom to date, how to put the moves on, what girl was putting out, and whether or not they had gotten laid were the topics discussed. Sex was never openly discussed in polite society. High school kids weren't supposed to "do it." They weren't even supposed to know what *it* was!

Janis had the inside information from guys at school about what was and wasn't happening, while she was participating in none of it. She and Karleen talked about sex, necking, and more, but Janis didn't have a beau for experimenting.

"Oh, Janis, you're a good old girl!" the intellectual guys often said. "Don't call me a good old girl, dammit!" she replied. Janis was as much a woman as anyone, but she wasn't considered so in the group. Women were seen as soft and nurturing, and Janis didn't aim for either. The boys knew no other way to relate to women beyond sexual aggressiveness. The only other kind of relating they did was with each other, as buddies. Slowly Janis began to treat the men she met the same way she saw guys treating girls. She got sucked into the role of being a tough girl as the only way to be taken as an equal.

While other girls in the 1950s focused on dating and pairing off, Janis rejected the whole coupling ritual. Society encouraged young women to seek a man who would protect them from the perils of life. Janis refused. To adopt the female traits needed to make a relationship work was to take that fateful first step in denying her individual identity.

Grant Lyons was into serious folk music—roots music, not the watered-down Burl Ives that trickled into most homes. He searched out ten-inch records of obscure artists such as Huddie Ledbetter ("Leadbelly"), Woody Guthrie, Odetta, and Jean Ritchie. Jim, Adrian, and Dave were into the jazz of Dave Brubeck and others. Their bantering carried over into music, with the gang studying and analyzing the techniques of certain artists, time periods, and instruments. Both Dave and Jim also had large classical collections. Music wasn't background for that group. It was the primary stuff.

Squeezing into Jim Langdon's bedroom, the gang gathered around his small portable hi-fi. Jean Ritchie's mountain music spoke of the harsh life of the Appalachian miners and the beautiful hills ruined by uncaring and ignorant mining corporations. Her music spoke to their guts, as the same conditions prevailed in our town's relationship with the oil companies. The refinery fumes fouled the air daily. Their oil tankers, in releasing their ballast, periodically left globs of gunk on our sandy ocean beaches.

For Janis, the most compelling artists were the old-time black blues singers. They hit her with the experience of social oppression described in Kerouac's books. Blues records allowed Janis to break out of the stereotypical limits of her white world, to move beyond race and meet the poetic hearts and minds of the black culture.

Sometimes the group brought their records to a church party or other large gathering that wasn't just their group. In a calculated manner, they would put their records on the hi-fi. As the wailing of one artist after another spewed into the air, the party would slowly clear out and they would have it all to themselves. "Are you hip?" their actions asked.

Janis did the same thing at home. She tested our parents by replacing the resonant tones of classical symphonies with Willie Mae Thornton's version of "Hound Dog." She found out the music wasn't appreciated. She eventually was able to gain equal time for her new taste in music, but only if she put on classical records between her selections.

While the gang was driving the "great American night," as Jim Langdon called it, they sang in unison the folk tunes they listened to so faithfully in the day. One evening, while they were doing an Odetta tune, Janis refused to join. She sat silently, expressing her disdain. Unable to bear their butchering any longer, she broke out in a voice that sounded just like Odetta. The guys stopped singing. They were shocked. There was no point in singing along if she was going to sing like that. Later she called Jim Langdon, "Guess what? I can sing." He replied, "Oh, really? What else is new?"

The group found new sounds by listening to the late-night radio stations out of Memphis, Nashville, Chicago, and Mexico, across the border. Locally they followed the Big Bopper's show in nearby Beaumont. He was Jay Richardson, a white man who sounded black. They heard the sounds of Bobby "Blue" Bland out of Houston. The radio brought them insight into the hip sounds all around. At that time, many of the national acts had roots in their part of Texas.

With Karleen, Janis pursued her interest in the radio. She loved everything about the radio; it was the vehicle of cross-distance communication that allowed people to find like souls across the land. Port Arthur College, where Mother worked, had an affiliated radio station, KPAC, where technical students could practice. Roy May and John Robert, one year ahead of Janis in school, were two of the local kids who worked as DJs. Janis and Karleen often stopped by the station to visit while they worked. Sometimes they went to the broadcast booth of another station, KOLE, to talk to "Steve-O the Nightrider," Steve O'Donohue, sitting quietly between his on-the-air spiels for the brief moments he could focus on their questions. He played rhythm and blues and rock and roll, and Janis wanted to pick his brain about the songs and musicians. Other times the two girls brought coffee to the guys manning the radio tower and sat and talked.

Janis was developing a bravura that left Karleen out. Like their contemporaries, the two girls rode aimlessly up and down the drag certain nights of the week. They peered into cars that passed as the other autos' occupants stared back. Janis often slunk down in the backseat, hiding, knowing that if any of her intellectual pals saw her she would never hear the end of it. With Karleen she did things she didn't do with them. Often she tried to steer Karleen off the drag and downtown to that den of sin in town, the Keyhole Club. They were too young to enter, so Janis would ask a passing patron to go inside and buy her one of their hot dogs that were so famous around town. Her brazenness embarrassed Karleen, who hid in the car until Janis returned, displaying her treasure like a trophy.

Janis saw herself as a painter in high school. She drew for hours. She was particularly interested in anatomy, forcing Karleen to sit for hours so she could sketch her hands or feet. "Don't move, I'm just about to get this right," she would say, showing her drive to perfect her work.

Janis took up oil painting, a challenge in both technique and pocketbook. The paints and canvases were expensive, and our parents didn't have the extra cash to afford nearly as much as Janis's artistic passions could consume. She occasionally took a small job, such as taking tickets at the Port Theater, in order to buy art materials.

Painting consumed Janis's days. The emotions within her demanded an outlet. Her canvases displayed people, generally only one, male or female, and any viewer of her work could behold the artist's passion for understanding humanity. Janis painted both religious themes, such as an angular Christ on the cross, and social themes, such as a picture of an old black man playing the banjo. Her brush strokes captured emotion, and her images shouted out her questions.

Janis was fascinated with the human form and became interested in painting nudes. The folks got quite flustered, thinking it was an inappropriate subject for a young girl. They wanted her to paint landscapes or buildings. Pop and I sometimes helped her pack her lunch and art materials and drove her to Pleasure Pier to a spot behind the old ballroom near the water. We left her there most of the day, to paint vistas of choppy water, sailboats, fishermen, and diving birds.

Janis decided to decorate her room with her art, painting the two panels on her closet door. On one panel she painted a nude figure. The folks were upset. They didn't want Michael and I exposed to such visions. Janis went round and round with them about the finished painting until she was forced to replace it. Over the nude she painted

★

a scene of tropical fish underwater with tendrils of lazy seaweed in the current.

Art still provided a forum for Janis to interact in the broader world. She won a football poster contest using a tiger skin in her senior year. She also entered Captain Kangaroo's Play-Doh modeling contest with a model of the digestive system. She won an honorable mention.

Alcohol began to enter Janis's social scene in her junior year. The drinking age in Texas was twenty-one, but like many adolescents, the gang spent evenings hunting for enough quarters to afford one six-pack of beer and someone to buy it for them. If successful, each of the gang would have one beer, sipped defiantly as they cruised the darkened byways of the Texas coast.

The first drink of liquor that Janis had was at Karleen Bennett's house. Karleen's mother wanted the girls to learn about alcohol in safe surroundings, not in clubs or the backseats of cars. Mrs. Bennett fixed Janis a whiskey sour, which she sipped with pride. "This is too great to believe, Karleen!" she exclaimed with pleasure. The girls felt especially sophisticated because the drink had a maraschino cherry in it.

The city of Port Arthur held pockets of independently governed communities like Griffing Park and Pear Ridge. Each had its own liquor laws under the Texas state law, which forbade liquor by the drink. Some areas were wet and others were dry. The system allowed a small enclave to loft the banner of abstinence by keeping liquor stores across the community boundary in Port Arthur. Even the wet areas didn't allow full-service bars. Patrons had to buy a bottle, which was kept with their name on it and from which the bartender prepared their drinks. "Private clubs" could serve drinks if you paid a "membership fee" at the door. The cynicism, denial, and downright insanity of these laws and the accepted ways of circumventing them just increased the outlaw adolescents' disgust with their hypocritical society, which seemed afraid to look at reality.

They learned about drinking from the books they read. They discovered the strong connection between literary genius and alcoholic weakness: F. Scott Fitzgerald, Thomas Wolfe, Dashiell Hammett, John Berryman, Jack Kerouac, Edgar Allan Poe, Ambrose Bierce, James Thurber, and Stephen Crane. Four of the eight American writers who had won the Nobel Prize by 1958 were alcoholics: Eugene O'Neill, William Faulkner, Ernest Hemingway, and Sinclair Lewis.

Eventually Janis's group found the local music halls. Luckily, or unluckily, Port Arthur was close to the Louisiana-Texas border, and the drinking age in Louisiana was eighteen. Louisiana also had liquor by the drink. Texas kids believed that the joints across the state line would serve anyone who was tall enough to get their money up on the bar. They were further enticed by a twenty-five-cent happy hour at a place called Buster's. Jim Langdon began to get jobs playing in bands in Vinton, and his friends came to listen. Good girls in high school did drink alcohol, but they didn't go to Vinton. Or if they went, they didn't talk about it.

Vinton, Louisiana, offered Janis a glimpse into another way of life. It was Cajun. Both the language and the social attitude that came with it were different from the Anglo culture of Texas. There was a whole group of bars catering to the Texas youth: the Big Oak, Lou Ann's, Buster's, the Stateline, and more. Each had a large dance floor and several pool tables. After growing up glued to radio and hi-fi, Janis found her first good live music in Vinton. It may have been Cajun soul, rockabilly, or something else. There was certainly the white soul music of Jerry LeCroix and the Counts. Whatever it was, it sounded good, and uniquely Louisianan. Mixed into the atmosphere of the club was the Cajun priority of having a good time. These French-Arcadian descendants didn't harbor the pent-up Anglo-Saxon attitude toward emotional expression. They let it flow and everyone accepted it.

Louisiana was as racially segregated as Texas in 1959-60, and in Vinton there were "whites only" bars that were off-limits to the blacks. However, there were several bars, such as Lou Ann's, that catered primarily to the African-American trade but allowed whites inside to hear the black bands. Soul symbols began to creep into Janis's life. They were part of the Beat scene, echoed in her experiences in Vinton. The group adopted the lingo, referring to hip people as "cats," African-Americans as "spades," and throwing in an artful use of "ain't" and "man" in every sentence possible.

Janis was developing fluency in the new adolescent slang. She and Karleen practiced at Karleen's home, holding cussing contests. Her parents laughed at the young girls practicing words they didn't understand so that they could appear tough in their social circles. They sat on the couch with a dictionary. One would say a word and the other would have to define it, or they would both look it up in the dictionary.

★

Away from the guys, Janis was more of a girl. She and Karleen painted their nails together. Sometimes they would do weird things, like paint polka dots on their nails. Once they sprayed their hair with cans of purple and green color for Halloween. Karleen washed hers out before school the next day. Janis didn't.

Our parents kept trying to support Janis and provide positive experiences for her to balance her hostile feelings. The summer between the eleventh and twelfth grades, they tried paying her to stay with Michael and me while Mother worked. They hoped Janis would develop a greater sense of responsibility. Janis played with the role, inviting the Bennett family over for a full dinner she prepared of chicken Hawaiian served as formal as we ever got.

Michael and I loved that time, but Janis wanted to break free and run with her friends. Mom eventually hired someone to replace Janis during the days. That's when Janis enrolled for summer courses at Port Arthur Business College. The folks wouldn't let Janis just loaf all summer, especially when Mom had to work and was unable to supervise. Janis enrolled on July 7 for half-days of clerical study. She lasted until August 7, when she withdrew. For the month she was enrolled she missed classes on nine days.

Janis did help with nighttime baby-sitting when required. One evening the three of us watched *Father Knows Best* on television and saw those kids enact a murder mystery for their parents. We decided to do the same thing. Michael became the deceased, with ketchup serving in place of blood on his shirt. Janis painted footprints on the front steps and we carefully hid a pipe—the murder weapon—in the living room. Our parents were delighted to come home and enter the game. This was the kind of breaking with tradition that they valued.

Janis had her own real police encounters. One summer afternoon Arlene got Janis and Karleen dates with some out-of-town friends. Riding around, the guys threw some firecrackers as a prank. Reported to the police, they were caught and brought to the Port Neches police station. Janis wailed, "What are they going to do to me?" as Arlene was let off because her father was a physician and Karleen was excused because her father's company had done the plumbing in the new police station. Janis stood there in disbelief. "My father only works for Texaco! I'll never get off!" Following a stern warning, Janis was also allowed to leave. Janis turned to Karleen. "What will I tell my parents?" With a typically cool approach to life, Karleen shook her head at Janis's ignorant query. "You tell them nothing!"

Janis's senior year of high school was most different from her junior year in the absence of the core intellectual group, who had graduated and were on to college. The younger contingent pulled together, the core of which was Jack Smith, Tary Owens, Philip Carter, and Janis.

Janis loved hanging out at Karleen's house. The Bennetts treated her more as an equal than as an adolescent. Karleen's father would talk to her for hours on end about his views of life. He believed in reincarnation and that life was hell. He told her stories of his father, who had been a revival preacher, and how he'd been tarred and feathered because he took to tarrying with another man's wife. Janis and Karleen sometimes took dates to the beach, along with the Bennett family. They cooked steaks and swam and had a regular celebration. Her involvement with the Bennetts was so constant that Karleen's grandmother commented, "Don't you ever leave her at home?"

Our parents liked Karleen, so it was easy for Janis to get permission to go to her house. It wasn't always as easy to get out with the guys, though. In the winter of her senior year, Janis went to Karleen's as a way to get to a coffeehouse—the Sage—that had just been opened by Elton Pasea, an older merchant seaman from Trinidad. He envisioned a relaxed social gathering spot, and served good coffee over a background of great jazz music. On the walls he hung original art, and on the tables he placed chessboards. It was modeled after the many similar places in Los Angeles, San Francisco, New York, and Paris. Cutting-edge culture was attempting to take root in Port Arthur.

The Sage was only a simple storefront, just one man's dream. On New Year's Eve, 1959, the gang held a party at the Sage. Though it wasn't a formal concert, Janis sang for the group. She also danced on the tables, reminiscent of our mother's style so many years before.

The Sage gave Janis the opportunity to display her artwork and sell a few paintings. She hung her rendition of the three kings following a distant star. Someone from Galveston bought the piece as he passed through town. Janis went to the Sage as often as she could, and it usually required a struggle with our parents to get permission. At least once she sneaked out of the house at night, took my bicycle, and pedaled to the Sage, hiding the bike under the cooling tower of the A&P across the street from the coffeehouse. Wrangling a ride home, she left my bike. I was aghast the next day to see that someone had stolen my bicycle! I looked everywhere until Janis and Pop and I went to the A&P to do the grocery shopping. Janis casually suggested we drive in the back way, where we would be sure to drive by the cooling tower. As we drove I screamed, "My bike! There it is! I can't believe we found it." She never owned up to her involvement in taking it, and I might have resented her theft had I recognized her action, but I didn't. Instead, I was overwhelmed by her helping to retrieve it.

The Sage and Vinton might have been quick jaunts to a brave, new world, but everyone knew that the really good music was in New Orleans, on down the highway. On January 26, 1960, near Janis's seventeenth birthday, she talked Jim Langdon and two other guys at the Sage, Clyde Wade and Dale Gauthier, into going to New Orleans to listen to music. Our parents would never have let Janis go, so she went around them. She borrowed Pop's work car and gave our parents a cover story about spending the night with Karleen. She figured they would never realize she left town. Who would believe she'd go to New Orleans for the weekend? It took almost that long to drive there and back! Perhaps she would have gotten away clean, had a minor wreck not damaged the radiator, leaving the car inoperable.

The Louisiana police started looking at papers and realized Janis was underage and across the state line with overage boys. "They were talking the Mann Act, statutory rape," said Jim Langdon, "and the trip was all her idea!" The police called Mom and she told them there was no ill intent. She explained that Janis and the fellows often did things together. Being in Louisiana was not out of character for them. The police escorted Janis to the bus, but the fellows were left to hitchhike back.

This was not an adolescent prank in anyone's eyes. Janis endured hours of misery and apprehension during the ride back home. It was so bad, our parents didn't know what to say about it. Clearly Janis wouldn't accept the limits they set for her and she wasn't good at setting her own limits. The wounds festered for some time as they tried to decide how to deal with the problems that Janis seemed to be creating for herself. They feared that the real pain from this excursion would be visited on Janis at school.

They were right. The story made it back to campus, easily embellished on the gossip circuit. Janis was righteously indignant. In people's dirty minds she had been doing naughty things with a group of guys in New Orleans. In truth she had spent the night going from bar to bar, listening to different bands. As she later said, "That sex thing they lay upon me is all in the viewer's mind." Society gave a freedom to boys that it withheld from girls. It was "sowing their oats" for the guys, but "tarnishing your reputation" for her.

It must have been awful being in school with whispered lies circulating around. Before this incident, Janis had only seemed a bit kooky to other kids because she wore beatnik clothes. After the gossip about the New Orleans trip in her last semester in high school, she picked up the banner of social outcast and began taunting them with it.

The school counselor called Janis to her office. She discussed rumors of Janis's drinking and improper behavior. Janis denied them. She sat in the office defiant, telling Karleen later that there had been a wine bottle concealed in her purse the whole time. (Neither Janis nor her friends drank much in high school—alcohol was too hard to get. When they did get some, they bragged about it, which has led to conflicting stories about the extent of their drinking.)

The unresolved tension at home was thick. Our parents couldn't believe the stupid things Janis was doing. The more problems her behavior created, the less she seemed to care about modifying her activities. She stayed out later, studied less, and developed a mile-wide mouth full of impolite expletives. Coming home at one A.M., she and Karleen were greeted by Mother, worked up into a lather about the idiocy of her daughter's transgressions. Mother screamed in confusion, "You're ruining your life! People will think you're cheap!" Slamming the door to her room, Janis cried to Karleen, "How can she do this? I'm her daughter."

In 1950s Texas, people were intolerant. Our parents saw Janis damaging her reputation, a thing so important and nebulous that a girl was supposed to do anything to keep it pure. Mother had tried everything and was clearly at her wit's end. To make matters worse, she saw her daughter do the very things that had so terrified her in her own adolescence. Mother knew the grief of losing one's social position through the action of her father's publicly amorous affairs. She cringed in fear at the possibility of Janis losing the thing Mom had treasured in her own life, her reputation. It was so real to her that explaining it to Janis was impossible. Mom talked in generalities: "You just don't do that!" Mother hadn't dealt with her anger toward her parents enough to speak from her core. She was still reliving the pain of her own adolescence. She couldn't empathize with Janis. She could only speak from the fear that still held her attached to her firm belief in not challenging society's rules.

Our parents worried about Janis's behavior. They talked, cajoled, lectured, set limits, urged, and tried everything else that came to mind. "Please don't set the world against yourself," they seemed to plead. They finally sent her to a counselor to help her move beyond her social anger. They pondered family therapy, to help in reducing the problems of the internal arguments, but opted for individual work with Janis. After a short time, the counselor seemed to have helped Janis to cope with her situation, though not to reach any cathartic illumination.

Pop offered Janis some solace. He had much less respect for society's value system than did Mother, but he accepted life and counseled Janis to do the same. Still, Pop believed the world was greater than any localized set of values. The fact that Janis questioned them was intriguing to him, although he told Janis that the difficulties were not worth the price.

Pop had always laughed loudly and easily with his kids, until the girls started to become women. Then he withdrew. Somehow our femininity made it more awkward for him to express his feelings, a task that took effort at any time. He was shy, so what comfort he could offer Janis was not enough.

Friends tried to talk to Janis. Kristen Bowen tried including her in planning parties, thinking that what she really needed was more social acceptance. But even if Janis went to the gatherings, she didn't feel included. Roger Pryor called one day and invited her out for a Coke. It was as big a disaster as you could imagine. Mother kept saying, "Don't blow this. Roger is a nice young man." Janis secretly felt Roger was interested in her only because he had heard the gossip about her loose morals and wanted to get laid. Instead, Roger lectured Janis about her improper conduct and urged her to reform. Janis scoffed at him belligerently, "Get lost!"

Things seemed to come to a head in mid-March. On the 17th, two days after my birthday, Janis was suspended from school for a few days. Then a little bit of reality seemed to sink in and she put her life together enough to finish school.

Karleen got wind of an attempt to deny Janis an invitation to the country club's Black and White Ball for seniors. Karleen, whose parents were members and thus entitled to invitations, called Mary Carmen Fredeman and the two plotted. Mary Carmen told the steering committee that if Karleen didn't give Janis an invitation to the dance, then she would. Mary Carmen was one of the most popular girls at school—they couldn't deny *her* an invitation. She was also from a prominent and wealthy family. So Janis got an invitation. She and Karleen double-dated. They danced in their formal gowns on the arms of their dates and felt the icy stares of the narcissistically proper young ladies around them. There were no incidents, but it wounded Janis nonetheless.

Marijuana was starting to trickle into the high school scene. Janis first ran into it at a sock hop, where she got a joint from a fellow she knew at school. Karleen and Janis took a car and drove to the outskirts of town on Procter Street. It was typically muggy and hot, but the girls rolled up the windows before they lit up. Karleen wouldn't smoke, but Janis was eager. "But Karleen, this is what all the beatniks do!" Janis implored. She drew deep drags on the forbidden drug and sighed in anticipation. The car slowly filled with smoke as the girls circled the edge of town.

On the night of their senior prom, Janis and Karleen went driving. They picked up a couple of guys who wanted a ride to Port Neches, so they took them. It was a fitting nonevent to end a three-year period of adolescent frustration. Of Port Arthur, Janis later said, "What's happening never happens there. It's all drive-in movies and Coke stands on the corner, and anyone with ambitions like me leaves as soon as they can or they're taken over, repressed, and put down." Reflecting on those days, she mused, "All I was looking for was some

★

kind of personal freedom, and other people who felt the same way."

Living with Janis in high school tested the bonds within the family. She bolted from the innocence of childhood insistent on finding a better replacement than a compromising adulthood. She demanded that her parents know what she was doing and accept her behavior. By her graduation a shaky truce was reached. Our folks accepted the fact that Janis would probably continue to do things they didn't like and were comforted by the fact that she had reached a level of social independence by graduating from school. They were more willing to let her solve her own problems. Together the three of them decided that they loved each other and would agree to disagree.

CHAPTER FIVE

COLLEGE AND THE
VENICE BEAT SCENE

★

Time keeps moving on
Friends they turn away
I keep moving on
But I never find out why . . .
But it don't make no difference
And I know that I can always try

—Janis Joplin and Gabriel Mekler,
"Kozmic Blues"

*I*N OUR FAMILY we never admitted defeat. Instead, we plotted strategy to remedy our problems. Janis's fantasy for solving her frustrations in high school was to move to a more accepting and open-minded community. At age seventeen, fresh from graduation, Janis followed her friends to college, at Lamar State College of Technology in nearby Beaumont, Texas.

Weren't colleges places where people wrestled with truth? Didn't the power of intelligent ideas reign supreme among students who came to fine-tune the use of their minds? Wasn't college a community where people coveted their free thought and free lives more than life itself? Wasn't college a place that could value Janis's gifts? Couldn't she finally escape the repression of parental oversight?

We helped Janis move to a two-story modern-style brick dormitory the summer after high school. The dorm rooms were laid out in suites, with two double-occupancy rooms joined by a bath. An open balcony along the front of the rooms served as the hall. I helped haul her things up to the second floor and envied the crisp newness of the room, its golden-brown stained-wood cabinets and large windows. In

★

her new home, she unpacked old treasures that took on new value in a world of unknown potential.

Janis shed no tears when we left; she almost hurried us out with promises of "See you soon!" With zest she attacked the task of settling into her digs. The centerpiece of decor that lit her new palace was a painting she'd just completed. Lacking a canvas, she had layered the oils on an oversized piece of plywood. Confidently she strolled to the campus wood shop with the picture in hand, ready to greet a fellow traveler, a woodworking artist who would trim off the lower edge of the plywood. Back in her room she wailed, beat the walls, and cussed up a storm. She hadn't found a wood artist who treasured her work. She had encountered only a mindless hand on a saw that splintered the wood and ruined the picture!

In the midst of her verbal barrage, Gloria Lloreda entered the room. She was a feminine, dark-haired beauty from a Catholic Mexican-American family in Galveston. Gloria was enchanted with Janis, her energy, power, and talent, which seemed to assure Gloria that college life would be lively. Their friendship began in empathy over Janis's deep frustration about the painting. It was an easy way for the girls to connect. Gloria and Janis became friends that summer. In the fall, they became roommates.

Janis and her new friends stayed up late that first night, talking endlessly about dreams and questions. Janis's first day at college promised her a greater sense of belonging than she had felt in years.

Regrettably, the gossip mongers who had talked about Janis in high school had followed her to college. They pledged sororities and walked around in clusters of like-minded coiffured heads whose uniform challenged, "It's just not proper to *do* that!" Gloria was soon warned that Janis was loose and that she should stay away from her and her friends. Luckily the talk never fazed Gloria. Besides, she was developing a crush on Adrian Haston, the man she later married. Gloria had already found Janis a warm and caring friend. But the gossip must have added an atmosphere of unease to Janis's encounters with other new students. It created an automatic distance between the sorority girls who gossiped and the artist intellectuals who scoffed at them.

Both Jim Langdon and Adrian Haston were returning to Lamar for their sophomore years. Their network of intellectuals was growing, with as many fresh faces from Beaumont as there had been from Port Arthur in the original gang. Tommy Stopher, a wonderful artist, and his brother Wally were there, along with Patti Mock and her future husband, Dave McQueen, plus Phillip Carter, Jack Smith, and Tary Owens from Janis's class in high school.

Janis listed her major as art and pursued her work seriously. She took figure-drawing classes in which Patti sometimes earned money as the model, always clothed in a bathing suit in prim Beaumont. Janis played with styles. She liked the broad, flat areas of color in much of Picasso's work. She also liked the crispness of Braque and the color of van Gogh. Her all-time favorite was Modigliani, the impassioned Italian painter and sculptor who revolutionized the art world with his eerie fluid figures that showed a forceful African influence. His brief artistic life was spent in the ravaged world of wartime Paris. Janis studied the man as well as his work and found that he had drunk alcohol and experimented with hashish to such an extent that they had cursed his life. He had a persona that many portrayed as larger than life—a man who carried around a copy of Dante's *Divine Comedy* and the Bible and was quoted as saying, "Your real duty is to save your dream."

Janis went to Houston with Karleen, who wanted to visit a friend. Janis wanted to see the Purple Onion coffeehouse. Karleen dropped Janis at a cheap hotel, not realizing that it was a whorehouse. When the management explained this to Janis, she said, "Well, it's cheap, isn't it?" They took her under their wing for the day. Karleen picked her up the next day and they headed home, feeling young, free, wild, and capable of anything. It was typically hot and humid, and Janis took off her shirt to let the breeze from the car window cool her down. She cradled a bottle of red wine she'd managed to salvage from the adventure. "We've got trouble," Karleen told Janis. "There's a cop flashing his lights at us." Hurriedly Janis put on her shirt and hid the bottle of wine. "Do you know how fast you were going, young lady?" the officer asked. The girls replied, "We're lost." He was kind and gave them an escort on their way.

Patti and Janis sometimes cut class together and went to a bar, where they drank and talked. Other times they would gather as many people as they needed to raise fifty cents and head to the Paragon

Drive-In on Houston Avenue, where you could get a gallon of beer for fifty cents if you brought your own jug.

Behaving outrageously was part of the image the artistic crew felt they needed to maintain. When a situation didn't arise on its own, they created it. One night Janis and her three suitemates slipped into their nightgowns at bedtime. The boys' dorm was right across a courtyard, visible through a huge window that was covered only by a drape. Gloria flashed the lamp in their room, on and off, on and off, and on. With the light creating a shadow, the four girls performed a pretend striptease, all the way down to the bathing suits they were wearing underneath. The next day some of the guys expressed their appreciation of the show, to the shock of the girls. The mock strippers had never believed anyone could determine who had put on the show. They didn't try it again.

The girls almost got expelled because one of them had a date with the captain of an oil tanker in port. Janis, Gloria, and several other girls dined on the ship as well. The thrill of excitement vanished when the captain's wife found out and complained to the dean of the college that the students had spent the night. "We didn't sleep over, we didn't do anything, and we didn't know he was married!" they wailed earnestly. When they were able to present evidence of having slept in the dorm, the dean let them off with a warning: "In the future, please choose more appropriate behavior."

Parties were seldom planned; they just happened when any group of three or more gathered. Some of the guys had apartments off campus, which were the preferred places to celebrate. Now that some of the gang were old enough to buy booze legally, the alcohol flowed freely. On a few occasions Janis drank too much and her friends had to struggle to get her back into the dorm. It was a challenge to loft the inebriated Janis from the lawn up and over the balcony railing to the waiting arms of her friends on the second floor. Somehow they always made it through curfew check.

Occasionally Janis and others would sneak out of the dorm for the heck of it. Many times the destination was to hang out "on the line"—the jive description of the bars just over the Texas-Louisiana state line. They grooved to the music of the Vinton clubs, especially when Jim Langdon was playing in the band.

By the end of the fall semester, Janis was disillusioned with college life. The school was designed to train engineers to work in the local petroleum industry. Lamar was not the hothouse of artistic stimulation that Janis needed and sought. She spoke to our parents on one of her weekends at home. "I don't want to go back." "What will you do instead?" they queried. "You have no skills to support yourself."

Mother worked at a business college and saw in its short-term training programs an answer to Janis's dilemma. Janis enrolled at Port Arthur College to study keypunch, typing, and other clerical skills. After her training she would be equipped to move to the more accepting atmosphere of a larger city and support herself. Janis trained just long enough to pass the skill level required to get work. She enrolled in March 1961 as a half-day special student. She missed all or a portion of nineteen days of class in the four months she was enrolled. The reason given was "ill."

Janis lived at home that spring. She and Patti spent a lot of time together hanging out in town. They sometimes went downtown to a record store. In 1961, music stores had listening booths. The girls spent hours playing everything, including jazz and country, but only bought things like Bessie Smith. Sometimes Janis and Patti used Patti's father's Webcor reel-to-reel tape recorder. Janis sang into it and then they listened critically. They weren't pleased with any of it.

Once Phillip and Janis dropped by to fetch Patti to a shrimp boil down on the pier. It was a typical rainy day and the two had picked up a young black hitchhiker on the way, planning to drop him at his home downtown. As Patti bopped out to the car, her father caught a glimpse of the black guy in the backseat. He then accused her of going out with him. Even their good deeds brought them trouble.

The parties were growing ever more bawdy. Few people had internal limits about how much to drink. They drank what they could afford to buy. With increasing liquor, many parties disintegrated into crude grab-ass kinds of things, with drunken men making a play for Janis or any other women around. It was a demeaning way to find physical intimacy.

Parties were often held at the house of whoever's parents were out of town or away for the evening. One gathering at Phillip Carter's house was notable for the demolishing of a four-by-eight-foot model of

★

an oil tanker that belonged to Phillip's father. The accident evolved from verbal sparring between Janis and G. W. Bailey, a Port Arthuran who later played Sergeant Rizzo on the television show *M*A*S*H*. G. W. was a good friend of Patti Mock's brother, and he warned Patti about hanging out with Janis. Mixing liquor and two hostile attitudes produced strings of insulting accusations from G.W. to Janis and back. Trotting defiantly over to Jack Smith, Janis said, "Be my white knight. Do something." Jack accepted the challenge and ended up fighting G.W. over Janis's honor. The ship model was the unfortunate victim of their fury.

One evening a group of eight—Jim, Dave, Adrian, Randy, Janis, and three other girls—walked up the steep pathway along the narrow two-lane roadway of the Rainbow Bridge. The bridge spanned a narrow river, but it had to be tall to allow the uppermost spires of the oceangoing vessels to pass easily underneath. Reaching the top, the group swung their legs over the side railing and climbed down a ladder to the catwalk underneath. It was dark, quiet, safe, and forbidden. Far below, the tiny tugboats pushed their heavy barges of oil. Silently, someone leaned over and dropped an empty beer bottle, aiming for a tug. Everyone held their breath to see if it would hit the target. Suddenly, sirens split the air—one, then two, three, and more piercing wails. A passing motorist had seen the last girl climb over the railing. Fearing a possible suicide, the police had been called. Every patrol car within twenty miles blocked both lanes of traffic as the kids were called to the road surface. "This is it," the guys mumbled. But feminine charm sometimes works wonders, and the police were cajoled into letting them off.

New Year's Eve at Phillip's house, Janis and Patti were goaded by the guys into showing female fighting tactics. They went at it on the floor in a true cat fight, pulling hair and popping buttons. The girls enjoyed the tussle. As they bopped down the stairs to get a fresh bottle of whiskey, the front door opened. The Carter parents caught them looking disheveled, their shirts hanging open, and swigging bourbon. They quickly threw the whole crew out.

People started traveling. One weekend Jim Langdon and Rae Logan, his future wife, along with Adrian and Gloria and Janis, drove to Austin and stayed in a hotel. They wanted to visit their old chums

Dave Moriaty and Randy Tennant. During a school vacation when Adrian couldn't stand being parted from his true love, the old Port Arthur group drove to Galveston to visit Gloria. As evening approached, Janis and the guys bid good-bye to Gloria and decided to get a cheap motel room instead of driving the few hours' journey back to Port Arthur. They flipped a coin to determine which two people would get to sleep on the bed. Janis and Adrian won. The other guys slept uncomfortably on the floor around them. The next day, Gloria went with them to wait for the Galveston ferry to dock and return them to the Port Arthur side of the ship channel. The car held six groggy, hung over, sleepy, and bored people. Janis, ever interested in enlivening things, said, "Gloria, guess who I slept with last night?" Adrian groaned, "Oh, no!" and everyone else in the car howled at the mischievous gibe. They'd all been there and knew that nothing except sleeping had happened.

A lot of the people in the group had moved out of Port Arthur. Dave Moriaty and Randy Tennant attended the University of Texas in Austin. Grant Lyons went to Tulane in Louisiana. Janis was itching to be on to grander places. She and our parents hatched a plan to move Janis to Los Angeles, where Mother's two sisters, Barbara and Mimi, lived. Our parents were hoping that removing Janis from the influence of the gang would enable her to find another base for herself. Los Angeles seemed like a great spot because Janis's two aunts could provide some oversight. However, Los Angeles also held a thriving artist community, one of the three largest Beat groups in the United States. Janis was thrilled at the idea of going to Los Angeles, a place she saw as full of possibilities.

We drove her downtown one Saturday morning to put her on a large, smelly Greyhound bus. I was dead set against Janis leaving me behind but was powerless to influence anything except my own anger and frustration. "Just don't go," I kept saying, a plea that fell on deaf ears that already heard the roar of the Pacific Ocean.

Barbara and Mimi met Janis at the bus station in Los Angeles. They found her standing by a pile of beautiful new luggage and talking to a young black man. "He's been on the bus with me the whole way," Janis said happily. Neither of them commented about her selection of friends, but they didn't need to say that it seemed improper to them that Janis visit with a black man. "That is awfully nice luggage," they said to Janis. She replied, "Mother insisted on buying it for me. I didn't want it. I was all set to stuff my things in an old bag, but she insisted."

Piling in the car, Barbara and Mimi began a guided tour of the city they loved. They showed her the sights and took her for breakfast at a posh place near Beverly Hills. Janis was shy and polite but a bit aloof.

Janis soon settled into an artist's shack behind Mimi's house in Brentwood. It was a small building where Mimi's husband, Harry, painted. He kept it well stocked with oil paints and canvases. Mimi didn't realize that Janis painted too and was surprised the next day to find that Janis had stayed up half the night painting. Janis thought she'd moved into heaven! She liked Los Angeles already.

Our parents insisted that Janis work, and with the assistance of her aunts, she soon got a job as a keypunch operator at the telephone company. She kept to herself in the back house most of the time, but came home from work one day and went into the kitchen to talk. "A guy's coming by in a little bit and I don't want you to think I'm crazy about him or anything. I'm not. I'm just using him. I asked him to come over and pose." Then Janis cracked up laughing. "He's in for a shock when he finds out I just want to paint his hands. He has perfect hands to finish the picture I've been working on." Janis was on her second attempt at painting a man playing a guitar.

Mimi took her niece out one evening to get to know her better. She brought Janis to a pizza place near the university, thinking she would like being around other people her age. It was a lively spot where a small band played. Before Mimi had settled down, she turned to see Janis stand up, kick off her shoes, and march in place as she sang at the top of her lungs "When the Saints Go Marching In." For five minutes Mimi and everyone in the audience clapped along as the young enthusiast from Texas stole the show.

Barbara eventually helped Janis find an appropriate apartment, but she didn't stay there long. Money was tight, and she moved into Barbara's two-bedroom apartment. It was an awkward fit with Janis squeezed in beside Jean, Barbara's teenage daughter. Life at Barbara's apartment couldn't be more different from the calm normalcy of Mimi and Harry's routine with Mimi's daughter, Donna.

Barbara sold real estate and had a special relationship with her broker, a married man named Ed. Barbara had been married twice. They worked well together and their days often started with Ed coming by at ten A.M. for martinis. Frequently they took a client out for lunch and drinks. Regularly Ed came to the apartment at four P.M. for the cocktail hour. Janis was impressed. She thought Barbara's life was wonderful; she had found freedom.

Janis grew very close to Barbara. The two shared a zest for living and a tough, decisive style of interacting with the world. Janis often joined Ed and Barbara for drinks and conversation. However, Jean resented Janis, and that tension made everyone's life difficult in the apartment.

One afternoon while returning from work to Barbara's house, Janis started visiting with a guy on the bus. He was going all the way to Venice Beach, on the outskirts of L.A. Janis passed her stop and went with him.

Venice was the embodied dream of Albert Kinney, who had made a fortune in tobacco. He had envisioned a Renaissance town like Venice, Italy, with gondolas and charming bridges over sixteen miles of linked canals. The area grew, embellished by rococo-style hotels and amusement parks, the Coney Island of the West. Hundreds of tourists savored its charm. However, the discovery of oil destroyed the development of this fanciful burg. Standing derricks and the stench of oil just didn't blend into the quaint Venetian stucco architecture. Many of the canals were filled in with dirt. The tourists quit coming. By the 1950s the beatniks took over Venice's cheap apartments along picturesque narrow streets and alleys.

Venice had never looked like a regular L.A. suburb, and seemed unwilling to act like one either. It attracted a unique group of residents who had little money but a strong aesthetic sense. They lived in "voluntary poverty." They liked the winding streets, the area of the city prohibited to cars, and the proximity to the beautiful Pacific Ocean. Alexander Trocchi, an American who had edited a literary magazine in Paris, came to Venice and wrote *Cain's Book,* his tale of craving and battling heroin. Stu Perkoff was the most famous poet to emerge from the Venice coffeehouse scene, a group that included Charles Bukowski, who later wrote "Notes of a Dirty Old Man," a column in the *Los Angeles Free Press.*

Lawrence Lipton gave what he termed "Venice West" national

★

recognition in his epic tale of Beat life there, *The Holy Barbarians*. Published in late 1959, it changed the local scene forever. *Time* ran a full review of it. It was the new guide to the Beat generation. The tourists returned to Venice, intent upon drinking coffee in a "real" coffeehouse and gawking at beatniks involved in their artistic tasks.

Lipton was intent upon turning Venice into the new North Beach, where his friend Kenneth Rexroth held court with the Northern California Beats. Lipton's novel was aimed at achieving recognition for the Southern California scene. Few others wanted it, though. Most had moved there to escape. Now they were in the limelight.

There were about fifty coffeehouses in the Los Angeles area in the 1960s. Venice West Café Espresso was the first hip coffeehouse and restaurant. It was opened by Stu Perkoff as a business to support his family and to enable him to continue writing poetry. He sold it in early 1959, prior to the publication of Lipton's book, at a time when the café was empty and losing money. By late 1959, it was packed and profitable.

The Gas House was the most notorious coffeehouse in Venice because it had become the target of a citizens' group that hated the influx of tourists and artists. The Gas House was the first place they wanted to close. It was supposed to be an art gallery where tourists could not only see art on the walls but also see artists at work producing new pieces. It was also supposed to serve as a venue for poetry readings and as a members-only flophouse. It struggled to do much of any of those things, but the court case lodged against it gave it so much publicity, everyone stopped by.

Another product of the Venice beatnik scene was Henry Miller's *The Air Conditioned Nightmare,* a saga of a family's automobile trip across country. Miller's heroes believed that California was the only place in the country where there was any hope for culture, where people had any zest or joy in their lives.

There was a deliberate mixing of the races in the coffeehouses. The literary movement in Venice owed much to the earlier bohemian movements and also a deep debt to the creative energies of Watts. Many frustrated blacks from the South streamed West to Los Angeles and founded a thriving community in the 1930s. Langston Hughes, the great black writer, came from there, and Arna Bontempts also wrote of Watts. Jelly Roll Morton's best years were in Watts.

Janis moved into the low-rent Venice district. Aunt Barbara and Ed came to visit her new home. Barbara's jaw dropped as she scanned the dirty dump that Janis had chosen. In the middle of the living room was a large steel barrel into which all trash was thrown. On the wall hung a collage Janis had made from a dried-up pot of split pea soup with a ham bone solidified on an old rope. She turned to Janis and raged, "You weren't raised to live like this!" A verbal barrage ensued between Janis and Barbara, a device that the two had perfected and seemed to find useful in resolving their differences. This time Barbara left angry and resolute. She wouldn't visit Janis at home again.

Janis had moved to Venice well past its heyday. She came on the limping tail end of the tide of publicity-enticed newcomers who had read Lipton's book. The area had become mean-spirited. Crime was commonplace—murders, robbery, and rape. The amusement park stood rotting. At night the beach belonged to the muggers. No longer on the fringe of the drug world, it was now one of the centers. Grass, Benzedrine, heroin, and codeine cough syrup all had their followings.

The Los Angeles and Venice Beat scenes were saturated with drugs and their effects on artistry. A totem of the movement was the all-night drive to create art in any form. Wine and marijuana were most popular, but heroin was used by a small percentage of the group. Painting, music, or writing occupied hours of everyone's days. Janis was undoubtedly influenced by the wealth of ability she witnessed there. She still considered herself a painter and focused on that. In addition she was emerging as something of a singer, performing spontaneously at the Gas House or at late-night gatherings among friends.

Sexual exploration fascinated and united these students of aesthetics. They welcomed uninhibited pleasure between men and women, as well as between men and men, women and women, or groups of enthusiasts. One's virginity was often the first thing a novice lost after wandering curiously onto the scene. An even better symbol of freedom was interracial sex. Straight society developed a paranoia about the Beats, a feeling that the police helped to start by arresting Lawrence Ferlinghetti in 1956 because he had published "Howl," the startling poem by Allen Ginsberg.

Janis frequented the Gas House and met "Big Daddy," the official spokesperson for the establishment. His real name was Harry Hilmuth Pastor, but he was also known as Eric Nord. He was six feet

★

seven inches tall and weighed three hundred pounds. He had been living in the North Beach community, where he owned the Co-Existence Bagel Shop. Hanging out around him and others, Janis heard about the North Beach scene. She called Mimi and Barbara one day and said, "I'm going to San Francisco and I wanted to say good-bye." They replied, "How are you going to get there?" Janis sighed and said simply, "I'm going to hitchhike." "Oh, no," our aunts cried, "we'll give you the money for the bus." Janis was firm. "I don't want your money. I want to go and go *my* way." She arrived in North Beach and strolled down Grant Street. Then she went into the City Lights Book Shop and rubbed shoulders with Lawrence Ferlinghetti.

Around Christmas in 1961 Janis returned to Port Arthur wearing a World War II bomber jacket turned inside out so the sheepskin lining showed. She came unannounced in a taxi that pulled up in front of our house, something that never happened. Pop went outside to greet her and was astonished to see his daughter emerge from the backseat of the car tumbling small shoe boxes tied with string onto the lawn. There she hugged him with a warm, gleeful smile, ignoring the oddity of her arrival. We were glad to have her home.

Janis returned a more experienced person, capable of impressing the local gang with her tales of the real life in California. Janis went with Jim Langdon to a private club on New Year's Eve to hear a Lamar friend of his, Jimmy Simmons, and his small jazz band. Jim brought Janis to the stage and Jimmy asked her to sing a few tunes with them. After the first one, he said, "Enough." Janis's rough style wasn't the pretty-voiced sound he had expected.

Janis had tasted freedom in Los Angeles and was uncomfortable living under parental oversight again. She and Jack Smith found an abandoned drive-in theater one day while tooling around town. She grew excited by the apartment in the base of the screen and argued with our parents about moving into it. Our folks never considered the possibility, and Janis ranted and raved about their getting in her way.

She enrolled as a student at Lamar and commuted back and forth. She lived at home. Janis increasingly looked to Jim Langdon as a mentor. Jim was a gifted musician coming into his own at Lamar. He played in the Beaumont symphony, various jazz clubs around town, and dance bands like the ones formed by Johnny and Edgar Winter, who lived in Beaumont. Sometimes, late at night when Jim was playing and the crowd had thinned out, Janis could be coaxed onstage to sing something like "Cherry Pie."

Janis and gang met George Alexander, a jazz trumpet player who had played with Gatemouth Brown and many others. He was back living in Port Arthur, teaching at the local high school. He played jazz on the weekends and tutored his fans.

Jim Langdon worked with a group called Ray Solis, which had a contract to do a radio and television commercial for a bank in Nacogdoches, Texas, that was celebrating its fiftieth birthday. The band recorded an instrumental track of the Woody Guthrie tune "This Land Is Your Land." They asked Janis to do a vocal version. She sang:

This bank is your bank
This bank is my bank
From Nacogdoches
To the Gulf Coast waters
Fifty years of saving
Fifty years of service
This bank belongs to you and me.

The vocal was never used.

In March, right before Mardi Gras, Patti Mock and Dave McQueen got married. They honeymooned in New Orleans, and Janis and Phillip Carter went along to enjoy the thrill of the city. They went in Phillip's father's car and had only ten dollars between them aside from Phillip's father's credit card. They slept in shifts in the car parked in Pirate's Alley. One slept in the front seat and another in the backseat while the other two roamed around. When Janis and Phillip knocked at the window to get their turn sleeping, Dave couldn't be budged. In frustration Janis marched off into the crowd. In the morning she returned with a tale of having picked up a sailor who got them a motel room. She said it matter-of-factly, as a way to solve a problem.

Janis got a job in Port Arthur at the local bowling alley waiting tables in the restaurant. Earning her own money gave her a feeling of independence, and she needed that. She worked till midnight and was then ready to unwind. Frequently she met Jack Smith after he got off work at the drugstore. They liked to go across the canal to the pier on the lake and talk. The view of gently lapping waves under a broad expanse of sky stimulated profound thoughts.

"Why is everyone a pair except me?" Janis wondered. There was Jack and Nova, Jim and Rae, Adrian and Gloria, etc. "I want to want the white house with the picket fence covered with climbing roses, but I just don't," she often said with a sigh.

There was a drawbridge across the canal that connected the pier on Pleasure Island to the town. If a tanker was passing by, cars had to wait twenty minutes or so for it to inch its way carefully under the narrow upraised bridge. One night as they sat waiting in Jack's car, Janis got the impulsive idea to take one of the portable flashing lights that were set up at the base of the raised bridge. She taunted Jack until he slid a broken one out of sight in the backseat. They hadn't considered that the bridge attendant would call the police. A squad car waited for them on the other side of the road. Jack was arrested and put in jail. Janis was frantic, feeling that she was the cause of his misfortune. She went to the police station and stayed for three hours talking to the desk sergeant. She tried every approach possible, pleading, taking responsibility, and even demonstrating that the light had been broken when they took it. Finally they let Jack off. Walking outside he expressed his gratitude, and the tough young girl said, "I was too frightened to call my parents at this hour of the night."

Our folks tolerated much of Janis's personal activity as long as she got her work done. Her activities still ranged from the expected attendance at church to the outrageous. They hoped that Janis, like most teenage rebels, would make an about-face and return to her former self.

They drew an invisible line between Janis and Michael and me, tolerating things in her behavior but ruling them out for us. Their seething hostility greeted Janis's attempts to encourage Michael and me to adopt her ways. Otherwise they tried to accept their eldest's behavior.

There must have been some discussions about drinking because Michael pulled Janis aside once and asked her if she had ever seen anyone drunk. He wanted to know how they behaved. She roared and said, "Hey, I've been drunk. It's cool." He was shocked. He had no idea she even drank. "Next time you've had something to drink, tell me," he implored. Not too long after that she knocked on his door. "Well," she said, "can you tell? [Pause] I'm drunk." He was floored. He couldn't tell at all.

Parties had become intense, mind-probing affairs. Grant Lyons might be found throwing darts across the room. Near him lay Jim Langdon head-to-head with another person. The wall was lined with records, and another person was carefully selecting among them. Placing the album on the stereo, the challenge would be presented: "Who is playing the three-quarter-time flugelhorn passage on the first cut?" Jim was a serious musician and his passion set the tone.

A typical evening started with people tossing coins to test Newton's law of probability or playing a few hands of bridge. Janis created a new bidding convention, which she called a googly, as in, "I bid a googly heart." It meant that she knew she wasn't supposed to bid but she wanted to bid, so she called it a googly to sanction its improper basis. Soon people would tire of cards and start drinking and listening to music. The last run for beer was ten P.M. If the energy level was still up around midnight, the group might head to Vinton to see what was happening.

The amount of alcohol consumed often determined the tone of an evening's antics. In one blurry evening at Patti and Dave McQueen's garage apartment, in the midst of the camaraderie, Patti and Janis spontaneously embraced, kissing on the mouth. It was the only remotely homosexual encounter that had occurred in the group.

The kiss shocked both girls. They stepped back. It was late, about midnight, and Dave McQueen, Patti's husband, and Jim Langdon had just entered the door after their late-night jobs. They had walked into the room just in time to witness the kiss. No one said anything. The party continued.

Janis and Patti never shared another kiss or hug. No sexual relationship grew between them. Patti said that they loved each other very much, but their feelings had nothing to do with sex. Janis was hot to explore the world and she wanted Patti to take off and live a fantasy life in California, but Patti was married. She found her future in her husband.

Much later that evening, Jim, Dave, and a few others were

★

talking in a small hallway by the bath in the rear of the one-room apartment. By that time, two or three A.M., the apartment held only a few people, and most were drinking, sloppy drunk, or passed out. Patti had fallen asleep fully clothed between two similarly incapacitated men on the bed in the corner. Finally Dave's anger exploded as he finished his beer and hurled the bottle toward Patti with all the force his powerful build held. The bottle missed, smashing instead into the sleeping Jack Smith's jaw and knocking out several front teeth.

Janis entered the fray, frantic as she took Jack under her arm and drove him to the hospital. "This wasn't supposed to happen. This is horrible! Why did this happen?" she kept mumbling.

In the spring of 1962, Janis and her friends Dave Moriaty, Randy Tennant, Grant Lyons, Adrian Haston, and Bob Clark went to the Cameron Shrimp Festival. It was a rambling affair where you could buy boiled shrimp and crayfish at booths all over town. People roamed, eating and drinking beer. Janis wore a "69" T-shirt, which she used to inflame the locals. Some festival-goers tried to negotiate with her male friends to "buy" Janis's services. The guys thought this was great fun and haggled over a price, all in jest. Adrian tried to negotiate an end to the prank, but eventually it was necessary for Janis's friends to fight to extricate themselves from the scene. Luckily, no one was hurt.

Janis and Patti developed a whole shtick for playing with the guys they encountered in the Louisiana bars. Sometimes the group didn't have enough money for everyone to get past the cover charge. The girls became proficient at duping a stranger to pay their way in. Once inside, they continued flirting and leading them on, seeing how many free drinks they could get. They felt safe because they knew they were with a whole gang of trusted male protectors. When things had gone far enough or it was time to leave, they would either indicate that they were with other men or quietly steal away. It came close to fistfights more than once, but the Texas gang seemed to know how to handle the hot-blooded Cajuns and navy men stationed nearby whom the girls had humiliated. They either stood up to them or slipped out, running like hell to the car.

One evening when they had been at the Shady Motel Restaurant and Lounge playing pool and drinking beer, Patti was flirting a bit too much for Dave McQueen's taste. He restrained his fury until everyone piled into his secondhand Oldsmobile. As he drove home, fuming silently, he pushed his foot harder and harder on the gas pedal. The numbers on the speedometer went up to 120, but the car wouldn't budge over 110 mph. He yelled and pounded on the dash. Leaning into a curve, the car spun out of control and rolled over and over down the side of a bank. Finally it came to rest, and the group of seven began calling each other and climbing out of the auto. Unbelievably, no one was hurt.

That spring Janis helped Jack Smith fill out an application to West Point. She was frustrated by his desire to leave, feeling he was deserting her. Perhaps she had more than a friend's interest in Jack; it sometimes seemed that she had a latent jealousy of Jack's girlfriend, Nova. But Janis and Jack never discussed any romantic reason she might have had for wanting him to stay. Instead, she argued with Jack that she thought it was hypocritical for him to go to West Point because he drank beer and smoked. "You can't be a soldier with honor and duty to country if you act like we do," she complained.

Purity of action guided Janis's behavior. If she was going to be good, she was very, very good. If she was going to be bad, she let all the stops out. Anything less than full commitment to an idea or activity was "hypocritical," the worst adjective anyone could hurl at another.

The spring of 1962 was a time to plan new beginnings. The activities of the Port Authur-Beaumont crowd were wearing thin. Jim and Rae Langdon were married and had a baby. Others were planning their lives after one remaining year of college. Jack Smith said to Janis, "You can't just hang out here and party."

CHAPTER SIX

AUSTIN, TEXAS

★

Home of the brave, land of the free
I don't wanna be mistreated by no bourgeoisie
Lawd, in a bourgeois town
Hee, it's a bourgeois town
I got the bourgeois blues
I'm gonna spread the news all around

—Leadbelly, "Bourgeois Blues" ©

RUMORS OF A spirited community in Austin were trickling back to Port Arthur. Intent on checking them out, Janis surreptitiously took Pop's car for the weekend. She hadn't planned it, but about midnight during a weekend party when everyone else was heading off to Vinton, she and Jack ran off to Austin. Jack guided her straight to the apartment house at 2812½ Nueces Street. It was lovingly called "the Ghetto," reflecting the group's view of its role in campus life. Stepping through the kitchen doorway of one apartment, Janis found free-flowing beer and intent conversation. John Clay, a local folkie, was sitting atop the refrigerator playing the banjo. "You're right, Jack," she exclaimed. "I'm going to like this place!"

Her weekend of music and partying was broken only by occasional pangs of belated guilt about being there without permission. So she cleaned fallen leaves off Pop's car, as though taking extra care of it would make up for the error of her ways. Returning home, she had to face the consequences, but that was hardly an uncommon experience by this time in her life. The clamor of her disagreements with the folks always ended with the question, "What are you going to do with

★

your life?" The question was so serious, Janis persuaded them to let her enroll at the University of Texas—UT.

Mother, Janis, and I drove to Austin, moving my sister to yet another college. Janis was excited, intent on what she knew to be there. She dragged Mom and me to the Ghetto, as though Mother would ever approve of that as a home for Janis. It was a small cluster of run-down apartments that rented for forty dollars a month and attracted a hodgepodge of nonmainstream students who roomed in fours and used the place like a revolving commune. Mother was emphatic that we find Janis another home. The university finally settled the question of where she would live. Like most institutions of high learning at that time, the UT administration saw its responsibility toward students through the concept of "in loco parentis" (in place of the parents). They required freshman and sophomore girls to live in supervised housing.

We found a suitably funky rooming house for Janis, a large clapboard building in need of paint. The wooden screen door had that bent dark-wire screen so common in the unair-conditioned, bug-infested Southern climate. The door banged and quivered when I trudged in and out, carrying her things up to her new home. I ran my shoulder, like others before me, along the shiny paint, yellowed with age, that covered the walls of the stairwell. Everything there said she was entering a new world, and in the rhythm of my climbing it sang, "Good-bye, good-bye."

The university, they called it in Texas, since in 1962 there was only one university in Texas. About forty thousand students attended, mostly Texans attracted by the cheap twenty-five-dollars-a-semester tuition. Rich grazing lands where oil had been discovered endowed the school and enabled it to build aggressively and expand academically.

Janis didn't care much for the school, but she craved the offbeat society. It was located on the edge of the picturesque Texas hill country. "Oxford on the Perdenales River," Jim Langdon described it. The Regents never anticipated all the groups that a great education might attract or develop. In 1962 the local powers burned with indignant confusion that a small subgroup of social inventors had taken root in the largesse of almost free university education. So surprised were they that the police monitored the group's activities. They feared subversives, but all they found were underage drinkers and college-level pranks.

Janis was exhilarated by the stimulation of a larger social group and broader cultural opportunities. She gulped it down like a homesteader whose throat was parched from a fruitless search for water until he finally drilled a good well. The art films and musical performances shouted that she had found Nirvana! Austin wasn't just a university town, it was decidedly Texan. The rugged, defiant orneriness of Texas worked to trample polite intelligentsia. In Austin, ideas screamed to be recognized.

Janis slid comfortably into a group already steeped in outrageous behavior. Their parties were known for such activities as shooting twenty-five pistol shots into the walls, knocking holes in a closet door, and putting a bare fist through a window. People were thrown into a fountain on campus, whereupon they entertained their audience. Graffiti flowered from their paintbrushes, which were propelled by drink to scrawl "Aw shit" and "Fuck it," with the inside slogan "Poddy rules the world!" referring to a local comic-book character created by Gilbert Shelton. Joe E. Brown climbed to the flat roof of a building and wrote, "Fuck you, Sky King," so that he would see it when he flew over.

The new group consisted of a loose association of musicians, writers and cartoonists for the *Texas Ranger* humor magazine, and a club of spelunkers. They were the loyal opposition. They were outsiders with an acute sense of the absurd who delighted in nothing more than poking fun at and mocking society. By necessity there was a great deal of tolerance within the group, a respect for individual differences and overflowing praise for personal creativity.

Wally Stopher, who was part of the movement of the Beaumont gang to Austin, became a memorable symbol of the times. Called "Oat Willie," he was Austin's unofficial mascot. A photo of Wally standing in a bucket of oats, dressed in an aviator cap and polka-dot underwear, was given the caption "Onward Through the Fog."

One evening a group of girls pledging a sorority were locked into a house across the street from a Ghetto party. Janis and friends delighted in teasing the pledges, trying to get them to leave the house and come to the party. Janis went over and sang them a couple of songs, and a few of them did leave. The cops arrived after midnight. They walked up to a few musicians sitting on the porch and reprimanded them by asking, "Do you know there's a little old lady dying next door?" Lieuen Adkins, one of the musicians and a good friend of Janis's, said, "No, but hum a few bars and we'll fake it." Janis thought the reply was hilarious and wrote some instant lyrics, which the two of them proceeded to perform. Janis and John Clay were caricatured (shown opposite) in a handbook of party tips in the *Ranger,* a piece titled "What to Do Until the Cops Come," written by Lieuen Adkins and drawn by Hal Normand.

Janis's Austin days coincided with a turbulent period in American history, including racial demonstrations and the Cuban missile crisis. The shadow that hovered over most conversations was an atomic one. In everyone's minds was always the question of whether the future they argued about so heatedly would have a chance to bloom before the bomb was dropped. Women were just starting to assert their demands for equal pay and equal orgasms. Racial integration was just beginning in Texas. The university admitted blacks, but if a class assignment involved seeing a movie at a local theater, they couldn't get in the door because of their skin color. In 1962 the state was taking down the segregated bathroom signs in the capitol building and the restaurants began to accept black diners. Those changes propelled Janis's gang onward to hot talk at parties and interracial excursions into the music world. Janis revealed to a close friend, "I wish I were black because black people have more emotion."

Janis came back to Port Arthur from Austin full of enthusiastic stories. She told me the latest fashion news from that big town, saying, "They're wearing a lot of yellow tops with gray-and-white ticking material for pants and skirts." I took it to heart and had a set by her next visit.

She tended to wear a different look, setting herself apart from the typical UT coed. Janis and her friends often wore men's white dress shirts, hanging out over blue jeans. Other times the uniform was a black turtleneck and black slacks with boots or sandals. Janis spiced her vision of the local dress code by wearing her WWII bomber jacket inside out. She'd torn the sleeves off to make it more comfortable in the Texas heat, thereby enhancing the scruffy look the worn lambs-

(4) SCREAMS. This game, as its name implies, is really screams. The rules are very simple: everybody sits on the front porch and screams. That's all. Everybody just sits there and screams. This keeps up till the cops come. You can even develop a sort of inter-party rivalry with this game, the object being to see which party attracts the most cops the fastest. This makes a handy classification for parties afterwards, when someone asks you, "How was the party last Saturday?"

"Oh, fair," you say, "it was a three-car party."

The standard by which all scream parties are measured is the immortal Geology Department Glee Club Party of April 17, 1959. So inspired were the partyers that their screams attracted 14 squad cars, a hook-and-ladder truck, six taxis, two ambulances, the dogcatcher, the Salvation Army, and a man from down the street who showed up dressed in his pajamas and carrying a hoe.

wool lining already offered. Janis didn't wear makeup, though she sometimes dressed more femininely for a date. Most UT girls had bouffant hairdos that led the *Ranger* to call them "Bubbleheads." Janis's hair was growing long and hanging loose.

Her social group was at odds with the frats, and vice versa. The mutual resentment resulted in fistfights on occasion, sparked by serious challenges, such as one of Janis's friends wearing a mustache. Texas students knew that not even a graduate could get a job if he went to an interview with a beard. Growing one after you'd been hired was cause to be fired. All of her friends were targets, but Janis's volatile temperament made their fury land harder on her. Everyone had tales of being yelled at while walking down the Austin streets. Janis was one of the few who threw verbal epithets back. She was "very defensive and radically hostile," Tary Owens said. Unlike Janis, most people in Texas in 1962 didn't punctuate their sentences with "fuck." Janis shouted the word at high volume and used it to incite the straights around her to respond. She taunted her social enemies with intentional exhibitions, even if she cringed from their willingness to taunt her in return.

Which group had the *right* ideas? In those days people rarely thought it was okay to see things differently. Powell St. John, a slender, handsome, and friendly guy from Laredo, Texas, who grew to be a friend, lover, and musical partner, often talked with Janis about the razzing they got from the straight community. "Janis," he said, "you don't have any use for these people. You know you're cool and they're not. Why does it bother you? What difference does it make?" She didn't know why it made a difference, but she couldn't let go of an intense and righteous anger at any taunts directed at her.

The group knew that the straight community didn't understand them, but a new rumor began to worry them. An FBI agent had come by the Ghetto to interview Powell about a former roommate of his who evidently wanted a security clearance. Later they heard that the FBI was actually investigating the Ghetto crowd. The FBI didn't like the nickname "Ghetto." It worried them. They asked, "What does the Ghetto group stand for? Who are their major speakers?" Hearing this, the gang didn't know if they should laugh or worry. The FBI totally misunderstood. The group wasn't political at all.

The summer of 1962 Ted Klein bought a house on Lake Travis, a local recreation spot. He threw a housewarming party with fifty regulars from the Ghetto and assorted other acquaintances. It was a regular Texas good time with singing and beer drinking until Janis hollered, "Let's go skinny-dippin' " and six or more "ran down the hill scattering clothes as they went." The lake was a cool respite from the Texas heat.

The following day Ted was contacted by the sheriff's office concerning a complaint about "a party full of 'naked beatniks.' " They dithered, hassled, and postured until Klein apologized, adding, "By sheer accident we failed to mention swimming attire on the invitations."

After little more than one month in town, Janis had distinguished herself sufficiently to have an article written about her in the July 27 campus newspaper, *The Summer Texan*. The headline was SHE DARES TO BE DIFFERENT! Pat Sharpe, assistant Campus Life editor, wrote the article, accompanied by a photo of Janis playing Autoharp.

She goes barefooted when she feels like it, wears Levi's to class because they're more comfortable, and carries her Autoharp with her everywhere she goes so that in case she gets the urge to break into song it will be handy.

Her name is Janis Joplin, and she looks like the type of girl a square (her more descriptive term—a "leadbelly") would call a "beatnik." [Ms. Sharpe appears to have misunderstood one of Janis's comments about Huddie "Leadbelly" Ledbetter, a blues singer whom Janis favored. The word *leadbelly* was never used as a descriptive term by Janis or her group.]

"Jivey" is what Janis calls herself, not "beat." She leads a life that is enviously unrestrained.

She doesn't bother to have her hair set every week, or to wear the latest feminine fashion fads, and when she feels like singing, she sings in a vibrant alto voice.

UNTRAINED VOICE
Since she has never had a music lesson and cannot read notes, [Janis sang in a school chorale for several years. She could read music.] her voice is untrained. But this lack seems to be an asset rather than a liability, for Janis sings with a certain spontaneity and gusto that cul-

tivated voices sometimes find difficult to capture. She is at her best with folk songs, to which she gives an earthy, twangy rendition.

Janis' current ambition is to be a folksinger, though she really prefers blues. She has performed at the Gas House in Venice, Calif., and in Port Arthur, her home town. But she really began to think seriously about singing when she came to the University this year as a freshman majoring in art.

She says that people in Austin are definitely more hip on folk music than the clods in other cities she has visited. In fact, it was here that a friend persuaded her to take up the Autoharp.

AUTOHARP

This particular instrument is not one that is seen as often as a piano or a guitar. As a matter of fact, it is about as common as a glockenspiel. At first glance, it looks like a zither, but longer and narrower and with fewer strings. At the squared-off end are 12 bars which are depressed to form chords.

Right now, Janis' career as a folksinging-Autoharpist is in its beginning stages. She is currently the female member of a local group which styles itself the Waller Creek Boys. The other two are Lanny Wiggins and Powell St. John Jr.

GHETTO

When they are not in class or at home, the favorite hangout of Janis and her friends is an apartment which they have nicknamed the Ghetto.

The walls are decorated with original modernistic paintings done by local cats, and the furniture defies description. For want of a better name, it might be called contemporary American hodgepodge.

Password around the Ghetto is "uninhibited." Man, if a person isn't uninhibited, he's sick. Whenever somebody gets the urge to stand up and do a little impromptu jig, he gets up and does it. And if suddenly he feels like dribbling out a piece of modern art, he goes right ahead and dribbles.

COMPULSION

If on the other hand, he feels inspired to write a piece of poetry, beat or otherwise, man, he writes. Why if a person doesn't feel the compulsion to do something crazy at least once in a while, he is a leadbelly.

All activities sacred to leadbellies—like bowling, twisting, or ratting their hair—are taboo for cats. Consequently, the cats are confined to being uninhibited and singing folk music for whole hours together, which sounds about as exciting as the average fraternity party.

Cliches such as "suave," "swinging," and "I just can't beleeve!" are held in the utmost contempt by the uninhibited, but at the same time it is interesting to note the frequency with which "man," "chick," etc. appear in conversation.

In short, comparing the vast majority of University students to the vast minority of University beatniks would be like comparing a large sack of potatoes to a small sack of onions. The onions may be a little spicier, but they are all onions just the same.

In spite of Janis's penchant to raise the dander of those outside the group, Tary Owens said that she got along pretty well with everyone. Even the verbal sparring that she and John Clay resorted to when they were both drinking was part of their relationship. Jack Jackson, an accountant who wrote a comic strip for the *Ranger* titled "JAXON," said, "When Janis walked in the room, she completely dominated it." She had a powerful presence embellished by her obvious talents in artistic areas prized by the gang.

Janis came to Austin with interests in both painting and music. One day she ran into a Beaumont friend, Tommy Stopher, in Austin. He had returned from studying at the National Gallery in Washington, D.C. His technique had soared, and Janis felt embarrassed about her weaknesses. At the same time, she began to leave the isolated work of a painter for the crowd drama of a performing artist; she was lured away from painting by the gratifications of performing for an audience. The power of applause, the flush of adrenaline, and the camaraderie of working in a group captivated her.

Janis's real education in Austin didn't come from the university's classes. It came from the Austin music scene. That summer Janis teamed up with Powell St. John on harmonica and Lanny Wiggins on guitar and banjo, both of whom lived and partied in the Ghetto. They spent countless hours sitting in the backyard of the apartment playing tunes. They sang bluegrass, old-time country, union songs, and traditional folk music. They soon worked up a lot of material to play for others.

Powell St. John fell crazy in love with Janis. He had spent two years in the ROTC program before dropping out and focusing on his art studies. He didn't just want to be a painter. He also desired to be an original personality. Powell was attracted to Janis's brash, outspoken nature. He liked her *because* she was different.

Antiwar sentiment was growing, but their group was decidedly nonpolitical. Janis could empathize with Powell's background. She told him, "If there was a war, I'd go to work in a defense plant to free the guys to fight." There was a conventional part of Janis that always tagged along with her more noteworthy, eccentric bravura.

Their romance was brief that summer because Janis just wasn't interested. She told Powell, "I do what I do because it feels good, man." When their physical intimacy ceased, they remained good friends. They were close enough that Janis could walk into his house a few months later and declare, "Guess what? I've just come from the student health center and they said I have had a spontaneous abortion. And it was your baby!"

The Austin Parks and Recreation Department held a talent contest at Zilker Park. There were many categories, including vocal groups and dance. Janis, Powell, and Lanny entered and won first in the singing category. They were on the way.

The group sang at the Cliché Coffeehouse on Guadalupe, where an open stage hosted unpaid folk musicians between poets reading their work. The art lineup was selected by friend and Ghetto resident Ted Klein.

They started singing at the school-sponsored hootenanny at the Student Union on Thursday nights. Janis had been coaxed into learning how to play the Autoharp in Austin and began performing with it. Powell St. John, Lanny Wiggins, and Janis called themselves the Waller Creek Boys. Being one third of a "boys" band didn't bother Janis most of the time. She was often heard saying, "I'm just one of the boys." Sometimes not being regarded as feminine enough stung, so they started billing themselves as the Waller Creek Boys, featuring Janis Joplin. Powell explained that when Janis sang, there was no doubt that she was featured.

The hootenanny drew all aspiring musicians and singers in the area. The rules required everyone to sing one song before anyone sang a second piece. Janis liked to sing, not to sit and wait. In one evening her group would get to do two or three songs. In between was a constant stream of plaintive female voices crooning "Barbara Allen."

Janis resented competition, especially if it was an attractive woman who had any talent. Lolita was her most visible rival. As soon as that woman sang, Janis was pushing the guys in her group to take the stage. She had to try to upstage Lolita's lilting tones with her harsh intensity. But Janis didn't need to worry. The crowd loved the Waller Creek Boys. They were clearly some of the most talented people there.

Janis tried to capitalize on her popularity by getting a job singing in local bars, but they wanted to hire the Lolita types—the beautiful face with the Joan Baez voice. When Maria Muldaur came through town and was attracted to a Ghetto party, Janis stayed in the shadows. She refused to sing and compete with the petite beauty who already was a successful singer.

Janis favored such tunes as "Careless Love" and "Black Mountain," a song she introduced by saying, "I sing it every time I sing." The words hit home about living on Black Mountain, where the people were mean, so mean "a child will slap your face." At the end of the song, the woman leaves the mountain with a gun to get justice from her worthless lover.

Singing was a constant activity among the Ghetto crowd. Janis and Gilbert Shelton, a gifted musician as well as a cartoonist, often teamed up on old-time church songs. Over and over they sang the traditional song—"You better start reading your B-I-B-L-E / There's comfort, hope, and joy in the book of G-O-D / It's there in simple language, so P-L-A-I-N / that the D-E-V-I-L gets those who live in S-I-N." Most any traditional music could be heard being sung by the group. Tunes from Flatt & Scruggs were mixed in among those popularized by the Stanley Brothers.

The hootenanny, the jazz and blues clubs on the east side of town, and the constant Ghetto playing influenced Janis, but a barkeeper/singer influenced her the most. Kenneth Threadgill was a country singer who ran a bar that catered to real rural-type people, truck drivers and a few UT students. In his bar reality lived and breathed with the regular swinging of its two front doors. Janis said Threadgill "was old, a great big man with a big belly and white hair combed back on top of his head. He'd be back [behind the bar], dishing out Polish sausages and hard-boiled eggs, and Grand Prizes and Lone Stars." He was a man without pretense. To him a folk musician was a New Yorker in Bermuda shorts. He didn't consider himself part of the folk-music revival. He cared about the country music he had always

★

known. In the eyes of his college admirers he took on the role of "the real thing," the authentic roots of the music that they wanted to know.

Threadgill's converted gas-station bar was the first in Austin to get a liquor license when Prohibition was repealed. Tobacco smoke had discolored the whitewashed walls, testifying to the history of the bar's clientele. The obligatory jukebox was pure Threadgill. *All* the records were by his favorite singer, Jimmie Rodgers. The room was full of odd tables and chairs, with an old bar of beautiful wood on one side. A small stage sat in the far corner. Most evenings Threadgill could be coaxed out from behind the bar to sing a few of his favorite Jimmie Rodgers tunes. He would "lay his hands on his belly and lean his head back and yodel, just like a bird. . . ."

Jimmie Rodgers popularized country music, creating the Nashville sound and bringing the yodel to international acclaim. He didn't travel much. His success was based solely on his recordings. Rodgers was the first person inducted into the Country Music Hall of Fame. He sang about railroads and wandering, lost loves, and tear-gushing tunes of Mom and Dad. The "Singing Brakeman," as he was also known, borrowed liberally from blacks, blues lyrics, and the flavor of laments. Through Threadgill's adoration of Rodgers, Janis learned even more about passionate commitment to a musical style.

Once a week, generally Wednesday, Threadgill had some bluegrass musicians perform. The tradition had been initiated in 1961 by an English professor named Bill Malone and four of his graduate students. Many gifted musicians performed on mandolin, guitar, banjo, and harmonica. Later Threadgill took it over, and by 1962 Janis's crowd dominated. Each group received two dollars per night and all the beer they could drink. Ken's policy encouraged Janis to learn to play the guitar. If she accompanied herself, she wouldn't have to split the money. Another problem, of course, was that she was still underage in Texas, and Threadgill was strict about serving minors.

Threadgill told Janis about playing roadhouses, dealing with Prohibition, and the many acts he had known by running a tavern with live music since the 1940s. He recognized that she was an extraordinary talent but rough around the edges, and adopted a fatherly attitude toward her. No comments from her friends could equal his acceptance of her talent. He said, "You can make it, Janis. You have what it takes."

Mrs. Threadgill also took a liking to Janis. She offered a maternal touch to Ken's musical praise. Mrs. Threadgill sat Janis down and brushed her unkempt hair. "Let yourself be pretty," her motherly advice suggested.

So Janis sang and sang some more. Though Threadgill required country and bluegrass tunes most of the time, he let her slip in a blues number the nights she was onstage. The melodies she chose allowed the strength in her voice to knuckle under the tones and let them resonate throughout her frame. They echoed in her head like the pulsating gong in a Buddhist temple. Her talent had finally given her a way to get the respect and acceptance of redneck truck-driver-type people, folk who would otherwise have scorned her.

The music found in Threadgill's had deep roots, a mixture of railroad songs, blues, Carter family folk songs, and country and western from the twenties, thirties, and forties. Coupled with rhythm and blues, these styles built a foundation for the rock music that was to emerge in the later 1960s. There was rock while Janis was in Austin, but it was musically simplistic and topically banal compared to what emerged later. During her days in Austin, the serious people and the best musicians were on the folk scene.

Folk musicians expected their audiences to identify with the songs and react emotionally. Performers needed listeners to sway, clap, and sing along with the tunes. Folk allowed youth to anchor their current experience within a context from the past. This historical continuity and the validation it provided was vital to the music's ability to capture the hearts and minds of its listeners.

Austin was deep into the tap roots of this music. The more commercial groups, like the Kingston Trio, differed markedly from the ragged, direct style Janis sang in Austin. Only one successful performer commanded the respect of the Austin group—Bob Dylan. Janis believed in Dylan for a long time. She thought Dylan and folk music were the answer.

But folk was only one stepping-stone on the path to discovering those hidden aspects of life that she was so intent upon finding. She later described her situation, saying, "There was a time I wanted to know everything. I was an intellectual. Feelings made me very unhappy." Her gang of intellectuals in Port Arthur had unknowingly adopted our cultural separation of the intellect from the feeling and spiritual aspects of life. Even when they listened to music, they analyzed it intellectually. That confusion was still woven into Janis's life until she found the Austin group. In Threadgill's bar she found the emotional roots of music, a way to express her feelings—by singing the blues. Blues replaced even Dylan's style of folk music. Feelings began to work for her! In blues, Janis could celebrate the bouquet of natural life rather than guard against spontaneity as her Anglo culture preached. Music was the compelling experience and folk music told the stories of everyday life. It was basically democratic, lauding the value of each individual. Music and the stage were the vehicle; the audience response was the guide. The blind led the blind.

That it should spontaneously occur in Texas is really no accident. Texas was one of the last outposts of the original American spirit. Big dreams were part of the culture, alongside a fervent belief in the individual's ability to act and reap the rewards. Its continued adherence to the foundations of American Protestant belief placed the local society years behind the changes that affected the rest of the country. Texas was also geographically isolated from New York and Los Angeles. Stuck in the middle of the continent with little experience of the dog-eat-dog competition in the large cities, Janis's gang held unlimited visions of success. Their ambitions included social change. They merely expected the country to be what it should be. They demanded that Camelot arise at once!

Their views were made known through the *Texas Ranger*'s social commentary, satirizing the dominant culture's follies. They stated their complaints in humorous language, not angry shouts. Founded in 1923, the *Ranger* was an early example in a long line of college humor magazines that cropped up on campuses in the early 1960s. It was the best, voted number one by college humor editors all over the country. The people were the magazine. Their loose communal commitment to the monthly deadline in spite of miserly or nonexistent pay was based solely on love for the work and each other.

Bill Helmer, the quick-witted editor in 1959–60, said, "[We] turned the *Ranger* from a cliquish, genteel publication to a popular commercial publication." The magazine was operated by a company known as Texas Student Publications. The editor was allowed only a one-year term. That should have meant staff turnover. In 1962 it meant that the job was traded among a group of people and that the staffers were holdovers from the past and incredibly capable.

Janis witnessed the development of a social phenomenon as the *Ranger*'s circulation rose from five thousand to twenty-five thousand. What engineered the grand rise in interest was based on the university administration's desire to censor it. They trumpeted free-speech violations in an argument over a poem. "The butcher the baker the candlestick maker. Why can't I?" The authorities thought it was an obscene use of a candlestick. The writers thought it was a funny play on words.

The *Ranger*'s growth showed Janis one strategy of getting noticed: using notoriety to succeed artistically. The *Ranger* was a rallying point as important to Janis's development as her experience with folk music.

Janis brought home a favorite page of the September issue of the *Ranger* when she came for a visit. She proudly taped on the wall one of Gilbert Shelton's cartoon strips (shown on the next page). He hit the nail on the head, capturing her complaint about society in the relationship between the painter and his subject.

Shelton, editor in chief of the magazine, was most famous in Austin for his "Wonder Wart Hog" cartoon strip, an underground superman character known as the "Pig of Iron." Rippling muscles erupting through the suit he wore on his day job, Foolbert Sturgeon metamorphosed into the hog, "that fighting, fearless, foul-mouthed champion of justice."

Where the Port Arthur group had been introspective, Jack Smith explained that the Austin group's motto was "Whatever this thing's for, let's reverse it." They were into fun and excitement. They lived an upside-down life, forcing their observers to stop their routine lives for a moment.

Many cultures have a hallowed place for the clown, like the Navajo Indian tales of the cunning coyote, who seems to thwart man's best efforts while teaching him a lesson in humility. Janis's gang were trickster coyotes, bringing the Navajo culture's lesson to the Anglos. Some Indians chose reverse roles, they washed with dirt and dried with water, merely for the educational benefit of making people think. It's too easy to focus on the routine and miss the profound. By breaking

★

the tedium, the group allowed others to change their focus. The *Ranger* gave Janis the gift of the clown and the coyote.

In 1962 the coyote must have nominated Janis for Ugly Man on Campus, a fund-raising prank of a fraternity. For one day they erected a stage on campus and wrote names on a large board. Each vote cost a quarter, and there was fun competition among the frats to have their man win. Traditionally, school personalities were nominated—all the deans, etc. Janis's humor group saw the contest as a challenge to be turned and played with. Running a woman in the Ugly Man Contest would be a perfect foil! Jack said selecting Janis as Ugly Man was like Rice University selecting a refrigerator as homecoming queen, which they did a few years after Janis was in Austin. Jack said she nominated herself, as a lark! Others felt it was a type of revenge from a frat rat who Janis had teased sexually.

Janis complained about her involvement in the contest bitterly when interviewed later. Austin didn't appreciate her then—they elected her Ugly Man on Campus! Well, Janis didn't win, even if she was in the running. Her friends gave conflicting stories. Several recalled the event humorously, but Powell St. John remembered Janis coming into the Union with tears in her eyes because she was getting votes in the contest. Even if initiated in parody and jest, Janis resented the experience.

Janis had the same emotional needs as any adolescent girl—to be loved and accepted for who she was. But she was living Wonder Wart Hog's fanciful life as a "fighting, fearless, foul-mouthed" woman. She chose a role lauded in the hog by her friends, but she refused to accept the consequences that others saw in her female brand of toughness. In her heart she was just as soft and loving as any other woman.

In Austin her men friends related to her as a woman, not just as "one of the guys," like she was in Port Arthur. She had boyfriends, first Powell St. John from the musical group and finally settling on a *Ranger* editor, Bill Killeen. He was a cool, intense, intelligent, six-foot-tall, thin man with dark hair and eyes. Originally from Massachusetts, he was an old humor magazine hand from Oklahoma State University who blew into Austin in a limping 1950 Cadillac Superior model hearse with red velvet upholstery. He took women on strange dates to graveyards in his hearse.

★

Janis met Bill at a party at Gilbert Shelton's house, where Bill was staying. They walked down to a restaurant near the capitol and watched a bat fly around and terrorize the eating patrons. Janis thought it was hilarious. They slept that night on the capitol lawn, near one of the monuments. A capitol guard made a feeble attempt to shoo them off, but they weren't doing much, just cuddling, and he soon strolled away.

Their romance was complicated by neither of them having a place for amorous entwining. Janis lived in a rooming house that didn't allow male visitors. Killeen was just crashing with Shelton. Then Janis got a boon from a friend named Wynn Pratt. His father was a UT professor who owned a rental house that was vacant. Wynn gave them a key. They lived there in September and October.

They hosted a party one evening that was boisterous enough to get police attention. "Who lives here?" the cops asked. Killeen said, "I do." "And what is your name, please?" he was asked. "Foolbert Sturgeon" he replied, using the moniker of Wonder Wart Hog. He enjoyed defying authority. He drove without a driver's license, the *Ranger* explained. "What need have I of a license? I can drive all right without one." He was fun, serious, and articulate, and Janis loved him.

Bill found Janis to be a fascinating alternative to most girls he knew. She had more drive and zest for life. She wanted to have fun and he was a willing companion. Janis didn't want to miss out on anything. When he read her an article in a newspaper about LSD causing people to jump out of buildings, he remarked, "I don't want anything to do with that stuff." Janis said, "Well, I want some right now!" Janis was heavier than in her high school years; she might have weighed 140 pounds. Her face was round, made rounder by the way she wore her hair, and with her penchant for loose clothes, she looked even larger.

With Bill, Janis played with her more feminine self. She dressed up, fixed her hair, and put on high heels when they double-dated to the first football game of the year, UT playing Oregon. There was a *Ranger* party afterward and Janis was grumbling by the end of the game, "What the hell did I come to this thing for? There's not going to be any liquor left at the party."

Janis and Bill ventured to the border town of Nuevo Laredo one weekend with Gilbert Shelton and Karen Kay Kirkland. It was a pleasant time, though Karen almost got them into a fight by calling some Mexican thugs "specious asses."

Their relationship fell apart as much by losing the free house to live in as anything. The final test was the UT–Oklahoma University football weekend. It was a staunch local rivalry supported by students who ventured to Dallas, where the game was held, and got drunk. Janis wanted to go to the party. Bill didn't. He was not a drinking man. Janis went with a group, and when she came back, they had been evicted from their love nest by Pratt senior and Bill was sleeping on an unheated porch. There was no room for romance. She moved back into the rooming house our parents had been paying for all along.

John Clay was a man whose journalistic style the October *Ranger* called "Texanese, to be read with a slow drawl . . ." He said Janis and Bill's relationship had started out all love and roses. Janis was Bill's girl. He was strong and older and, according to John, "kept her in line." So romance with one of the gang still resulted in a general belief that a woman needed to be kept in line. What did that tell Janis?

Outside of a relationship, sexual conquest was considered a party sport by Janis. She took humorous pride in flirting with a frat rat at Threadgill's one night, the same incident purportedly linked to the Ugly Man Contest. He followed her back to the Ghetto as the party continued. Upon leaving, he raised his eyes at his fraternity buddies in a manner that implied, "Look what I'm going to be getting!" Then Janis slipped out and left his masculine ego a-hurting.

Sexual experimentation also included relations with women. She boldly announced her intentions, strolling up to a group of her friends in the Student Union that included Ted Klein. She sat down and said, "I've decided to become a lesbian." Given her visible appetite for men, people guffawed. "You wait and see," she replied to their jests. They wished her well on her decision. A few days later she returned to the gang in the Union. They asked how her lesbian experiences had been. Ted Klein said that Janis "shrugged her shoulders, mumbled a fairly neutral 'ehnn' and went back to pinching the boys."

There were several women who had a homosexual reputation in the group, in particular short, muscular Juli Paul. Everyone accepted them, possibly even enjoying the way their presence heightened the group's sense of its own nonconformity. Juli was kind, soft-hearted, and considerate. She could also be aggressive and tended to get emotional, especially when she drank.

Juli Paul described their first meeting. "When I first saw Janis, I was driving down the Drag, down Guadalupe, and Janis, Lanny, and Powell were walking along and the Autoharp and banjo were in evidence. I really just thought it was the thing to do, to pull over and see what they were up to, where they were going. And I'm sure it was Janis and her bawdy voice that said they were going to a party, did I want to go?"

Their relationship was steadfast and stormy—sometimes lovers; sometimes just friends. The tone ranged from buddies forever to drunken yelling matches. One evening Juli got very drunk. Janis was with her in the Ghetto. A few rounds of verbal sparring found Janis calling Juli a phony, a hypocrite. That was too much! Juli stumbled in a blind roaring stupor after Janis, ready to flatten her. She chased her through the apartments until Janis sneaked away. Juli began an apartment-to-apartment search and started making people mad, upsetting the whole tenor of the easygoing social scene. One thing led to another and a few shoves later, Juli was sliding down the stairs. In *Buried Alive,* Myra Friedman wrote that Janis pushed Juli down the stairs. Others recall someone else making the fateful push. Either way, Juli landed at the bottom, surprised and sore but okay.

Stan Alexander, one of the Austin gang, said Juli was "wild but interesting, a lost soul." Janis told him that she and Juli had hitchhiked to Port Arthur. The two of them had been forceful in getting rides, to the point of lying down on the highway across the lanes to get people to stop and listen to their pleas. The Port Arthur group didn't welcome Juli with open arms. She confronted them with rough mannerisms that at least a few found repulsive.

There was a constant stream of traffic between the Austin and Beaumont–Port Arthur contingents of the group. Several times the Austin crowd was taken on a tour of the Vinton clubs by Port Arthur folk. Once Janis took Wally Stopher, Dave Moriaty, Travis Rivers, Tary Owens, Johnny Moyer, and Wynn Pratt to Vinton. She settled into her former routine of sexually baiting the Cajuns, thinking that the Austin guys would perform the same function that her former group had. But they didn't know the unwritten laws of Cajun country. They didn't flaunt their toughness in a way that protected them from the taunts of the locals. They kept it hidden until it was needed.

Wynn Pratt was a Golden Gloves boxer. When the Louisiana guys started pushing him, he tried to back off and avoid a confrontation. They thought he was just chicken-shit and pushed him up against the wall. He punched back with a fist crowned by a high school ring and opened somebody's jaw. Stunned silence was followed by mass pandemonium and brawling. Travis hid under a pool table as the Austin group made their way to the bar's front porch. Dave and Tary sat on the hood of a 1953 Chevy and watched some fool try to run down people with his Oldsmobile. Someone smashed a beer bottle against Johnny Moyer's face and broke his jaw. Back in Austin, stories of the event were greeted with drawn looks and shaking heads. What used to be good fun was beginning to be a pain.

Alcohol had taken the spirit of nonconformity and escalated it until problems erupted. Drugs of one sort or another were always involved in the excesses of the group. The *Ranger* ran a story titled "How to Get Drunk in Dallas," showing the group's assumption that being drunk was not only desired but required. Men proved their masculinity by regularly getting sot-faced, expecting the resulting antics to provide them the social esteem of raging Texas bulls.

Alcohol was frequently the aim of getting money, the requirement for starting a party, and the subject of tall tales spread liberally among the friends. Beer and liquor consumed the meager profits the group made by selling copies of the *Ranger*. It was quickly guzzled at the monthly staff party after each issue's publication. A bottle of booze was the prize of a Saturday bike race sponsored by the *Ranger*. This race was a mad dash through town in search of a hidden treasure—whiskey. Twelve contestants pedaled furiously around the police station, the capitol, and Scholz's [Beer] Garten with their eyes peeled for the glint of amber liquid in glass. Gilbert Shelton won. Beer was the payment Kenneth Threadgill laid on his musicians in place of money. It was everywhere. Alcohol was the cause of turning good-natured fun into outrageous antics. Things often got out of hand. Juli Paul once stopped her Triumph on the Austin streets and physically pushed Janis out of the car. Juli roared off, leaving Janis to walk.

Gilbert Shelton and friends played a prank on Lieuen Adkins,

★

who had squirreled away a full bottle of gin to keep it from the lips of his friends during a brief absence. Finding the clear liquid in his closet, they enjoyed it. Then they replaced it with clear water and waited for Lieuen to return. When he returned, he fixed himself a drink. As he sipped, Bill Killeen volunteered to chug the whole bottle of gin if Lieuen would buy them dinner. Lieuen raised his eyebrows at the possibility of seeing the modest drinker, Bill, get smashed on gin and agreed to the bet. Bill drank the "gin," but Lieuen caught on. He bought them dinner anyway. He tried to get back at them by buying a new bottle of gin, emptying it, and replacing it with water. They upped him once again, finding the real gin, drinking it, and replacing it with water once again.

Some people used peyote, which was legal then. Out on Highway 183, John Clay explained, anyone could go to Hudson's Cactus Gardens and buy peyote for ten cents a plant. "Forty cents' worth was an effective dose." People simmered it on the stove until it turned into a foul green broth. Four ounces were required to get high.

Peyote had been used by Indians in the western United States and Mexico for centuries. After it was discovered by white men, it went from the scientists to the intellectuals to the bohemians, a process that took thirty years. Psychiatrists believed mescaline, the active ingredient in peyote, mimicked schizophrenia. They used it therapeutically to help clients draw their emotions and visions from the depths of their subconscious. Others saw it as a learning tool to escape the rational plane of a literal world. Psilocybin, similar to mescaline, was discovered in 1958, and by 1961 had become the toast of the New York jet set, who zoomed off for weekends of visionary splendor. Texas was slow to catch on to new trends. Peyote still held sway. Janis surely tried peyote, but she wasn't taken by a spiritual rebirth or even a sufficient interest in using it frequently.

Marijuana was smoked by several people, though because it was illegal and the gang was watched, the level of paranoia was high. Most of the time a joint was lit in a bathroom with the blinds drawn. Janis and Tommy Stopher gave Powell St. John his first joint. It was extremely thin, but the three of them shared it reverently. Janis and Tommy said they got high off it, but Powell didn't feel any effects.

Janis enjoyed grass because it was something "verboten," but alcohol was her drug of choice. She stuck to beer, as did most of the crowd. Underage drinking was their primary crime. Alcohol was also their biggest problem. No one seemed to know when to stop drinking.

By the winter of 1962 a new fellow had arrived in town. Chet Helms was a Texan and a former UT student now living in San Francisco. He was just passing through and was taken with the quality of the folk music in Austin. These musicians had achieved something the San Francisco musicians wanted, a true roots sound. The Northern California musicians were stuck in a pop-folk sound, yearning for authenticity. Chet told Janis that she would be a hit in San Francisco.

The flicker of fascination flamed in her mind. She set about planning to go. She needed money, and one way she found it was to not buy food—she stole it instead. In this way she intended to be ready to leave with Chet.

Many people shoplifted occasionally in the Ghetto group. For most it was for thrills. Janis liked to lift a jar of maraschino cherries or some T-bone steaks from the Checker Front Store across the street and down a bit from the Ghetto. Then she paraded her cache mirthfully in front of the gang. Bill Helmer invoked situational morality to take avocadoes because the outrageous prices kept them out of reach. He also felt that if he did get busted, it would make good newspaper copy: BUSTED FOR SHOPLIFTING AVOCADOES! "We needed them for the avocado dip!"

Janis liked the excitement of life on the edge, living between the known and the unknown. Where Port Arthur may have formed her impulses, only in Austin did she get to test her wings and practice her style. Austin tutored her in performing, gave her the necessary support and recognition, and shaped her Texas-style public satire. Janis's life in Austin was the proper jumping-off point for her. It was a place to test the waters, to gain experience, so that when opportunity beckoned, she would be ready.

CHAPTER SEVEN

THE SAN FRANCISCO
BEAT SCENE

★

I ain't got no reason for living
I can't find no cause to die . . .
I ain't got no reason for going
I can't find no cause to stay here
I got the blues
I got to find me that middle road

—Janis Joplin, "No Reason for Living"

*I*N MID-JANUARY 1962, when the winter term ended at the University of Texas, Janis and Chet Helms put their thumbs to the wind and hitchhiked to San Francisco. Janis wanted more than Austin offered. *On the Road* had been her map for finding life, and she had already been to Venice, California. Her next goal was the North Beach community of San Francisco.

Janis and Chet landed first in Forth Worth, where Chet's parents lived. The traveling pair were received politely and entertained over dinner, but Janis wouldn't court their approval. They were put off by her profanity and wild-woman style. Janis and Chet were refused hospitality for the night. They headed out to the highway and thumbed down truckers heading to California. Not more than fifty hours later they made it to San Francisco.

"Wall-to-wall people" is how Nick Gravenites described the scene. Nick was a tall, gentle man full of burning emotions that he let loose in short bursts to dramatize his points. He had been into folk music since 1955. In 1959 he headed to San Francisco from the University of Chicago. The people in North Beach were much like the ones

★

Janis knew in Austin and Port Arthur, but there were a lot more of them.

The scene owed its existence to the literary soirées that Kenneth Rexroth, noted radical poet, had been holding in apartments in the city since the 1940s. The city on a hill with a cultured undercurrent attracted poet Lawrence Ferlinghetti in 1951. In 1953 he stumbled onto what became the City Lights Pocket Book Shop. By 1955 Ferlinghetti was the sole proprietor. It was open from morning until midnight, seven days a week—the first all-paperback bookshop in the country at a time when hardcovers were still the norm. From the start, the owners wanted the bookshop to be the heart of an intellectual and artistic community.

The 1950s saw publication of such books as Sloan Wilson's *The Man in the Gray Flannel Suit* and William Whyte's *The Organization Man*. They raised the charge of bartering one's soul to the corporation at a time when American corporations controlled one of every two dollars of wealth in the country. They jabbed at the idea of a managerial approach that enslaved the thoughts and habits of its workers, in contrast to the national magazine stories about continued prosperity.

In 1950s America, nonconformists were despised and feared because they rocked the boat in which everyone sat busily rowing. Nonconformists were attracted to City Lights, and providing an alternative was the whole point of the endeavor.

National awareness focused on the San Francisco scene from the time of an October 13, 1955, poetry reading at Six Gallery. Six poets read that night; second among them was Allen Ginsberg reading "Howl," a complaint that cried, "I saw the best minds of my generation / generation destroyed by madness / starving, mystical, naked / who dragged themselves thru the angry streets at / dawn looking for a negro fix . . ." Jack Kerouac was there, shouting amid a clapping, foot-stomping audience rhythm section—"Go! Go! Go!"—as Ginsberg read in rapid patter. It was a watershed. The rest of the nation awoke to the challenge when customs agent Chester MacPhee seized 520 copies of "Howl" as they entered the country from the British printer. He labeled the poem "obscene." Ferlinghetti was arrested as the publisher. From that moment on it was required reading for every soul with a flickering sense of disagreement with the establishment. City Lights Book Shop became nationally known.

Janis entered a scene that had been started and led by a group that Ferlinghetti called "New York carpetbaggers." Rexroth called it "the San Francisco Renaissance." When Janis arrived in January 1963, the artistic scene had peaked. Many of those defining the pulse of the movement had fled North Beach to less visible locales. Michael McClure, noted local poet, moved to Haight-Ashbury. Lawrence Ferlinghetti took a part-time home at Big Sur. Gray Line bus tours of the beatnik scene signified an end to the underground vitality living off its own energy. Janis came to a place that was filled with others like herself, seekers from across the country attracted by the reputation of the area. They arrived unconnected and searching for roots. Janis stayed briefly with Chet Helms and his friends and then moved on.

North Beach offered Janis a true cross-race experience, with a greater variety of ethnic and social backgrounds than she had ever known. It was one of the first integrated communities in America. George Wallace was elected governor of Alabama with the slogan "Segregation now; segregation tomorrow; segregation forever!" The San Francisco integration was vilified in the press and watched by the police. Those within it grew that much more committed to their ideals. Their frontier mind-set quickly developed into a sense of community, which was welcome, as most had cut their ties to home.

Sleeping on concrete floors or in lofts over neighborhood warehouses, the Beats cultivated a sense of "All for one and one for all." Whoever had money provided the food, with each person contributing whenever he or she could. Janis ran with a group that often gathered at an apartment rented by a close friend, Kenai, a talented artist. Kenai was Filipino, but his parents were diplomats, so he grew up everywhere but the Philippines. He entered Northwestern University in Illinois at the age of thirteen. Transferring among several colleges, he eventually received a bachelor's degree in English history and another in psychology. He dropped out of architecture school in 1956 to be a beatnik and live in North Beach. For a time, he helped published a twenty-page magazine called *Beatitude,* which sold in the Bay Area. He lived an artist's life, asking very little and giving what he had, all with a smile on his friendly face. At three A.M. he would sweep the bars and gather everyone to his place. People would bring food and someone would always go to the bakery at Union and Grant to get plenty of French bread. Sometimes the events were food feasts, when a friend

★

would donate fifty pounds of shrimp or lobster from his job at Fisherman's Wharf. Other times there was very little, but whatever there was everyone shared.

No one put down anything except conventionalism. People wanted to feel everything, merely for the value of experiencing. The first oral contraceptive was approved by the FDA in May 1960. This drug paved the way for the sexual revolution Janis was encountering. Allen Ginsberg blew into town again in August 1963. He had been traveling in India and had a fresh angle to his message of free love to save the world: He was into sex orgies, a world united into one big family through physical bonding. Experimentation was the byword, whether through heterosexual or homosexual acts.

The excitement of creating and being part of a vibrant artistic current was enhanced by the use of various drugs floating through the Beat scene, especially speed. It magnified hugely the intensity of an earlier day, when coffee was the drug of choice. That powerful brew loaded with caffeine had horrified citizens at the turn of the century in what was known as the bohemian coffee cult. Users were warned that the drink could cost them their self-control, that they would be subject to fits of nervousness and depression. Speed was an infinitely bigger step down that same path.

Jack Kerouac wrote one version of *On the Road* in 1951 in twenty coffee and Benzedrine-driven days, chronicled by his biographer Tom Clark. Kerouac followed a formula discussed in the North Beach community: He worked and lived a somewhat regular existence for a while, then chucked it all, holed up with his typewriter, downed speed, and wrote rambling memories of his earlier life. *Big Sur,* published in 1962, was written in much the same way.

Alcohol was also a common drug in North Beach. Janis's tolerance for alcohol had reached a level where she could drink a lot with little visible effect. In fact, at only twenty years of age she was beginning to be compulsive about her liquid friend.

The Coffee Gallery became one of Janis's favorite haunts. She sang there frequently, though it was never a source of real income. Kenai sometimes passed the hat during her performance but never raised more than eight dollars. James Gurley, who later played with Janis in Big Brother and the Holding Company, frequently played

[B]enjamin Jopling, our great-great-grand-[fa]ther. Benjamin brought the family from [V]irginia, through Alabama to East Texas, [m]arrying four times and fathering twenty-[t]wo children. He helped build the fort at [Fo]rt Worth. (*Courtesy of Joplin family*)

Charles Alexander Joplin, our great-grand-father, was the sixteenth child of Benjamin and helped found the settlements around Lubbock, Texas. He was known as C.A., and called all of his seven sons by their initials as well. (*Courtesy of Joplin family*)

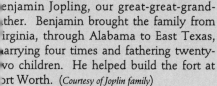

[C].A. and his bride, Margaret [A]mira White, our great-grand-[p]arents. They proudly display [al]l of the possessions that [st]arted them off in life in an [ar]ea near Joplin, Texas. [*C*]*ourtesy of Joplin family*)

Seeb Winston (S.W.) Joplin—our grandfather— was the eldest of eleven children born to C.A. and Margaret Joplin; he managed a large cattle ranch near Tahoka, Texas, went on a cattle drive to Montana, ventured to Alaska, then returned to marry Florence Porter and live in Amarillo, Texas, managing the stockyards. (*Courtesy of Joplin family*)

Robert Ury Porter, our great-grand-father, brought his family to Texas via flatboat on the Mississippi River and sailing ship to Velasco, Texas. From there they ventured by ox-drawn wagon to Central Texas, where they home-steaded land they called Porter's Prairie. (*Courtesy of Joplin family*)

Florence Elizabeth Porter, our grandmother, wa[s] born to Robert Porter and his second wif[e] Arminta Roberson Porter, when he was sixty-two years old. She was the fourteenth [of] sixteen children. Later in life, she only learne[d] to drive a car so she could get to cooking clas[s] which she needed because she ran a boardin[g] house. (*Courtesy of Joplin family*)

Arminta Roberson Porter—our great-grandmother—and her daughters after Robert Porter died and the family moved to Georgetown, Texas. Florence is on the lower right. (*Courtesy of Joplin family*)

Porter family reunion at Porter's Prairie, at Robert Porter's house—the first two-story frame house built in Burleson County, Texas. The picture was taken sometime before Robert's death in 1899. (*Courtesy of Joplin family*)

The Easts—Our Maternal Grandfather

Our great-grandparents Ulysses Sampson Grant East and his wife, Anna Belle Bowman East, and their children, Violet, Cecil (our grandfather), Vern, and Floyd. The Easts settled Illinois in the early 1800s. It is rumored that Grant's great-grandfather married into the Cherokee Nation. (*Courtesy of Joplin family*)

John Milton Hanson (our great-great-great-grandfather), who homesteaded the wilderness of Henry County, Iowa, and left his wife in charge of the farm while he sought their fortune in the California Gold Rush.
(*Courtesy of Joplin family*)

Cecil and Laura East and their four children. Dorothy is standing in the center. The others, from the left, are Barbara, Mildred (Mimi), and Gerald. They lived in Nebraska, Oklahoma, and Amarillo, Texas, where they eventually separated after Dorothy was married. (*Courtesy of Joplin family*)

AT LEFT—Four generations of Hansons. Henry Hanson (our great-great-grandfather) upper right, served as an orderly in a general's headquarters in the Civil War. Henry's son Herbert married Stella Mae Sherman. Their eldest daughter, Laura (our grandmother), is shown with two of her children, baby Gerald and Dorothy, the eldest. She was our mother. (*Courtesy of Joplin family*)

Dorothy and her sisters and brother on their favorite horse, Beauty, in Nebraska, shortly before her father lost the farm in the Depression. (*Courtesy of Joplin family*)

Dorothy East sang lead in the annual social event sponsored by the Lion's Club when she was a senior in high school. Dorothy is the first girl to the right of center. (*Courtesy of Joplin family*)

Our father, Seth Ward Joplin, son of Seeb and Florence Joplin. This photo was taken when he first started work for Texaco, shortly before he married.
(*Courtesy of Joplin family*)

Dorothy East (our mother) was twenty-two years old when she worked at the Amarillo radio station and met her future husband, Seth. Her reputation as a "swinger" was made when she was madly trying to figure out why the station wasn't broadcasting, and said, "I can't get the damn thing to work," only to discover that it *was* working and had broadcast her expletive to every house and farm in the area. (*Courtesy of Joplin family*)

Janis, a few months old, and our mother, Dorothy, at their Port Arthur, Texas, home on Procter Street. (© *Joplin family*)

Janis and our parents on a family visit to Amarillo, Texas. This photo was taken shortly after Janis turned to them and said, "We are going home now. I'll have to start being good." (© *Joplin family*)

...udio portrait of Janis, about three, and our ...other. Dorothy doted on her young daugh-...r. (© *Joplin family*)

Janis, about six or seven, at the new family home on Lombardy Street. Dorothy made Janis many lovely dresses, such as this Easter outfit. (© *Joplin family*)

...erial shot of the city of Port Arthur, Texas, in the 1940s, with Pleasure Island in the fore-...ound. The large white building in the center is a dance hall. The roller coaster and midway ...e directly behind it in an area called Pleasure Pier. The intracoastal canal separates the island ...om the town. In the distance storage tanks for the refineries can be seen. (*Courtesy of Artie Hebert*)

Sitting in the backyard on the dense St. Augustine grass, Janis is holding her best friend. (© *Joplin family*)

On a trip to Los Angeles to visit Dorothy's family, Janis and I pose with our mother, dressed in matching outfits she made. (© *Joplin family*)

Janis, about ten, in one of the dresses our mother made for her. (© *Joplin family*)

Janis adored our baby brother, Michael. He was like a living doll for her. (© *Joplin family*)

Janis (at left) liked to play dress-up with the neighbor girls. The house on Lombardy was built in a family neighborhood with lots of playmates of all ages.
(© *Joplin family*)

Seth and his children in the backyard, in front of the hedge he dug up and replanted from a cow pasture across the street. Janis was thirteen. (© *Joplin family*)

Grandfather Seeb Joplin with his three grandchildren about 1957, on a visit to Port Arthur. Janis was about fourteen. (© *Joplin family*)

Janis in a school photo, probably in the ninth grade. (© *Joplin family*)

Janis (second from left) used her artistic talents in school pep rallies. Here she and her classmates are planning death for their upcoming football opponents. Her attire is noticeably different from the other girls', with a shorter skirt and no bobby sox or loafers. Family friend Kristen Bowen is second from the right. (*Courtesy of Kristen Bowen*)

Janis standing in front of a pen-and-ink drawing she did during her summer volunteer job at the local library, drawing illustrations for the children's section bulletin boards. A newspaper story and photo read, "Library Job Brings Out Teenager's Versatility." (© *The Port Arthur News*)

The summer after ninth grade, Janis (second from the left) joined the Port Arthur Little Theater. In this production, *Sunday Costs Five Pesos*, she played an ingenue. (*Courtesy of Jim Langdon and Grant Lyons*)

Janis's yearbook picture for her junior year in high school. She often dressed in black, emulating Beat artists. She ran around with a group of guys who listened to folk music and jazz, read good literature, and discussed intellectual topics at length. (*Courtesy of Joplin family*)

Grandfather Joplin visited in 1960 after his second marriage. This was Janis's senior year in high school. She is wearing a royal blue two-piece outfit that she favored. (© *Joplin family*)

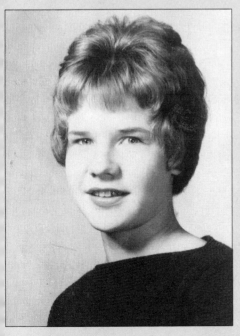

Studio portrait about 1960–61, when Janis was attending Lamar State College of Technology in nearby Beaumont, Texas, and Port Arthur Business College. (© *Joplin family*)

Janis played around in California, posing as the ultimate beach-going sophisticate. (*Courtesy of Joplin family*)

Janis tried living in the Los Angeles–Venice area the summer and fall of 1961. She initially went to live with our mother's sisters. They are shown here, sitting on opposite sides of the table from their daughters. From the left are Jean Pitney, Mildred "Mimi" Krohn, Janis, Barbara Irwin, and Donna MacBride. (*Courtesy of Donna MacBride*)

At the University of Texas, Janis ran with a group of folk musicians and writers for the *Ranger* magazine. They often gathered at a group of apartments fondly called "the ghetto." From the left, in Ted Klein's ghetto apartment, are Ted Klein, Ray "Papa" Hansen, Gilbert Shelton, and Pat and Bill Helmer. (© Texas Ranger; *courtesy of Texas Student Publications; from the collection of Ted Klein*)

AT LEFT—The summer of 1962, Janis enrolled at the University of Texas in Austin. She majored in art but spent most of her time in the growing folk music scene. She learned to play autoharp and distinguished herself enough to be the subject of an article in *The Summer Texan*, the school newspaper, with the headline SHE DARES TO BE DIFFERENT. (© The Summer Texan; *courtesy of Texas Student Publications*)

Wednesday evenings the group sang at the university-sponsored hootenanny at the Chuckwagon in the student union. Here Janis performs with Powell St. John and Lanny Wiggins. (© 1963 Cactus *yearbook; courtesy of Texas Student Publications*)

On Thursday evenings, Janis and her Austin gang often sang at Ken Threadgill's bar, a converted gas station on the outskirts of town.
(© 1980 Tom Hatch)

Kenneth Threadgill got the first liquor license in Austin after Prohibition was repealed, and he began selling alcohol and bringing in local musicians. With his years of experience, he provided the knowledge and support that Janis needed.
(© Burton Wilson)

Janis moved to San Francisco from Austin in January 1963. She worked at odd jobs and lived the life of a beatnik artist in search of herself. She began singing professionally in local clubs. She learned to play guitar in California, so she wouldn't have to split the modest fees she earned singing with a musician to back her. (*Courtesy of Michael Ochs Archives and the Joplin family*)

Janis had a new twelve-string guitar and gave me her old six-string. On a 1964 visit home while driving cross-country, Janis taught me to play. Janis wore typical beatnik clothes: black turtlenecks and gold medallions with blue jeans and sandals. (*© Joplin family*)

Janis returned home in the spring of 1965, after a disastrous experience shooting methedrine in San Francisco. We spent girlish hours styling our hair and experimenting with makeup and clothes. (*Courtesy of Joplin family*)

Before she became a singer, Janis turned her artistic talents to painting and drawing. In high school she drew this quick sketch of classmate and sophomore boyfriend Rooney Paul. (*Courtesy of Joplin family*)

I begged Janis to paint my portrait, expecting Janis to pose me like a Southern belle at the fireplace. Instead Janis painted what she saw, a bored eleven-year-old looking over her shoulder to see what her sister was doing. (*Courtesy of Joplin family*)

In college, Janis was especially taken with the angular portrait style of Modigliani. Here she adapted his approach in a picture that hung in the family dining room for years. (*Courtesy of Joplin family*)

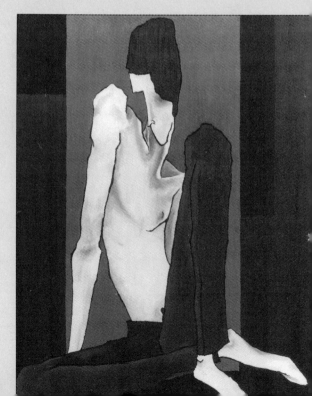

there. He performed eerie original music and distinguished himself with a clean-shaven head. Sam Andrew—also a future member of Big Brother—played jazz there with Steve Mann.

At the Coffee Gallery, Janis met her eventual roommate and longtime friend, Linda Gottfried. Linda, a Los Angeles girl, had just turned nineteen and was focused on life's frustrations. A lover said, "Go to San Francisco. You're not the only one who feels like you. Go to the Coffee Gallery and look up my friend Janis Joplin." Following those instructions, Linda appeared, and Janis was performing that night.

Janis was living in a basement on Sacramento Street. It wasn't a basement apartment, Linda said, it was the basement of a house that was rented by people who were fans of Janis. They let Janis live there free because they liked hearing her sing around the house. Linda moved in and the two of them lived together off and on.

Together, the two girls planned their days around the idea of nurturing their creativity. They sampled many modes of expression alongside Janis's devotion to painting—photography, poetry and song, and more. There were places to see, things to do, and people to know. At night they would collapse at home and share SpaghettiOs and Fudgsicles.

To be an artist was to interpret experiences for others. The more a person tuned in to the charismatic forces in life or in a piece of art, the more that person lived in the ecstasy of energy we call life.

In 1963 Janis appeared on a local radio show with Peter Albin, one of the founding members of the group she would eventually join in 1966, Big Brother and the Holding Company. Janis was a bit over-weight and her face was broken out at the time. She wore a man's dress shirt that was unbuttoned several notches, allowing glimpses of her breasts. She sang in a rough manner that accentuated the bluntness and defiance of her physical appearance.

Janis had been singing with Roger Perkins, Larry Hanks, and Billy Roberts. They performed around town, at the Folk Theater and other places. They had a spot in the upcoming San Francisco State Music Festival, organized by Peter Albin's brother. They never showed up for the festival, perhaps because Janis had injured her leg trying to mount her Vespa motorcycle while she was drunk.

Or perhaps it was the call of the road that compelled her to miss the festival. Rumors say Janis hitchhiked to New York sometime in 1963 for a brief look at the tap root of the Beat movement, Greenwich Village. Chet Helms said that Janis quaked in her shoes about being on the road from Austin to San Francisco when they arrived in January 1963. She confided to him, "I've never hitched this far." She clung to him with female softness, asking for male protectiveness. A trip across the country later in 1963 would have been a giant leap from the fear she showed to Chet.

A trip, solo or with someone, must have appeared more possible considering the network of folk musicians that had developed coast-to-coast. The Beat movement was old enough to have spawned a whole series of coffeehouses across the country. Most were loosely allied with universities. Since hitchhiking was "the experience" for the young Beats, the group mingled a lot. Each enclave knew who the hot talents were in other spots. Janis could have availed herself of this under-ground railroad.

On November 22, 1963, John F. Kennedy was shot and killed in Dallas, ushering in an age of anti-Texas sentiment—that Texas was where the crazies lived. It must have helped fuel Janis's belief that Texas was beyond help—if JFK could be shot in broad daylight, then nothing was safe down there. It would have been easy to sit in a bar in San Francisco and put down her home state.

Folk music was also in the news. The August 27 issue of *Look* magazine wrote, "Yesterday, it was the esoteric kick of history buffs and music scholars. Today, it's show biz. With a hoot and a holler, folk music has taken over from coffeehouse to campus to prime time television." *Hootenanny* was a regular Saturday night television show. Peter, Paul and Mary made seventy-five hundred dollars a night in concert. The popular folk groups were giving fewer campus concerts and making big bucks in cigarette commercials and nightclubs.

The national acceptance of the folk scene may have helped Janis decide to head to New York and witness Greenwich Village for herself. She passed through Port Arthur in December, showing up unexpectedly at the Christmas gathering of her friends at Jim Langdon's house in Lafayette. He had quit school and taken a job working on the local newspaper to support his growing family. Most of Janis's friends were in their third year of college, attending either the University of Texas, Lamar Tech, or other good schools in the South. Several were married with children.

It must have been obvious by then that her life was far different from those of her friends. While Janis was pursuing a degree in the Beat experience, they were looking for careers and thinking about raising children. Their social beliefs and artistic interests were still similar, but the individual commitments were changing.

Janis was accepted as an equal, but more as an equal to the men. The women in the group were mostly wives, often with children. They were working to put their husbands through school. They prepared the food and cleaned up after the all-night drinking, talking, and listening-to-music sessions.

Janis was taking off for Venice, San Francisco, and New York. She had male and female lovers, and lived a life ostensibly focused on developing her artistic expression. I wonder how she felt when she came home? Most of the women she knew in Port Arthur were not role models for her. They were hardly pals or confidantes. They were often just appendages to the real focus of the group, the men and their jovial and intellectual haranguing. Rae Logan and Gloria Haston explained that sex-role issues had not yet come together for anyone. They would, but not in 1963.

Soon she was off for New York. Linda Gottfried explained that Janis went there for the purpose of earning and saving money so that she wouldn't confuse her image as a San Francisco artist by working in California. She intended to return to San Francisco and continue exploring her creativity. In New York, she got a job as a keypunch operator, working for a large company. She moved into a residence hotel full of musicians and druggies. She was on the edge, supporting herself, and pursuing the artistic life in the Village. She ran into Austin friends Gilbert Shelton and Joe E. Brown. She looked the same as she had in Austin, Gilbert said, only a bit thinner, having lost the pudginess that characterized her at the Ghetto.

New York was full of meth that year. It was the newest drug and could be found everywhere. In February 1963, Allen Ginsberg had written to Timothy Leary, as recorded in *Ginsberg* by Barry Miles, "All the young kids are shooting (needle) a drug called methedrine. An

★

amphetamine semi-hallucinogen—haven't tried it yet. It's all the vogue." There were also huge pot love circles with free sexual exploration enhanced by the stimulating properties of marijuana.

In *Buried Alive,* author Myra Friedman repeated stories by Linda Knoll, who knew Janis in New York during this period. According to Linda, Janis shot speed throughout the summer of '64 in an apartment on the Lower East Side. My sources refuted Knoll's closeness to Janis, saying that she was a peripheral person. Janis probably used some speed, but Linda Gottfried believes that Janis didn't get heavily into speed until much later.

Janis was also performing in New York. She invited Gilbert Shelton and Joe E. Brown to come to a club to hear her. They arrived, enjoyed the music, and then realized it was a gay bar. Uncomfortable, they politely beat a hasty retreat. Sexual exploration was part of her life; she bragged later to friends about her black female lover.

In August Janis left New York driving a yellow Morris Minor convertible, a VW Bug look-alike. She drove several hundred miles out of her way to visit us again. I was in the ninth grade then, in summer band practice. In line with the many Chrysler sedans and Chevrolet station wagons waiting to pick up my fellow band musicians was a convertible with the top down. A hand waved and a voice yelled my name in excited, happy tones.

"How are you?" Janis asked me, and then quickly launched into describing her life. "New York was great!" she raved. "I just had to stop and tell y'all about it. Isn't my car wonderful? I love it! It's so great to just drive cross-country with my hair in the breeze."

We loved having Janis home. The house was always livelier when she was around. The trivia of everyday life was more exciting. Discussions at dinnertime, always interesting, took on a grander note, with more laughter and puns punctuating the banter.

"I have a surprise for you," Janis said, laughing. "I got a twelve-string guitar for myself in New York, so my old six-string is for you." I was wowed. She was broadening my horizons beyond band music for the saxophone! The neck was warped and the strings were so far from the frets I had to use a capo just to play, but it was my first guitar and my sister had given it to me.

We practiced in the front bedroom off the kitchen. Janis sang some deep-throated blues and showed me how to barre chord and slide across the frets. She said, "Here, you play a while," and went off to the next room. I was fourteen and envied her larger, stronger hands, but I was always game to try. I slung back my head and hollered, "Highway Fifty-one," then did the guitar slides, "done turned its back on me." Three lines into the verse, Janis laughingly jumped around the corner. "I heard that!" Okay, so my voice was more a church soprano at the time, without the guttural strength needed for that song. But it was fun. Janis was my only exposure to such music, and I reveled in it while she was home.

Pop shook his head as she headed out of the driveway, waving as she started back to San Francisco. He had his fingers crossed, hoping she would make it, but he worried like a father. It was a funky, broken-down car, leaking so much oil he figured she might run out of money feeding it.

She passed through Austin on the way to California. She impressed the gang there with her tales of singing for money in New York clubs. They were proud one of their own had broken out of playing for free in college gatherings and was making money performing. Pat Brown complimented her on her new look. Janis was wearing a simple dress, had lost weight, and had her hair up. She was bright and optimistic, and obviously proud of herself.

She arrived in fine shape in San Francisco, sending two postcards home during her drive.

September 1964
Spent the night in Reno—unfortunately the Nugget was filled so I slept in the back seat of my car parked in a Royal gas station—but still—a night in Reno! Lost 60¢ in the slot machines—phoo. San Francisco by noon. A letter should arrive shortly.

XXX

September 1964
Thurs—10:30 A.M.

SIGH!!

XXX

★

Janis quickly settled back into the West Coast scene. The longer she stayed in California, the more committed she became to the Beat focus on living in the present. She consumed alcohol flamboyantly. She equated drunkenness with personal spontaneity because it temporarily freed people from social restraints. With the artistic community, she sampled other drugs for their potential to enhance the unbridled freedom she sought.

Janis pursued truth, but didn't ignore fun. Linda Gottfried said she was "sardonic, sarcastic, and funny." Janis made her laugh. It was social-commentary humor—inside jokes that had a truth beyond factual life. "We *knew* J. Edgar Hoover was gay"—that was her type of humor. Janis's group knew that the rest of society hid their desires, compulsions, and pleasures in extramarital sex, homosexual acts, and mind-altering substances like alcohol or other drugs. The humor reinforced their belief that they differed from the rest of America only by admitting what they did.

In 1964 Congress passed the Civil Rights Act, and racial integration finally became law. Linda Gottfried remembered the intensity of Janis's views on the subject by saying, "Janis called herself the first black-white person." It wasn't enough to sing black music or live Kerouac's view of the black man's noble existence. Janis sought *internal* self-integration, to quit being just white. She wanted to become all the good things from all heritages. In February 1964, Bob Dylan released his album *The Times They Are A-Changin'*, a fitting description of the events.

Music was integral to Janis's experience of North Beach. Nick Gravenites, who played in the local clubs, knew music as a way of explaining things that weren't otherwise communicable. "It's a way to make sense of your life," he stated, his deep, powerful voice and commanding look belying his words' simplicity. Janis, Nick, and many others performed for each other at the local clubs. There was no music profession. It was all done for love, three dollars, and a cheeseburger, said Nick.

City Lights Book Shop published a literary journal called the *Journal for the Protection of All Beings*, a "revolutionary review." It was an open forum for uncensored discourse on any subject. The second issue came out in 1964 and the cover was graced with a picture of Ezra

Pound. "The artists are the antennae of the race," Pound wrote in "The Teacher's Mission." Janis's antennae were alert and receiving on all channels.

In the midst of the Beat pursuit of open discussion, Pop came to visit. He left Port Arthur claiming a business trip, but his only goal was to check on his daughter. He came to help Janis find herself, and to be sure she was all right. He looked Janis in the eye and never made any judgments about her life-style. He chose his comments carefully, trying to help. Pop complimented her artwork and the wonderful songs she wrote. He affirmed that she was a beautiful person. Pop told Janis, "You will achieve."

He also held on for dear life, entering the world of his wild, young daughter. She took him around town in her Morris Minor, driving as fast downhill as up. "Slow down," he implored. "Never," she laughed.

Pop took Janis and Linda to dinner, and counseled them not to divorce themselves from the mainstream of society—the audience who would buy Janis's paintings and sing her songs. He made one suggestion to help them stay in touch with society: "Every week you should buy *Time* magazine and read it cover to cover. *Time* will give you all you need to know about the world, and still allow you to make independent decisions."

Even after Pop left, his suggestion was de rigueur on Thursday afternoons. Following the afternoon movie and a quick check to see if they had won on *Dialing for Dollars,* Janis and Linda would walk to the newsstand. They would purchase a copy of *Time* and read it front to back.

Away from Pop's steadying influence, Janis's artistic pursuits began consuming her. "Janis called herself a candle, burning on both ends," Linda Gottfried said. Janis would ask, "When am I going to burn out?" Linda felt Janis knew she was going to die young, because she said it so often.

She drank to excess, frequently. Was she copying her inspirations, Billie Holiday and Bessie Smith? Billie Holiday was a spontaneous and emotional singer who turned her tragic life into music that moved her audiences. She fought a heroin addiction all her life and served time in prison for it. By the time she died at the age of forty-four, her voice showed the signs of alcohol and drug abuse. Surely Janis absorbed the details of the life of a blues singer by reading Billie Holiday's 1956 autobiography, *Lady Sings the Blues.*

Linda Gottfried believes Janis was a reincarnation of Bessie Smith. Bessie was called "the Empress of the Blues." She used her innate drama and power to project her personality into her music. She wore bright satiny clothes and feathers in her hair. She was foul-mouthed and bisexual. Her brief period of public acclaim came between 1923 and 1928. When the public's taste changed, Bessie's life entered an era of excessive drinking, fistfights with men and women, and other reckless behavior. She died in an automobile accident at the age of forty-three. I'm sure that Janis rose emotionally to her defense on hearing that she died from blood loss supposedly because she was refused treatment in a whites-only hospital. I wonder if Janis was able to glorify Bessie and Billie only by copying them down to their weaknesses.

Janis wandered around the apartment she shared with Linda Gottfried, singing, "Fame, fortune, and humility." It became her motto and goal. To be successful and haughty was too white, too elitist. Janis's intellectual views demanded that she remain humble while her internal drives and her Anglo-Saxon culture impressed upon her the need to achieve.

Janis said, "A lot of artists have one way of art and another way of life. They're the same for me." Was it art that drove Janis to try speed, or speed that consumed her art? Linda said that both she and Janis started chipping (using infrequently) in 1964, and by the latter part of the year, drugs owned them. "I remember when we knew," Linda said. "We had planned to go to the de Young Museum and then the Laundromat. On the way we looked at each other and said, 'Let's go home and do some meth.' " Linda continued, "No one knew about drugs then. They were an experiment. We thought we were growing by leaps and bounds. We worked day and night. We did more paintings, more poems, and more songs." Meth made them think they were being more creative.

By 1964 Janis had increased her speed use. Like many users, she began to deal a little. "I heard this pounding on the front door of my apartment building," recalled Pat Nichols. Pat was a large-boned woman of impressive presence and earthy beauty. She had grown up in Los Angeles, where she had felt the outsider role like the one Janis wore on her sleeve. They would become fast friends. Janis hardly knew Pat then, but she was insistently pounding anyway. When Pat yelled, "Who is it?" Janis yelled back with forthright bravura, caring little for those who might hear, "It's Janis Joplin. I want to sell you some speed!"

Pat Nichols, Kenai, and other friends said that people who were into speed often got into heroin. Meth was so easily available then, it was too easy to get too high. How to come down? Ahhh, you take a bit of heroin. Like a self-regulating emotion machine, people used a little additive to go up and a bit of something else to come down. The American belief in science led people to trust the use of chemicals. Drugs initially gave Janis the sense that she was getting somewhere, merely because things seemed so different. Life looked brighter, sounds seemed louder, and she felt more creative. It's quite possible that Janis first sampled heroin as part of her pull-out-the-stops speed experience.

Anglo-Saxon America dealt with the emotional aspects of life by hiding them, ignoring them, or defining them as problematic. Janis rebelled against those habits, yet there was no guidance beyond the ramblings of Kerouac's novels. Releasing one's feelings from years of bondage was a righteous and dangerous experiment.

Some of Janis's desire to explore the emotional aspects of life must have come as a reaction to our analytical family. Our parents were more comfortable thinking about their passions than feeling them. Mother would say, "Think before you talk, Janis," as though that would change what she said. Mom and Pop tried to validate what Janis felt, but often summarized by saying that she should ignore her feelings because the world didn't agree. That had worked for them, but it wasn't enough for Janis. She needed more. Janis had found the structural weakness in our cultural heritage. Searching for guidance, meaning, and a way to release the whole range of emotions brought Janis to others as confused as she was.

In early 1965, Janis met a fellow meth enthusiast, John Smith.* He was special. He dressed in suits, had money, studied international

---

*Not his real name.

news, and drove a fancy car. He had a genteel demeanor. He was also charismatic and intelligent, though his behavior was often manic, heightened by his use of speed. He was taken with proper social etiquette, and romanced Janis so much that she felt lovely, soft, gentle, and womanly. He wasn't perfect, but he had some of everything that Janis needed in a mate. He was creative and suave, and talked of big dreams for his life. Linda said, "It was a great love affair! It was the first time I saw Janis's heart open. John was a gentleman. . . . They loved each other."

Janis followed him into his intense use of speed. They both sailed over the edge of manageable use into a habit-forming compulsion to hit up. One dose lasts up to seven hours and gives users the feeling of energy and mental sharpness. They lose the desire to eat. They hurry about life consumed by the profound importance of trivial tasks and the thoughts that streak through their minds. Inevitably they come down to a world of blandness and boredom. Prolonged or heavy use almost always causes depression and fatigue.

John's speed use began to take over his life. It advanced to a state of paranoia and delusion. He outfitted his car with guns and told friends about messages he had received from the moon. He wound up in a hospital from a drug-induced inability to deal with reality.

Janis reportedly encountered a young man, Tom Jones,* living on the streets during this period of uncertainty in her life. He found her sitting in a drizzling rain in the park, exhausted from pacing the San Francisco streets, thin, gaunt, unhealthy, and driven by speed's nervous energy. Tom was shy and quiet, suffering from a severe stutter that made employment impossible. He was an emotional refugee running from child abuse, hunting for an unknown solution. For a few days he taught her the tricks of living on the street, how to stay clean and out of trouble, and where to find a meal.

Tom was the perfect partner for a strung-out speed freak who tended toward constant chatter. She talked as he listened; unimpeded by comments from Tom, since he didn't talk, Janis was free to let her thoughts flow uninterrupted. From initial friendly bantering, Janis soon

---

*Not his real name.

moved into deep speculation on the significant questions of her life: What is friendship? Why do people treat each other the way they do? Where do I fit into the universe? A lot of anger emerged as she vented her sense of outrage at social hypocrisy in race relations, the behavior of politicians, and more.

But Janis was just a visitor in her street friend's life, and they both knew it. "Look, man, I've got things I have to do in this world and I can't do them with you and living like this." Tom grabbed her and held her as tight as he could. They both cried but Janis persevered, saying, "Just let me go." She headed up Grant Street to deal with the problems she had been able to talk about with Tom for days on end.

Tom was picked up shortly thereafter by the police, and a thoughtful judge enforced counseling and speech therapy. Janis became one of his inspirations, motivating him to learn to talk. It was his dream to be able to share his thoughts with the woman who had shared so much of her inner self with him.

Janis and Linda visited John in the hospital as he was regaining his sanity. Janis told her friends, "One day I woke up and realized I was going to die." The girls decided to quit. They tried to check John out of the hospital, but as Janis walked with him down the street, she realized he needed to go back. Weeks later he emerged a sane man again. With John out, the three reformers planned their futures. Linda would go to Hawaii to be with her boyfriend, Malcolm Wauldron. Janis would go to Port Arthur to prepare for her wedding to John.

John threw a bus-fare party for Janis. Everyone they knew was invited. Entrance to the party was a contribution to the pot to help send Janis home on a Greyhound. The people who came knew that Janis needed to get out of there. The pitfalls of her environment were too obvious to all.

It was a funny, triumphant failure. Janis had truly hit bottom. Weighing only eighty-eight pounds, she was terrified by what she'd done to herself. Speed had overtaken any pursuit of truth and creativity. Drugs had become the reason and the problem.

Janis was on the edge; a few more steps along the same path looked like sure death. In the novels she consumed, all female heroes

★

either died or got married. Was that bred into her subconscious? Was the only solution Janis could see to her bohemian involvement with drugs a return to convention, to wedding bells and happily-ever-afters?

Janis left San Francisco in early May 1965.

We welcomed her with open arms.

CHAPTER EIGHT

HOME AGAIN

★

I guess I'm just like a turtle
Hiding underneath its horny shell
But you know I'm very well protected
I know this goddamned life too well

—Janis Joplin, "Turtle Blues"

WHEN JANIS CAME home in May 1965, she moved into my room at first, the one I had decorated in white, plum, and green, copied from a *Seventeen* magazine article. During those first few days of getting her acclimated, I took her to the Jefferson City Shopping Center to buy some new clothes. I couldn't understand why she insisted that all the dresses have long sleeves. In Port Arthur? In May? Surely she had forgotten the weather. "Sleeves," she insisted. I didn't know she was trying to hide needle tracks from her days of speed use. She never mentioned them, and I wouldn't have understood if she had.

She was uncomfortable in the middle-class comfort of the store. I was almost supervising. When we went to try on clothes and Janis didn't have underwear on, I went to Woolworth's and bought her a few pairs while she waited in the dressing room. I chose size 8, not knowing what she wore, remembering only that she was larger than me. She laughed. "How big do you think I am?" The panties draped loosely around her lean frame, evidence of her recent drug abuse.

Janis returned home convinced that her past ways were wrong.

★

For the first time, she was asking for advice from our parents and listening to their replies. She was no longer passing through town, content with her way of life. She had come home to recoup and repair. Her attitude brought a wonderful, pleasing peacefulness to the family. For the first time everyone was pulling in the same direction.

Janis became a serious college student, planning a career in sociology. She enrolled in the second summer-school session at Lamar Tech. She took swimming to get fit, world history, and a survey of British literature, one of her loves. She studied and earned B's in all the courses. Janis envisioned a career in helping others, as she had witnessed the importance of the helping professions during her lover's hospitalization in San Francisco. She knew firsthand the kind of help she had wanted over the past several years. She decided that providing that to others could fulfill her need to do something meaningful with her life. Her former investment in art courses began to seem like youthful folly.

Pop bought a 1961 VW Bug, beige in color, for Janis to drive to college and share with me the rest of the time. She was twenty-two years old then. I had turned sixteen and gotten my driver's license. No matter how often we washed its off-white plastic interior, the dirt seemed determined to hold on to its place in the car's dimpled fabric, as though it were needed for ambiance. That trusty vehicle could never be anything but working-class. It was the perfect car for Janis, one that reflected her humble, funky, and functional ideals.

Janis spoke often of John, with a wistful and romantic look in her eyes. He arrived in Port Arthur sometime shortly after she did. He was tall and slender with a dignified air. He had straight blond hair, parted to the side, that kept falling across his face. There was a certain nervous rhythm about his efforts to keep it out of his eyes. He wore a rumpled suit, but exuded a demeanor of calm strength. He stood politely in the living room, a bit uncomfortable but warming up to us as time went by. He was terribly proper and truly seemed devoted to Janis.

He asked to speak to Pop alone, so the rest of us retired to the front bedroom. We whispered and tried to overhear their conversation, knowing something was up. Pop called us back and announced, "John has asked for my daughter's hand in marriage, and I have consented." Janis jumped up and down, hugging John and clutching his steady arm as if it were a tether to reality. The moment excited us all. It felt so right! We really liked John.

John stayed with us for several days in preparation for joining the family. Mother apologized for not having nicer guest quarters and for serving coffee out of the aluminum drip coffee pot instead of a server. Pop spent time with John socializing and discreetly judging his mental acumen and ethics. Janis was peeved that John wanted to spend time with the family. He took Michael swimming for three hours and went on a lengthy tour of the plant where our father worked, getting Pop's enjoyable discourse on mechanization in the workplace. Janis fretted about how he spent his time in Port Arthur. He didn't get to spend an afternoon playing golf with Mom or have time to go to a movie alone with her.

John left shortly, explaining that he had to take care of some family business, alluding to the recent death of a relative. He talked of getting things squared away so that he could announce the marriage in the society section of the Detroit paper. In keeping with his proper demeanor, he wrote a lengthy thank-you note after the visit, saying he'd been made to feel our house was as much his as Janis's. He was surprised and deeply grateful that his reception had been so whole-hearted. A package arrived a few days later. John sent Mother a beautiful silver-plated coffee/tea service.

He exchanged letters with my father, describing his plans for the marriage. He wrote that he and Janis loved each other very much, and had shown that despite occasional arguments, there was a strong bond between them. He wanted to see Janis finish school. What she didn't have before they were married, he claimed he would see that she got afterward.

Janis implied that John's family was prominent in local society in Detroit. He requested that our parents not announce the engagement in the Port Arthur papers until he did so there.

Getting some things squared away? Shortly after Janis left San Francisco in May, Linda Gottfried met John's pregnant wife! Linda quickly wrote to Janis. Did the letter arrive before he went through the ceremony with our family? Did Janis know then? Does it matter? She appeared to have believed his earnest entreaties of getting things cleared up—i.e., divorced—so that they could wed.

He wrote and Janis wrote, and the two of them talked on the

★

telephone. Mom, ever the keeper of tradition, wanted to help Janis ready her trousseau. Janis started a quilt. She chose turquoise and green, a large ever-bursting star made of elongated diamonds. She journeyed to Houston, where Dave and Patti McQueen were living. Janis and Patti went shopping for china and linens and cutlery at Pier 1.

As Janis carpooled to college with Adrian Haston, who was attending graduate school at Lamar, she often spoke about John. She thought she would fit more easily into the gang that consisted of married couples. Ensuring her social membership seemed as important to her as the feelings from the relationship itself. With simplistic trusting logic, Janis told Karleen that if he loved her, then it must be right. Karleen shook her head, thinking that the important question was whether Janis loved John and wanted the same kind of life. But to Janis the only question was whether he loved her.

She told friends about her experience with speed—how she had gotten into it and how bad it was. The stories she told frightened Adrian; it was the first he had heard of anyone going that far. "If I got back into it," Janis told him, "I don't think I'd live very long." Her fear of speed was the fear of death. "California is behind me," she declared to herself and anyone who would listen.

Janis started seeing a counselor in Beaumont that summer, a psychiatric social worker named Bernard Giarratano who worked through a United Way-funded agency, Children and Family Services. She came to him saying she wanted to be like normal people, but she wasn't. There were things about her past she wanted to change. She thought the answer was to emulate another model. At that time she felt that our parents and I represented the model, but she also felt we were too restrictive. She also looked for models within the lives of her friends, but clearly had rejected the detrimental habits of the music world. She wanted to be happy being what she called straight.

She was full of inner conflicts and fears. She was restless within Lamar's academic program. She wanted harder courses, more challenging texts, and class discussions that pushed issues to their limits. She was bored and impatient, waiting for something interesting to happen in her classes. She was frustrated with American culture's blandness and homogeneity. She worried that her own zestful, impulsive nature would get her in trouble with the campus society.

Her only guiding light was creativity. She felt alive when she let herself come forth into any sort of creative effort, from singing to writing letters to friends.

Giarratano counseled her to accept herself and her creative strengths, saying, "Creative people are okay, even if they are eccentric." He encouraged her to experiment, to find what she called a balance between the straight life and a creative one.

She told him emphatically about her identification with Bessie Smith, Odetta, and other singers of that genre. She brought her guitar into the counseling session and sang a few songs so he could understand the intensity of her feelings about art as life. She worried that she didn't have what she needed to succeed on their level, but that did not prevent her from receiving satisfaction from music.

She talked about philosophical and cultural questions. Janis told Giarratano that when she had been in California, she had tried to live in a style she thought would help her break into the world in which she wanted to succeed. She'd pursued drugs as a component of that culture. For a while she had been heavily into pills, Quaaludes, heroin, Demerol (an opiate derivative), and other things that made people feel smooth, especially people who were agitated and believed their feelings might go out of control. After that period, she told Giarratano, she got heavily into speed. Her abuse of that drug brought her back home. While she was in counseling that year, a physician prescribed a tranquilizer for Janis—a drug not so different from some of the street drugs she'd been using.

Sex came up in their discussions, but it was never the central issue for Janis. Her problems were philosophical and cultural. Marriage was important only as part of the ideal she strived to mold her life into. She wanted more from life than she had found, and she didn't know where to get it except by seeking her personal gratification through creativity.

Janis became studious and responsible. "Her life as a nun," Jack Smith joked. Gloria said she looked good. Janis's complexion had cleared up. She was more carefully groomed and wore makeup. She put her hair up in rollers and dressed to fit in as much as she could. At social gatherings she told her friends, "Don't drink too much," and, "Watch your language."

A modern-day Samson, Janis took the most visible sign of her

★

freedom, her wild loose hair, and bound it tightly to her head. When she was home, she and I spent hours in our bedroom experimenting with ways to braid our long tresses in different styles of twists and knots. She settled on using a hair form, carefully pulling her fine brown hair through the doughnut and tucking it underneath. Sometimes she let it hang loose with soft waves around her face.

Janis's new look wasn't only a sign of forgoing the wildness of other days. She was evoking classical female beauty, which depended on the lines of her face and the look in her eye. Nightly, she undid the bun and brushed her hair. Standing at the mirror, she shared her image of what her life would be like in the future. Janis would have longer hair and never, ever cut it. Pop often told us that men loved women with long hair because they liked to watch them brush it. When she was old, Janis planned to wear her hair beautifully braided and pinned around her head. Each evening when it was past the social hour, she and her husband would retire to their quarters. Sitting at her dressing table in a long, silky robe, she would slowly and methodically take the pins from her hair and let it fall down. Only her husband would ever get to see. Each evening, for him, she would brush it one hundred strokes. As Janis told me her story, I knew that she wasn't brushing hair but fingering the pearls in her treasure chest of dreams.

We were the same size, so we traded clothes. We talked a lot about fashion and our bodies and what looked good on our build. We both liked straight skirts or dresses with simple belts or sweaters dyed to match. We talked about hose and shoes to set them off. Weejun loafers were in then, but Janis favored simple pumps with only a slight heel. We both liked the string of Venetian glass beads that Mother bought us, so we had to barter a lot about whose turn it was to wear them.

Janis and Patti talked often about life and death: "Is there a God or not?" They moved beyond that ultimate question to its everyday counterpart: "What, then, is a human?" People weren't just egos with human parents and quirky personalities. People were embodied souls on unknown quests.

There was a wistfulness that crept into Janis now and then. She wrote and taught me a song, "Come Away with Me." Later she laughed. "Sing it all you want to, Laura, but don't tell anyone I wrote that." It was too idealistic for the cynical Janis image.

Come away with me
And we'll build a dream
Things will seem
Like they never seemed
They could be

VERSE 1:
The grass will be green
The trees will be tall
(forgotten stanzas)

VERSE 2:
(forgotten stanzas)
There'll be no hunger no sorrow at all
No one will cry alone in their sleep
There'll be no loneliness hidden down deep, inside

VERSE 3:
Just like the Pied Piper
I'll walk through the streets
Gathering all the happy people I meet
We'll all join hands and
Fly through the sky
Leaving our troubles
Here to die, all alone

Janis continued her lengthy discussions about life and possibilities with her friends. "Janis and I were talking with Jim Langdon," related Jack Smith. "Jim saw life in terms of a box, with limited aspirations. Janis and I saw it more as an open-ended triangle, where the sides went on forever. There were some things you couldn't do, like be born and raised in China. Otherwise, there were limitless aspirations." Sometimes, with Jack especially, Janis let herself echo the sentiments of that ninth-grade girl who read *Ivanhoe* and talked of princesses and knights in armor.

Janis tried to stay away from her earlier wild activities, but she still liked music. She began playing for friends and picking up gigs here and there. Her performing helped her craft a life focused on music but free of the excess that had led her to heavy drinking and drug use. Over

★

the Thanksgiving holiday she had a gig at the Half Way House in Beaumont. Jim Langdon was then writing a column reviewing music in the *Austin American-Statesman*, "Jim Langdon's Nightbeat." His column covered Janis's performance.

> But while it is fresh in my mind, I would prefer to talk about a rare experience I had over the weekend.
>
> That experience took place down in Beaumont, where I had the opportunity to hear a young lady whom I consider to be the best blues singer in the country.
>
> Her name is JANIS JOPLIN, and she is a former Austin resident. Her home is Port Arthur, but she has run a course from Austin to San Francisco to New York and back, before returning home, still relatively unknown as a singer.
>
> This is a condition that I hope will soon change, for her talent is as great, in my opinion, as anyone in the folk field today.
>
> I heard her sing over the weekend in a coffee house–type club in Beaumont called the Half Way House. It was the first time she has performed before the public in quite some time, but her weekend showing there was enough to land her a future engagement in a Houston coffee house in December.
>
> When I entered the club she was singing her own lyrics to a "Cocaine Blues" with a knowledge born of pain, suffering, and the scars of experience. . . .
>
> So she went home and decided to start all over again.
>
> Starting all over again at that stage meant not singing, so she didn't sing. But now she's bringing it all back.
>
> She plays little guitar—just enough to accompany herself—and she is still reluctant to seek out engagements, but it's all coming back.
>
> From her coast-to-coast odyssey remains [*sic*] many marks, some of which cannot be erased. But those same marks have embodied themselves in her interpretation of the blues, and in that context, I hope they remain forever.
>
> Texas has been a hard place for a good many blues singers, from Leadbelly on, but because of this, it has produced some great ones.
>
> In my mind, Janis Joplin is one of the great ones.

Even Janis's social life was becoming traditional. That winter she decided to have a party at the house. She desperately wanted John to come down for the occasion, but he said events forced him to postpone his visit. Mom even sprang for some shrimp to boil for hors d'oeuvres. On a Saturday night, Janis entertained the regular gang, interesting newcomers, and some of her professors. I sat in the den, out of the way, watching television. A guest brought me a plate of food and we talked for a moment. All in all, the party was very successful. Janis was pleased and so were the folks. They enjoyed her friends. Gloria was impressed that anyone would have a party at her parents' house!

Janis had long since given up painting, but she relented as a favor for Mom, who wanted a nativity mural to put on the front porch at Christmastime. Grouped in a family portrait, her plywood Joseph, Mary, and Jesus graced our house that year. Janis impressed Michael, ten years her junior, with how easily she painted something so beautiful, elegant, and loving. She drew with deliberate, fluid strokes and chose warm, earthy colors to set off the figures.

Janis spent part of the Christmas holidays in Austin with Jim and Rae Langdon and their young children. They lived on a hill near town. The group decorated for the holidays, trimming the tree and then turning on the holiday lights in their darkened house. Then everyone sat around the tree as Janis played the guitar and sang Christmas songs.

The next semester Janis studied math, industrial sociology, physical science, United States history, and the sociology of marriage. John had written of his plans to fly down to Port Arthur for the holidays and give Janis an engagement ring, but he didn't make it. It was beginning to seem obvious that he wouldn't follow through on his romantic promises. Janis tried to take it in stride, but her heart was broken. She had tried to marry and live the straight life, but not even that would work for her. Why can't it work for me? she thought, over and over and over.

Janis began dating a sociology major at Lamar. She told us stories of walking in on him early in the morning and finding him asleep in bed, such a skinny guy that his body looked no larger than a wrinkle in the quilt.

Janis went to Houston and Austin occasionally. She visited Patti and Dave McQueen in Houston. She sat around with Guy Clark and other local musicians, picking and singing. She belted out, "Bring it on down to my house, daddy, there ain't nobody home but me." She played a few gigs at an R&B club on West Alabama called Sand

★

Mountain. She may have played at the Jester, though Patti thinks she was rebuffed by the manager. Her Houston appearances netted little local attention, though she enjoyed them immensely.

Janis wrote to Jim Langdon in Austin and asked for help in getting some bookings. Jim was still relating to her as a mentor. He turned Janis on to new singers she needed to hear and introduced her to people she needed to know. His friendship enabled Janis to retain some involvement in the music world without jeopardizing her serious student resolve.

The weekend of March 5-6, Janis played at the 11th Door in Austin. Half of the crowd was crazy about her, and the other half didn't know what to think. They were bewildered, since Janis wasn't at all like the Joan Baez clone they had come expecting to hear.

On March 13, 1966, Janis played a benefit for Teodar Jackson, a penniless blind fiddler who was quite ill. Jim Langdon was the emcee for the event and reviewed it for his column in the *Austin American-Statesman.*

> The concert staged at the Methodist Student Center before a standing-room-only crowd of more than 400 featured perhaps the finest package of blues talent ever assembled under any one roof in Austin. It would be practically impossible to single out any one performer over any other—all were in such rare form.

On the bill were Allan Dameron, Kenneth Threadgill, Mike Allen, Tary Owens with Powell St. John, Mance Lipscomb, Robert Shaw, Roky and the 13th Floor Elevators, and Janis. Jim wrote,

> But the most exciting portion of the program may well have been created late in the second half of the show by Port Arthur blues singer JANIS JOPLIN—the only female performer on the bill—who literally electrified her audience with her powerful, soul-searching blues presentation.
>
> After opening with the grim and gutty "Codine," Miss Joplin changed over to her "soft voice" and a delicate treatment of "I Ain't Got a Worry" which produced an almost spellbinding effect.
>
> Then back with a raucous interpretation of "Going Down to Brownsville," and for her encore, one of her own compositions called "Turtle Blues," which she calls "semi-autobiographical."

On May 5, Janis played a blues festival at the Texas Union Auditorium titled "An Evening of Barrelhouse and Blues." She shared major billing with Robert Shaw. It was her first professional gig before a mixed audience, and it was her crowd, Jim explained in his column. They loved her.

Jim Langdon's reviews helped her book other jobs in Houston and Beaumont. She never liked going to the gigs alone, and wanted me to come along. I was all for it but knew the folks wouldn't approve. We asked anyway. Despite our pleadings and reassurances that there would be no alcohol and that Janis would look out for me, they drew the line. They said they didn't think Janis's musical life had helped her any and they didn't want it to influence me.

Janis had written "Turtle Blues" that year. She taped it on Pop's reel-to-reel tape recorder and sent it to her former roommate, Linda Gottfried, who was now married, named Wauldron, and living in Hawaii. The song talked about hiding, and I guess Janis felt sequestered away in Port Arthur. She hadn't found a way to come out of the shell and live, and so lamented,

> *I'm a mean, mean woman*
> *I don't need no one man, no good*
> *I just treats 'em like I wants to*
> *I never treats 'em, honey, like I should*
>
> *I guess I'm just like a turtle*
> *Hiding underneath its horny shell*
> *But you know I'm very well protected*
> *I know this goddamned life too well*

Janis started plotting a single future for herself. She wanted all the options available to men, the ones that most people didn't allow for women. For all Jim Langdon's goodness to Janis and her career, he still wanted a wife who was a nurturing caretaker, not a liberated woman demanding equal time.

Summer break came around, and Janis needed a change of pace from her regimen of study. She wrote to Jim, and he got her a booking at the 11th Door, where she had sung before. She told our folks, "I'm

★

just going to go to Austin for a week until summer school starts." They didn't like it, but they accepted that Janis was an adult and could make her own decisions. She had been so studious the whole school year, they assumed she was serious about college.

Once in Austin, other opportunities presented themselves. The 13th Floor Elevators needed a singer and Janis considered that possibility. Then she talked on the phone with Chet Helms about an opportunity for her to sing with a band in San Francisco called Big Brother and the Holding Company. Travis Rivers, a Texas folkie with San Francisco credentials, was in town and backed up Chet's story. Janis weighed thoughts about her future carefully. Jim counseled her not to go to California. It was too early for her. He felt Janis should go slow in developing her talent. She needed time to bring her voice to its full potential. Besides, she needed strength to handle the craziness of the business. Her career would be easier if her talent was honed before the business started pressuring her.

Then there was that nagging question about drugs. Janis's experience with the music scene had always involved drugs. She was terrified of them. Jim Langdon said, "The two aren't wedded, you know." What? Do music and not do the drugs? If only she could. She had proven she could stay clean in the past twelve months.

She spent a week staying at Langdon's house before she went to stay with other folks in town. Old friend Dave Moriaty was back in Austin, hunting for fun before he shipped out with the marines. He was at a friend's house when he "heard someone storming up the stairs making lots of noise. It was Janis with Travis Rivers saying she was going to the Coast to join a band." After she left, people at the party groaned. She'd shown she couldn't handle California. Why was she going back?

When Janis didn't come home, Mom called Jim in Austin. He had to tell her where Janis had gone. She panicked. Her heart raced ahead of her terrified mind, which flashed, "Danger! Danger! Daughter in danger!" She felt helpless, wanting desperately to change what had already happened. Mom directed her angry terror at Jim, ranting about his encouraging Janis with his articles and helping her get bookings. "Without your influence, my daughter would still be at home!" she screamed. Jim was shocked and furious at her accusations. He tried to say that he told Janis not to go, but none of that mattered. Janis was gone and Mom was scared for her. She feared for her daughter, who had already experienced some of the bad things that come with a musical subculture.

We moved Janis's things into the den, hoping she'd be back in the fall. I sneaked her books off the shelf and got my first introduction to the other way of life, in Henry Miller's *Tropic of Cancer*. All we could do was hope and be ready to help if the opportunity presented itself.

Summer's sticky Southern heat grew, and life settled into its lazy routine. Janis had left us again. Away from the family and friends who knew and loved her, no one was there to call her hand when she went too far. Janis had come home and asked for help. She had been given all that any of us had to give. Still, her questions had gone unanswered.

CHAPTER NINE

THE SAN FRANCISCO HIPPIE MOVEMENT

★

Work me, Lord
Please don't you leave me
I feel so useless down here
With no one to love

—Nick Gravenites, "Work Me, Lord"

*W*HEN JANIS HIT San Francisco in June 1966, she must have felt a moment of panic at the changes she saw around her. The earnest folkie enclave that she had left merely a year ago was gone. Chet brought her to a new scene, away from North Beach, where rising rents, hassles with the police, and the constant stream of gawking tourists had driven the artists away. Many had moved west to a section named for the intersection of two streets, Haight-Ashbury. While Janis had retreated to Texas, those she left behind had run pell-mell into the future. New drugs and music changed the all-black motif of the Beats into a wild, swirling cacophony of color and sound. Mind-blown, intense rockers now cruised the San Francisco streets. They dared the future to envelop them.

June 6, 1966

Mother & Dad . . .

With a great deal of trepidation, I bring the news. I'm in San Francisco. Now let me explain—when I got to Austin, I talked to Travis Rivers who gave me a spiel about my singing w/a band out here. Seems Chet Helms,

★

old friend, now is Mr. Big in S.F. Owns 3 big working Rock & roll bands with bizarre names like Captain Beefheart & his Magic Band, Big Brother & the Holding Co. etc. Well, Big Brother et al needs a vocalist. So I called Chet to talk to him about it. He encouraged me to come out–seems the whole city had gone rock & roll (and it has!) and assured me fame & fortune. I told him I was worried about being hung up out here w/no way back & he agreed to furnish me w/a bus ticket back home if I did just come & try. So I came.

Had a nice trip–camped out at night along the Rio Grande, collected rocks, etc. Now I'm staying w/some old friends from Austin, Kit and Margo Teele–he works for Dunn & Bradstreet, she for the telephone co.

I don't really know what's happening yet. Supposed to rehearse w/the band this afternoon, after that I guess I'll know whether I want to stay & do that for awhile. Right now my position is ambivalent–I'm glad I came, nice to see the city, a few friends, but I'm not at all sold on the idea of becoming the poor man's Cher. So I guess we'll see.

I just want to tell you that I am trying to keep a level head about everything & not go overboard w/enthusiasm. I'm sure you're both convinced my self-destructive streak has won out again but I'm really trying. I do plan on coming back to school–unless, I must admit, this turns into a good thing. Chet is a very important man out here now & he wanted me specifically, to sing w/this band. I haven't tried yet so I can't say what I'm going to do–so far I'm safe, well fed, and nothing has been stolen.

I suppose you could write me at this address although I don't know how long I'll be here. I expected a letter from Linda–maybe John–if they've arrived, please send them also. The address is c/o C.L. Teele, 23rd St., S.F.

I'm awfully sorry to be such a disappointment to you. I understand your fears at my coming here & must admit I share them, but I really do think there's an awfully good chance I won't blow it this time. There's really nothing more I can say now. Guess I'll write more when I have more news, until then, address all criticism to the above address. And please believe that you can't possibly want for me to be a winner more than I do.

Love, Janis

Will write a long happy & enthusiastic letter as soon as I stop feeling guilty. My love to Mike & Laura. Want to write Laura & tell her about the dances–FANTASTIC! and the clothes & people. Will in due time.

I love you so, I'm sorry . . .

Big Brother and the Holding Company, the band Chet Helms enticed Janis to come and join, had a local cult following for its "freak rock" music. People grooved on the crazy guitar playing of James Gurley, but the band felt it needed a more commanding singer to balance their wild sound. Two of its four members, Peter Albin and James Gurley, knew Janis from the North Beach scene. They had told the other members, Dave Getz and Sam Andrew, about her. They believed she would fit perfectly into the group.

Peter Albin, bass player, was a San Francisco native. He was about five feet ten inches tall with fine brown hair that had a soft curl to it. His slender build and ready smile came with a style that was decidedly clean-cut, regardless of his dress and the craziness of the scene around him. The local folk and country blues music had always been his avocation, though he worked as a postman to support a wife and daughter.

James Gurley, lead guitar, was from Detroit. He was into blues, the music of Lightnin' Hopkins, and free-style music like Ornette and Coltrane. He was a tall six feet three inches, with sandy hair and blue eyes on a lanky frame. He exuded sex appeal to that group of women fascinated by a suffering artist. He and his wife, Nancy, had a toddler son, Hongo.

Dave Getz played the drums, a New Yorker drawn to the Bay Area to teach at the San Francisco Art Institute. He was a talented and creative fellow who had been a Fulbright Fellow. He was medium height—five feet seven inches—and an athletic 150 pounds. He had dirty blond, tightly curled hair and a laughing intensity in his manner.

Sam Andrew had the classic good looks in the group, standing six feet one inch with long, thick, straight blond hair that hung enticingly. He had probing blue eyes and a gentle manner that spoke of his experience as an army kid moving around the world. He had lived in Okinawa, but many of his relatives were from Texas. He had a degree in linguistics and was prone to reading the classics in their original languages. Sam had a background in music theory. He had perfect pitch and was capable of knowing chords merely by hearing them. His background was in old-time rock and roll.

Chet Helms was not a musical member of the band but the spiritual leader, providing inspiration and support for the music. His long strawberry blond locks set off his favorite knee-length uniform

★

dress coat with a long row of brass buttons down the front. The other guys knew Janis from her North Beach singing days. They were enthusiastic about the idea of her joining the band. Only Chet, with his Austin connections, had been able to find Janis and entice her back to San Francisco.

Janis met the guys where they practiced, on the lower level of an old firehouse on Henry Street. Upstairs was a living space and an artist's studio where dwelled Mouse, or Stanley Miller, a poster-artist extraordinaire who drew advertisements for the dances put on by a group of people who called themselves the Family Dog. Janis walked through two huge doors that swung open so that a panel truck could enter and load all the sound equipment the group transported to gigs.

Dave Getz had a foreshadowing dream that Janis would arrive with a glow, beautiful like a goddess. When she came in the flesh, she was dressed in the light cotton clothes she had packed for her week-long trip to Austin, but they were out of place in cool San Francisco. Her shy innocence shone in a face blemished by acne. Then she sang, and her pure notes captured the band's full attention. With her commanding voice, they knew that, everything else aside, Janis had the sound they wanted. The band was complete.

On June 10, six days after she arrived, she joined them onstage. Big Brother played in the new rock style. Janis, Peter, and James knew some standards from the folk days, so they initially connected with tunes like "Blindman" and "I Know You Rider." Janis added some Texas favorites, like her "Turtle Blues" and Powell St. John's "Bye Bye Baby." Those blues tunes joined a repertoire that included such humorous satirical songs as Peter Albin's "Caterpillar," written for his kids, which pleaded, "I'm a caterpillar, crawling for your love."

June 1966

Dear Mother & Dad . . .

Haven't received any word from you yet but presume we're still speaking, so another letter. This one to advise you of my address—I've found a room in a rooming house. Very nice place w/a kitchen & a living room & even an iron & ironing board. Four other people living here—one schoolteacher, one artist, don't know the rest. Anyway the address is Pine St., S.F.

*Still working w/Big Brother & the Holding Co. & it's really fun! Four
guys in the group–Sam, Peter, Dave, & James. We rehearse every afternoon
in a garage that's part of a loft an artist friend of theirs owns & people
constantly drop in and listen–everyone seems very taken w/my singing
although I am a little dated. This kind of music is different than I'm used
to. Oh, I've collected more bizarre names of groups to send–(can you believe
these?!) The Grateful Dead, The Love, Jefferson Airplane, Quicksilver
Messenger Service, The Leaves, The Grass Roots.*

*Chet Helms heads a rock & roll corporation called the Family Dog–replete
w/emblem & answering service. Very fancy. Being my entrepreneur (and
mostly having gotten me out here without money–I still have $30 in the
bank I'm hoarding) Chet rented me this place for a month. He says if the
band & I don't make it, to forget it & if we do, we'll have plenty of
money. Chet is an old friend–married now to an actress named Lori.
Tomorrow night at his dance, some people from Mercury will be there to
hear the Grateful Dead (with a name like that, they have to be good . . .)
and Big Brother et. al. and I'm going to get to sing! Gosh I'm so excited!
We've worked out about 5 or 6 numbers this week–one I really like called
"Down on Me"–an old spiritual–revitalized and slightly bastardized w/new
treatment.*

*I'm still okay–don't worry. Something of a recluse. Haven't lost or gained
any weight & my head's still fine. And am still really thinking of coming
back to school, so don't give up on me yet. I love you all*

*XXXX
Janis*

Haight-Ashbury was an area of ornate but shabby Victorian
houses that had either survived the 1906 San Francisco earthquake or
been built in the teens. It was originally a prestigious area full of the
politically powerful, but it had been in decline for many years. By the
time artists started moving there in the 1960s, the homes had been split
into two or three apartments that housed blacks displaced from a
nearby area razed by urban renewal, along with a hodgepodge of other
ethnic groups hunting for economical homes.

The new scene on the Haight was a direct descendant of the
Beats in North Beach. The same ideas dominated: creativity and self-
exploration, free sex as communion, racial integration, an antiestablish-

★

ment attitude, and music as ecstasy. But the scene had been unequivo-cally changed by the introduction of a new drug—LSD, or lysergic acid diethylamide.

LSD's effects were accidentally discovered in 1943 by Dr. Albert Hofmann, a research scientist for Sandoz Pharmaceuticals in Switzer-land. He had been hunting for a cure for the migraine headache when he formulated the twenty-fifth drug in a series of compounds derived from a fungus that grows on various types of grains. Dr. Hofmann encountered the psychedelic effects of LSD-25 when he absorbed the chemical through handling it.

From Switzerland, LSD found its way into the bodies of the young in Haight-Ashbury by a circuitous route. Mind-altering drugs fascinated a small subgroup of scientists who sought answers to men-tal-health abnormalities. The effects of psychedelics were thought to mimic psychosis. LSD profoundly alters perception, especially color, texture, and detail. The artistically inclined describe its effects as open-ing a previously unknown door to a fresh vision of reality, one seem-ingly bathed in the pure light of whole knowledge. The patterns, similarities, and structure of the world become visible for the first time.

Many psychiatrists were overjoyed that a drug was finally capa-ble of giving them insight into the problems their patients confronted. They postulated that LSD cut through the inhibitions with which people structure their daily lives to allow the hidden truths of the subconscious to be made conscious. Therapists began giving it to some patients in order to pull repressed memories up to be analyzed. Then the patients could be freed from the control of their subconscious.

It wasn't long before LSD found its way into the hands of artists. Aldous Huxley, who had become interested in psychedelics through mescaline, took his first LSD trip in 1955 and was profoundly affected by its potency. Dr. Timothy Leary of Harvard, who was conducting research on LSD, found poets and musicians to be willing subjects. He gave it to Allen Ginsberg in 1960, and together they made a list of people who should be turned on. Ken Kesey, author of *One Flew Over the Cuckoo's Nest,* took LSD through the experiments of Dr. Leo Hollister at Menlo Park in California. Once introduced to LSD, Leary, Ginsberg, and Kesey continued their experiments outside the laboratory. The LSD experience gave users strong new convictions about spirituality and the world. Their experiences were so powerful that they withstood the challenges and taunts of the uninitiated long after the drug wore off. They were so elated by them, they wanted to share them with others.

Important differences developed among the three about sharing LSD. Huxley counseled that LSD should be given only to an elite group of people who could handle its potency. Leary felt that LSD was right for everyone if the circumstances were controlled and an experienced guide was provided. Kesey pulled out all the stops and felt that no controls were necessary.

Kesey shared LSD with friends at his house, and a group of people formed through the shared experience. Where other users had analyzed and tried to describe LSD and its effects, Kesey's group played with their new visions. They called themselves the Merry Pranksters. In comic-book fun they imagined a place called Edge City, a town reminiscent of that described by Robert Heinlein in *Stranger in a Strange Land,* which was about a Martian living on earth. They redesigned their dress to reflect a user's absorption in design and detail. They especially liked Day-Glo orange and green. They christened their new selves with fresh names like Gretchin Fetchin, Mal-Function, and Cool Breeze. They took off from California in July 1964 to visit Leary's group in New York, driving a converted 1939 school bus that had the sign FUURTHER on the front and CAUTION: WEIRD LOAD on the rear.

The Pranksters were back in California by the end of 1964. Word about LSD was getting around. Aldous Huxley had written *The Doors of Perception* in 1954 about his mescaline experiences; it was published together with his *Heaven and Hell* in 1963. In 1962, Huxley's *Island* appeared, a saga of what a psychedelically enlightened community could be. Other books about exploring the inner self began to appear: Adelle Davis's *Exploring Inner Space* and Alan Watts's *The Joyous Cosmology.* The popular press was beginning to run articles about LSD. People were becoming aware that something was afoot.

The Pranksters took it upon themselves to initiate a small number of citizens into the new culture. They began to hold what they called "acid tests." The initial gatherings were held in people's houses and advertised only by means of a poster that said "Can You Pass the Acid Test?" At first only Pranksters and their friends attended. Later others began hearing about the experience, and participation grew.

Organizer Stewart Brand, who later developed *The Essential*

★

Whole Earth Catalog, took over the management of a grand acid test in San Francisco. He rented the Longshoreman's Hall in San Francisco, a popular convention center, and hired a publicist who, among other things, released three weather balloons that spelled the word *NOW.* Scheduled for the third week in January 1966, ten thousand people paid to listen to the Grateful Dead and Big Brother and the Holding Company, watch various theater groups, and amble among booths that sold sweatshirts, incense, and psychedelic literature.

Kesey's experiment was not just attracting nonconformists, it was creating them. The moment of social action had arrived, and the powers resisting change were already fighting back. Kesey was arrested three days before the January test for possession of marijuana. After the watershed event, he jumped bail and headed for Mexico.

Janis arrived on the Haight scene in June 1966. By then the acid ritual had evolved into a multimedia experience, with rock music and other sensory visuals and movement. Gathering in large ballrooms for rock-and-roll dances, people were bedecked in velvet and brocade, madras from India, and anything paisley. They were typically aged eighteen to twenty, encountering the profound through ingesting tablets of LSD.

Big Brother's modernized spiritual "Blindman" echoed the listeners' cravings, intoning, "Blindman stood by the way and cried, cryin', 'Show me the way, the way to go home.' " Big Brother's audience knew "home" meant returning to the truth, living in love and harmony, and discarding the irrelevant trappings of the bourgeoisie. Their audience was constantly tripping. Acid was legal and essentially free in the Haight-Ashbury district.

These denizens of the Haight had left the controlled, clean environments of middle-class America and, with the aid of acid, began playing with the memory-stored images of their lives. They turned themselves into elaborately adorned replicas of the visions they saw. They dug through the discards of society's closets, easily found in the local Goodwill stores, creating the new out of the old. They stared with wonder at design patterns reminiscent of the gaudy Victorian era. They found interest in intricacy, much as their parents found delight in the simple, direct lines of the modern or Bauhaus movements. The young wanted decoration in every conceivable corner of their lives, from beadwork on their shoes to braids, feathers, and beads in their hair, multiple rings, acres of bangles adorning arms and legs, and layers of clothing that blended but never matched.

With or without the drug behind it all, the music performed in San Francisco had changed. Though it was called rock and roll instead of folk music, it had discarded the bubble-gum lightness of early rock so evident in such tunes as the 1955 hit "Earth Angel." Folk songs delivered a true *picture* of human drama, but only the new rock, with its psychedelic influence, promised a way to confront the audience with a sensory *experience* of reality.

The new rock was more than music. Listening alone couldn't convey the whole experience—all the senses were involved. Carl Belz, in *The Story of Rock,* wrote that the new rock concerts were much like the happenings created by 1950s New York artists Claes Oldenburg and Alan Kaprow, combining music, art, drama, and life. The musicians pushed the electrical pulsing to such a volume that it seemed to ignite the molecules in the air, which surrounded the audience like prickly vibrations, forcing them to dance.

Janis brought her roots in blues. She knew the blues, and wanted her audience to know them through her. If the audience sought to have all its senses aroused at a concert, then Janis, as trance enhancer, brought total commitment to her music. Hers was not a music born merely of the vocal cords anyway, but an ensemble piece within her physical presence alone. She coaxed the music with urging arms and strutting steps. She delved deep within herself, so that pieces of her soul seemed to dance along the harmonies and ride the tidal waves of sound that defined her voice.

Big Brother and the Holding Company slowly began weeding through their song list. Their loud freak rock overwhelmed even a singer as strong as Janis. The most she could do was stand in the back and play the tambourine on those numbers. They began to change their repertoire to include more blues, enabling the lead singer to move in front of the music. The singing was shared among the group. Janis was featured only on about a third of the songs in any one night.

Her first out-of-town gig was a dance in an indoor exhibition building at the Monterey County Fairgrounds. The poster read, "Karma Productions & Brotherhood of the Spirit Presents: Big Brother

★

and the Holding Company, Quicksilver Messenger Service, The Glad-
stones, Bill Ham's Lightshow, Famous Underground Movies. Don't
Miss the Great Event, July 2 & 3." Tickets were sold at the Psychedelic
Shop in the Haight, City Lights Book Shop in North Beach, and in
Berkeley, San Carlos, and Menlo Park.

July 3, 1966

Hello!

*In Monterey this weekend for an "Independence Dance." Beautiful
country–have a photograph from this Sunday's paper to send for
illustration. Work's going fine except a lot of hassles w/the union (I think
I'm going Republican). A letter brimming w/news as soon as I have time to
write. Like to hear from you–Love*

XX
Janis

The new rock artists invited the audience to be a part of the
music. Listener and performer built a feedback loop that evoked new
responses on each other's part. The artists depended upon spontaneous
reactions in the audience. They lived Baba Ram Dass's words "Be here
now." Here, at last, was the true initiation into another life, out of an
ordered, planned, and logical culture. To leave the mental control of
that life even once was to know a truth that permeated the rest of your
days. Spontaneity was more than a characteristic. It was a religion unto
itself.

The press coined the term *hippie* as a takeoff on *hipster.* Few in
the Haight liked the word, but it stuck. By June 1966 there were about
fifteen thousand hippies in the Haight-Ashbury area. They spawned a
local culture. By September 1966 they had their own newspaper, *The
Oracle,* giving the true inside story. It emerged from the model of *The
Village Voice* in Greenwich Village. The *Voice* had led the way, showing
that virtue and inspired amateurs could produce a meaningful community newspaper, wrote Abe Peck in *Uncovering the Sixties: The Life and
Times of the Underground Press. The Oracle* also took energy from Art
Kunkin's development of the *Los Angeles Free Press,* which found its

power and financial viability by focusing on the racial uprisings in Watts. *The Oracle* was destined to be the herald of the new social order of the Haight, and was different from the other papers because of its grounding in the developing hippie culture. Abe Peck quoted Allen Cohen, the managing editor: "The *Oracle* was designed to aid people on their [LSD] trips." He continued, describing the paper's focus as "a more conscious, loving, intimate, non-alienated world . . ." One sign of the difference was the paper's use of colored inks in nontraditional ways, sometimes just squirting them on the paper and adding aromatic perfumes.

The new culture spawned a changing emphasis in local specialty shops catering to the hippies. The Psychedelic Shop opened in January 1966 and sold underground newspapers, rolling papers and pipes of all kinds for smoking grass and hash, and the other small necessities of daily existence. The first hippie boutique, Mnasidika, was owned by Peggy Caserta and her partner, who became Janis's friends—everyone in the area was a member of an extended family tribe.

Janis must have felt that the audience response was as much for her as for the music. This was the ultimate community she had sought to find or create since her break with convention at age fourteen. What blissful delight! They accepted her for her true self, her soul. They related to the real person that she was.

Janis found individual acceptance as well, falling in love with James Gurley. He was tall and angular with a distant, haunting look. He had spent months in Mexico taking psychedelic mushrooms with the Indians in the mountains. He didn't use LSD, but his days with the folk who had learned from psychedelics for centuries added to his awesomeness. He sometimes donned a full set of buckskin mountain-man clothes and wore feathers in his long curly hair. Janis felt James had everything she needed in a man to make her feel as if she fully belonged. James even left his wife, Nancy, to live with Janis for a while. For weeks they cuddled and played music. With him she could reveal the tender, soft Janis, the one that didn't need the protection from the tough, ballsy mama. Ahhh, such a dream she was living. Janis had left Austin on a whim and dropped into never-never land to become romantically linked with one of its leading citizens.

★

The music within Big Brother and the Holding Company was evolving. Well-intentioned critics told the guys, "You have to get rid of the chick!" But there was never any question for the five members that they were right for each other.

San Francisco was the place to develop their music. Chet Helms, through the Family Dog commune, had put on the first dances at the Fillmore with the aid of Bill Graham. As head of the San Francisco Mime Troupe, Graham had a long-term lease on the building. Later Graham chose to put the dances on himself, and Chet et al. moved their scene to the Avalon Ballroom. Together they provided a rich atmosphere, flush with musical opportunities. In frequent small concerts, the music evolved according to audience feedback.

Big Brother became the unofficial house band at the Avalon Ballroom. It was a large open room on the second floor of a typical storefront at 1268 Sutter Street, at Van Ness Avenue. Built in 1911, the Avalon held about twelve hundred people. It was originally a dance studio, part of a chain of ballrooms in the 1930s. Ornate gilded balconies ran along the top of the room. It was very Deco, with gilded columns, mirrors, and red flocked wallpaper. A full bar was upstairs, but they served no alcohol. There was a dance floor and seating area on the first floor. Here and there were other activities to entertain patrons: light shows, strobes to play in, chalk for face-painting, and more. The acoustics were wonderful, as the ceiling was draped for sound.

The Avalon provided the base to develop the final polish, but the gelling as a unit came when Big Brother and the Holding Company rented a large summer home in the canyon town of Lagunitas. Other rock bands had moved there from the city. Big Brother's house, nicknamed "Argentina," was down the street from the Grateful Dead's place. Surrounded by acres of woodlands, they practiced their music daily in the living room of their rambling hunting lodge, which was rumored to have once sheltered Teddy Roosevelt and John Muir. The house seemed to evoke great things from a grander era. Here the group's musical cohesiveness was strengthened by living together and talking, breathing, playing, and partying around music.

August 13, 1966

Dear Family . . .

At last a tranquil day & time to write all the good news. I am now safely
moved into my new room in our beautiful house in the country. I'm the only
member of the band out here so far. Our landlady & one of her daughters
are still here but they've gone out to dinner so I'm all alone, sitting in a
comfortable chair by the fireplace, doors wide open and a 180° view of
trees, redwood & fir. Bliss! I've never felt so relaxed in my life. This is the
most fantastic house & setting. I really wish you could see it. Of course
part of my comfort is due to the fact that this is the first day in 10 or 11
that I've had to relax at all. We've been working every night for 11 days.
S.F., Vancouver, S.F. again–and we really worked! Last night, for example,
we played a benefit. They had scads of talent–5 rock bands, 2 poets, 2
comedians, a puppet show, etc. Went on from 3 pm to 1 am. We went on
at 5 and again at midnight. Really was exciting though . . . two of the
bands have hit records out–the Grass Roots (who incidentally are big fans
of ours and even wear our buttons when they play) and the Jefferson
Airplane–and were very well received, but I/we got an ovation, bigger than
any other groups, for a slow blues in a minor key. Wow, I can't help it–I
love it! People really treat me with deference. I'm somebody important.
SIGH!!

We have a P.O. Box here in Lagunitas but I don't know the number–will
add a P.S. w/it. I've got the best bedroom in the house (I got here first)
w/sunshine all day. The weather up here is much warmer than in the city.
In S.F., you have to wear a heavy coat even in the afternoon, but it's just
perfect here. I plan on getting a wonderful tan. And it's not too hot like
Texas. Just lovely–75-80°, don't you envy me? If you have a map, look on
the coast for Stinson Beach–we're about 10 mi. inland from there.

The guys from the band are going to be in a movie–a short, about 2 girls
who fall in love w/a rock and roll group. I can't be in it because I'm a girl
& consequently no romantic figure for 2 girls. In the movie, the band will be
called The Weasels. Not much money but it should be fun. Also in the fire,
we're talking to ESP records–they want us to do an album. Did you read
in TIME about the new upsurge in underground newspapers–the East
Village Other, Berkeley Barb, etc? Well, ESP is either owned by them or
owns them & is sort-of an underground record company. Not big and
flashy, only does albums, & only does slightly out-of-the-way groups, which I
must admit we are. We wouldn't get a big nat'l following like the Lovin'
Spoonful, but we'd have a steady following among the hippies.

★

And lest you think that not much—beatniks are making money *these days. And by being beatniks, it's really amazing. There's such an upsurge among teenagers trying/wanting to be hip. Several of my friends own dress shops & make really far-out clothes for them, others make beads & sell them, others make leather things, but most of them are in the rock & roll business. Really fantastic—a social phenomena really. The society seems to be leaning away from itself, straining for the periphery of hell, the edges, you know. At least in California. Now* that is *a qualifying statement.*

—Later, sorry. Address is P.O. Box 94, Lagunitas, Calif.

As I mentioned earlier, we played Vancouver 2 weekends ago, enclosed something I brought back for Mike & Laura. For Laura's jewelry box-money collection, a Canadian dollar; for Mike's coin collection, a Canadian nickel. Note the edges.

A fashion note—thought y'all would like to know what everyone looks like out here. The girls are, of course, young & beautiful looking w/long straight hair. The beatnik look, I call it is definitely in. Pants, sandals, capes of all kinds, far out hand made jewelry, or loose fitting dresses & sandals. The younger girls wear very tight bell-bottoms cut very low around the hips & short tops—bare midriffs. But the boys are the real peacocks. All have hair at least Beatle length—[drawing indicating chin-length hair], most rock & roll people have theirs about this long [shoulder-length] & some, our manager Chet's for example as long as this [below shoulders], much longer than mine. And very ultra Mod dress—boots, always *boots, tight low pants in houndstooth check, stripes, even polka-dots! Very fancy shirts—prints, very loud, high collars, Tom Jones full sleeves. Fancy print ties, Bob Dylan caps. Really too much—just like in the magazines, folks.*

Conforming to the style to the extent of my budget, I have a new pair of very wide-wale corduroy hip-hugger pants which I wear w/borrowed boots. Look very in. On stage, I still wear my black & gold spangley blouse w/either a black skirt & high boots or w/black Levis & sandals. But, as soon as I get money. . . . she said, shaking her fist at the sky. Rock & roll has gone so casual—everyone dresses nice but street-wear & all different. And the girls all wear bell-bottoms & boots, so I want to get something out of gold lamé. Very simple but real show biz looking. I want audiences to look at me as a real performer, whereas now the look is "just-one-of-us-who-stepped-on-stage." Well, we'll see—A girl friend of mine owns a clothing store—she makes the clothes to your design. So either she or I will make me something. If I ever get around to it.

Oh this weekend Bell Telephone Hour is filming the "San Francisco Scene" (because there really is something going on here that's not going on anywhere else) at the Fillmore Aud. Unfortunately, we're playing at the Avalon. Damnation!! But some good friends, the Grateful Dead are playing there–they're also neighbors, one of the 2 other groups that live out here. Just down the road a piece.

Oh, Laura, may I suggest some reading? J.R.R. Tolkien wrote The Hobbit, *followed by* Lord of the Rings Trilogy—*really very charming reading. I'm reading it now.*

Had a bunch of visitors from Texas up last week–Jim, Tary Owens & his wife & some other friends from college. Jim was purportedly looking for a job but fled within a week back to the sanctity & comfort of Texas & his wife.

No more news–guess I'll amble down to the post office & mail my letter. All of my love, will send photographs of our haven as soon as I can.

XXX
Janis

The group had moved to Lagunitas in the hopes that by pooling rent they could save some money and find a good place to rehearse. A blastingly loud rock band can't practice just anywhere. Finding good rehearsal space was always a problem.

All five of the band members with their respective spouses, lovers, children, dogs, and cats lived under one roof. James was back with Nancy and, with their son, Hongo, lived upstairs. Across the hall from them were Peter and Cindy Albin and their daughter, Lisa. Janis lived in the sun room just down the hall. Dave Getz lived in a room off the kitchen on the first floor. Sam Andrew and his girlfriend Rita lived in a small cottage out back. Together they confronted the reality of "extended family."

Fun was the real watchword of the times. "Winter, fall, spring or summer, there's nothing worse than a mealy bummer," is the nonsense Janis penned with Dave Getz after biting into a bad apple. He explained, "That phrase became synonymous with a lot of things, so it got hauled out a lot." Inside jokes, references, and joy. That's what it takes to turn a group into a synchronized band.

★

Janis's identity with the group was growing. On her car she painted the "God's Eye" symbol for the band that poster-artist Mouse had designed. The posters that were made to advertise the dances around town were gaining artistic respect on their own terms. Museums from around the world were buying the original drawings of the posters for their collections. The art-world professionals Janis had learned to respect as a child were now coming to her scene and saying it was the most exciting thing happening. That added to her convictions about the correctness of it all.

"Janis was easy to live with," Peter Albin said. Living in the sun room, all of her windows open to the forest and the sun cascading in through the abundant leaves of her carefully tended houseplants, Janis was happy there. Relaxed in her solarium, she wrote songs for the band. Her voice wafted through the house as she strummed new melodies and tried new lyrics.

She found a special friend in James Gurley's wife, Nancy, despite the obvious tension between them about Janis's past yen for James. Nancy, with a master's degree in English literature, was a companion who thrived on meaningful discussions of the books that were as much a part of Janis as her music was. Nancy was an Earth Mother figure, married with a child. Like the women in Janis's Texas group, Nancy represented the other female role, but she, more than the Texas wives, blended the nurturing role with the strength Janis wanted to see in her vision of the modern woman.

Nancy was also into speed, Janis's nemesis from earlier days. Janis cringed in fear when she first arrived in San Francisco and saw someone shooting anything. Dave felt that Janis's attraction to it was so strong that its mere presence was too great a temptation. For a while, Janis held the line on drugs, with only occasional drinks of alcohol, but living in Lagunitas changed that. Intrinsic to the times and that place were crazy-drug and free-spirit exploration. There were big parties, and lots of intoxicating and mind-expanding chemicals. So, she did some drugs. It wasn't the main focus of her life; she was just being part of the scene. Sometimes Nancy, Rita, and Janis stayed up all night doing speed and stringing beads manically into necklaces and elaborate wall-hangings.

The free-spirit, Earth Mother speed experience of Nancy Gurley clashed with the early-to-bed, straight, dope-free life of the Albins. Peter and Cindy wanted a quiet house at ten P.M. so that their daughter could get to sleep. Many of the others wanted to practice rock and roll deep into the night, mimicking the hours they lived onstage, starting at nine P.M. and ending at one A.M.

Nancy had been one of the first teachers at the Summerhill School in Los Angeles. She raised Hongo in a very relaxed manner compared to what Cindy wanted for Lisa. Everyone kept dogs, but James and Nancy's bitch had puppies that got distemper. For a while it seemed there were always half-dressed, dirty children running around, dead puppies, and the clutter of too much stuff, too few people cleaning, and constant rock-and-roll parties. The overall intensity of eight adults, two toddlers, and an untold number of animals created mind-boggling chaos for anyone who cared to look closely.

In spite of the gelling of the band and her role within it, there was still the independent Janis who wasn't sure that being merely a part of Big Brother was enough. Janis's early Coffee Gallery days had netted her the attention of others in the music world. While back in California she had been approached to try another career route. Paul Rothchild, then the recording director at Electra Records, had funds to develop a blues roots band. He gathered Taj Mahal, Stefan Grossman, and Al Wilson (Wilson later formed Canned Heat). Janis rehearsed with them in San Francisco without the knowledge of the guys in Big Brother. Paul told them, "The music is great!"

August 22, 1966

Mother . . .

Haven't heard from you yet, but I'm brimming w/news so here I am.

First of all, we begin a 4 week engagement in Chicago next Tuesday—at $1000 a week!! So don't write till you hear from me. Really looking forward to going . . . . Chicago is Blues Heaven & I can hear & be heard by some important people. They (the club we're playing in—Mother Blues) pay our transportation, so we're flying out Tue. morning. I really dig flying—& being a R&R band & flying to a gig is even more exciting. SIGH!! And a friend of mine gave me a dress & cape to wear for the occasion—a wine-colored velvet, old, from a Goodwill store, but beautiful! Queen Anne kind of sleeves & a very low & broad neckline. Really fantastic.

★

Now, I have a problem. I'm hoping the Chicago job will resolve it for me, but right now it's plaguing me. Last weekend we played in the city & a man from Elektra, a good label, spoke to me afterwards. Liked me/us a lot. During the week, someone called me . . . . seems Rothchild (the guy from Elektra, who discovered Paul Butterfield who is very big now—he does old-fashioned blues) is interested in forming a blues band and wants me. The two guitar players & the other vocalist & Rothchild & the Owner (!) of Elektra & I had a meeting today. Very involved, but, to summarize—Rothchild feels that popular music can't continue getting farther & farther out & louder & more chaotic, which it is now. He feels there is going to be a reaction & old-fashioned music blues, shuffles, melodic stuff is going to come back in. Well, Elektra wants to form the group to BE this—and they want me. They want to rent us a house—in L.A.—& support us until we get enough stuff worked out, then, first, they want us to do a single & an album. Now they're a good company—& since we'd be their group, they'd push the hell out of us. . . . And, he says, we couldn't help but make it. Now I don't know what to do! I have to figure out whether R&R is going to go out, how deep my loyalties to Big Brother go (the band is very uptight at me for even going to the meeting & I can understand it) & just, in general, what to do. Blues is my own special love for one thing & for another, I'd be under contract to a record co. from the beginning—I'd be starting on the top almost and I'm not sure yet whether the rest of the band (Big Brother) will, indeed want to, work hard enough to be good enough to make it. We're not now I don't think. Oh God, I'm just fraught w/indecision! And let's face it, I'm flattered. Rothchild said I was one of the 2 maybe 3 best female singers in the country & they want me. Well, what I'm hoping is the Chicago job will show me exactly how good Big Brother is . . . . . & then I can make up my mind. Wow, this is really too much. Hope you don't mind my rapping on you like this, but I just needed to talk to someone. Wish I could ask someone for advice that knew & wasn't biased for any reason. Ah, Dream on, Janis.

Will write, maybe I'll even call from Chicago.

My love to everyone
XXXX
> *Help!!*
> *Janis*

When the fellows found out Janis was talking to Paul Rothchild, they initially thought Paul was interested in them as a band. Finding out that Paul wanted only Janis was devastating to their newly developed sense of family. In heated discussions, they accused her of betrayal. Janis yelled back, "Don't bandy words with me!" She wished she knew what truly was best for her. Big Brother was just hitting its stride; to leave then would rob the band of the ability to test its newfound merits. They argued and implored. After all, ESP, a small record company, had already approached them. Finally, they persuaded Janis to delay the decision until after the big Chicago gig ahead.

Mother Blues was an old folk club that had changed to rock and roll because there was too much competition with straight blues. Big Brother arrived, bringing the Haight scene with them, and entered the world of "before there was acid." Long hair on the guys got the typical catcalls: "Is it a boy or a girl?" Cut velvet, boots, beads, feathers, and fly-away hair just weren't the norm in the Windy City. Nick Gravenites's head turned as he saw the five of them strolling the street. Crossing to say hello to his old friends, they cringed as though unsure whether he was a local intent on hippie-bashing or just a gawker. But it was Nick, a vagabond like them, back home in Chicago from his former days in the bohemian North Beach scene.

Nick brought a record producer friend, George McGowsky, to hear the group perform. Like much of Chicago, he was confused by the sound. "Too bad she won't ever make it," George confided to Nick. "They're just too far out for the business." Still, the money was good and the trip was fun. Away from Lagunitas, Janis and James renewed their romance.

Arriving in the mail was a letter with parental questioning for Janis.

As you have so studiously avoided the topic we are assuming that you feel your present venture promises success and that you will not be back here for college next month. If this assumption is incorrect let us know immediately as we need to know. On the other hand if the assumption is correct all we can do, I guess, is to wish you the very best of luck and all the success you hope for. Love, Father

★

September, 1966

Dear Mother . . . . .

We're playing in Chicago now—5 sets a night, 6 nights a week. GASP! Really is hard work. We're at Mother Blues in old town. Our music isn't really going over either. There are so many good blues bands in Chicago that we pale beside them and that makes playing all the harder.

We have been fortunate in one respect—Peter has an Aunt & Uncle who live in Chicago & we're staying at their house. They're really nice people—w/3 super-creative & bright kids. Have a big air-cond. house in the suburbs, loaned us a car. Really fantastic. We're all kind-of sad about having to leave our house in the country, though.

The record thing I wrote you about caused quite a bit of emotional trauma within the group. All sorts of questions of loyalty came up. I decided to stay w/the group but still like to think about the other thing. Trying to figure out which is musically more marketable because my being good isn't enough, I've got to be in a good vehicle. But I don't know anything about the music business, so I'm just plodding along.

Daddy brought up the college issue which is good because I probably would have continued avoiding it, in my own inimitable adult fashion, until it went away. I don't think I can go back now. I don't know all the reasons, but I just feel that this all has a truer feeling. True to me. A lot of the conflicts I was having and going to Mr. Giarratano about I've resolved. Don't take my tranquilizers anymore. I don't feel like I'm lying now. This is all fine & good & very sincere but the trouble is—I'd like to go back to school. I really would, but I somehow feel that I have to see this through first and when I can, put myself through. If I don't, I'd always think about singing & being good & known & feel like I'd cheated myself—you know? So, although I envy many aspects of being a student and living at home, I guess I have to keep trying to be a singer. Weak as it is, I apologize for being so just plain bad to the family. I realize that my shifting values don't make me very reliable and that I'm a disappointment and, well, I'm just sorry.

We have an address here where you can write me—wish you would. I tried calling last Sunday but no one was home—since has occurred that you are probably in Bandera, lying in the sun. Will try to call again—or you can call here if you ever want to. The address is Pleasant Lane, Glenview, Ill.

Thought I might be able to see John Smith while I was here. Sent him a wire in Rochester, but haven't heard from him. He's probably moved.

Oh, forgot another bit of news. Mainstream Records is trying to sign us—we have a contract and are having it looked at. Will see.

Write Please—Love You
All X X

Janis

How wonderful! Janis didn't feel like she was lying anymore. She had found her emotional home. No matter how tenuous that life might prove to be, for that moment it looked like it would last forever.

Janis had a curious way of reporting that she wasn't taking tranquilizers. It implied that she preferred a clean mind. She failed to mention the other drugs—the social drugs that were now a daily part of the hippie scene. Tranquilizers were not hippie kinds of drugs, as they dulled the senses. Hippies were into mind-expanding. Yet Janis rejected the psychedelics, preferring depressants, most notably alcohol.

Janis had always faced her devils, even if it caused problems in her life. Now she was taking the first of many steps aimed at avoiding the core issues of her life. Janis already knew the danger of drugs from her speed experience in 1964, but she decided to tolerate the drug scene in 1966 because she craved the music world. She traded legally prescribed tranquilizers for a socially accepted, politically correct drug—alcohol! She couldn't get past our culture's assumption that the problem was only which drug to use. Few were then questioning the reliance on drugs in our society. Few were asking why drugs were needed. In those days, drugs were the new discovery. Who dared question the new shaman?

In Chicago, the club date started out clean. The owner paid the band one thousand dollars a week for the first two weeks. The third week of the four found the club owner out of money because his experiment with Big Brother didn't draw sufficient customers. The local audiences weren't stoned and didn't understand Big Brother's style of rock. Chicago was a blues town. Audiences, especially at small nondescript clubs, expected to hear typical blues tunes with the traditional musical background. They didn't know what to do with the reborn San Francisco hipsters.

Peter pursued the band's financial rights through the Musicians' Union, but legal assistance couldn't give the owner money when he had none. Stuck in Chicago with no way to go home forced the band to work for gate receipts. "We had to start developing a stage show," Peter Albin explained, "with me doing a lot of witty remarks. But it still didn't come off. And finally, the last week, we . . . got a go-go girl. We named her Miss Proton, the Psychedelic Girl." She wore leotards on which Peter sprayed paint and glitter. They gave her weird makeup and attempted a Saran Wrap hat.

Janis explained to a *Mojo Navigator Rock and Roll News* interviewer, "You can't imagine what it's like trying to sing. You know, little tiny stage, it's real small and real long like this and you can't move at all, and I'm standing there singing and the dance floor's right in front of me like this, and there's this half-naked chick dancing there right in front of me, and I was really cracking up. It was hard, very hard to sing."

Janis took her revenge. "Janis and I had some differences," recalled Peter, and "her reaction in Chicago was one of them." It was her old sense of a higher authority. If the club owner didn't pay her salary, then she would get back at him by helping herself to a cashmere sweater that belonged to a friend of his. Since the friend had let the band stay in his apartment, he must be involved in the rip-off. Janis was taking care of Janis, balancing the tables in the most direct way possible.

She didn't consider the sensibilities of the guys in the band. Taking the sweater made problems for her within her family. "It just wasn't good business," Peter explained to me. "It all eventually comes back to you." Years later, Peter ran into the former owner of the sweater. The guy said, "Yeah, I got a good story. Janis Joplin stole my cashmere sweater."

The pressure of Paul Rothchild's offer to Janis intensified the band's sense of urgency to get a record deal. Earlier in San Francisco, along with other bands, Big Brother had auditioned for a couple of small record companies, including Bob Shad at Mainstream. Chet Helms, as manager, had rejected any offers that were presented. Reflecting the San Francisco business view, he was holding out for a good offer giving them artistic control and more.

In Chicago, Bob Shad reintroduced himself to Big Brother. Chet Helms was no longer the group's manager. They'd let him go due to his time conflicts in managing the Avalon Ballroom. Away from his guidance they were susceptible to a precipitous move.

Bob Shad had been in the business a long time and wasn't a bad sort. He offered them a contract that was standard at the time. The band would get 5 percent of the royalties and the record company would get ownership of all the songs they wrote. They thought they were taking the necessary precautions by having an attorney check the deal, but all he could do was look at it from a legal standpoint. What they really needed was a manager's view, and that was missing.

Bob Shad courted the group with promises that Mainstream was a label that understood their type of blues music. He could capitalize on their niche. So Janis made the all-important choice. She told Paul Rothchild, "I fell in love with one of the guys in Big Brother, so I'm going to go with that band, and not with yours."

Bob Shad's plan was to release some singles of the band's music. Eight hours in an eight-track studio in Chicago netted four or five songs. They might be considered true renditions of the form of their art at the time, since they played only two or three takes of each song and just chose the best of the group. However, sound engineers weren't yet aware that some distortion was necessary to duplicate the music's impact. The audio level was kept too low, losing much of the intensity of their live performances.

September 20, 1966

Dear Mother, family

Finished the Chicago job Sunday & started out last night for California. Home! Home! We're now in Nebraska. In fact, we just passed the Clay Center turnoff—I almost drove in to meet my relatives but I couldn't remember their names so we're still on the road. We're driving a '65 Pontiac Grand Prix—real class. It's a driveaway—you put up a certain sum of money which is refunded when you deliver the car & all you pay for is your gas. (Car is in motion, excuse handwriting. . . .)

★

HOW THINGS ARE GOING, PROFESSIONALLY, DEPT:

1. We completed one recording session—quite an experience. It took us 9 hrs. to get less than 12 min. cut. And we didn't mess up a lot either. First of all, you record the instrumental part alone. Then when you have it to your (and your engineer's) satisfaction, you lay the vocal on another track over the instrumental. Then for a dynamic effect you dub another vocal track, same voices, same words, over the first to give the voice a deeper sound. Really involved. So at any rate, we cut 4 sides. He's going to release 2 of them—1 single 45—in a month or so. Now he's badgering us to get some more recording done. He says I came out very well on the first ones & thinks I am the most marketable aspect of the group & wants to get some of my songs. He wanted to do it before we left Chicago but we have a gig this week-end & so will have to do it later in L.A. Whew.

2. Our Chicago job, though good for us from a professional point of view was a real burn. (Burn—idiomatic for unfavorable balance of exchange—i.e. we got cheated.) The first 2 weeks were okay—we got paid. At the close of the third week, the mgr. of the club told us he didn't have any money to pay us or to buy our plane tickets home,—so we were forced to work the 4th week for the cover charge & simply hope it would be enough to get us back home. And about the $1400 he owes us—well, he'll send it when the club gets back on its feet & gee I'm really sorry & mumble mumble. So, here we are in our driveaway sweating across country cursing. But we have an I.O.U. from him & still think (hope?) he'll pay us. I gleaned about $200 out of the gig though. Will get $120 this week-end & another $80-100 for the recording session. Think I'm going to buy myself a car. Also via the Chicago job, we got a very good job feeler for 2 wks. in Toronto & 2 more in Montreal—at $1500 a week, 4 days a week. In December. Sounds good now, but theoretically our record may be a hit by then & we'd be stars. But, we'll see.

FASHION NEWS: Before we learned that we weren't to receive any more salary, I felt very flush—I have $200 and $200 more coming—pure profit, bills already paid—So, I went out & bought myself a $35 pair of boots. Oh they are so groovey!! They're old-fashioned in their style—tight, w/buttons up the front. Black. FANTASTIC! When I get back I'm going to rent a sewing machine & make myself some sort of beautiful/outlandish dress to go w/them.

HOWDJA LIKE TO DO ME A FAVOR DEPT: Y'know that box you're ready to send me? Well, I thought of a few more things I'd like to have if they're still around. I'll list them, for efficiency:

1. the makings of my quilt. If I get the sewing machine, I'd like to work on it.

2. my knitting bag & the gray & blue Orlon sweater I was working on.

3. the black photograph album of Linda & I. Should have been in the second shelf of the desk. Also down there, a manila envelope—closed—full of rather inconsequential but very personal things—I'd like to have it too.

4. In the record holder, a small manila envelope w/a booklet & other things from a record club I joined—that too.

5. And, if they haven't been given to Goodwill or Laura, a couple of articles of clothing: the grey & brown striped knit top and grey skirt? and the green cotton shirtwaist I liked so much.

6. Do I have a black knit hat at home? If so, send it too?

7. Recipe box & book. Hope this isn't putting you out too much—I really appreciate it. Send it by Greyhound, that's fine—my address is P.O. Box 94, Lagunitas, Calif.

What I want to do, if we get our employment on an even keel, is take a few days off & come home—to try & explain myself to you, to see everyone, & to sort my belongings. But heaven knows when I'll be able to do that. But I'm still hoping.

All for now, I guess—if you find any little personal thing of mine that you think I might want, send it.

Love XXX
Janis

    The gig over, the contract signed, the band started for the West Coast intending to record again in Los Angeles with Mainstream. Peter had saved his money, so he flew from Chicago in style. The rest of the group jammed into the Pontiac Janis mentioned in her letter.

    Until October 2, 1966, LSD had not been covered by any laws, but on that date possession became a misdemeanor. Seven hundred or

★

so hippies celebrated by congregating for a Love Pageant Rally in Panhandle Park. The flyer encouraged them to come "to affirm our identity, community and innocence from influence of the fear addiction of the general public as symbolized by this law." Big Brother, the Dead, and the Wild Flower performed. Reporters from radio, television, and newspapers were on hand. Most celebrants were flying on acid in group defiance.

Janis and Pat "Sunshine" Nichols sat at the edge of the event. They traded a bottle of Ripple wine back and forth, staying away from psychedelics. They watched those around them trip on the geometric patterns of the leaves in the trees and the astounding allure of veins in the blades of grass. Janis and Pat were old friends from the Coffee Gallery. They didn't need to justify their preference for alcohol over acid. They were part of the movement but rejected the chemical that gave the era its style.

CHAPTER TEN

SUCCESS WITH
BIG BROTHER

★

Come away with me
And we'll build a dream
Things will be like they
Never seemed they could be

—Janis Joplin, "Come Away with Me"

IG BROTHER AND the Holding Company went back into the studio in the late fall of 1966. Bob Shad flew out from Chicago, intent upon getting some good singles to release. From the two studio sessions, Chicago and Los Angeles, Mainstream released the first single, "Blindman" and "All Is Loneliness." Despite Janis's enthusiastic mailing of 45-rpm singles to family and friends, and almost wearing out a copy on the Lagunitas stereo, nothing much came of the effort.

Big Brother was getting good local reviews for their record and their performing. *Mojo Navigator Rock and Roll News* said the record ". . . is excellent, both in terms of commercial potential and actual re-creation of their in-person sound." In *The Berkeley Barb,* Ed Denson wrote in his column, "The Folk Scene," "The chick really can sing, thou. She is a blues wailer working material from Shirley & Lee back to Ma Rainey and Bessie Smith, with the ability to scream and throw her body into the music." He continued, "But it was the instrumentalists who made the group out of sight. . . . I was hooked on the guitarists. . . . Overall was the feeling that the group was making their

★

music, not just their living, & that they were doing some inventive things."

Big Brother plunged into a tumultuous search to find bits of the soul, unearthed through gut-wrenching musical determination. Soul was Janis's musical guide. It led her to black music and the black experience in white America. "Blue-eyed soul" was her entree into the white middle-class rock-and-roll scene. The roots came from folk and rhythm and blues, but it was uniquely white. Her music was an attempt to blend the styles meaningfully and echo the life of white America. People were working at creating the new sound, finding its definition. But there were limits. When Sam Andrew tried some unusual chords on a blues piece, Janis shot him down quickly, ever the purist, saying, "TV blues!"

Jive talk accompanied her absorption into black music. Every sentence started with "Hey, man," recalled Paul Rothchild. In the middle was always the word *like*. "Hey, why don't we, like, go downtown?" Drugs redefined the language; a frequent user was an "acid head," a single dose a "hit" or a "tab," and marijuana was "pot," "grass," "reefer," or "good shit." Life was art, and dialogue was improvisational theater. They thought a new society was beginning.

The *Mojo Navigator* of October 5, 1966, paraphrased the Declaration of Independence:

> When in the flow of human events it becomes necessary for the people to cease to recognize the obsolete social patterns which have isolated man from his consciousness and to create with the youthful energies of the world revolutionary communities of harmonious relations to which the two-billion year old life process entitles them . . . we hold these experiences to be self-evident, that all is equal that the creation endows us with certain inalienable rights, that among these are: the freedom of body, the pursuit of joy, and the expansion of consciousness, and that to secure these rights, we the citizens of the earth declare our love and compassion for all conflicting hate-carrying men and women of the world.
>
> We declare the identity of flesh and consciousness; all reason and law must respect and protect this holy identity.

October, 1966

Dear Mother–

Gawd, I feel so delinquent not having written in so long–& you just getting over a serious operation. I'm sorry, sorry. I'm so thankful that you're okay–your letters sound chipper–& that they feel they caught it in time. I really am relieved & also very proud of you for the stoic way you handled everything. I know it's rather late to be saying all this, but since I have my car I'm highly mobile, so if you ever need me or want me, call, Please.

Things are just as messed up around here as ever. We all just stumble from one day to another, not getting much of anything done. I've discovered I can't do anything unless there's a modicum of quiet & w/eight people in one house–talking & carrying on w/their babies, I can't do any little things, like writing letters, mending, sewing, anything. For example, everyone is gone now (Allah be praised!) so I can do this.

I got a beautiful old sewing machine in a second-hand store. An old Singer w/gold fillgree (sp?) designs all over it. Also bought some blue velvet to make a dress for on stage–if I can get around to it, probably not until our lease is up & we each get our own place again.

Our record is out now–Blindman/All is Loneliness on Mainstream Records. We're supposed to get 50 free records & I'll send you one. We haven't received any yet–they were due 2 wks ago. Do you suppose our record producer lives w/eight other people & just can't seem to . . . oh of course not. We have one copy which we've played so much I can't stand it any more. I can't even tell if it's any good.

Am sending you a couple of things. First, a picture of me looking beautiful–off a proof sheet that a photographer did for us. Second, an I.D. magazine w/some of the local bands in it. All the people w/names by them are friends. I send this so you can see how groovey the people in California look. The bands that are friends of ours are the Grateful Dead (isn't Pig-Pen cute? They make Pig-Pen T-shirts now w/his picture on it–for fans. I have one–red.) the Quicksilver Messenger Service, the Charlatans (remember the blue poster I had of them? Is it still around by any chance? I'd like to have it.) the Outfit, & the P.H. Phactor Jug Band. Take a look at them, then at the Calliope Co. & then, if you're steeled, the Family Dog picture. The Family Dog is Sancho on top of the truck–the symbol for all those people that form a rock & roll corporation & put on dances every

★

week end. Those people are all friends of mine! Aren't they amazing?! The people w/stars after their names are members of the band.

I'm in the back on the right. Really an amazing picture. They aren't dressed up–they look that way all the time. Now, taken in perspective, I'm not so far out at all, eh?

My poor little car. I lost the keys so it's hot wired. Lost a hub-cap. And the starter motor burned out so I have to push it to start it. It was a nice clean healthy little car & now its an out-&-out beatnik car–& it knows it. Poor thing. It's out front, parked on a hill.

Linda & I are still writing–she and Malcolm and Sabina are now living on the boat that Malcolm built. She sent me a picture–she is so beautiful! Holding Sabina w/a bikini on–all brown. She just looks great! Sigh.

I think we're supposed to go to L.A. in November sometime to record. Hope to stay w/Barbara or Donna [Janis's cousin] while I'm there. Really want to see Donna.

Isn't this ridiculous–I haven't written in about 2 mos. & I can't think of any news. Absurd. Well, I love you all, think about you a lot, will send you a record, & try to write sooner.

> Love, XXXXX
> Janis

> November 20, 1966

Dear Mother . . . .

How is everyone? Fine, I hope. And happy.

We've been busy working lately–and glad of it. This business just isn't any fun unless you can perform. The monitary aspects of not working are important too of course, but the real value is just in being appreciated. It's worth all the hassles and bad rehearsals just to have 1500 kids really digging you. And for me to have a musician from another band tell me that I'm the best chick blues singer, bar none–not even Bessie Smith. Happened this weekend SIGH!!

Last week end, we were very busy–Fri. nite from 7:00-9:15 we taped a T.V. program–a local pop art show called POW! We did our record & had to lipsync it which is very strange. Then off to Sacramento in a rented car for a job that night. We were very late–11:15, so to fulfill our contract we had to play for 2 hours straight which is none too easy. The next night into the city for what ranks as our crowning achievement here-to-fore–a Hell's Angels Party. A complete madhouse! Then Sunday night we played a zenefit–a benefit for the Zen Temple here in town. This weekend we played at a place in Santa Cruz called the barn. It's about 60 mi. away, so we stayed at someone's house & slept on the floor Fri. nite–which is just barely called resting. Moan. We're at the Avalon Ballroom next week end and the first part of December we're supposed to be going to L.A. to record. Our record doesn't seem to be making it despite quite a push from fans around here. The record company wants to feature me on the next sides so we're working on my stuff and so on and so on, business, business.

Also new–I have a dog. So cute! Only 8 weeks old and fluffy as a dandelion. Part German Shepherd and part English Shepherd. He's going to be pretty big. He has German Shepherd coloring but long curly hair, named of course, George. Actually, he was named George when I got him, so I kept it. Also, while in Santa Cruz this weekend, I caught a mouse. Just about this _____ big (not counting tail) and really cute. Haven't named him yet.

My car now has Big Brother and the Holding Co. painted on it, and our symbol, the God's Eye, very good, done by Mouse, one of the poster artists around did it. Very nice. Car, haven't named it yet either, is running well but won't start because of my non-working starter motor. So I jump-start it rolling down hills. Luckily we live on top of one. Will get it fixed as soon as we get monies.

I also have a $35 dermatologist bill. Doesn't seem much better yet. He's doing a new thing–at least to me. I'm taking internal medication called Tetracycline that he says has revolutionized the profession. We'll see. But the advantages, if it worked, would be tremendous.

Last bit of news–we got a new manager, Jim Killarney & just shrugged all responsibility & information & money & everything off our shoulders onto his & last week he broke his back–literally (my analogy & story line got a little crossed there . . . .) he had a car wreck so he's in the hospital now & we're all disorganized.

Now to matters at home:

Mother, did I read in your last letter that you'd gone back to work!? Good Heavens! Please don't do too much too early. Take care of yourself for heaven's sake. But if it means that you're feeling that well, then I'm glad.

★

Mike, mother told me of your grade in English & just want you to know how Pleased *I am. Really proud of you–& I'll bet you are too. Don't you find it a kind of interesting class after you get your momentum up? Keep it up! Keep it up! Are you taking art this 9 wks or have you finished it? You could write you know. . . . Love you.*

Laura, no news from you at all. How is school? How is your bugle section? How are you, the cats, the car? How do you like our record? Are you pleased w/my new occupation or do you secretly think I'm being a bit silly? Address all replies to Box 94, Lagunitas, Calif.

Dad, no news from you at all, so I presume you're the same–entrenched in a tome of The History of Upper Slobbovia, *from the First Great Invasion to the Civil War to End All Civil Wars, Vol. I. If not so occupied, please advise . . .*

All for now, will be thinking of you on Thanksgiving–and other days too of course.

Love XX
Janis

P.S. Mother, notice the stamps. Aren't they pretty!?

When Big Brother was in Los Angeles to cut a professional record, Janis was courted by Bob Shad as the most marketable aspect of the group. Then she played nine holes of golf with Aunt Barbara! I know she crowed to Barbara, building up the grand future and the astounding promises from the hippie culture.

Time declared "The Younger Generation" to be their man of the year for 1966. The San Francisco music scene was getting national recognition. *Time* ran a piece on December 16, 1966, entitled "What Ever Happened to the Andrews Sisters?" The article talked about the numerous new rock groups that could be distinguished only by their "oddball names." They listed twenty-six groups with such monikers as the Dirty Shames, the Swinging Saints, Sigmund and the Freudian Slips, the Virginia Woolves, and Big Brother and the Holding Company. Janis pasted the article in her scrapbook.

In the December 19, 1966, issue of *Newsweek,* the scene was covered in an article called "The Nitty-Gritty Sound." Peter Albin was quoted. " 'People are getting more into the nitty-gritty of emotional and personal life,' says 22-year-old guitarist Peter Albin. 'They're expressing themselves through physical movement and this creates a real bond between the musicians and the audience.' "

Janis's scene had now been validated by the source that our family trusted weekly: *Time.* Whether the tone was mocking or not, at least they were being noticed. They weren't insignificant outsiders; they were becoming important.

Her sense of self had been changing. Janis had been slowly adding to the clothes she had brought with her from Texas. She emulated Nancy Gurley's look of granny gowns—hand-me-down dresses redone into Earth Mother fashion. She took Pat Nichols's passion for cheap spangled bracelets and loaded her arms with shiny metal. She was free of the disheveled look of her earlier Beat days. Now she cultivated a soft, feminine look that fit into local fashion. Photos of Janis captured her in tight pants and a T-shirt with a soft curl in her loose hair. She wore hats with dresses and boots. She was indistinguishable from the average hippie on the street.

December 1966

Dear Mother . . . .

Just a note to keep you informed. Played a "happening" at Stanford this weekend. It was held in Wilbur Hall, & called—A Happening in the Wilburness. Cute. They had a room featuring sensory awareness, a womb room, a jazz band, an old car that you could wail on w/sledge hammers, & a rock dance. Really fun.

Now about Christmas. The only thing that I can think of that I want is a good, all-round cookbook, Betty Crocker or Better Homes or any good one. Also could use a couple of pairs of tights—if they still sell them. Colors! Can't think of anything else. Any hints from the rest of you? What do y'all want? Please rush me Mike's shirt size, by the way. And what is this $20 check for? I think I can afford to buy everyone presents. I'm planning on spending Christmas in L.A. so Barbara suggests that you send my presents there.

My car suffered a tragic breakdown on the streets of Berkeley & is now parked in the alley behind the repair shop waiting for me to raise $75 (!!)

★

Should have it as soon as we get paid for the Stanford job. But as my finances are tenuous, I think I'll keep Daddy's check to be sure I can get to L.A. After that, I'll destroy it! After memorizing the contents of course. Actually I don't think I'll need it, but thanks anyway.

All for now, I guess . .

Love,
Janis

Will try & do something about the bank balance.

Big Brother had taped their first television show in November 1966. *POW* was a tribute to the new music, yet they were forced to lip-synch their songs. They bristled at having to present what they considered a false image to the viewer by pretending to be singing. Music was the means to "be," and to commune directly, soul-to-soul, with others.

Buddhism had long been an influence on the Beat movement. The hippies looked outside their heritage for new ways of understanding the spiritual life. The new believers flailed away at the guiding principle of Western religions that God could be found only in a relationship with Jesus or his conduit, the pope. Hippies sought the Eastern ideal, that people could realize their identity *with* the Maker. "We are all one spirit," their lives seemed to croon to the community. The hippies were living the clash of Eastern and Western cultures, with the American birthright of freedom of religion carried as the battle cry by yet another generation of alienated pioneers.

Instead of avoiding their emotions, hippies made music and forced their needs to emerge through sensory expansion. They developed new symbols in rock dances, uniting as one spiritual organism. Surely Americans had returned to their tribal roots. The shamans had arrived, carrying their message electronically.

"I found out what they want from me," Janis said in 1967. "It's my freedom of feeling. Big Brother can't read music. We're not dispassionate professionals, we're passionate and sloppy!" The new reality could not be expressed in words, and Janis, especially, had the gift of using other means.

Through it all, the conclusion was that love was the ordering principle of human life. Love was being truly alive! Why should something so central be hidden and metered out in tiny doles? Hippiedom became an emotional finishing school. If love wasn't sufficiently forthcoming at home, they would create a new love-based society. This generation saw no reason not to share love with all. Free love!

"Singing with Big Brother was the first time I was able to make my emotions work for me," Janis explained. "I put everything I have into the songs. I think if I hadn't gotten a chance to really sing like that, I would have destroyed myself."

"I'm on an audience trip. I talk to the audience and look into their eyes. I need them and they need me," Janis explained to interviewers. "There are a lot of good Christians putting the hippies down, but hippies are bringing the Christian ethic up-to-date. They believe in being good to people."

So they equated free love with free sex. "I think Janis wanted to be seen as completely free," said Pat Nichols, "so sexual lines shouldn't matter. She had to live up to this free ideal." John Cooke added, "Sex in the late 1960s? We thought we were throwing off invalid social shackles. Sex was a desire to make contact." Bobby Neuwirth explained the twelve-step point of view: "Sex was used as a drug, a mood changer."

Janis was becoming a celebrated princess in the Haight. She and some of her girlfriends used to walk around the neighborhood sweeping up attractive-looking men to bring back to Janis's apartment for a party. They related to men as sex objects, much as they had seen men relate to women.

Janis wanted no more "Saturday night swindles," using our father's phrase to describe the big buildup to romance on that promising date, only to be disillusioned instead. She invoked the power of women's romantic complaints in "Piece of My Heart": "Didn't I give you nearly everything that a woman possibly can? . . . But I'm gonna show you, baby . . . Have another little piece of my heart now . . . if it makes you feel good."

The songs got mixed up with her life when John Smith sent a few letters, trying to get back in touch. Only this time Janis didn't offer him another piece of her heart. She and her girlfriends just talked about him as another of those "charming, gorgeous rats."

Janis adapted the traditional spiritual "Down On Me." "When you see a hand that's held out toward you / Give it some love, someday it may be you . . . / Believe in your brother, have faith in man / Help each other, honey, if you can / 'Cause it looks like everybody in this whole round world / Is down on me." Not anymore. Now it was a collective group that seemed to say, "We're down no more. Now we're rising to claim our rightful role in society as the legitimate children. We're banishing the adopted sons spouting one-sided truths that lead to hypocritical lives."

Yes, the scene was growing. A sense of inevitable triumph was in the air. More people were hitting the road from towns and cities across the country and heading to the Coast, where it was happening. Hard-core hippies were beginning to make money being hippies! The early residents set up shops for the suburban kids coming to the Haight to soak up the culture. They opened head shops and clothing stores, and the profits gave the owners a living and the $2.50 cover charge at the Avalon Ballroom.

Music was the unifying force in this revolution. Eagerly, Big Brother promoted their record to their audience. "Call your local radio station on October 10 and request 'All Is Loneliness' and 'Blindman.' " The band hoped "that the San Francisco sound makes the national scene, and that San Francisco becomes the Liverpool of the United States," reported a county newspaper.

The *Mojo* reporter asked, What happens if the record doesn't click and the San Francisco scene just stays local? Janis replied, "Something's gonna happen. It isn't just gonna go on. Either we're all gonna go broke and split up, or get rich and famous." Dave Getz added, "The audience is getting bigger and bigger and if the audience keeps growing there's really no limit to how big the thing could become, in this country."

. . .

(The following letter was written to Janis's aunt, Barbara Irwin, who lived in Los Angeles.)

December 1966

Dear Barbara . . . .

How ARE You?!! Fine, I hear. Also hear from Mother that Jean & Chuck are well, Mimi is well, & Donna has a boyfriend. Everything sounds under control. I'm sure you've heard that I'm a new-breed-swinger now, the idol of my generation, a rock-n-roll singer. Yes fans, yes, it's true. I sing with Big Brother and the Holding Co. (!) and really enjoy it.

We're playing a dance Dec. 18th at the Santa Monica Civic Auditorium. Now we may stay on for a few days to do some recording—we don't know yet, it depends on our A&R man, when he wants to do it—he's in New York. And I've been trying to arrange things so I could be with y'all for Christmas. It depends on when & where our jobs are and also how my finances are. (Right now, things look rather bleak—I have Christmas presents to buy & a broken car needing $75 worth of work, doctor's bills—$35 and only $65 on hand. Moan!) At any rate, if it can be arranged, I thought I'd stay w/you—if it's alright—that'd be Sunday night (the 18th) for sure & later depending on plans. Okay? Write & tell me if you have conflicting plans.

Also, tell everyone so they can come to the dance if they want to. I can probably get people in free—and doncha wanta see me be a star? (How can I be a star & only have $65? Hmmm . . .)

Write me & advise how this all sounds to you. . . . . Address is P.O. Box 94, Lagunitas, Calif.

> *See you soon,*
> *Love,*
> *Janis*

Janis loved Barbara's company, but bristled at her insistence that she wear a bra when visiting. However, some things are worth the price, and Janis wore the bra to obtain the pleasure of Barbara's company. Then she got even by blatantly taking it off as she crossed

★

Barbara's lawn and walked down the street. Barbara was a special friend for Janis, one worth the hassle of wearing undergarments. Yet Janis accommodated only so far, and made sure Barbara knew her limits.

The lines were being drawn, and not wearing a bra was only one of the important distinctions. On November 17, the police raided the Psychedelic Shop and Ferlinghetti's City Lights Book Shop and made arrests based on sales of an allegedly pornographic book, *The Love Book,* a collection of poems by Lenore Kandel. The hippies adopted a line from J. D. Salinger's book *The Catcher in the Rye:* "Don't trust anyone over thirty."

The more divisive things got between traditional and nontraditional society, the better Janis's life and career went. The band had plenty of work and Janis had lots of friends who loved to party. An invitation read, "Big Brother is holding a Christmas Party, Sunday December 25, 1966. Go to the Lagunitas grocery and park. A Big Brother bus will pick you up." They played "a multi-dimensional experience of fun and good will, New Year's Eve" at the Kezar Pavilion in Golden Gate Park. Just past her twenty-fourth birthday, on January 29, 1967, Janis played a gig called "Krishna Consciousness Comes West." "Bring cushions, drums, bells, cymbals. Proceeds to opening of San Francisco Krishna Temple," read the flyer. Big Brother played the Avalon regularly. They told a *Mojo Navigator* interviewer that they preferred the Avalon to the Fillmore. The audience was only eight hundred, compared to fifteen hundred at the Fillmore, and the sailors cruising for a pickup preferred the Fillmore.

January 1967

Dear Family . . . .

I bet you thought I'd forgotten all about you, eh? Sorry, but you have no idea how busy we've been. Really, for almost a month now. First down to L.A. to record (we did 6 sides—all w/me featured. Next record released in January despite our rather inauspicious showing on the last. SIGH . . .) then back here for a gig, down to L.A. for a gig, stayed w/Barbara, back up here just in time to start cooking for our mammoth party—then the party, then 2 more gigs, 3 days of intestinal flu & New Year's. AAAAAGHH!!

So, as I said—we've been busy. But that's what really makes it fun, y'know. When we're not working, being a singer isn't very rewarding.

Enclosed—the best, so far, article on the "San Francisco scene" from Newsweek. Really good—they've got quotes from the top 4—the Airplane, the Dead, the Quicksilver, & Big Brother. Very good. Also enclosed—a scorecard from Barbara & my golf match. How about that! On one of those small courses that are short. You just use an iron & a putter. But I did pretty well for my first time. And it was fun. Had a nice stay in L.A. Didn't get to see Mimi but I went over & saw Donna who reminds me so very much of Mimi—just like her, to me. Same mannerisms, everything.

Thanks for everything at Christmas. And sorry I couldn't call, but people started coming for the party at 2 in the afternoon & I just couldn't. The cook and anti-cook books are just perfect but my favorite is the candlestick—just lovely. Thanks so much. Also, thank you, Daddy for the $20—haven't gotten it cashed yet but I will. I have $150 in debts now (doctor, car & union). So, it is greatly appreciated.

Tell Laura how cute I think she looks w/her short hair-do. I really like it that way—makes her look impish. And of course Mike looks debonair as usual. And, Mother, you really look good, too—didn't look like you were suffering too much. And Daddy looked so nice next to that musty old pile of burning leaves—really takes a nice picture.

Speaking of pictures, a girl friend of mine is a photographer & did a whole bunch of things of me & I think they're going to use one on a poster for the Family Dog! Gawd, I'm so excited! Also, from (which is a page of 1½" sq. photos) Mouse, who has a button machine, has made Janis Joplin buttons. Oh thrill of thrills—very rare, only the IN people have them, my dear. No name just a picture so you have to be in to know who the hell I am. But I dig it. FAME, FAME, heh, heh. . . .

Played a hippie party in Golden Gate Park yesterday—very nice. Co-sponsored by the Hell's Angels who, at least in S.F., are really very nice. They have a different social code but it seems to be inner-directed and they don't try & impose it on anyone.

Seem to be running out of ink, so I'll close. Hope it won't be so long till the next letter. . . .

LoveXXXX
Janis

★

On January 4, 1967, twenty thousand people came to the "Human Be-In, a gathering of the tribes" held on the polo field of Golden Gate Park. Music was provided by the Grateful Dead, Quicksilver Messenger Service, Jefferson Airplane, and Dizzy Gillespie (one of the first experimenters with LSD with Leary and Ginsberg). It was the beginning of a new cultural ritual, an answer to the question Kesey had asked when coming back from exile in Mexico: "What next?" It wasn't just a dance or a concert; it was a community meeting and celebration. Guided meditations, chanting, poetry readings, and speeches were part of the forum.

Timothy Leary spoke to the gathering, expanding on the theme of his slogan " Turn on, tune in, drop out": "Turn on to the scene, tune in to what is happening, and drop out—of high school, college, graduate school, junior executive, senior executive—and follow me." Leary was trying to form a psychedelic religion. Kesey wanted to hold a "Graduation Test," signaling the next step after the acid test. The hippies refused to move on. They saw no reason to go beyond spreading the word about rock and roll, dances, drugs, and free love. The Buddha's eight-fold path to total enlightenment may have been motivating Ginsberg and other elders in the movement, but the hippie on the street was not driven to go further.

They began perfecting the art form known as psychedelic rock-and-roll dances, which would become San Francisco's chief export, and bands paved the way by holding concerts and dances up and down the California coast.

Peter drove a '56 Ford Galaxy station wagon to the gigs. It was big enough to hold everyone crammed in among their equipment. With an American flag on the side of the car, they attracted the attention of families on the road. As they sped along the coastal byways, kids surreptitiously flashed them the peace sign, risking the angry admonitions of their parents in order to make the connection.

Love and peace were in the air, but the band decided that living together was stretching it. In February they all moved back to the city to separate quarters. Living together had served its purpose. Big Brother and the Holding Company was now an organic entity.

LOVE, *Janis*

HAPPY BIRTHDAY MOTHER FROM JANIS

Again, my apologies for not having written, but we've *been busy. Making a lot of money, ($600 for 1 night in San Jose for example) (SIGH!) getting a very good reputation (one of the Monkees came & heard us at the Matrix & supposedly left w/his mind blown!) got ourselves a manager who is so fine—does everything & really knows his business—really helped a lot, bought a '52 Cadillac hearse for transporting band & equipment, and looking for new places to live in the city—we move out of here on the 15th. So, as I say, busy. Our new record is coming out soon & best of all, we're really getting better. New material & new proficiency—it has us all turned on. We have a lot of confidence in our ability now & we're irrepressible! (sp?) Well, we're awfully excited anyway.*

Don't write to Lagunitas anymore. Write to Ashbury, S.F. until I send my new address.

The picture is from a bunch of promotion pictures we've had done. Hope you like it. All my love & best wishes, Mother. . . .

XXXX
Janis

By March 1967, Janis was back in the city. She had a new apartment, and a friend of Sam's, Linda Gravenites, Nick's former wife, was staying with her while she finished a sewing job. Linda was a tall, big-boned, attractive woman with dark hair and alluring eyes. She was a California native who grew up in the desert but abandoned the traditional life her adoptive parents planned, dropping out of college her sophomore year to be an artist. By the time she met Janis, Linda had been married and divorced twice. She had established herself as a gifted clothes designer for boutiques and a costume designer for the theater. However skilled, she wasn't able to provide sufficient income to raise her two children, who were then living with relatives.

Linda's life was in flux, and Janis and she crafted a relationship that gave each the balancing strength and friendship they needed. She had a wonderful sense of humor and was a delight to be around. She had a gift for craft work, sewing new hippie fashions with precision and artistry. One day while looking at a sink full of dirty dishes, Janis

★

wailed, "I need a mother." Linda said, "I can do that," and so her temporary living arrangement became a permanent one.

Linda was a costume designer and began dressing Janis for her career. Casting out the madras Earth Mother influence of Nancy Gurley, Janis began grabbing the spotlight with shiny pants, blouses showing cleavage, and flowers in her hair. Linda saw Janis as flamboyant and lush but funky at the same time. Janis loved Linda's plans and wore her creations with style. Nick Gravenites saw Janis enjoy the positive strokes she got with her new look. He also recognized that part of her resented how easy it was to change people's attitude. Wasn't she the same Janis, with the same voice? It was almost too cheap a trick to get praise just for changing a few external decorations.

Regardless, Janis worked on her image. Big Brother landed a job in the movie *Petulia* in March 1967, starring Richard Chamberlain and Julie Christie. Janis latched on to Sharrie Gomez, a socialite model working with photographers on the set. Sharrie introduced her to Stanley Ciccone, a fashion photographer at Macy's, who took promo photos of Big Brother. Janis wanted him to help her become glamorous. She wanted to learn how to use makeup artistically. Ciccone counseled, "No makeup. I love you the way you are." In spite of that advice, Janis believed the glamour-magazine hype that makeup techniques would make the difference between an ordinary face and a glamorous one. She had finally found people who knew, and wanted to take advantage of their expertise. She asked questions like, "How much eyeliner?" "How and where do I apply it?" "How could you improve my skin?" She began wearing makeup.

Janis also worked on improving her love life. Country Joe McDonald became her lover. He was a man of the times, a politically minded Berkeley rock-and-roll musician who led the band Country Joe and the Fish. He wanted to unite the scenes in the Haight and Berkeley. He often sported flowers at political benefits and protest buttons at hippie dances. Joe was about five feet eight inches tall, with a muscular build and sandy-brown hair that curled and hung shoulder-length. He had rugged good looks, with a beard and a winning smile. He was a considered man but wasn't afraid to jump into the middle of emotional issues.

Janis and Joe strolled the streets arm in arm, hugging each other and grinning. Some say it lasted a few weeks, others say longer. Joe said they lived together several months, a six-month period of laughing and loving. Lying in bed in Janis's city apartment listening to the radio, they gleefully turned up the volume whenever the DJs played a single from Big Brother or Country Joe and the Fish. Janis wrote in her scrapbook, "For awhile it was Country Brother and the Holding Fish." They broke up in a very touching way, in love but unwilling to compromise their individual pursuits.

The success of Janis's career was beginning to dominate her life. She asked her roommate, "Linda, how can you be so happy. You don't have anything." Janis was so consumed with succeeding that she couldn't understand anyone not similarly inclined. It wasn't just money and possessions that she wanted; it was also the approval.

Janis was becoming very serious about managing her career. She clashed with Peter Albin again because they both wanted to handle the business aspects of the gigs. They also vied for the role as front person for the band, pattering with the audience. "What are you doing?" Janis challenged Peter, not approving of his Lenny Bruce approach to talking with the audience. When they sang "Amazing Grace," Peter liked to do a rap about a guy who was trying to see God and so he went to a psychedelic church and took LSD. He also enjoyed guiding the audience in breathing exercises. Janis preferred a more traditional entertainer style, talking about the history of the song they were going to do. She also liked copping the blues approach of setting herself apart from the audience by letting them in on the "truth" she had learned from her "experience" of hard knocks in the world.

Finding themselves without a manager again, Big Brother sought advice from someone they respected, the manager of Quicksilver, Ron Polte. He recommended Julius Karpen. Julius had a powerful nervousness about him that showed not in fidgeting but in the unwavering stillness of his body. "I felt they were on a mission from God," Julius later explained, "helping lead the San Francisco revolution. They were as priests to the masses. My motto was to guide them and not let the outside world change it, to let the band stay true to itself. From the first day I met them, I knew Big Brother was the biggest thing happening in rock and roll. All that was needed was to show it to the world."

The Haight-Ashbury scene was truly on the map by March 1967. Gray Line bus tours promoted a trip through the area as the "only foreign tour within the continental U.S." The prankish Diggers, formerly the San Francisco Mime Troupe, who were masters of political street theater, chanced upon a bin of broken mirrors. The next tour through the district was met by hippies who ran beside the bus, holding up the mirrors so the tourists could see what they looked like while they were gawking.

March 1967

Dear Mother . . . .

Your beautiful letter came today & prodded my guilt feelings once again, so here I am. You were on my list though—I've been trying to get something written, honest.

I had written of a friend of mine, Bobbi, who had a place in the Haight Ashbury that I might move to. Well, I have for the time being. I have a room plus use of the kitchen & living room, complete w/TV. So I'll be living here (Ashbury St., S.F.) until I let you know.

So far, moving into the city has really hung us up—we have no rehearsal hall. Very hard to find a place where you can make a lot of noise, don't have to pay much rent, and the equipment will be safe overnight. So, we're all sitting in our respective places trying to find something to do & waiting. And it's come at a very inopportune time—we were really getting into a good thing together—we're getting lots better & we all have new songs we want to try & we can't get together to do it & it's so frustrating! So I sit around my new house & play folk songs on my guitar & watch television & make beads & take George for walks. George! Now, he is my salvation. He gets me out of the house when I'd have just sat & moped. And he's so nice to come home to. After a job when I'm feeling especially lonely. I come home & he's so happy to see me! Just can't contain himself—he's so sweet. He's getting bigger & bigger but is really a good dog. When I take him in the car, he won't get out unless I tell him to, never runs away, & is housebroken. And so sweet—all he wants is to be petted & loved. (That's about all anyone wants though isn't it? . . .)

Still faced w/the problem of what to wear on stage. I think I am going to have some clothes made by someone. A lot of the hippie girls sew & work from your design. Now all I have to do is design them. I'm pretty heavy again—so I want flattering things, plus they can't be too hot, plus I have to be able to move around a lot in them. I have one idea—I have an old lace curtain—very pretty that I want to use for sleeves & make some sort of simple dress to go w/them.

Our new record is out & we seem to be pretty dissatisfied w/it. I think we're going to try & get out of the record contract if we can. We don't feel that they (Mainstream) know how to promote or engineer a record & every time we record for them, they get all our songs which means we can't do them for another record company. But then if our new record does something we'd change our mind. But somehow, I don't think it's going to. But, we'll see . . . More importantly, I feel, we're playing better than ever. Seem to have more of an idea of working together not fighting each other w/our instruments.

To answer questions in your masterpiece of a letter:

The thing in the picture is an old tablecloth made into a parka or a shawl.

Tell Michael his puzzles puzzled me—is this what he's doing in school?! Good heavens.

About your coming to California—that's great!! As I understand, you'll go to L.A. & then come up here. Oh, I think that's wonderful! You'll just love San Francisco, I know you will. Actually I've always hoped Laura would try & go to college out here, so maybe she could see some of the campuses while here. And of course I'll take you to one of the big dances. They will blow your mind! It's really startling at first to see. They're based on pure sensuousness—or at least bombarding the senses & they just astound you. I remember the first one I ever saw just completely stoned me! Whew! And you can see us perform! Oh, I'd really like for you to.

Re your cartoon about haircuts I enclose a handbill from our last dance at the Avalon called the Tribal Stomp. The picture is of our lead guitar player, James Gurley, who says he laughs in every barber shop window. James is quite a romantic figure in the hip scene in S.F. (which numbers from 5-10,000 people according to the S.F. Chronicle) & reports are that soon 3 × 5 posters of his face will be on sale around. Fantastic, eh?

Well that's it for now I guess. I'm sorry I don't write more often but I do think of you all the time. All my love. Looking forward to seeing y'all.

Janis

P.S. I know I've asked before, but do you have the black scrapbook w/pictures of Linda & I—I really would like to have it. Please look.

★

Big Brother emerged within the context of the democratic San Francisco music scene. Problems were discussed in group meetings and settled amicably. The group secured a warehouse on Van Ness in which to practice, and they returned to seriously focusing on their music, rehearsing daily. "There was a lot of input from everyone about the music," recalled the band's new attorney, Bob Gordon. "There was real good genuine cooperation from everyone. . . ."

Julius sent Janis for voice lessons with Judy Davis, who coached the stars. Janis attended begrudgingly, with Julius feeling compelled to call her before each lesson to be sure she went. For six months Janis practiced sliding through the upper and lower registers and singing the vowels, holding them until her breath would come no more.

The band was making money, enough to begin putting some aside to buy new instruments as the old ones wore out. "It's not fair," Janis complained as Julius explained this new arrangement. "I'm only a singer, I don't have an instrument." She relented as Julius explained that a good PA system and good instruments meant a better sound behind her.

Already people were telling Janis that she was better than the rest of the band. In spite of the band's family attitudes, Janis was still looking out for Janis. In Los Angeles, she called a band meeting. "Look, I think I'm doing more for this group, and I would like to be in charge, sign the union contracts like Peter does, and get the additional money." "What?" Peter exclaimed. "You think I'm getting more money?" Ooops. Union rules allowed for the leader of the band to get 20 percent more, but in egalitarian hippie bands, it was equal shares all around. "No," Peter said, "we share everything."

The five of them put up with each other's quirks. "I'm not giving them any money," Janis yelled at Julius when he asked about her court summons for a stack of traffic tickets. "We can just pay the fines, Janis. It means loss of income to the band if you spend time in jail," he implored. "I'm going to jail," she retorted. "Janis, you're tough," he sighed. Jail it was—for one day, until Julius paid the fines.

Philip Elwood, in the *San Francisco Examiner* on March 22, wrote, "Most dynamic of the musical performers is granny-gowned Janice [sic] Joplin with Big Brother. . . . And the Big Brother band is in good shape, too. Their guitar-bass blend has become an harmonic fascination and the once ponderous rhythm is now moving in a rolling good dancing pattern."

The hippie audience loved Janis. "Janice," one wrote on a card accompanying flowers, "your voice defies the use of stupid words. You're just too much." The band was making money and getting love and acclaim from their audience.

"Karleen, don't put the phone down, I want you to hear something," high school friend Arlene Elster said, telephoning from San Francisco to Port Arthur. In 1967, she lived across the street from the Avalon Ballroom. She opened the apartment window and moved the phone receiver closer. "Can you hear that, Karleen? That's Janis singing!"

Janis's Texas friends were still in her life. "She sent me a poster of her, with a nipple showing," said Tary Owens, "along with a note, 'I'm the first hippie pin-up girl. What a kick!' " Posters by Berkeley Bonaparte presented sixteen choices for $1 each, except Janis and Yab Yum, which were $1.50. Her intent stare sold alongside photos of Oscar Wilde, Allen Ginsberg, and Ho Chi Minh.

When Janis sang, she put her all into the performance. "She was a great singer, but basically she was a performer," said Linda Gravenites. "Going onstage, Janis was like a thousand-watt light bulb going off. . . . Her insecurity made her a great performer because she needed the return that she got." Janis, along with the rest of Big Brother, brought a cup of the night's choice of liquor onstage during performances. Some brought whiskey, others brandy, but whatever the flavor, alcohol was a proven lubricant for everyone in the group. Janis sometimes drank a bit before going onstage, just to loosen herself up. She would stretch as though preparing for the aerobic workout of her performances.

April 1967

Dear Mother, family

Things are going so good for us & me personally I can't quite believe it! I never ever thought things could be so wonderful! Allow me to explain. First of all, the group—we're better than ever (please see enclosed review from S.F. Examiner) and working all the time. Just finished 3 weeks straight *engagements, 6 nights a week & we're booked up week-ends for well over a month. And we're making a thousand or over for a week-end. For single nights we're getting from $500-$900. Not bad for a bunch of beatniks, eh? And our reputation is still going uphill. It's funny to watch—you can tell where you are by the people that are on your side. Y'know, the scene-followers, the people "with the finger on the pulse of the public." One of the merchants on Haight St. has given all of us free clothes (I got a beautiful blue leather skirt) just because 1) she really digs us & 2) she thinks we're going to make it & it'll be good publicity. Our record is enjoying a fair reception—much better than our first one which was much, much better. We made #29 in Detroit but we don't really know what's happening because we never hear from Mainstream. It's a long & involved story but we really feel like we've been used & abused by our record co & we'd like to get out of the contract but don't know whether we can. We talked to a lawyer about it & he seemed fairly negative & we can't even get ahold of our record co. to talk about it. So until further news, we're hung up. There's a slim possibility we might go to Europe & play this summer. There's a hippie boat going back and forth & rock bands get free passage if they play on the way over. And Chet, head of the Family Dog, is trying to organize `` '' dances over there & if he does, we'd have a place to work. Probably won't work but it sure would be groovy. Speaking of England, guess who was in town last week—Paul McCartney!!! (he's a Beatle). And he came to see us!!! SIGH Honest to God! He came to the Matrix & saw us & told some people that he dug us. Isn't that exciting!!!! Gawd, I was so thrilled—I still am! Imagine—Paul!!!! If it could only have been George. . . . Oh, well. I didn't get to see him anyway—we heard about it afterwards. Why, if I'd known that he was out there, I would have jumped right off the stage & made a fool of myself.*

Now earlier, I spoke of how well things are going for me personally—it's really true. I'm becoming quite a celebrity among the hippies & everyone who goes to the dances. Why, last Sunday we played a Spring Mobilization for Peace benefit & a simply amazing thing happened. As the boys were tuning, I walked up to the front of the stage to set up the microphones &, as I raised the middle mike up to my mouth, the whole audience applauded! Too much! And then as we're getting ready to play, a girl yelled out "Janis Joplin lives!" Now you can't argue with that, and they clapped again. Also, a rock publication named World Countdown *had a collage on its cover using photographs of important personages in & about the scene & I'm in there. Also they're bringing out a poster of me! Maybe you've read in* Time *magazine about the personality posters. They're big, very big photographs, Jean Harlow, Einstein, Belmondo, Dylan, & Joplin. Yes, folks, it's me wearing a sequined cape, thousands of strings of beads & topless. But it barely shows because of the beads. Very dramatic photograph & I look really beautiful!! If it wouldn't embarrass you, I'll send you one. I'm thrilled!! I can be Haight-Ashbury's first pin-up.*

Speaking of the Haight-Ashbury, read the enclosed article from LOOK magazine. There've been lots of articles written about the scene here. Newsweek has had two & this new one. And even the Chronicle—they've all had articles with more understanding than the one in Time. As a matter of fact, I just plain quit reading it because of that article—not because I was mad. Because I was aware of how distorted they were & I figured they were probably that wrong about everything. I really am not social critic enough to know/discuss what is going on, but in answer to your question—Yes, they are our audience & we're hoping they can turn on the rest of the country because then we'd be nation-wide. We'd be the Monkees! Well, at any rate, a good article.

Okay, on to news: For one thing, we've gotten a raise—the guys with wives were feeling constrained, so now we get $100 a week! Good heavens.

Second in importance, I have a new apartment. Really fine!! Two big rooms, kitchen, bathroom & balcony. And I'm right across the street from the park! You can't really understand living there with a yard, but here you can go 10-20 blocks without ever seeing a living plant and I just look out my window or step out on my balcony & I've got fresh air & trees & grass!! So wonderful, sigh. My new address is 123 Cole St., S.F. Still in the Haight-Ashbury. Have lots of plans for the place—two rooms need painting but I may just end up hanging stuff up on the walls. I've sort of got the front room fixed up now & it's really nice to live in. SIGH! See what I mean about things going my way? Also, I have a boyfriend. Really nice. He's head of Country Joe and the Fish, a band from Berkeley. Named Joe McDonald, he's a Capricorn like me, & is 25 & so far we're getting along fine. Everyone in the rock scene just thinks it's the cutest thing they've ever seen. It is rather cute actually. Speaking of boyfriends, I've been hearing from John again. He's written several letters. For some reason I get the feeling he's planning on coming out here & is sort of putting out feelers.

Next, guess what (special for Dad) I've done—I've quit smoking!!! Still want one now & then but it's been about a month now. I felt it was just too

★

*hard on my voice. I'd been smoking for 10 yrs! I got a real bad cold &
bronchitis & I just* couldn't *smoke for about a week & when I got well, I
refused to start again. I may break down but I hope not. This is really
better for me.*

*More news, George is really getting to be a fine dog. Learning things every
day. Today he learned the hard way not to run across the street to the park
by himself—he got hit by a car. But the vet said he wasn't hurt very
badly—bruised & scared. Poor thing, he's just moping around with a very
paranoid look on his face.*

*I'm having a few clothes made for me now—had a beautiful dress made out
of a madras bed spread & now she's working on one out of green crepe
with a very low V neckline. I've been making things out of leather lately.
Made a beautiful blue & green Garbo hat & pair of green shoes.*

*I'm also sending our new promo picture. Not very flattering of me but a
very strong picture. Pretty good looking group, eh?*

*Really enjoyed seeing the pictures of all of you. Looking beautiful, Mother.
And Laura looks really cute! Is her dress white or silver? And I've never
seen Mike look so charming. Must be the Big Brother T-shirt.*

*Now, please let me know when you are coming. Oh, I have so many places
to take you to & show you! But we'll be working so let me know as soon
as you can your plans. Well, I guess that's it for now. Write me . . .*

LoveXXX
Janis

June 2, 1967, the Beatles released their new album, *Sgt. Pepper's
Lonely Hearts Club Band.* From the bizarre cover to the new cosmic
uniforms worn by the Beatles to the blatantly psychedelic music, the
album forced the genre of rock music into the future.

Ralph Gleason predicted in the *San Francisco Chronicle,* "The
music capital of the world, starting Friday, will be the Monterey
County Fairgrounds, not Nashville, not Tin Pan Alley and neither
London nor Hollywood. The first annual Monterey International Pop
Festival is bringing to the Fairgrounds Arena the greatest aggregation of
popular song stars ever assembled in any one place for a weekend
event. . . ." It was sold out at the time of his writing. Gleason was one

of the most important rock critics who helped establish the San Francisco sound.

The event was organized by John Phillips, one of the Mamas and the Papas, and Lou Adler, a Los Angeles record producer. They envisioned a nonprofit gathering where any money made would be distributed "for the betterment of pop music" by a board composed of musicians, including Paul McCartney, Paul Simon, and Smokey Robinson. For two and a half days and more than twenty-five hours of music, the seven-thousand-seat arena was full of peace and love. More than forty thousand people attended, yet Saturday and Sunday, Frank Marinello, police chief, sent forty uniformed policemen home. They weren't needed. "I'm beginning to like these hippies," Philip Elwood of the *San Francisco Examiner* quoted him as saying.

"Monterey was really clean. Everybody who slept there had tents. The cops were nice, and all the bands were in motels. There were no big crowds, no fighting your way through," said Dave Getz.

Much more than music was presented; it was high drama. Psychedelic movies played near a midway of booths selling food and paraphernalia. The Who smashed a guitar and Jimi Hendrix—appearing in a gold shirt and red pants, with fuschia feathers around his neck—climaxed his appearance by burning his guitar. In his unpublished memoirs, Sam Andrew wrote, "One of the best things about Monterey was the audience. You cannot imagine how much easier it is to play for a large audience that is with you than for a small indifferent one. Playing for an audience that doesn't dance or enjoy itself is like running uphill. But when everyone is together and especially when they dance and yell and scream, there is a great communion of effort and everything is lubricated. We were playing for our peers at Monterey and there was truly an absence of any kind of competitiveness or stress."

The organizers scheduled Big Brother for Saturday afternoon. "Big Brother performed a set that was a miracle," Julius Karpen said. "It was not to be believed. The audience went wild, mind-blown." Julius worked his way into the middle of the audience during the band's performance, and had tears in his eyes, like a proud papa. "I've cleared the way for a miracle!" Big Brother played "Down On Me," "Road Block," and "Ball and Chain." This performance was the one that sparked Mama Cass's overwhelmed response to their sound and

★

Janis's voice. Mouth agape, her ears were in music lover's heaven. Cass's response was clearly captured by the film crew in the film *Monterey Pop*. The band's performance, however, had not been filmed.

"You mean they didn't film that?" the band screamed at Julius after the set. Their manager had wanted to retain control. Julius was sick of promoters ripping off musicians. The Monterey promoters had offered the band nothing in return for the film rights, so he had refused. He made sure that during Big Brother's performance, the cameras pointed to the ground.

The promoters were furious with Julius's refusal and went directly to the band. Albert Grossman, one of the more powerful personal managers of the day, may have influenced Big Brother to override Julius. Everyone knew that Big Brother's performance *had* to be filmed because it was the pinnacle of the show. Finally, the five band members pressured Julius to allow a second set to be filmed. Reporters would talk about the qualities of the music as well as the uniqueness of Big Brother's encore as evidence of their artistic triumph. The press didn't realize that the main reason for the encore was to allow filming. They thought it was only because the band was so good. Nevertheless, the accidental encore helped to propel their acclaim.

Even Mom heard about the performance. She immediately wired, "Congratulations on being first page Los Angeles Times Monterey Festival Report. Barbara sending us a copy." The telegram was signed, "Your Port Arthur Fan Club."

Not only the family was lauding Janis, but most newspapers and magazines had picked up the story. *Newsweek* and *Time* wrote descriptions like the one that appeared in *The Berkeley Barb,* saying, "Janis Joplin, of Big Brother, brought the house down belting out blues with her magnificent voice." Scott Holtzman from the *Houston Post* wrote two columns mentioning Janis, both saying that she had been discovered in California but ignored when she played in Houston. She pasted both in her scrapbook. The band had been the hit of the festival, but Janis was being singled out as *the* star of the show. She had triumphed as a performer as well as the leader of a social movement. The "conspiracy of reality" that Jim Langdon described in Texas had become a national happening.

Mainstream released four new singles by Big Brother between

May 1967 and February 1968. "Down On Me"/"Call On Me" was the first, followed by "Bye Bye Baby"/"Intruder" in August 1967, "Women Is Losers"/"Light Is Faster than Sound" in November 1967, and the last, "Coo Coo"/"Last Time." They put out an album of these pieces in August 1967 entitled *Big Brother and the Holding Company*. The band was furious. The material was old and the arrangements were outdated. Rather than presenting the group to the public, they felt Mainstream was merely capitalizing on the band's Monterey recognition.

Big Brother met Clive Davis of Columbia Records, who signed every act he could at the Monterey Pop Festival. Clive invited Big Brother's manager, Julius Karpen, and their attorney, Bob Gordon, to the upcoming CBS convention in Hollywood, Florida. The big-time folks were courting the group, and this time they were prepared.

Bob Gordon brought the band broad experience in the entertainment business. In Janis he received a giving friend who transformed him from being very conservative and uptight into a more relaxed uptight person. Janis's life was changing, too. Julius had joined the band in January 1967, when they were earning four hundred dollars for a two-night weekend. By the end of 1967, they were pulling in twenty-five hundred dollars a night without having released a significant album. The business normally didn't work that way! It could only have happened as part of a general revolution in the music business itself caused by a push for change from a new generation of listeners.

CHAPTER ELEVEN

AFTER THE MONTEREY

POP FESTIVAL

★

Oh, Lord, won't you buy me a Mercedes Benz?
My friends all drive Porsches
I must make amends
Worked hard all my lifetime
No help from my friends
So, Lord, won't you buy me a Mercedes Benz?

—Janis Joplin, Bobby Neuwirth, and Michael McClure,
"Mercedes Benz"

ONTEREY USHERED IN what became known as the Summer of Love. Some fifty thousand young people passed through San Francisco, attracted by the marching cries of love and acceptance cranked out in the press reports at an ever-greater frequency. They came from cities, suburbs, and farms across the country, leaving homes and routines for the unknown and the promise of Haight-Ashbury.

The Council for the Summer of Love had planned for the hordes. New gatherings were scheduled and the Diggers managed food and housing. They brought free soup to Panhandle Park every day at four P.M., served from large aluminum garbage cans. They ran a Free Store, with clothes and housewares. They got use of a free farm and were working on access to a five-hundred-room hotel. They were the epitome of American industriousness, the new pioneers making do with the resources of the city-grown wilderness.

The Haight was also the source of an LSD epidemic that swept across the country to the extent that *Time* magazine recognized the

★

problem by March 1966. Frothing tirades of fear were being sent over the press wires: "Guard your children against LSD!" Some people did have bad trips. In 1966, Dr. William Frosch, a psychiatrist at New York's Bellevue Psychiatric Hospital, testified before a Senate subcommittee studying LSD. Frosch reported statistics he'd developed that indicated that only seven people of every thousand taking LSD suffered an emotional breakdown, most probably those with a history of psychiatric problems. Incomplete reporting of Frosch's findings, coupled with questionable anecdotal evidence, convinced the public that taking LSD commonly gave you an irreversible psychosis. The real kicker was a story about LSD causing chromosome breaks when the two were mixed in test tubes, an illogical corollary with actual use of the drug. Nevertheless, those seeking evidence grabbed it and roared.

Stories in the press spoke of rape and murder under LSD's influence, which was vastly different from the effect that was commonly reported in most research on the drug—benign contemplation. The problem was that though there was a vast body of research on the drug, there were few proven conclusions about it. Rather than rational conclusions, many press stories pitted the extremes against each other—psychotic insanity versus spiritual awakening.

The furor over LSD was magnified by the changed characteristics of people in the movement. The kids who strolled into the Haight were no longer those drawn together after years of artistic struggle. Now they were young and unhappy rejects who needed someone to take them in hand. Drug dealing was no longer limited to sharing LSD; it turned into sinister ghetto hustling of anything people could be sold. The goal was no longer insight but merely sensory fun and games.

Speed was readily available in spite of notices warning against the drug by elders in the community. STP, a new, longer-duration psychedelic, gave people terrifying three-day journeys into hell. San Francisco General Hospital was treating 750 bad trips a month. Pimps hustled the young travelers, using drugs to turn them into prostitutes. By the end of 1967, crime in the Haight ended its initial downward dip with the hippies and showed 17 murders, 100 rapes, and almost 3,000 burglaries.

Heroin use cropped up all at once in the Haight. The residents were psychologically defenseless against it because their subculture rested on an outspoken assumption that being cool meant being high. Janis, James, and Sam all sampled the drug whenever they happened to run into any. None of them had sufficient money to use heroin more than that.

It's hard to accept heroin as a means to improve one's mind, given the ample evidence of negative effects of its use. Yet, with some perspective, we can see that using a pill of some sort had become an accepted cultural practice. People quit trying to solve problems because they didn't know how. Instead, they just wanted a quick fix, and the medical establishment had always been eager to provide help in the form of drugs.

Women with hysterectomies and menopause symptoms were given tranquilizers to delete the symptoms. In the 1950s and 1960s, doctors readily prescribed tranquilizers and amphetamines to alter the feelings of their patients. They wanted to have something to give patients who gave them money and asked for help. Our society was on a search for the right drug, the better drug. Drug use was not symptomatic of a problem in hippie Camelot. It was a deep-rooted problem of our society that spawned the 1960s, and it was, regrettably, carried forward by the new innocents.

In 1967, heroin was a drug in which Janis dabbled, but her drug of choice was still alcohol. She was developing a particular affinity for Southern Comfort, as much for its name as for its flavor. When Linda Gravenites made her a purse, Janis said, "Make it big enough for a book and a bottle." Alcohol was part of the outlaw Texas culture. To hold your liquor was a point of pride and Janis learned to hold it well.

Janis had wondered about drinking's pitfalls and benefits for years. She summed it up in a song she wrote during her Austin years, "What Good Can Drinking Do?" Janis sang, "I drink all night / But the next day I still feel blue."

In spite of the pervasiveness of drugs in the hippie community, some people refused them. Peter Albin, within the band, didn't indulge. In the spirit of "whatever turns you on," his preference was respected by the fellows. But Janis lit into him with scoffing vengeance. She never did like anyone to question her actions, even if it was only by behaving in a different way. Perhaps his abstinence merely made her feel guilty about her overindulgence.

Summer 1967

Dear Mother—

I do hope you remember me after all this while—what can I say? . . Wanted to send you these clippings—they're from the Examiner *&* Chronicle *& mark a real shift. Since Monterey, all this has come about. Gleason has been plugging us & has used me as a description for a style (the inimitable Joplin style) & he never wrote about us before. Now we have 3 big record companies, Atlantic, Mercury, Columbia after us & prepared to pay $50,000-75,000 plus any privileges we want to sign w/them IF we can get out of our contract w/Mainstream. And we are trying! Lawyers & all kinds of show-biz stuff. We'll see. Sure hope this doesn't seriously impair our career. And so now we're getting interviewed & my picture will be in* Esquire, *&* Playboy *(not the center fold-out but something about the festival) & Julius (our manager) said some lady from McCalls called & might use me in an article about "Young Women Breaking Down Barriers" or something like that. Oh, you saw the thing in* TIME *but you didn't see* Newsweek*—it had a picture of me! I hope all this & my excitement doesn't seem shallow to you, it really thrills me. Wow, I met 2 of the Rolling Stones, most of the Animals & they all (& these are big groups—well respected & rich, baby) & they say I'm the best they've ever heard! E Gad!! Ahhh . . . Well, anyway I'm ecstatic!! Also, watch for an ABC Special on the Monterey Festival—we'll be in it. Gosh I can't seem to find anything to talk about. This band is my whole life now. It is to all of us. I really am totally committed & I dig it. I'm quite proud of myself because I'm really trying. Before when I came out here I just wanted to hang out & be wild & have a good time but now that's all secondary (I still want to have a good time you understand) but singing gives me so much satisfaction. Well, the recognition gives me a lot of satisfaction too I must admit. Well, to summarize, Big Brother is doing great & I just may be a "star" someday. You know, it's funny—as it gets closer & more probable, being a star is really losing its meaning. But whatever it means, I'm ready!*

Now another topic, I still have George & I got a new kitten, no name yet, gray w/a little brown & white and very aggressive—when she's hungry she follows me around and shrieks at me. George takes really good care of her—licks her, carries her around in his mouth & she in turn eats only dog food & chews on his bones. It's a strange family, but it's mine.

Chuck & Jean were up last week end & came by. Chuck has a goatee now which he says Barbara has been haranguing him to shave (she sounds like a real bitch of a mother-in-law). They came & saw us at the Circle Star Theater (review #5) & then went to a party afterwards. James Gurley's sister-in-law was throwing a "Come-as-a-hippie" party and we were the guests of honor. We came as straight people. Anyway Jean & Chuck came, as hippies & had a great time. It was a gas.

HELLO to Mike and Laura hard at work at school! Hello, Hello, how's things? Work hard! I love ya! Oh, say why don't you two work on Mother to slightly alter your travel plans so you can stay here for Friday night & see us play somewhere. You see we work every week end & we'll be working somewhere & you can all come to a dance & wear beads & see us & see a light show & be proud of me & I know you'd have a good time so work on it—okay?

And Mother, I really do like to hear from you, please write me even if I am not so good myself.

Well, look everybody, I just got home from rehearsal & I'm tired & I want to just sit & drink a beer. So I'll close. Oh!! About your question—you'll need coats, real coats, not heavy ones, but fairly substantial & I guess if you have room bring my linen & did I give my leather coat to Laura? If not, I think maybe I could use it. Well, byeXXXX

Janis

Drugs were everywhere in the Haight, but when the family visited Janis in August 1967, we didn't know that. She was giddy with excitement, proudly showing off the Haight-Ashbury scene and her exalted status within it. We strolled the streets, with Janis pointing to favorite head shops, dress shops, ballrooms, and the attire of interesting people on the street. She couldn't stop sharing her excitement over Paul McCartney's recent visit to the neighborhood, that he had strolled the sidewalks right where we walked.

Then the new reality hit us square in the face as we entered her apartment. The gaily decorated hippie pad was complete with Indian madras bedspread on a bed serving as a couch. My eyes rested on the front wall, papered in countless copies of the personality poster of Janis, bare breast and all. "It hardly shows, Mother," she chided in spite of no comment from either of the parents. "I'll give Mike one if you'll let him keep it," she offered. Yes, things were really different.

Janis looked at my short navy-blue double-knit dress and asked,

★

203

"Laura, don't you have any long pants?" We were getting ready to go to the special concert at the Avalon. Big Brother wasn't on the bill that night, but they had arranged for the band to play so that we could hear Janis. "No, why don't you loan me some?" I replied. "It doesn't matter," she decided. Then she went ahead to the ballroom. We met her there.

We climbed the stairs. The tall, angular Chet Helms was taking money at the top, and Janis danced with glee, telling him we were her family. There was a feeling of importance associated with Chet waiving the admission charge and extending a gallant "Welcome." Entering the dance hall, the overpowering sounds and cruising bodies stunned me. Though people were dancing, sitting, or milling, I remember it as being calm and still.

I felt like a stranger, as I was, set apart by my clothes and by not being stoned. The room was dark, but the lack of regular light was overpowered by the light show of moving colors and images on the wall. People sat immobile and stared, not necessarily at anything, just ahead. Their heads moved slowly. Their attention was consumed by the sense bombardment of the room. Big Brother performed a few tunes, working in synchronized fashion with the swirling lights to force the viewer's attention into the present. I was awed by the whole experience, though the music was only a bit of it.

Michael went backstage with Janis, where he promptly tried to get someone to let him smoke a joint. Alas, even in this haven of freedom, no one would relent to his pleadings under Janis's watchful eye. We didn't stay long after Janis performed, not finding a way to relate to the scene. She must have asked, "Did you like it?" We must have said yes, because we would have never said no. Yet I am sure that after that experience, our parents ceased believing that they could influence her or that she would return to Texas and college. They came to be sure that she was okay. What they found was that things were so different, and Janis so internally successful, they could have no effect.

Outside the Avalon, Janis kept saying, "Isn't it wonderful?" She asked, "Oh, can't you see?" She stood, staring at us walking down the street, with the roar of the rock music pouring forth from the raised entrance to the ballroom. Caught between two worlds, she stood, perplexed, believing that we should like it. I think Janis realized then

LOVE, *Janis*

that we didn't, and couldn't, and probably weren't going to see. How did we hug and kiss and say good-bye, knowing we loved her, yet were no longer a part of the world around her? I don't know, but I remember we did.

Big Brother played the Monterey Jazz Festival on September 16. They hoped for a repeat of their triumph at the summer pop festival. The signs were good; local articles about the lineup featured photos of Janis. Big Brother was the closing act for Saturday afternoon, after B. B. King and T-Bone Walker. She was being noticed, but they couldn't spell her name right, writing it as "Janice" instead of "Janis."

Press after the festival gave Janis cover photos in the *San Francisco Chronicle*'s Sunday supplement magazine. Ralph Gleason's column gave her a three-inch photo with the caption "Wildly exciting singer." The *Los Angeles Free Press* put four photos of Janis in their spread on the festival. She clearly had arrived.

By the fall of 1967, the band's success had changed their attitude. No sooner had they started cooking toward the big time than they started asking Julius about money. "Are we rich yet, Julius? How do the books look?" "Don't worry, I have the books under control, you don't need to see them," he answered.

"You deserve to be robbed blind and taken for every penny you're worth if you keep a manager who won't show you the books," Peter's Uncle Henry exclaimed. He struck the match that lit the fire under their collective action. "I'll leave you the books and I'll leave too," Julius retorted, ending a relationship that had become untenable with the band's new managerial needs.

It was a situation in which every party was right. Julius had accounted for all the money, but tracking it was a matter of wading through baskets of unanalyzed receipts. "We didn't want to worry about it, but there were no books and it wasn't under control," laughed Dave Getz. Eventually, Julius explained, he worked with an accountant from Big Brother's subsequent manager's office and developed thorough accounting summaries.

Julius knew there were no accounting problems because he hadn't done anything improper with the money. He felt hurt that the band questioned him. It was sixties ethics, and Julius was solidly within the sixties frame of mind.

Even without the questions raised by financial confusion, Big

★

205

Brother had problems with Julius's need to protect the band from the clutches of sponge-hungry promoters. From the band's perspective, his demands were hindering the group's ability to get gigs and exposure.

In 1967, after the difference of opinion over filming the Monterey Pop performance, another problem arose. Julius was negotiating with Bill Graham, the controversial and dominating influence in the San Francisco music scene. Julius said that Graham reneged on a verbal agreement giving the band a forty-five-minute set for a show to be televised in San Francisco. Graham sent a contract stating twenty-minute sets, and Julius flatly refused. Forty-five minutes or nothing, he said. More money made no difference to Julius. The band needed the time to excite the audience. The shorter sets wouldn't allow for that. Julius wanted to protect Big Brother's ability to make the right type of impression.

Julius and Bill parleyed until the time Graham had planned to send an airplane to take the band from the Monterey Jazz Festival to the San Francisco show. Big Brother missed the show. It was overprotection, the band said. Julius quit but then un-quit on the silent drive back to the city. Their disagreement over money followed a few weeks later. That time there was no repairing the relationship. By the end of 1967, Julius Karpen was no longer with the band.

The band went manager shopping. At the Monterey Pop Festival, they had met Albert Grossman. They wanted to rekindle his interest in the band. Julius, in a final act of love for the band, called Grossman and asked him to consider managing them. Other people also recalled contacting him on the band's behalf. Whoever called, it worked. Albert came to San Francisco to discuss the possibility.

Albert Grossman was a stocky, six-foot, imposing man known as "the bear." He was rotund, but more bulky and thick than fat. His hair was prematurely gray, with a squirrely wave that he pulled back in what would have been a ponytail had it been longer.

He was a Chicago native, born into a family that valued education and security. He attended the University of Chicago, where he received a master's degree in economic theory. Music, politics, and acting were also among his interests. He opened a folk nightclub called the Gate of Horn, which was very successful. Through it Albert got to know the business and entertainers, and developed a great ear for talent. He had an affinity for the blues because Chicago was a blues town.

Grossman made his reputation as a manager with Odetta. He eventually managed such blues artists as Michael Bloomfield, Paul Butterfield, Richie Havens, and Buddy Miles. He designed and managed the group Peter, Paul and Mary, hunting for two years for the right match of people to form his answer to the Kingston Trio. In Chicago he met Bob Dylan and spent months cultivating his trust before he began managing him as well. He was only interested in managing performers who had the potential to be concert and recording artists that earned top fees.

Grossman moved to New York, where he hung out in the Village. He was known to sing in a booming voice when he first came on the scene. He became part owner of a club called the Bitter End. By 1966, he preferred to sit quietly in the back of the Gaslight and hold court in quiet conversations at his usual table. He was a poker player who perfected the bluff. Silence and his imposing physique complemented the power that he obviously wielded thanks to the list of top acts he controlled. He never sought attention for himself, only the trappings of success that came with good business management.

When he agreed to manage Big Brother, Albert Grossman lived in a town house on Gramercy Park, an exclusive area tucked away between midtown and Greenwich Village on the East Side. The centerpiece of the area is a small, well-tended park that dates from 1831. The Gramercy Park neighborhood was especially prized for its privacy, a commodity Grossman valued. Albert lived alone in the city and had a catering service deliver his meals.

He also had a house in Bearsville, New York, near Woodstock, north of the city. It was an old stone house known as the Streibel place, to which he added a greenhouse and a sauna. It was picturesque, quiet, and pastoral, with the atmosphere of a country squire's farm. Inside, everything was beautiful. Knickknacks packed the house, each with a museum-type label, showing they were collectibles indexed for tax purposes.

Grossman's office in town was a posh spread in a new high rise that housed many music-related businesses. It was within walking distance of both RCA and CBS. There were at least fifteen rooms, all

decorated in contemporary style. His personal office had huge windows and a mammoth desk with several cushy chairs for guests.
Officious businesswomen ran the scene. A lot of people were in and
out of the office. Sam Gordon ran Grossman's music-publishing arm.
Peter, Paul and Mary had their own private office for their solo manager. Grossman formed different partnerships on and off during his
career. Some of the road managers worked in offices, planning their
upcoming tours.

He seemed personally elusive, so that even if you knew him
long, you might not have known him well. He used silence to imply
he knew something he wasn't saying. Sometimes he was deliberately
vague; other times it was just a ploy to see what would happen. He
developed eccentric mannerisms as part of his role, smoking a cigarette
by holding it in a strange cradle of a curled thumb and overlapping
forefinger.

Grossman could be arrogant and insolent in such a way that
made others perceive him as sinister or overpowering. Some thought
he was clearly full of his own self-importance. For many he was just
a good businessman who managed the challenges of the industry
without stooping to the vulgarities that others used. He did what
needed to be done to make the business work for everyone, protecting
his clients from the steamrolling corporate behemoths that dominated
the industry. He was interested in money, but was by nature a connois-
seur, selecting only the best performers for his agency.

Grossman was an excellent judge of talent, with a real knack for
picking the wheat from the chaff. He had developed an ear from his
years as a club owner. He was totally involved creatively and his advice
was heeded because he had proven himself.

In 1959 Grossman became involved with George Wein, the
promoter who had started the Newport Jazz Festivals in the 1950s.
Together they planned the first Newport Folk Festival. In 1963 Bob
Dylan arrived at the folk festival as an interesting underground performer. He left a star. Perhaps Albert saw the same thing happening
again with Janis and Big Brother at Monterey.

Albert demonstrated his unique negotiating style when he met
with Big Brother. Band members asked, "Will you guarantee us a
yearly income?" "Name a figure," he said. "Seventy-five thousand

dollars," someone said. "Make it a hundred thousand and I'll put it in writing. If I can't make you that, I'm in the wrong business."

All right! The group had found someone who talked dream city as though it were a place he'd been for lunch. There were other discussions, but with that financial carrot, the band was mentally packing the business records, destination Albert Grossman Management, NYC.

Albert defined some of his conditions for working with Big Brother as well. "I won't deal with anybody who's into heroin," he stated emphatically. "It has to do with people I've worked with in the past." The band members shook their heads left to right, three of the five lying as they earnestly proclaimed they never touched the stuff. Since none had more than sampled the drug occasionally, I guess they felt they were being honest.

It wasn't that Albert was against all drugs, just certain ones. When entertaining at Bearsville, he kept a tobacco jar filled with a special concoction of tobacco mixed with hash and wine. He always had marijuana, and cocaine of good quality. He was seen doing drugs only on social occasions, never at work, though he was known to go to the bathroom frequently during business meetings. At least some people thought emptying his bladder was not the goal.

Big Brother signed the contract with Albert on November 11, 1967. "Janis and I called him Uncle Albert," recalled Linda Gravenites. "He was solid, as though he could take care of anything." He was a man who wore spectacles that gave him the trustworthy look of Ben Franklin. With genuine affection, Janis cut out the portrait of the man on the Quaker Oats box and hung it on the kitchen wall. It looked just like Uncle Albert.

He never tried to manage Janis's life, only her career. I am sure that she loved his approach to management. He was an enabler, letting her follow her artistic interests. Linda said that Janis saw him as a father figure. I wonder if Janis was creating a new core family for herself, with mother, father, and band-member siblings?

With Albert's organization involved in her career, the whole scene became more professional. For one thing, Big Brother got a road manager. It was a somewhat new idea in music touring, but one that Albert's office adopted earnestly. John Cooke had been a Harvard student and local Boston folk musician. He was ready for a change. While interviewing John for a job as a road manager, Albert let him choose among several acts who needed the help. John quickly picked Big Brother because he wanted the excitement that surrounded the group. On December 1, he was whisked from the San Francisco airport to the band's rehearsal.

The relationship between shy, patrician John and communal Big Brother was rocky before it fully engaged. "It's a matter of life-style differences," the band complained to Albert. John took the issue by the horns, calling a band meeting. "Look, man, if you want somebody whose hair is long, who just hangs around and smokes dope all the time, and carries the guitar cases, we can hire somebody to do that. But if you want somebody to do the job that I do, let's try this a little longer."

A few months later, driving between gigs in San Diego, John told the band members, "When I first took the job, I thought of staying for six months. But I like it and I like working with you." Dave smiled. "We love you too, John." Janis said, "You want a raise, right?" John laughed. "Well, now that you speak of it." John Cooke was an important cog in the band's new machinery, someone Janis could always rely on to get his job done and be a friend unchanged by the development of her career.

John handled the travel, pushed everyone to be on time, organized the equipment, and monitored the gate receipts at the still loosely run rock concerts. Big Brother played mostly in California in late 1967—Fresno, Turlock, Merced, and Huntington Beach, with the biggest gig at the Whiskey-a-Go-Go in Los Angeles.

Janis had a lot to be happy about. She had appeared in a fashion spread in the October 8, 1967, *San Francisco Examiner* living section. "Wearing a poncho of antique Moroccan fabric over velvet peone [sic] pants" and a red flower in her hair, Janis stood jauntily on a hillside in Buena Vista Park for a group portrait of stylishly hip women and their dress as designed by Jeanne Colon.

In her scrapbook, Janis wrote, "At last, recognition," next to a *San Francisco Chronicle* column by Herb Caen about the changing nature of the hippie movement, away from peace and LSD. He wrote, "I remember a party at Hillsborough where Big Brother and the Holding

Company played, and singer Janis Joplin kept belting the champagne, one glass after another. I was shocked. Pretty soon they'll be wearing mink stoles and making love furtively instead of openly."

She received fan letters from men saying they had hunted forever for a woman like her, asking her to share the energy of love and to "see God in each other's eyes." She could talk about the December review of their gig at the Golden Bear in Huntington Beach that headlined, JANIS JOPLIN TOO FULL OF SOUL FOR HOLDING COMPANY PARTNERS. Yes, Janis had plenty to discuss with her old trusted friends.

The fall of 1967 was a good time to review personal commitments. Though the social revolution was gaining speed, the scene in Haight-Ashbury was souring with age. The venereal-disease rate was up six-fold in one year. Police were conducting daily raids on the streets, picking up underage runaways and anyone carrying pot or LSD. On October 2, police arrested musicians, managers, and friends at the Grateful Dead house on Ashbury Street for possession of marijuana, then a felony. The band protested through a subsequent press conference, complaining that since they were charged with a felony, society incorrectly equated smoking marijuana with the crimes of rape and murder. They challenged the country to look at the unpunished guilt of an automobile company that made cars that were knowingly unsafe and compare it with the benign experience of smoking grass.

Big Brother almost got arrested in October over a noise complaint during their three-day engagement at the Matrix, a popular club in San Francisco. It was located in a residential area, and neighbors had finally had enough of the thundering rock that regularly accompanied their weekend evening hours. In such situations, the police normally threatened to arrest the club managers. In this situation, they threatened to arrest the band as well. Under duress, the band canceled the last night of the gig.

The elders of the movement were heading out of the city to communes in the country or the healthy life-style of Marin County, just across the bay. The Beatles, the cultural leaders of the movement after Kesey and Leary were arrested, announced they were giving up LSD and getting into transcendental meditation, or TM.

The brief vision of a new-style community within the city had vanished. Hounded by the police, overpublicized by the press,

★

swamped with unwanted and needy new converts, abused by criminals, and trivialized by tourists ogling at the scene, the core of the movement was moving on. In the spirit of rebirth, they held a wake and parade for "Hippie, devoted son of Mass Media." October 6, 1967, in Buena Vista Park, ten pallbearers carried a coffin around Haight-Ashbury, ending in Panhandle Park, where they set the poor soul afire. Before Hippie was given his last send-off, high-pressure water from the fire department put out the whole event, a fitting symbol.

Janis was ready for a rest and a place to crow when she came to Port Arthur for Christmas 1967. She brought presents for the family—a gold pin with a pearl for Mom, a blue leather fringed vest for Michael, and a velvet and pheasant-feathered purse for me. She also brought 45-RPM copies of the band's single "Down On Me." Those she shared liberally with family and friends.

Michael ran next door to Jimmy Pryor's house to show off his sister's success. They sat around the record player in Jimmy's living room as the needle settled into the grooves. Easing back into their seats, they tried to make sense of the new, raucous musical style. Even Michael was a bit chagrined. He wanted to shout for joy that his sister was on a record, but his close friends had difficulty finding a polite and honest adjective to mumble in their thanks for sharing the music.

Janis had a special warmth for Michael, the only family member who seemed to be trying to join the movement. He was an artist, echoing her earlier interest. She confided to him, "You look pretty hip, but you should let your hair grow." Michael replied, "I can't because the school won't let us, but I let the front grow as long as I could."

Janis's old gang held a holiday party at Adrian and Gloria's. Janis gave out copies of her 45-RPM record, saying she didn't like it, but it was all they had out then. They were recording a new one.

"It was really exciting and fun hearing her stories," Adrian said. "By then, Janis dressed differently, I'll say outrageously," he laughed. "She went down to the Seven-Eleven for cigarettes, and when she came back she was all upset because some guy had said, 'By God, a costume party!' She flew into the guy, but I think she got enjoyment out of that too."

In our living room, Janis posed, shifted, smiled, and cocked her head as the photographer and reporter from the *Port Arthur*

News, Leonard Duckett, took her picture. "Janis Joplin Drawing Acclaim . . ." read the lead. "Janis Joplin is another Port Arthuran carving her name across the country with talent." Duckett and Janis had a friendly discussion about blues singers and their history, the meaning of soul, and the development of her career. "The band is making money," she said. "That's what it's all about, isn't it?" She laughed. I leaned on the doorframe of kitchen, watching the unfolding of the public Janis, curious about the nature of press interviews, and pondering the new role my sister was developing. Before he left, Duckett shot a photo of the family together, the four of us in normal Texas clothes, and Janis in San Francisco attire—wild hair, with inordinately wide bell-bottom pants under a ruffled white blouse.

Returning to California, Janis had to contend with more than the gigs Big Brother was playing on the West Coast. She was pregnant. The father was a young guy and their relationship was nothing that would last. Janis flirted with the idea of having the baby and carrying it lovingly from dressing room to dressing room, but she soon faced up to the impossibility of having a child and continuing her career. While playing in Southern California, she went to Mexico and had an abortion. She knew the decision was best, but it grieved her terribly. She really wanted children. It was even harder for her because the procedure hadn't been done properly and she suffered physically from it, hemorrhaging and having pain for some time.

January 31, 1968

Dear Mother, Father, Mike & Laura

Quite a surprise, eh?! Well I got your letter this morning & it's stopped raining & I have an hour until rehearsal so George & I are in the park, respectively—chasing doves & writing to Mom. Thanks for that article on Aretha, she is by far & away the best thing in music right now. (Although, a review in Rolling Stone, a national rock & roll newspaper, called me "possibly the best female voice of her generation". But I suppose she & I are of different generations. Well, I don't know . . . . . 25 y'know)

Twenty-five. 25. XXV. A quarter of a century! Oh, it's all too incredible. Thanks for the presents both Christmas & birthday. I loved the nightgown but I dyed it purple & aged it 10 yrs. It's lovely. And the clock I really needed—but twenty-five?! I never thought I'd even survive this long.

★

I've been sick for the last week & a half & confined to bed so I finally had a wonderful rest. We had to cancel 3 days at the Fillmore & lost about $8000 but I feel so nice & calm now. The first time off I've had in months! Very fun, this was the first time I've ever been stay-at-home preferably in bed sick since I was away from home. I didn't really realize it until one afternoon lying in bed drinking a beer. I suddenly flashed on the fact that lying in bed drinking a beer is the way to be sick! And I'd never done it before. It was really a nice time—people sent me flowers (3 vases full) and very many charming young men came to call. Linda and I had a fine time.

On my birthday we were in L.A. playing a club & everyone was so nice! The owners of the club sent me 3 dozen red roses—all over the stage when I came in, the band gave me 2 doz., some friends in S.F. sent me 1 doz. & (are you ready Mike?) Peter Tork sent me 1 doz red roses. And after the show we had lots of champagne & a birthday cake. Really nice.

Well, career news now. First of all the word from Albert is that we're only a few weeks from finally recording again. Confidentially (if this shows up in the Houston Post I'll kill you) Columbia has agreed to pay everything over $100,000. Mainstream's lowest figure for us has been $250,000. We pay the $100,000. A lot of money but a good record right now would really set us. We're getting an incredible amount of national press now and more to come. I just did a thing for Eye magazine, a hip young adult magazine put out by Harper's Bazaar which will be out in March or April. An article on Grace Slick (of the Jefferson Airplane) & I w/full page color photos of both of us, so things look good. Very good.

And in February, we take off for 7 weeks on the road in the East. Playing Philadelphia, Boston, N.Y., Buffalo, some colleges, Toledo, Detroit. Should certainly test our mettle. Will be gone from Feb 15 to the 2nd week in April, so if my birthday presents don't quite get there right, please understand.

Mike, your poster was GROOVEY & really good luck w/your light show. Sounds like a great idea. If you need any advice write, because I know lots of people that do them. Some of them the originators of the whole thing. Do you plan to start with liquid projections? They're the best because they can reflect the mood of the music, & keep the tempo. If you can get this & incorporate slides with it you'll really have something. You & your friend should get the equipment & rehearse w/records. Again, good luck, it's a good idea. And I hope the flu doesn't cut into your grade, too much.

Well, no more news I guess. You'd better frame this—it may be another year . . . Bye & love,

Janis

CHAPTER TWELVE

BREAKING UP WITH
BIG BROTHER

★

Well, you told me that you loved me
I believed you darling, but you lied, you know it's true
I hold you to my heart, I believe until you leave
And then I cry . . .
Oh darling . . .
Make it the last time . . .

—Janis Joplin, "Last Time"

EBRUARY 17, 1968, Big Brother and the Holding Company opened on the East Coast at the Anderson Theater in New York City. They were the headlining act for a program that included B. B. King and a new rock group, the Aluminum Dream. New York was a whole new experience for the group, but one they were ready to make their own. Myra Friedman, in her book *Buried Alive,* wrote about the Anderson event, the first time Myra had seen the band. "She [Janis] crouched for a second and I jumped up in astonishment as the entire theater blazed open. Never before had I heard a sound like that! She was a headlong assault, a hysterical discharge, an act of total extermination. It was as if some invisible claw had risen up from her throat, its talons hooked to tear unmercifully at the outer reaches of the auditorium." Myra related the tunes, opening with "Catch Me, Daddy," followed by "Summertime" and "Piece of My Heart." The last of four encores was Big Mama Thornton's "Ball and Chain." Friedman wrote about the finale, "A stunned pause followed. Then the crowd reared back like a huge stable of just-branded horses and heaved forward with a shrieking charge to the stage."

★

Robert Shelton of *The New York Times* besieged Myra, who was then the band's press agent, for pictures and details about the band, all of which she was unprepared to supply. No one had expected the extent of press reaction to Janis and Big Brother. On March 9, 1968, Shelton wrote, "Rock Star Born on Second Avenue: Janis Joplin Is a Smashing Success in Debut Here . . . As fine as the whole evening was, it belonged mostly to the sparky, spunky Miss Joplin. She sounded, at first, like an athletic soul shouter, a white stylistic sister of Aretha and Erma Franklin. But comparisons wane, for there are few voices of such power, flexibility and virtuosity in pop music anywhere." Big Brother had arrived in the East, and Janis had taken it by storm.

The band members were all overawed by their new success. Used to scraping by on a month-to-month basis, they were tight with their increased income. None of them was sure that what had come so surprisingly might not evaporate as quickly. John Cooke labored to convince them to spend a little extra to fly first-class. At that time, the difference was often less than twenty dollars a ticket. They finally settled on a routine of flying first-class when they were going coast to coast. The shorter flights were to be coach.

The eight weeks Janis spent in the East were marked by many milestones in her career. January 30 was the termination date of Big Brother's ill-advised recording contract with Mainstream Records. They bought themselves out of their contract with Bob Shad and Mainstream. As Janis mentioned in her letter, it cost them $250,000, of which $100,000 was due to innocent conversations while visiting in Texas at Christmas. Janis had mentioned the possibility of signing with Columbia, a label of CBS Records. Mom told a family friend, who told her daughter, who shared it with a friend who was a reporter for the *Houston Post*. Once published as a gossip note, Bob Shad upped his price. ARRGGHHH! I remember the anguished telephone call about that, and the drawn faces of our family talking among ourselves. None of us could even imagine $100,000.

Everything over $100,000 was paid by CBS as a cost of doing business. February 1 was the effective date of their new contract with Clive Davis and CBS. Twenty pages long, it outlined the details of their legal relationship.

February 20, 1968

Dear Mother—

Well, here it is—our first New York review from our first New York gig. Too much? Eh! So now we're in the process of taking the East Coast by storm. Also, as of yesterday afternoon we're with Columbia, officially. Signed the contract on the 26th floor of the CBS building, met the president, had a press party, & got drunk. Am now in Albert's office, just completed an interview. From all indications I'm going to become rich & famous. Incredible! All sorts of magazines are asking to do articles & pictures featuring me. I'm going to do everyone. Wow, I'm so lucky—I just fumbled around being a mixed-up kid (& young adult) & then I fell into this. And finally, it looks like something is going to work for me. Incredible.

Well, pin the review up so everyone can see—I'm so proud.

All my love,
Janis

I'm staying at the Chelsea Hotel, 23rd St. N.Y., very famous literary type intellectual hotel. Dylan Thomas lived & died there, Brendon Behan also.

The March 2 issue of *Billboard* ran a photo of Clive Davis, the ubiquitous president of CBS Records, welcoming Big Brother and the Holding Company. Clive was forceful and visionary. He was one of the first in the record industry to recognize the staying power of rock and roll, and thus signed many top acts. Unfazed by the entourage around her, Janis reacted with working-class honesty to the unlimited free records offered by Columbia. "I sat on the floor, in the middle of Clive Davis's office, and went through the catalogue," Janis told Linda Gravenites. She came back with boxes full of records, including *The Baroque Oboe* for Linda and two albums for me, by the Krainis Consort, playing my favorite madrigal recorder tunes.

Columbia threw a press reception for Big Brother at a tony Manhattan restaurant. Mike Jahn wrote a story that went out over the Bell-McClure Syndicate wire:

Janis is beautiful. In a business where popularity usually is accompanied by studied aloofness, she is a breath of fresh air. . . . In appearance she is a small, sexy doll, almost a toy that bounces happily around the

★

microphone all the while assaulting the ear drums with the drilling intensity of her voice. Her disdain for bras and affinity for lightweight blouses adds a certain universal appeal to the basic raunchiness of her voice. She may become, since such distinctions are inevitable, the first major girl sex symbol in rock. For a lot of people, she is that already. . . . "I tell all the performers I meet to drink Southern Comfort because it preserves their voices," she said. "It's just an excuse for my own drinking."

The February 23–29 *East Village Other* called Janis's music "feminine vocal blues." Peter Albin explained the band's roots: "We're not a white soul group. Just white, middle-class, suppressed, and repressed old-time beatniks." The *New York Free Press* hailed Janis as the "Voice of a Lady Leadbelly." *The Village Voice* of February 22 said that "the girl gap had been closed. The girl gap is an easy term for a hard problem that's been facing the pop music industry. The plumage and the punch in the last few years' rock has remained in the province of men. . . . Now, with Janis all that is over."

Newsweek ran a story on "The Queen Bees" of rock, quoting Janis, Grace Slick, Mama Cass, Spanky, and Mama Cowsill. "The guys are starting to sing and there is something to build around, me," Janis was quoted as saying. Peter agreed, "Without her, we're nothing." Already the "bizness," as Janis liked to call it, was defining her image of herself.

Albert had added someone new to Janis's retinue of business attendants, a press agent. Myra Friedman was a stubborn, persistent woman who cared about Janis to a fault. Her involvement in Janis's press totally changed the publicity. Myra dropped the impromptu interviews after a performance and scheduled in-depth interviews, often back-to-back for afternoons on end.

From the first press feature in New York, the stories focused on Janis, not the band as a whole. They wrote as though Janis were a singer with a band backing her and not the family-unit San Francisco band. John Cooke recalled, "The guys in the band were mumbling, 'Hey, how come the reporters only want to talk to her?' They should have been smarter," he added. The billing that Julius Karpen had been so insistent on keeping as "Big Brother and the Holding Company" was changed by Grossman's office to "Big Brother and the Holding Company, featuring Janis Joplin."

March 5, 1968

Dear Mother—

So very busy & N.Y. is very strange–competitive & ugly & is turning us all around. On my evening off, I went & saw Hello Dolly w/Pearl Bailey. She's wonderful.

Love, Janis

April 4, 1968

Dear Mother,

I just can't tell you how much your letters have meant to me here–so nice.

Your first born is really doing great in the music business. Did I tell you about all my reviews? Can I tell you again? This is all so <u>exciting</u> to me. Now just since we've been in New York, all of the following has happened.

1. Vogue–*picture session w/Avedon who is #1 for the "People Are Talking About" section, 3 mos or so.*

2. Glamour–*interview & picture for their column on "happening" people–great picture, I've got a copy, June issue maybe.*

3. New York Times–*the review that you saw plus I was interviewed last week by Nat Hentoff (maybe you've heard of him?) who's writing an article on me for the* Sunday Times–*be in about 2 more weeks.*

4. Jazz & Pop–*was notified by the editor last night that I had* <u>won</u>*!! their reader's poll for female vocalist–be out in April!!!!*

5. Eye *magazine–picture & article in "Elevator" section people on way up. Out now.*

6. Life–*interviewed for an article on 7 rock groups which is scheduled though I have my doubts it will appear.*

8. New York Magazine–*a new magazine, an outgrowth of the Sunday supplement to the* N.Y. Herald Tribune *which folded, covered a gig in Detroit for an article.*

9. Cashbox, Billboard, Record World & Variety *reviewed our opening at the Fillmore East in N.Y. last month.*

FOOTNOTE to: 1. *In the current* Vogue *I'm mentioned in the People Are Talking About, also my fondness for Southern Comfort, also my press person at the office thinks I may be for something bigger in the "American Woman" (!?!) issue.*

★

10. Village Voice—*a fashion interview & picture thing*

11. underground press reviews by 3 N.Y. papers—Rat, East Village Other (EVO), *&* N.Y. Free Press

ISN'T THAT TOO MUCH?!

I just have to crow.

Our record is coming slowly & at this point we don't know whether we're going to be able to finish in L.A. (we're going back to Calif next week) because our producer wants us to do it in New York which means coming back & also canceling some gigs (losing a lot of money in the process) so we don't know what's up. But the 3 tracks that we have down really sound good. As a matter of fact, some friends of ours—a band—just returned from England (they cut their album there w/the Rolling Stone's producer) & we listened to their tapes & ours are better. At least we think so.

Just bought $115 worth of fur—a deer skin for the wall, 5 used coats to cut up & sew back together for a huge rug & a fantastic white alpaca rug about 3" thick & huge! Fantastic, I love fur & soft things.

I didn't get any clothes while I was here—just some shoes. In fact I didn't do anything except the music bizness. *Recording, gigs, interviews & picture sessions took all of our time. Oh, new interview to mention—an article for the Women's page of the* Washington Post.

So, sorry, no news except my music. Except I met a very charming young man in Chicago I'm going to visit on my way back to Calif.

Bye for now—try to write again when I'm not so enamored w/myself.

Love, Janis

Janis shared her views on the "bizness" with *Glamour*: "In New York, music is ambition, pressure, pushiness. Be nice to this one or that one. We were never in the music 'business' and all that raka-raka, and we're beginning to get weird about it." Yet, she found time to attend the theater and be inspired by Pearl Bailey in *Hello, Dolly!* Janis had read about New York and its cultural offerings for years in *The New Yorker* magazine, to which our folks subscribed. Not only was she in the city and ready to enjoy it, but she was also a part of that cultural elite!

Big Brother and their friends prowled the streets hunting for

During a year living at home in 1965–66, Janis often pulled back her most visible sign of power, her wild hair, and put it discreetly into a bun on top of her head. During this period she wore makeup, dressed conservatively, and warned her friends, "Watch your language," and "Don't drink too much." *(Courtesy of Joplin family)*

In the spring of 1966, Janis began performing publicly again, with the assistance of old friend Jim Langdon, who was then writing a column in the *Austin American-Statesman* newspaper. He got her a job May 5 at a blues festival, her first gig before a mixed-race audience. They loved her. *(Courtesy of Joplin family)*

Janis performed at the 11th Door, a folk club in Austin. Jim Langdon knew the owner, Bill Simonson, and he helped get her a few bookings. *(Courtesy of Joplin family)*

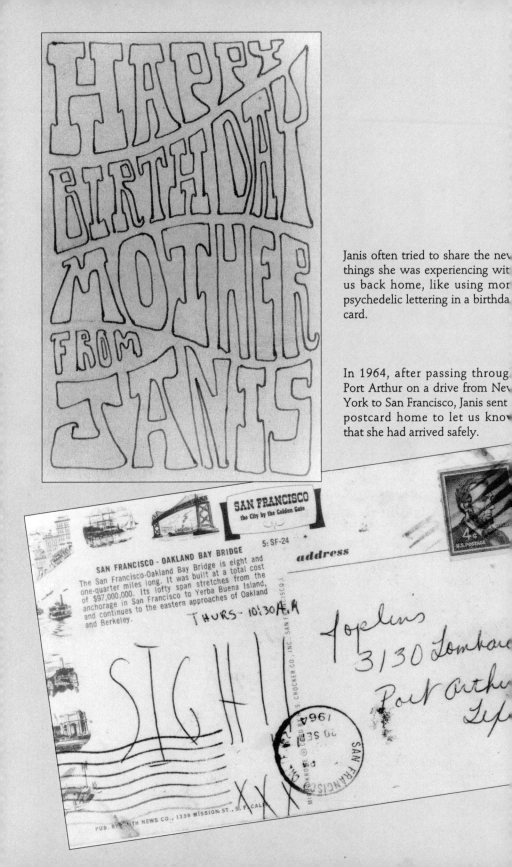

Janis often tried to share the new things she was experiencing with us back home, like using more psychedelic lettering in a birthday card.

In 1964, after passing through Port Arthur on a drive from New York to San Francisco, Janis sent a postcard home to let us know that she had arrived safely.

old-fashioned in
style — tight, w/
up the front. Black

FANTASTIC!

I get back, I'm going
a sewing machine
myself some sort
beautiful/outlandish
to go w/ them.
HOWDJA LIKE TO DO ME
FAVOR DEPT: y'know
box you're ready
send me? Well, I
ught of a few more
still around.

— 11 —

park by himself — he got hit
by a car. But the vet said
he wasn't hurt very bad —
bruised & scared. Poor thing
he's just moping around
a very paranoid look on his
face.
I'm having a few clothes
made for me now — had a
beautiful dress made
out of a madras bed spread
now she's working
one out of with a very low V neckline.
been making things out of
leather lately.
made a beautiful blue &
Garbo hat

green — blue
blue heads — green heads

SIGH!! AND A FRIEND OF MINE
GAVE ME A DRESS & CAPE TO
WEAR FOR THE OCCASION — A
WINE-COLORED VELVET, OLD, FROM
A GOODWILL STORE, BUT BEAUTIFUL!

QUEEN ANNE KIND OF
SLEEVES & A VERY
LOW & BROAD NECKLINE.
REALLY FANTASTIC.

NOW, I HAVE A PROBLEM.
I'M HOPING THE CHICAGO JOB
WILL RESOLVE IT FOR ME, BUT
RIGHT NOW IT'S PLAGUING ME.
LAST WEEKEND WE PLAYED IN
THE CITY & A MAN FROM
ELECTRA, A GOOD LABEL, SPOKE
TO ME AFTERWARDS. LIKED ME/US
A LOT. DURING THE WEEK, SOMEONE
CALLED ME ... SEEMS ROTHCHILD
(THE GUY FROM ELECTRA, WHO
DISCOVERED PAUL BUTTERFIELD
WHO IS VERY BIG NOW — HE

Janis's letters used various writing
styles—printing, script, or more artistic
designs. When words alone wouldn't
do, Janis added quick sketches that got
her point across. Like her stage show,
Janis's letters conveyed her emotions.

Young, happy, healthy, and optimistic, Janis found the 1966 hippie scene in Haight-Ashbury a community of kindred souls. (© *Bill Brach*)

Texan Chet Helms introduced Janis to the band he helped form, Big Brother and the Holding Company. Here Janis and Chet pose near the Windmill at Golden Gate Park in San Francisco. (© *Herb Green*)

One of Big Brother's first promotional photos. FRONT ROW: Peter Albin, bass; Dave Getz, drums. BACK ROW: James Gurley, guitar; Janis; Sam Andrew, guitar; and Sancho, the family dog of the commune that sponsored dances, the Family Dog. (© *Bill Brach*)

BERKELEY'S
JEANNE COLON:

Designer

...nis (FAR RIGHT) models clothes in this photo taken ...Buena Vista Park. Jeanne Colon designed and ...ade clothes for rock stars. For Janis, Jeanne made ...poncho of antique Moroccan fabric over velvet ...one pants."

(© San Francisco Examiner; *John Gorman, photographer*)

Timothy Leary, an early proponent of LSD use, was out of jail on appeal when he was busted again for drug possession April 16, 1966, in New York. He was supported in his fight by the San Francisco hippie community. Big Brother played many benefits for all types of causes. (© *Dennis Nolan, artist*)

...or several months in 1967, Janis had a deep romance with Country Joe McDonald, the leader ...f Country Joe and the Fish. They eventually split up because of commitments to their sepa-...ate careers. (© *Jim Marshall*)

Janis came home for Christmas in 1967. Our live[s] entered a new era as reporter Leonard Duckett, fro[m] the local paper, *The Port Arthur News*, came to th[e] house to interview her. He snapped this family po[r]trait as a favor. (© *Leonard Duckett*)

Janis signs her name to the band's contract wit[h] Columbia Records. Janis wrote home, "Signed the co[n]tract on the 26th floor of the CBS Building, met th[e] president, had a press party and got drunk." (© *John Cooke*)

Columbia Records threw a press party announcing th[e] signing of Big Brother and the Holding Company. Fro[m] left to right: their manager, Albert Grossman; Jame[s] Gurley; Dave Getz; Peter Albin; Sam Andrew; Jani[s] and Clive Davis, the president of Columbia. (© *Elliott Landy*)

At home in her Lyon Street apartment in San Francisco in 1967. Janis decorated with the art of the times, lace, feathers, and posters of friends and idols. (© *Jim Marshall*)

Janis in full regalia at an outdoor concert in San Francisco. (© *Jim Marshall*)

Janis and Ron "Pigpen" McKernan of the Grateful Dead at the Northern California Folk Rock Festival, May 18, 1968. (© *Jim Marshall*)

Janis loved capes like this Mexican one that a fan threw over her shoulders as a gift one night. (© *Baron Wolman*)

Janis was also proud of this velvet cape she wore for a promotional shot of Big Brother and the Holding Company at the Palace of Fine Arts in San Francisco. (© *Baron Wolman*)

...nis fondly referred to Albert Grossman as ...ncle Albert. He provided the support and ...pertise she needed to propel her career ...rward. (© *Elliott Landy*)

...February 1968, Big Brother made its first East Coast tour, opening at ...e Anderson Theater in New York. Backstage the band joked with fellow musicians Ed ...nders of the Fugs and Barry Melton of Country Joe and the Fish. (© *Elliott Landy*)

...sign of the times, Janis is reading an underground ...mic. Several of her Texas friends had moved to ...n Francisco and started Rip Off Press, a chief ...pplier of posters and comics. Dave Getz is peer-...g at a report entitled "The Horror of Growing ...rug Abuse." (© *Elliott Landy*)

...g Brother's first album with Columbia ...as *Cheap Thrills*. Much of it was ...corded live at the Grande Ballroom. ...is was one of the new-style posters ...vertising hippie concerts. The poster ...sign was by Gary Grimshaw. *Artrock, 1153 Mission Street, San Francisco, CA)*

The Janis Joplin image was becoming decided
sexy as Linda Gravenites began creating elabora
embroidered stage clothes. This one is crush
black velvet with beaded flowers sewn on th
bodice. (© *Joe Sia*)

Linda Gravenites was Janis's costume designe
friend, and roommate for three years. She prov
ed a steadying influence to the turbulence of Jani
life-style and escalating career. (© *Jim Marshall*)

nis formed a group she called the Squeeze, which lat-
became known as the Kozmic Blues Band. Here
ey play on the July 18, 1969, *Dick Cavett Show*. From
ft: Luis Gasca, trumpet; Terry Clements, tenor sax;
ornelius "Snooky" Flowers, baritone sax; Lonnie
astille, drums; Brad Campbell, guitar; and Sam
ndrew, guitar. (*Courtesy of Joplin family*)

nis and her new group played the Fillmore East in
ew York February 11 and 12, 1969. Janis often
ayed Latin American percussion instruments like
is guiro. She also played maracas and claves—
ooden sticks that are hit together. (© *Elliott Landy*)

In 1969 Janis toured Europe April
11–24, through Amsterdam, Frankfurt, Paris, Stockholm, Copenhagen,
and London. She clowns here for
friend and road manager John
Cooke. (© *John Cooke*)

In Amsterdam, Janis sings beside Sam Andrew, the only member of Big Brother she asked to join her new group. In Europe her new band received acclaim wherever they went. Janis remarked that the audience rapport hadn't been this enthusiastic since the early days in Haight-Ashbury. (© *John Cooke*)

John Cooke was Janis's close friend and road manager for the three principal tours of her career. (© *Jim Marshall*)

This portrait was taken in New York, December 1969, during a time in Janis's life marked by confusion, drug use, and excessive drinking. Still she manages to shine for the camera. (© *1969 Jay Good*)

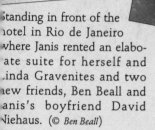

Standing in front of the hotel in Rio de Janeiro where Janis rented an elaborate suite for herself and Linda Gravenites and two new friends, Ben Beall and Janis's boyfriend David Niehaus. (© *Ben Beall*)

Ben, Janis, and David soaked up the street carnival life in Rio, partying and dancing till dawn. (© *Linda Gravenites; courtesy of Ben Beall*)

For two weeks normal life ceases for Carnival in Rio. Much of the partying takes place in the streets, which are elaborately decorated for the festivities. (© *Ben Beall*)

The last show of the Kozmic Blues Band was Madison Square Garden, December 19,1969. For Janis the whole point of singing was communicating. She was always good to her audience. (© *1969 Jay Good*)

In May 1970, Janis opened a new band called the Full Tilt Boogie Band. When they toured the East Coast, they set up a base in New York and traveled from there. Here she is on Fifth Avenue going to her limousine, wearing a new signature item, feather boas in her hair. (© *Clark Pierson*)

Janis toasted life with her Full Tilt Boogie Band, Clark Pierson, John Till, Brad Campbell, Richard Bell, and Ken Pearson. (© *Jerry Tobias*)

The band got an unexpected break in the Midwest when a concert fell through due to poor support work. Sympathetic to the fans who'd bought tickets, Janis tried to give a free concert the next day in a local park, but they couldn't get enough press to make it work. Here Janis relaxes with Ken Pearson and Brad Campbell of Full Tilt. (© *Clark Pierson*)

Friend and lover Kris Kristofferson dropped in to visit Janis while she was on tour. One of Janis's best-known songs, "Me and Bobby McGee," was written by Kris. (© *Clark Pierson*)

Record producer Paul Rothchild joined the Full Tilt tour for a few months to get to know Janis and her sound so he could capture it on record. He produced Janis's third major album, *Pearl*. (© *Clark Pierson*)

Janis returned to Port Arthur, Texas, for her tenth high school reunion the middle of August 1970. Here she and I strolled from a press conference into the celebration at the Goodhue Hotel. (© *Watkins Photo*)

Janis and some of her former classmates her high school reunion. (© *Watkins Photo*)

Sculptor Doug Clark captured Janis in many poses for a bronze statue of her that was unde written by her high school classmate John Palmer. Donated to the city of Port Arthur, th statue is now a part of the Port Arthur Historical Collection at the Lamar University Library : Port Arthur. (*Courtesy of Port Arthur Historical Society*)

bookstores and clothing boutiques. They encountered the variety and vehemence of the New York natives. One incensed woman accosted Sam and his girlfriend Carol Cavallon at a street crosswalk, cursing him and hitting him on the back. Sam was in a gay mood and decided to try to persuade her he was human. With dark-suited gentlemen hurrying by offering sympathetic glances, Sam assumed the missionary role of the hippie in a foreign land, intent on demonstrating that the world would be a better place if we could love and understand each other.

The hippies tried to lead the masses forward in spite of those who obviously weren't listening. "Celebrity in those days was about being allowed into a peer group of the leaders," said noted record producer Paul Rothchild. He continued, "It was like Camelot." Every day seemed to bring new, miraculous surprises to delight the confident knights of the hippie Round Table. Janis seemed to explode into rock "by being so intensely, joyfully" herself, wrote Nat Hentoff in *The New York Times* on April 21.

New York folk scene veteran Bobby Neuwirth, Janis's friend and touring companion who went along to do troubleshooting for Albert's office, was the kind of guy who was content living in the moment and trying to have a good time. His nature was also colored by true creative talent. He mused, "Maybe the reason Janis had her success was her very lack of polish. She was earnest and sincere." Bobby said she was an idealist and a dreamer. "Janis was an artist," he exclaimed. "An artist is not only a person who has something to say, but a person who can't *not* say it."

March 1-2 Big Brother played at the Grande Ballroom in Detroit. They brought tons of equipment, engineers, and producers to make a live recording, planning on using it as the basis of their first album with Columbia. Everyone in Detroit made them feel at home, but somehow the music just didn't click. Nothing was usable. Janis said, "Albert is miffed," a favorite expression of hers.

In New York, the band met with producer John Simon and his assistant, Elliot Mazer, a fellow who calls it as he sees it without much soul-searching. Elliot explained that Janis worried about the "untogetherness of the band." He recalled her as "nervous, frightened, confident, and very powerful, a person who was very specific about what she liked and disliked musically." He added, "Janis was as together in the studio as anyone I have ever worked with, interested in everything and totally committed."

The producers and engineers struggled to capture the band's music. The guys knew that their sound was an on-again, off-again commodity. When it gelled, it was great. The rest of the time it got the audience off, but was of questionable musical quality. They talked, listened, tried innovations, and stretched to capture the precision that lived in their minds as they played.

D. A. Pennebaker, the noted filmmaker who did *Monterey Pop* and profiled Dylan in *Don't Look Back,* met Janis while the band was recording in New York. They agreed that he could do a film on Janis similar to the one he did on Dylan. He began appearing when they were working or playing. In the studio he captured the band negotiating about the nature of the instrumental arrangement on songs. Janis danced a few steps, smiled, and winked. "We can do it either way, they're both valid approaches," Janis said, presenting her opinion of how to proceed. "But I think, it's ten o'clock, and I think by four we could have 'Summertime.' It will be hard. But if you want to approach it by doing a little bit of 'Summertime' and then a little bit of 'Brownsville' we can. You all voted to do a bunch of them tonight but I personally don't agree with it. . . . What you hear is what's up front and that's the vocal. Unless the instrumental really makes a mistake, you aren't gonna hear it."

Everyone got "superaggressive, separate, sour." Fred Catero, the engineer on the recording, said that the vocals worked fine, but the instrumental parts always had mistakes. On one song, "after four tries, Janis stormed out, screaming, 'I ain't going to sing with those motherfuckers!' " Slowly they learned how to handle New York and the pressures around them. Janis told reporter Nat Hentoff of *The New York Times,* "San Francisco's different. I don't mean it's perfect, but the rock bands there didn't start because they wanted to make it. They dug getting stoned and playing for people dancing. Here they want to *make* it."

After a gig in Philadelphia on March 16, everything fell back into place. The band worked and played together. They were friends more than anything. Discussing the prior evening's debauchery in jovial, reminiscent tones, Janis told James, "You look so cute when you're passed out, just like Hongo." They had carried him from the lobby of the Chelsea Hotel, where they were staying, up to his room. They opened the door and announced, "Coming up, one James Gurley," just like short-order cooks.

Janis was a loyal friend. She once declared to the guys, "Man, you want to hear how shitty some people are," then launched into a story about a mutual friend who'd been busted in Canada. He played with another band that was in New York at the time and had been advised by his managers to skip bail on a drug bust so he could stay for a gig in the city. The next day they fired him because he couldn't get a visa. Janis ranted on about it, saying, "He isn't even mad and I'm furious." They treated him "shabbily," she cried.

On April 4, 1968, Martin Luther King, Jr., was assassinated in Memphis. The band was stunned but rose to the occasion. On April 17, along with many other musicians, they played a benefit at the Generation Club in New York. "Emotions were running very high and a lot of cities all around the country were in flames," wrote Sam Andrew in his unpublished memoirs. "B. B. King sat backstage and talked about the tragedy in a very emotional, beautiful, calm manner. He made us feel the dignity and the poignancy of the moment. It was like being in church to hear him talk of the need for understanding and love between the brothers and the sisters, oh, yes, all over this world." Big Brother came onstage for what Sam called a consecrated moment, playing "Brownsville," "Piece of My Heart," and "Down On Me."

An interview appearing four days later in *The Village Voice* quoted Janis. "Make-up for Janis is a 'lot of insignificant crap. Sometimes I wish I was black or of some exotic race, where, baby, it's your face alone that's working for you, no camouflage.' "

The dichotomy of "us and them" was never so clear as in King's murder. Janis knew what camp she lived in and told Nat Hentoff of *The New York Times,* "In Texas, I was a beatnik, a weirdo, and since I wasn't making it the way I am now, my parents thought I was a goner. Now my mother writes and asks what kind of clothes a 1968 blues singer wears. That's kind of groovy, since we've been on opposite sides since I was 14. Texas is O.K. if you want to settle down and do your own thing quietly, but it's not for outrageous people, and I was always outrageous. I got treated very badly in Texas."

★

She responded to Hentoff's question about abusing her voice, saying that she tried to lay back and not push her singing, but she didn't like the feeling in performing. She said, "Maybe I won't last as long as other singers, but I think you can destroy your now by worrying about tomorrow. . . . We look back at our parents and see how they gave up and compromised and wound up with very little. So the kids want a lot of something now rather than a little of hardly anything spread over 70 years."

1968

Mother & family

At last a few moments of peace! We have a few weeks' vacation after finishing a month's recording in L.A. plus gigs on the weekend. Mother, even you w/your incredible pace would be amazed at all we've been doing. Working, working, working, all spare time devoted to sleeping & eating & readying for the next trip. Positively incredible. So I'm in the middle of my one week off. I'm spending a few days at a friend's cabin in Stinson Beach w/George. I've been doing nothing except sleeping, eating, & reading cheap novels. Lots of sleeping. Tomorrow back to the city to spend the rest of my vacation moving. We've been evicted because of George (dirty old thing). Our new address is

892 Noe.

phone # I'll send later. Some vacation–I'll just get all the boxes upstairs then it's back to L.A. for mixing. That's the final thing on the record–it means setting the balances of all instruments & voices to each other. It could be a very simple or a very complicated procedure–we'll see.

I guess by now you've seen the things in Vogue, Glamour, *&* Mademoiselle. *(Did the Port Arthur News have anything on these? If so, please send) I'm sending along two you won't have seen–the Nat Hentoff piece from the* New York Times *Sunday entertainment section &* Jazz & Pop *where I won the reader's poll. There was also a groovy thing (one full page) in the* Washington Post *but I only have one copy. Some people from* Look *have been following us around so we can expect something &* Life *did us for an article on Rock. So, keep checking your neighborhood newsstands, folks!*

I've been gaining a little weight & Linda is hard pressed to keep me in clothes. She's working on something now to end all. Some Indian material, *sort of a soft silk chiffon—all vaguely floral blues, greens & purples covered w/a gold thread sewn on in intricate floral patterns—cost me $18 a yd. (!) but it'll be beautiful—pants very full at bottom, see-through belled very full at wrist sleeves all lined in purple w/gold piping. Just gorgeous. Also of help in this current clothes crisis—I went shopping at Paraphernalia in Beverly Hills in a pair of old Levis & a tee shirt only to be recognized & fawned over by the manager who will make me up anything I want in any color & made to fit me at rack prices. ("Well, we make all of Tony Curtis' lovely shirts.") Too much!! Sure beats being a beatnik! Like somebody once said "I've been rich & I've been poor, and rich is better."*

Hope Mike got & liked his vest. (Dad, I'll get to you I promise!! Soon as I have time—you greedy devil . . .) I think it may be a bit short but that's okay in a vest, just supposed to wear them loose. I hope you let him wear it for heaven's sake. I was going to send a mess of posters too but then I remembered you were legislating against them when I called last. Ahh, maybe Daddy would like them. . . . .

All this time in L.A. & I haven't seen any of the family. I really feel bad but I don't know how to get a hold of any of them. I tried to call Barbara but her #'s been changed. Just had a brainstorm. I'll write her & have her call me at the motel. Why didn't I think of that before? Well, I do hope to get in touch.

Glad to hear that Laura's surviving society's rigors, i.e. school & sorority. Hope Mike's doing as well. Just to put out a feeler—how about if Mike came out one summer for awhile?

Well, back to my novels—have you read Rosemary's Baby—*it's a mind-blower, as they say in the vernacular. Album should be out sometime in July. Hope to get it out before we play the Columbia convention in Puerto Rico—July 25. After that we'll be doing another Eastern thing to promote the record. Oh, !! I almost forgot! I may be in a movie! Starring Michael Pollard who was C.W. Moss in "Bonnie & Clyde." He's very big now. Some sort of a hip Western a la "Cat Ballou." I'd play the part of a Texas barroom singer—no lack of authenticity there & probably get a lot of money & get to sing a tune. But it's all in the talk stages now.*

> *Bye, my love to everyone*
> *XXXXX*
>
> *Janis*

Also sending a brand new thing from Eye *magazine.*

Big Brother worked to play "live" in a studio, by recording everyone playing at once. May 20 through June 12 they worked in Los Angeles with John Simon and Elliot Mazer. Sam Andrew described John, saying, "One couldn't have found someone more unsympathetic to what we were trying to do." He was a very deliberate, precise, control-oriented producer. Sam Andrew aimed for a Dionysian guitar ecstasy. The band felt John Simon didn't understand them, their music, or the way they needed to record to capture it on tape.

With studio and live recordings in hand, Janis, Sam Andrew, and Fred Catero, a Columbia engineer, spent thirty-six hours straight doing a final mix for the album. The audience noise on the released songs wasn't authentic. It was secretaries and other people screaming and clapping in the studio. Even Bill Graham's opening monologue on the album was added in the studio. But the final product captured the powerful rawness of the band's performing impact.

The album was titled *Cheap Thrills,* though they had wanted to use a longer title, *Sex, Dope, and Cheap Thrills.* It was a phrase that came from the 1930s, Sam Andrew explained, when films like *Reefer Madness* warned about the ravages of marijuana addiction. Columbia nixed the first two words, but everyone was happy with the compromise.

Bob Cato, art director at Columbia, suggested an album cover of the whole band in bed in a typical hippie pad. Sam Andrew and Dave Getz arrived first at the photo studio and immediately began laughing at the Madison Avenue view of hippie night chambers—pink with ruffles and soft light. When Janis walked in she said, "Let's trash it, boys," and they did. They tore out the frilly stuff, took some props from the studio, hung some of their own things around, undressed and jumped in bed smiling for the camera. The shots were innocent enough but didn't capture anything the band wanted to say about themselves. They weren't used.

They searched around for other ideas and became inspired. Perhaps Janis delved back into her humor magazine mind-set by choosing R. Crumb to draw the cover. "You're really big," he told Janis, and he liked big women. Crumb drew what he liked, the voluptuous Rubenesque woman in a hippie caricature. He watched them in concert and drew impressions of them and their songs for the back of the album. Instead they put his captivating comic art on the cover.

The fun-loving humor of the gang showed best when they were taped for KQED-TV and asked the staple query, "Who is Big Brother?" All at once they replied, "He always stays in the bathroom. Go get him, we've been trying to play with that cat for so long. Get him out of there. He never shows up for a gig."

Janis confided to Sam Andrew while driving the Mercedes-populated streets of L.A., "Listen, if I have to sell out, I'll sell out. I love this!" Janis's comments hit him hard. This was far from the righteous attitude that had given birth to the group's career. "Before, nobody ever cared about whether I lived," Janis explained to reporter Beatrice Berg in *The Philadelphia Inquirer*. "This is exciting and I want to do it until it isn't there anymore. I could be very cool about it, but I don't want to know it's all bull. Maybe when I'm 45 I'll wake up and find this was all wrong, but now's the time to be excited. I'm excited!"

The new rock groups were difficult for the record executives to manage. They didn't take guidance from the in-house A&R men. The company artistic directors couldn't dictate recording plans, music choice, or mixing. The musicians didn't take input from anyone! That terrified the business structure, because it meant things were less predictable. The executives became more dependent upon the whims of the new artistic temperament. The San Francisco rock groups forced the industry to accept greater artistic freedom.

This loss of business power came while merchandisers were realizing the enormous buying power of adolescents. Teenagers accounted for more than 40 percent of the records sold. The baby boomers were a huge untapped group that had cash to spend, and they didn't want the same music that their parents, or even older siblings, preferred. The sales of *Cheap Thrills* amazed the executives. Columbia handled mostly slick and polished material. Few people there understood rock and roll, but the times were changing.

In 1968 Dave Moriaty showed up in San Francisco, just back from the Marine Corps, angry and ready to join the thriving California scene. In Nam he'd heard that Janis was famous. "I went to her house," he said, "and found her down the street at a washeteria. She was wearing some kind of fur coat and blue jeans. She came running and jumped into my arms and I was just physically bowled over. She had to act like that, to differentiate between fans and friends. She was euphoric."

Dave probably told Janis that Austin was changing. All the musicians were getting into rock and the police were getting heavy. The whole scene seemed to hit the trail on out to San Francisco. Dave and his friend Gilbert Shelton, cartoonist extraordinaire from the *Ranger* magazine, went there together and found Dave's college room-mate, Jack Jackson, running the business operations of the Family Dog, which became insolvent in November 1968. Even selling $60,000 worth of posters a month, they couldn't support the money-losing Avalon Ballroom. Dave, Jack, Gilbert Shelton, and Fred Todd formed Rip Off Press with $35.00 apiece as a down payment on a $1,000 used printing press. Their first job was posters for the reincarnated Avalon, which had been taken over by another group of Texans. Soon they were also printing R. Crumb's comics.

Many underground presses were flourishing. By 1969, reported Abe Peck, at least five hundred underground papers had emerged in cities and towns throughout the country. An additional five hundred to one thousand were published in high schools. Peck wrote in *Uncovering the Sixties: The Life and Times of the Underground Press,* "The papers could offer an honest subjectivity in place of an 'objectivity' that ignored its own underlying political and cultural assumptions."

With *Cheap Thrills* released in July 1968, Janis and Big Brother were now a certified musical success. The album went gold in three days! The band played the CBS convention in Puerto Rico to an audience of the stars Janis had listened to in awe merely a few months earlier. Big Brother was now playing to them, and not just as equals—they were the best of the new competition. What had happened? Janis had hardly changed what she had been doing for years. Now, instead of looking down their noses, people were applauding her.

July 1968

Dear family . . .

HAD *to write you a card from Puerto Rico. So far all I've seen, unfortunately, is the inside of 3 hotels & a short stretch of beach—but lots of free rum punch on Columbia. We play tonite & leave tomorrow morning for Newport but at least I'll get to see the island from the air . . . Special note*

to Mike—honey, just congratulations & pride & all the love I have for your
work, in Agape [a newspaper Michael and his friend Jimmy Pryor
put out], particularly the poem—oh so fine!!! I have it on my wall. Love to
everyone,

Janis

P.S. I'll be at the Chelsea, 222 W. 23rd, N.Y. for about a month.

XXX Janis

"The self and the public image blended more in those days," explained Bennett Glotzer, Albert's one-time partner. Bennett saw the world mostly according to business loyalties: "Stars used to hang out in public, meeting at designated gathering places. Everybody wore the same clothes on the street that they wore onstage." Janis was the same as her audience. She shared the same taste in clothes, drink, and musical entertainment.

Her popular acceptance wouldn't have been possible had her public persona not been based on some true aspect of her personality. It was part of her, but she seemed to begin to believe it was all of her. Instantly, she had become the subject of constant press observation. Janis always had to be "on" because someone was always there observing. "If you practice long enough being a big, brassy blues mama," Bobby Neuwirth said, "you become one. You start to expect it of yourself just as others expect it of you." "For me," Janis explained to the press, "life-style and singing are the same."

Janis believed the newspapers. "I'm the biggest groupie in the world," she told Dave Getz. Janis would "meet somebody and fawn all over them, and want to hang out with them," he laughed.

Paul Rothchild kept smiling and laughing when he described the mutual pleasure Janis and Jim Morrison had, meeting at a party at John Davidson's house. They talked and joked, egging each other on with verbal sparring. A few hours of drinking and several games of pool later, Jim proceeded to develop his characteristic alcohol-induced belligerence. The finale was Janis's attempted getaway. He wouldn't take no for an answer and stuck his head in the car as she tried to leave. Janis had to smash a bottle over his head to make her point. The next morning Jim told Paul he really wanted to see her again.

Janis had some rough moments, but her time onstage was still

★

driving her life. "I do believe in some very amorphous things that happen when you're onstage . . . like something moves in the air," Janis tried to explain to the interviewer from the *Los Angeles Times West* magazine, Rasa Gustaitis. "It seems like a real thing that moves around in the air. It's nonexistent but it's so real it's like love or desire. You know damn well it's there, you know it's RIGHT THERE, man—something's going on." Rasa became a friend after this interview, Janis liked her questions so much. Rasa called Janis a shaman woman, "wailing as though possessed."

Rasa quoted a fan who was later echoed by fan letters sent after Janis's death. "She's us. She's not a star, she's us. I've never met her but I know her. It's like, hearing her, you leave your body and you just move, man. She's just all energy. I don't know, she's all of us."

It was beginning to seem as if the only time Janis was herself was onstage. Offstage a personal duality arose that made little sense. It didn't feel as real as the locked-in vibes of the audience trance. She explained, "I'm full of emotion and want a release. And if you're onstage and it's really working and you've got the audience with you, it's a oneness you feel. I'm into me, plus they're into me, and everything comes together."

The fans got so into Janis and the band that they began storming the stage. The first time was in Cleveland, where people ran through the band while they were playing a song and began trying to pull the bangles off Janis's arm. She was shocked and startled, saying, "What are you doing? I'm trying to sing."

"Performing with Janis was an adrenaline-raising thing," James Gurley said. "I would never be able to go to sleep till past dawn. . . . And so, there was always wanting something that would cool you out." Janis faced the question of how to reenter the everyday world after her shamanic ecstasies onstage.

Alcohol was always her drug of choice, her friends individually reported to me. Janis favored Rainier Ale when Linda Gravenites first met her, and that evolved into Southern Comfort. Alcohol was a social drug. People went out and had a drink together. As her career advanced, Janis's comfort in the general social realm seemed to diminish correspondingly with her need to be her public image. Every alcoholic, and surely Janis became one, has this thing, explained Bobby Neuwirth. She told him, "Someday they're going to find out that I don't really know what I'm doing." And she once whispered to Linda, "What if they find out I'm only Janis?"

With heroin, explained James, "it was a casual thing that started. None of us were strung out. Because it was just infrequent, you know. Every couple of months we might come across some heroin. It was always after the show." Sam Andrew told me quietly, "It was a spirit of adventure and Janis got into doing things other people weren't." There was also that sense of childish kinship, a belief in club membership based on the drugs you used or your way of life. "She said it was the blues-singer mystique, like Billie Holiday, to get real messed up," recalled Linda Gravenites.

"In Cincinnati, we went to a party with a fan after the concert, to a funky hippie pad. We all sat around," passing a needle and shooting junk. "It didn't seem insane to us at all, then!" laughed David Getz.

"Someone told me that Albert Grossman sent him to get Janis some heroin," said Bennett Glotzer. "I say, 'Bullshit!' That's not what Albert would do." So he didn't get Janis heroin or support her in her habit. Did it matter? He did other drugs. The message was always *what* drug you did. In California, while they were recording *Cheap Thrills,* someone found a packet of heroin on the seat after the band got up from a restaurant booth. Albert was called and he canceled an upcoming gig; instead he flew the group to New York for a talk. Heroin was serious business to him. If lectures could have worked, he could have succeeded in ending any use of the drug.

Janis's situation was complicated by the public's need to watch her flaunt her newfound freedoms. The more outrageous Janis was, the more "in" she was. Soon even the parents of her fans began talking "hippie." The press promoted the idea that breaking down barriers was the gift of youth to society. Janis still read *Time* magazine every week, cover to cover. Where was the balancing force for her? All messages praised the dissolution of barriers and the creation of a new world. And her public image represented one of the forces for change.

In 1968 the scene began changing. Things didn't feel right. On April 27, 1968, during the days of peace and love, fans came backstage and stole Janis's beautiful handmade cape that a fan had given to her.

★

In Ann Arbor, Janis quipped, "They loved me so much, they stole my black pants before I got my purple pants on."

Janis told Rasa, "It isn't worth it," and *that* seems like it was truly from the heart. "Everyone she met," lamented Linda, "had a preconceived idea of who she was . . . and that was what she related to. So that's what she reacted back. So she lost huge chunks of herself by disuse."

She was beginning to feel the repercussions of becoming a youth-culture Moses. Her success burdened her life like a ball and chain. "Fame is a contract between the audience and the famous, where the seeker knows less about it than the appreciators," wrote Leo Braudy in *The Frenzy of Renown*. Janis was no longer controlling her life. It was controlling her.

Still, she hadn't lost her sense of humor. "She called herself a 'social phenomonemone' [fe-nom-o-nem-o-nee]," laughed Linda, remembering Janis's parody of the phrase *social phenomenon*. Commenting on her new life, she tossed aside grand illusions with this pithy statement: "There's a lot of TV in being a musician."

The novelty of being a white, female blues singer made Janis fabulously successful. It also held her in a prison whose limits she was just discovering. This predicament brought out the worst in Janis—her narcissism. She didn't just demand love, she demanded worship. The world had become unreal and she had no idea of her limits. Most people get feedback from the world that helps them define their personal aspirations and limits of acceptable behavior. Janis's success threw her former assumptions away. She wanted her life to be as gratifying as her stage performances.

She seldom thought about the repercussions of her actions. Linda Gravenites explained, "She'd do things without reflection and worry about it later. But it never stopped her from doing anything. The only time we had a fight," she continued, "was because I had this man I thought was gorgeous and wonderful. One night at the Avalon, Janis got a ride home with him on his motorcycle. I thought, hmmm, she's not thinking, she doesn't realize what she's doing to me. The next day she said, 'Linda, you're taking this well.' I thought, she wasn't unaware. She knew what she had done to me! I went *smash* with the coffee cup." Linda disagrees, but I wonder if Janis was testing the fidelity of her relationship with Linda. Like a three-year-old, Janis demanded to know if Linda would love her, even if she did something awful.

Not everyone played into the new worship routine. Janis could depend on Linda Gravenites and her other longtime friends. Linda Wauldron came for a visit with her two-year-old daughter, Sabina. No matter the time or distance, that relationship was still down-to-earth. Janis could confide and wonder about life with Linda Wauldron, just like when they had been roommates way back when.

Pat Nichols was also a dependable companion. After the ego-enhancing possibilities of one performance Janis and Pat went to a bar and drank Ramos Fizzes. With Pat she could expound on how fantastic her life was becoming. Other times she went to concerts or played pool at Gino and Carlo's Bar in North Beach. Pat chuckled about the times Janis came to a place where Pat waitressed and gave her a break by waiting the tables for her. "They don't know who I am," Janis hooted to her. "They tipped me a quarter!" There were small reminders of reality, but they seem to have been too few.

Janis's life became ever more tied to the East Coast, away from the antibourgeois scene of the West Coast. At least when she was in California, the San Francisco beliefs supported her style. They provided some help to guide her through the new situations her increasing success forced upon her.

New York held Janis's business influences—Albert Grossman, her manager; Clive Davis, the head of CBS; and the bulk of the national press. Together, their influence on Janis seemed to undermine her relationship with the rest of the band. Elliot Mazer explained, "Janis's ultimate goal was new. She didn't strive to play Las Vegas or prime-time TV; she wanted to play clubs and turn kids on." Elliot believed that popular music was more about communicating emotion than about technical competence. Big Brother was unequaled in that. "Anybody who saw how good that band was to an audience should have maximized it rather than change everything," Elliot exclaimed. "Technical competence has little to do with what the audience gets."

People were whispering in Janis's ear, "You're better than the guys in the band. You should leave them. They're holding you back. They're going to ruin your career and you'll just be penniless again."

Janis believed her press clippings, and in spite of her guidepost of "being true to herself," she started thinking that others knew what was best.

According to Elliot Mazer, Albert's office was no haven from the doubts expressed by Clive and the press. Nick Gravenites got the same feeling about Albert from other encounters with him. Nick remembered, "Albert would say, 'You love these guys but I'm more interested in you. I will get you a deal for two million dollars, but only if *you* get it. I won't put the money into the other guys' pockets.' " That's the way he was. Janis was only twenty-five years old and forced to decide between band loyalty and a dreamlike financial success that seemed to hinge on leaving the band. All the while, the press was harping that the band was holding her back.

Big Brother taped an appearance on the *Hollywood Palace* variety show on September 29. The guest host was Don Adams, of *Get Smart* fame. Big Brother appeared with Barbara Eden from *I Dream of Jeannie.* Nothing felt right about the evening. The band stood on pedestals and there were no electrical cords on their instruments, though they were expected to pretend they were playing. Instead of live music, the instrumentals were from a canned track sent over from Columbia. Only Janis sang live. Don Adams attempted some witty remarks that made the band feel he was apologizing to the audience for Big Brother's music and promising something better in the next act.

The pressure from the press accusations and the group's true weaknesses raised questions about alterations. Dave remembered Albert asking about changing lead guitarists. James was in a period of heavy alcohol use, and after an evening of his almost falling offstage, Albert asked if the band would consider replacing him. "Never," they all chimed, holding their sense of family too dear.

Nick also recalled Janis pleading with him to ask Albert if he would like to manage her separately from the band. Janis talked to Sam about her intention to go solo, asking him if he'd stay with her if she formed a new band. He agreed. She also talked to Dave about continuing with her at one point. James remembered that all the press brouhaha about the band needing a split made the eventual breakup more a relief than a surprise. Peter, however, hit the roof. When Janis met with the band and made her formal announcement, she told Sam she wasn't taking him along. In spite of that, Sam helped her form a new band. He suggested new guitarists and even called them to talk about the possibility. Ultimately, Janis decided she wanted Sam to join the new band, which he did.

Janis had entered the big time. She made tough business decisions like the rest of them. She continued to love the guys, see them socially, and occasionally play music with them. Yet her career decisions were now solely her responsibility.

9-28-68

Dear Family–

My goodness, it's been some time. Oh & so many changes!

We're back in Calif. for 2 more weeks–going to do the Hollywood Palace show so watch. Then off on our final tour, a college tour of the East & we're even playing Austin–about the 25th of November. Our last gig together will be Hawaii, the 6th & 7th of December. We're going to spend about a week over there w/all the wives & friends & then play. After that begins my hardest task. I told you, you remember, that I was leaving Big Brother & going to do a thing of my own. Well, I have to find the best musicians in the world (I already have 2) & get together & work. There'll be a whole lot of pressure because of the 'vibes' created by my leaving Big Brother & also by just how big I am now. So we've got to be just super when we start playing–but we will be. A lot of pressure too because of the way it's to be set up this time–I'm now a corporation called Fantality which will hire all the musicians & pay all the bills–much more responsibility but also much more chance of making money for me as my price goes up, I pocket the extra, or rather Fantality does. Albert told me–are you ready?–that I should make ★½ million!!★ next year counting record royalties.

I'm already doing pretty well for money. I have a tendency to spend whatever I have as soon as I get it but I've been getting so much recently that I just can't–I have everything I need plus several thousand in the bank. Last week I bought a 1965 Porsche convertible–very fancy & high class & a great car too. And a new stereo & a color TV & more clothes & Linda and I are now on a vacation–Lake Tahoe & Reno. Incredible. Who'd have thought?!!

Our record is a success story in itself. We got a gold album in 3 days! We go up to #4 on Cashbox next week with a bullet–that means it's expected to go higher.

★

*We've been playing bigger & bigger concerts lately although 20,000 at
Newport was the best. Played the Hollywood Bowl & the Rose Bowl
recently. The most fantastic thing of all happened at the Rose Bowl. We
closed the show on a big Pop Festival–lots of the biggest acts. The stage was
set in the middle of the football field & the cops wouldn't let the kids out
on the grass near us–rules. But on our encore I kept asking them to let the
kids dance, they wouldn't so here I am, looking at the audience singing
"Down on Me" & all of a sudden they broke, just like a wave & swarmed
onto the field. They ran to the edge of the stage & started trying to touch
me. I reached down & shook a few hands then turned to go down the back
stairs but when I got there, nothing but kids, thousands of them reaching,
reaching. They were pulling on my clothes, my beads, calling, Janis, Janis,
we love you. I was completely surrounded & being buffeted around when the
cops rescued me & put me in a car–had to drive to the dressing room. Car
was surrounded at all times by kids on the windows, roof, fenders, hood.
Made a Beatle type entry into the dressing room as they were trying to
break down the back door. Incredible! Can't say I didn't like it though.
Man, I loved it!!*

*Linda Wauldron has been around–Malcolm shipped out & she's visiting.
She & her 2 yr old Sabina stayed w/me for (ran out of ink in
Tahoe–finishing in San Francisco . . .) a week. The first time I'd spent
much time around a young kid–nearly drove me crazy! I sure am glad I can
sing–I'd make a lousy wife & mother. Not too bad, actually. Linda & I
have been having dinner parties–lots of food & charming men, some
famous, all charming. I'm recovering from one last night now.*

*My new place is really shaping up beautifully–shot some pictures for
Playboy (clothed) in my bedroom which were fantastic! Looks like a harem
room (whatever they call them) all fringe & fur & madras & pillows.
Should look fantastic in Playboy.*

*Now that I've frittered away one summer, lets start discussing next
summer. I really would love to have Mike out to visit & I have enough
room but I can't set any specific dates till we find out where we'll be. But
lets plan on it okay?*

*Bought some beautiful antique furniture the other day–all Victorian &
carved. A desk & a coffee table, being delivered today.*

*All I can think of now–be sure to watch Hollywood Palace–we tape it next
week but I don't know when it'll be shown.*

All my love XX write me at home for another week, then New York, the Chelsea.

XXX Janis

Janis sometimes telephoned with the latest news when she was too busy to write. Following the calls, Mother would write letters to Janis expanding on her thoughts and feelings about the subjects they'd discussed.

GOOD NEWS

to hear your report of singing being happiness and your own dream come true! While we do not know what part of each of the many news stories are quotes, etc., we do KNOW that you have achieved a *tremendous* success in a field of your own choice and every one of the steps you have taken have made it possible. So, your family salutes your happiness and your success and your developing business acumen and even your awareness of the continued need to grow in the field of your choice as you mentioned when you phoned about adding new instruments to your band and getting it professional as well as native talent. So, we would like to hear from you regularly about each of the steps, plans, itinerary, formats, styles and continued happiness. Glad to talk to you.

Mother

Some of the fall 1968 tour was a wonderful high for Janis. When the group played at the Newport Folk Festival, Janis was thrilled to be on the same bill as her Austin mentor Ken Threadgill and old friend Juli Paul. Janis also met Kris Kristofferson there.

But the band was feeling strained. The suppressed frustration with Janis leaving the band was affecting relationships on- and offstage. Dave Getz felt Janis was trying to upstage him during a long drum solo when the rest of the band was supposed to exit while Dave played. In the middle of his solo Janis reappeared carrying an extra drum for Dave to play and the audience roared at her entrance. Dave got real pissed as she walked offstage, and he kicked the drum over. She turned around and yelled, "Fuck you!" They finished the set and leapt into an argument backstage. Janis complained, "Why did you kick that drum

★

over? You really made a fool of me. I was just being nice bringing that drum out." Dave scoffed, "You didn't bring that drum out to be nice. You were just trying to upstage me and get your ass out onstage again. You put it where I couldn't even play it!"

Another time, in Minneapolis, after finishing the grueling song "Road Block," Janis stood at the microphone saying thank you. She was winded and was breathing quickly and heavily into the microphone as she talked. Peter said in an aside, "Now we're doing our imitation of Lassie!" She glared and said something to quiet him. They both backed off and finished the set.

Big Brother was booked solid that fall, performing ten out of sixteen days at the beginning of November. It was tough and took its toll. Janis told one audience demanding yet another encore, "I ain't got nothing left to give, lover." The strain wore her down, and illness forced her to cancel the very gigs she craved most—Austin and San Antonio.

She recovered from her illness quickly enough to play the Houston Music Hall on November 23. Mom called to reserve tickets for the family and the news got back to Janis. She telephoned and said, "Mom, I think I can get you in. You don't need to buy tickets!" We got front-row complimentary tickets, and sat beside the Bowens, Patti and Dave McQueen, and other Texans who knew the promoters.

We arrived backstage in time to see Janis verbally level a stage-hand for closing the curtain while she was on the other side. She had been stuck out there, until her groping among the material revealed the opening. Patti turned to Pop. "I think you should take her home." Pop sighed and said, "It's too late. It's just too late for that." Pop winced, then tried to ignore the whole thing as we hugged and Janis escorted us to her dressing room. I had never seen an official star dressing room, and was a bit surprised. There was a couch or two, makeup mirrors with bright lights, and scattered people who were silent and staring. It felt uncomfortable.

Janis and Patti hugged and talked about their vastly different lives. Janis said, "I'll be the star, Patti. You be the mama." She gave no one an opening for questioning her new life. She defined it as beyond their experience.

After a bit, everyone decided the crowd had subsided sufficiently to risk leaving the hall. Janis carefully told us that if she yelled, "Run," we were to go as fast as we could to the car. The fans might be waiting and we couldn't afford to let them catch us. As we emerged from the hall, a group of screaming girls rounded the corner, shouting, "There's Janis!" She yelled to us, "Run," and we barely made it into the car before the raised hands of running teenagers reached us. We stopped at Janis's motel and ate dinner with her and the band at the coffee shop. It was mundane. It was quiet. But we needed the small talk of visiting. Too soon we were off for the ninety-mile drive back home.

The story Janis obligingly repeated for the press through 1967 and 1968 was that of the mistreated outcast who made good. She embellished the "They hurt me" story, which reflected the Haight-Ashbury hippie view of an "us versus them" world. Some of her quotes were milder than others, but one went so far as to say that her family kicked her out of the house at age fourteen. Our parents were crushed. Not only was Janis flouting most of the morals that their generation prized, but she was lying about her relationship to her family in a very public way. They felt powerless and wronged. The little resentments stewed.

Janis began to recognize a change in the scene and her attitude in a November 24 *Los Angeles Times West* magazine article. She said, "The best time of all was Monterey. It was one of the highest points in my life. Those were real flower children. They really were beautiful and gentle and completely open, man. Ain't nothing like that ever gonna happen again. But for awhile, there were kids who believed they could make it all better by being better. And they were better and it didn't make a bit of difference." The reporter asked, "Are you bitter about it?" Janis said, "In a quiet way. But I've always believed people are screw-ups and are always gonna lie."

Janis was turning her back on the dream, the fantasy of the love generation. But she was fully embracing her personal success attained by riding the hippie wave. Her new 1965 Porsche Cabriolet, Super C, was her pride and joy. The only proper way to distinguish its plebeian ownership was to turn it into a hippie auto. Dave Richards, a friend and the original lone equipment man for Big Brother, hand-painted the car with images of Janis and the band. What a trip it must have been

★

to race along the California freeways, a flash of turquoise, yellows, and reds, with the top down and her hair blowing. The dash was painted with a regurgitating face, spewing the viscera of life out to the world. Yes, that was the Janis image, the one who let it all hang out.

Regrettably, the band's planned trip to Hawaii never happened. On December 1, 1968, Big Brother and the Holding Company played its last gig, a benefit for the Family Dog in San Francisco. How fitting that their beginning and end were in the same place with the same crowd. It was the end of a grand group. Though things changed, Janis still loved the guys. Pat Nichols emphasized, "Janis's feelings never changed for Big Brother."

CHAPTER THIRTEEN

THE BAND
FROM BEYOND

★

Well, I'm gonna try just a little bit harder
So I won't lose, lose, lose you to nobody else
Well, I don't care how long it's gonna take me
But if it's a dream I don't want nobody to wake me
Yeah, I'm gonna try just a little bit harder

—Jerry Ragovoy and Chip Taylor, "Try"

ECEMBER 21, 1968, Janis premiered her new group. It had taken almost two years to develop the Big Brother sound. She only had three weeks to get the new band's music together before they debuted. Janis had never formed a band. Her method of choosing a group was to get help from her friends and manager. She used the expertise of Michael Bloomfield and Nick Gravenites in selecting members and putting together a new sound. Both were gifted musicians. Michael was a very bright scholar and a musicologist. Nick always brought a deep dimension to his music, sharing the inspiration he found in the Bible and the Torah. But getting together was not all it took to be a band. They needed to know each other, and that demanded time.

Janis went with horns and a rhythm-and-blues sound. Aretha Franklin was big that year, and Janis wanted to be like her. Her roots were still entwined in the bountiful music of the Louisiana swamplands, in the bars she knew in Vinton on the state line. She had always been captivated by black culture. This was her chance to let her heart soar and her feelings marry the sounds that had always enchanted her.

★

Clive Davis and Albert Grossman also undoubtedly influenced her new sound. Elliot Mazer felt that Clive sought to reduce her raw style and throw out the mean and nasty blues, aiming for a more middle-of-the-road audience. Albert just wanted Janis to find her style. If adding horns interested her and would help her evolve into the authentic Janis, then he was for it.

The debut on Saturday night, December 21, 1968, consisted of a fifteen-minute set as the next-to-last act of the Stax-Volt show in Memphis, a town revered as the gateway to blues country. She was the only white act on the bill, the only "outside" act invited to the show. She wanted to be accepted by the real folk, but the black half of the audience had little idea of who she was. They weren't familiar with her or most of her material.

Janis sang well but the band wasn't together. "One Memphis musician suggested," *Rolling Stone* reported in February 1969, "that three months at Hernando's Hideaway, the Club Paradise, or any of the Memphis night spots where they frisk you before you go in might give them an inkling as to what the blues is about." Even if they had been perfect at the sound they were striving for, they would have failed with that audience. A San Francisco soul/blues band could never be a Memphis band. There was little applause and no encore. Glibly facing the reporters covering her band's debut, Janis smoked a cigarette, jiving about the future and the importance of the blues to her. "At least they didn't throw things," she chortled.

Janis came home that Christmas. Michael pulled Janis aside and confided that he wanted to quit school and hit the road with her. She was delighted by his faith in her but counseled, "Don't drop out of school. You need to finish. You can visit in the summers!"

I told her about my college experiences. I had moved back home from the college dorm because I found our parents to be more liberal than my schoolmates. One of my high points had been attending a theatrical performance of Oscar Wilde's *The Importance of Being Earnest*. I exclaimed, "My favorite word is *earnest*."

Janis had kept in touch with her Texas friends, telephoning with tidbits of her success. The gang gathered for a Christmas party at Adrian and Gloria's house. Janis strode proudly around the party protesting loudly that she never sang without her band. The gang said, "Okay," much to her chagrin.

This was the first time Janis said anything negative about Jim Langdon to his wife, Rae. He was upstairs that night, screwing another woman, and Janis confronted Rae. "How do you stand for this shit? Still?" Rae began asking herself why she did put up with her situation. Why did she accept and nurture him, while he was free to be the nonconformist, the profane and irreverent artist?

Whenever Janis came back to Texas the same female dichotomy confronted her. She visited Karleen, who was married and had children. Karleen told Janis about the joys of motherhood, gazing lovingly at her young daughter. She was a woman who had stayed at home, an example of the road Janis hadn't taken. Janis was incapable of hearing her exclamations of delight about her life. She kept pressuring Karleen to get a tattoo like the one she had. It was almost as if Janis had to prove that she had made the right choice.

Janis and I went to the grocery store on Christmas Day to get cinnamon for the cookies we were making. We drove to the only place that was open. Janis and I were dressed for the festivities of the season, in long granny dresses. The streets were deserted, giving us a feeling of being the only people alive. Happy, loose, and carefree, we joked as we searched the aisles for our necessities. At the cash register I thought we took the checkout ladies' decorations in stride. How often do you see fifty-year-old women with their hair in French twists that have been sprayed with "snow" and have red Christmas balls stuck in carefully sculpted nests in their piled-high locks? We paid, and they snorted to each other about our long dresses and loose hair! We held in our howling laughter until the parking lot, then screamed, "*They're* laughing at *us?*"

There were quiet times too. Janis and I went to the beach one afternoon. We drove the long, narrow highway that snaked through the oil refineries, past the Menhadden canning plant and on through the village of Sabine Pass. We gazed at the miles of marsh grass that filled the Texas coastal plain up to the narrow sandy shore itself. We parked and stood with our faces to the wind. We smelled that telltale Texas coast odor and relaxed with the seemingly endless view of the debris of the tides—the scalloped lace made of seaweed, shells, and jellyfish bodies. "I forgot how nice it is in winter down here," Janis said with a sigh. "Yes," I replied, glad that she had said something good about our home.

★

Leaving the sanctuary of our house, Janis jumped back into the turmoil of her life. The San Francisco press was openly hostile to her leaving Big Brother. They saw her defection as a public denial of the values that had created the scene and her fame. Her leaving was evidence that the movement was not triumphing but disintegrating. Her career aspirations were interpreted as ego-driven self-glorification. She was falling prey to the financial lust and personal acclaim that the hippie culture openly disdained. For that reason, Albert's office scheduled the new band's tour to start in the East.

The new group spent the weeks before February 8, 1969, rehearsing and experimenting with their new sound. They still hadn't decided on a name for the group. Various monikers were jokingly suggested, including Janis Joplin Blues Church, Janis Joplin's Pleasure Principle, the Squeeze, and Janis Joplin and the Sordid Flavors.

Tuesday, February 11, was the official opening of the tour. The Fillmore East sold out tickets for four performances. Reporters from the magazines *Time, Life, Look,* and *Newsweek* dominated the complimentary tickets. Mike Wallace was there with a *60 Minutes* crew, taping a segment entitled "Carnegie Hall for Kids."

The band opened with Sam Andrew on lead guitar, Terry Clements on tenor sax, Richard Kermode on organ, Roy Markowitz on drums, Terry Hensley on trumpet, and a temporary bass player, Keith Cherry, who was later replaced by Brad Campbell. The only song that Paul Nelson of *Rolling Stone* deemed acceptable was "Work Me, Lord" by Nick Gravenites. The rest he panned as "failed to mesh, stiff and preordained." The audience response was called "respectful." Nelson described his after-concert interview of Janis, saying, "Janis seems that rare kind of personality who lacks the essential self-protective distancing that a singer of her fame and stature would appear to need, [and] the necessary degree of honest cynicism needed to survive an all media assault. . . ."

Nelson also reported Janis's abundant apologies and explanations for the band. She said the sound was not developed yet. She was still hunting for a musical director to enliven the arrangements. She protested that the group needed time playing together to get into each other, etc. Nelson was also surprised at Janis's open plays for support in saying, "Don't you think I'm singing better? Well, Jesus fucking Christ, I'm really better, believe me!"

The article in *Rolling Stone* also reported that some fans thought Janis was at her best ever. Other fans, however, liked her better with Big Brother. One said, "Her thing now is showboating." Another felt that "success had most definitely spoiled Janis Joplin. This new thing was a brassy burlesque show . . ." The reporter wrote that while "the opening wasn't a success, neither was it any sort of a disaster."

The biggest difference from Big Brother, of course, was that the new band was a hired one of professional musicians. There was no commitment to the democratic band ideals she'd lived with before. Offstage they were different as well. Terry Clements was into yoga and health foods, contrasting sharply with Janis's ever-increasing drinking. Also, "they weren't as interesting to be with," Sam Andrew remembered, "because they didn't have breadth. They were more one-dimensional, into their music. In Big Brother, Dave had a master's degree in fine arts, Peter was into photography, James was one-of-a-kind, and I was a linguist."

"Janis wanted to love the people in the band," explained John Cooke. How could she develop that degree of affection and respect with less than two months' rehearsal? Though the new band recognized her as the leader, she was uncertain in guiding them. Big Brother had made decisions by voting. Janis had no experience in telling musicians how she wanted them to sound behind her. The guys in the new band knew more than she did about music and had more experience in performing and touring. Her failure to assert her role as band leader would be harder to overcome as the band solidified its attitudes.

Cut loose from the confines of Big Brother, Janis was developing and embellishing her image. She didn't talk about San Francisco and the movement any longer. Now she talked only about herself. She told a *Newsweek* reporter, "I didn't start out to be a singer. I started out to be just a person on the street, like everybody else. But suddenly I got sort of swept up into this singing thing. And after I got involved in it, it got really important to me if I was good or not. . . . I just like to say one thing on stage, 'Let yourself go and you'll be more than you've ever thought of being.' "

She began to display her bottle of Southern Comfort prominently onstage. The press always seemed to mention what or when she was guzzling. The *Detroit Free Press* called her "100-Proof Janis Joplin." *Newsweek* reported her late breakfast as "an unlovely concoction apparently made of wood alcohol and chocolate syrup." Backstage stories described her uninhibited manner of smoking and "always indulging in the hard liquor from bottles that had collected on a table." The band reportedly joked that she wasn't psychedelic, she was a psycheholic. Press stories often mentioned an alcohol-related story, such as spending an afternoon drinking sweet vermouth over glassfuls of ice. Janis said she believed in "getting stoned and staying happy."

A caring, more experienced black blues singer approached Janis backstage one night. "You're going to lose your voice if you keep drinking like that," she told Janis. The warning crept into her thoughts, but she wasn't yet frustrated enough with her life to try to deal with it.

The New York Times Magazine quoted her as saying, "Yeah, I know I might be going too fast. That's what a doctor said. He looked at me and said my liver is a little big, swollen, y'know. Got all melodramatic—'what's a good, talented girl doing with yourself' and all that blah blah. I don't go back to him anymore. Man, I'd rather have 10 years of superhypermost than live to be 70 by sitting in some goddamn chair watching TV. Right now is where you are, how can you wait?"

She toyed with the press's and the public's fascination with the sexual component of her music and stage persona. She moaned about the boring life on the road, saying, "Guys on the road at least have girls they can pick up, but who are the boys who come to see me—fourteen-year-olds, man." She described music in sexual terms: "I can't talk about my singing, I'm inside out . . . like when you're first in love. It's more than sex, I know that. It's that point two people can get to they call love, like when you really touch someone for the first time, but it's gigantic, multiplied by the whole audience. I feel chills, weird feelings slipping all over my body, it's a supreme emotional and physical experience."

"Being an intellectual creates a lot of questions and no answers," Janis told a *Newsweek* reporter in February. "You can fill your life up with ideas and still go home lonely. All you really have that really matters are feelings. That's what music is to me."

That same month, she told Paul Nelson of *Rolling Stone* that she was still hunting for a band name, and laughingly toyed with the moniker "Janis Joplin and the Joplinaires."

248

At least she had the opportunity to delve no-holds-barred into the blues. In February Janis was blessed with the addition of another great musician to her band, baritone saxophonist Cornelius "Snooky" Flowers, who also happened to be black. He provided essential expertise in making the band the success that it became. "With us, she opened up musically," Snooky remembered. "With Big Brother, they only had two or three chord changes, but we brought her along." Snooky called her "Little Mama," and always made her feel at home. He had a special rapport with Janis because he grew up close to our hometown, in Lake Charles, Louisiana. Snooky helped bring the band together, possessing what Sam Andrew described as a "joie de vivre," a unique quality that made the hours they spent working together more fun.

Most of the musicians in San Francisco supported her efforts and wished her the best, yet the public and press anger at her new experiment continued. Had she violated that unwritten contract with the audience? Was she daring to try something new when the audience just wanted to hear her and Big Brother play "Down On Me" yet another time? The first few months performing with the new group tested her conviction in becoming a solo artist, no matter how confidently she talked. There were always those lurking questions: "Will I fail by myself?" "Should I have stayed with Big Brother?"

In the middle of March the band ventured to California to play to a hostile West Coast audience and press. The media pressure might have been one reason she gave herself for increasing her use of heroin. It might also have been her view of "the thing to do," since the whole Haight-Ashbury scene was experiencing a heroin epidemic in 1969. Linda Gravenites found Janis purple on the floor one day in March. At least she knew how to revive Janis from that heroin overdose. "Walk," Linda commanded, forcing her to pace up and down the California hills around her house until three A.M. Janis mumbled, "What happened, Linda?" She replied, "You were trying to die!" "No," Janis said, ignoring Linda's warning.

Unknowingly, Janis was flirting with a lethal combination of drugs—alcohol and heroin. Heroin by itself seldom kills people, even in large doses. In combination, what is known as a polydrug effect takes over, and breathing can stop, resulting in death characterized by pulmonary edema—swelling of the lung tissues with water. By adding

★

heroin to her preferred alcohol, Janis was challenging the odds to get her.

Oblivious to the problems around her, Janis focused on continuing her professional success. During the five performances the band played in California in March, she was still struggling. Her repertoire included "Maybe," an old Chantels R&B tune from the late fifties; Robin and Barry Gibb's popular song "To Love Somebody"; and even a Rodgers and Hart show tune, "Little Girl Blue."

Janis called home to wish me a happy birthday and brag about her upcoming appearance on *The Ed Sullivan Show*. "Mama, Mama, guess what they're paying me for this one show." Mother replied, "You're worth every penny of it, darling."

March 16, 1969, Janis appeared on *Ed Sullivan,* an achievement recognized as the pinnacle of acceptance by the public and the powers within the industry. Janis appeared in a hot-pink satin blouse with darker pink pants and an open vest held together by strings of gold links. She sang a thundering "Maybe" to a wildly responsive audience. It was broadcast with a state-of-the-art attempt at a psychedelic backdrop of swirling black and white lines fading to superimposed pictures of the band. At the end of the show all the acts came onstage together and Ed Sullivan walked out too. Janis enthused to Aunt Mimi, "You can't believe! You're nobody unless he asks you over to shake his hand." When Sullivan reached out to Janis, she beamed as bright as any star in the sky. That meant everything in the world to her. Sullivan said, "Thank you," and Janis's heart was screaming, "Yes, yes, yes!"

After the show, everyone gathered at Max's Kansas City. In his unpublished memoirs, Sam Andrew described a large disparate group of people—Larry Rivers, Edie Sedgwick, Andy Warhol, Bobby Neuwirth, Rip Torn, and Debbie Harry. Tiny Tim roamed around carrying his ukelele in a paper bag. Salvador Dalí emerged from the crowd and chatted for awhile in the middle of all the madness.

Janis was still developing the songs. She worked with a fellow in New York who wrote out the music, arranged it, and made corrections in the vocal harmonies. Everything was coming together. A month in Europe gave the group cause for hope. Finally, the audience could feel the music that they intended. The press was full of glowing reports wherever the band went. The European audience listened, free of Big Brother expectations. They came to the concerts to love Janis and found her eminently worthy of their adoration.

A high point of the tour was the show in Frankfurt, full of American servicemen. After a rousing encore, Janis told the audience that she was going to do another show to be taped for television. Anyone who wanted to stay was welcome. The majority of them did. At the end they stormed onstage to dance alongside the mistress of "Get It While You Can" rock and roll.

The concert in London at Albert Hall was also a raving smash. Bobby Neuwirth's tape made in the dressing room after the show clearly captured a bubbling Janis saying, "It was dynamite, man! I haven't been this excited in two years, man. . . . Don't you know how happy we must be? . . . We really broke through a wall that I didn't think was possible. Like ever since we've been here [Europe], like the audiences we've had are the best. We've always felt, 'Oh, too much! That's really wonderful of them.' But everybody says, 'Don't expect that of the British audience. Don't expect them to do nothing, man.' When they first got up and started dancing, it was just like a big hot rush. And we just went, 'Oh, yeah!' It's like a whole other door opened up, a whole other possibility that had never occurred to you, like air just came in that you could breathe, maybe. . . ."

This was the first time Janis had been in Europe. In spite of the schedule, she and Bobby Neuwirth frequented art museums to see the great works she had studied in her days as a painter. She went to the theater in London to see a production of *Hair*. She was regaining her old cockiness. Responding rudely to a punk in a pub after the theater, Janis ran to Linda Gravenites and exclaimed, "He hit me! Did you see that?" That type of reality-testing hadn't happened for a long time.

John Cooke exclaimed, "That band could be fun! Especially in Europe, there were some wonderful concerts, and everybody felt good." Janis could feel justifiably that they had become the synchronized performing blues band she had wanted. Surely everything was okay now! Then the night of the Albert Hall show, constant friend Sam Andrew, whom she affectionately called "Sam-O," overdosed at the party celebrating the band's tremendous success. Once again, Linda Gravenites was there. Janis and Linda put Sam in the bathtub and covered him with ice-cold water. They jostled him constantly to keep

★

him conscious. He seemed to fight their efforts, almost refusing to breathe. In the end, he made it through the ordeal. So did Janis, but she didn't seem to learn anything from it.

"I was the one who had to tell her she was wrong in a way she could accept," sighed Linda. "She could get real defensive, real quick. I hated dope! I just hated it!" Linda continued, "I asked Janis why she did dope, and she said, 'I just want a little fucking peace, man.'"

Heroin, like alcohol, dulls the senses. It appeals to people who are cursed with an unquenchable inner turmoil, a fast-paced introverted dynamic that asks questions on top of questions. Both heroin and alcohol can partially stop some types of stress and conflict. Janis was undoubtedly anxious, a condition worsened by her position in life and a lack of other grounding mechanisms. She enhanced her sense of being adrift by a liberal use of alcohol and a diet that was heavy on sugar. The more she used external aids, the more she swung emotionally and the more she needed to calm herself. Rather than making it better, they made it worse. She began a process of self-medication, mostly using alcohol and, in 1969, heroin.

Janis was never interested in psychedelics, which have the opposite effect. They heighten the inner life, blowing up the complexity and intensity of everyday experience. "With dope, she turned into this grayish-colored shell, and I liked the real her, not this slack nobody," Linda Gravenites explained. Linda had gotten to the end of her willingness to put up with the dope. Sam's close call in London convinced her she needed a break. Linda chose to stay in England when the tour returned to the States. Her convenient excuse was that George Harrison, one of the Beatles, had requested one of her artistically crafted jackets.

Returning to New York, Janis heard that James Gurley's wife, Nancy, had died of an overdose of heroin. They had been camping in the woods alone, both sailing on smack while lying in sleeping bags under the picturesque pines. James was charged with murder because he had injected the dope. What did Janis and Sam do when they heard? Why, they went out and scored some dope and both shot up together. It was such horrible news that they just had to escape. Janis sent twenty-five thousand dollars to help pay for James's legal expenses.

It's not as though Janis wasn't around people encouraging her to quit. "Snooky was great," remembered Sam. "If he'd had his say, things would have been very different. He didn't have any bad habits or anything. He'd been in Nam and had seen drugs and he didn't do any. He was like a preaching person." Yet Janis told Sam the narcissistic drug taker's fantasy: "Nothing's going to happen to me, I'm from tough pioneer stock!" Bobby Neuwirth encouraged her to substitute one drug, alcohol, for the other, heroin.

Back in the States, the band expected the American public to continue the enthusiasm of the European public and press. They were wrong. Americans were unaware of the triumphs Janis had experienced elsewhere and continued to scorn the group. "Janis really believed the media put-downs," Snooky said, sighing.

The end of April and the first half of May, she toured the East Coast again. Based in New York at the Chelsea Hotel, Janis flew out for gigs on the weekends. She hated New York. It represented everything she didn't want to be, and contained the trappings of society that she rebelled against. The people were different and the pace of life was more frantic. In New York she had to concentrate on the "bizness" instead of art.

Albert's office was in New York, as were Columbia's headquarters. She also had to contend with press interviews and receptions arranged by her press agent, Myra Friedman. Myra was a special type of friend, a break from the monotony of male musicians. Bennett Glotzer, Albert's partner, explained that one of Myra's assignments in the office was to be Janis's companion when she was in New York. Janis was, for most people, a humorous, captivating, and inspiring friend.

Janis's schedule gave her May 12 to June 16 off for a much-needed vacation. She said, "Traveling around, you don't see anything but the inside of airports, Holiday Inns, and men's gymnasiums. . . . Success gets in your way. There's so much unspoken crap in the air that you're really alone." Janis told Pat Nichols when she went back to California, "Never again! I can't stand the one-night stands and little rooms!" Still, Janis wasn't about to give it up. I'm sure she did hate it, yet I think there was an ambivalent tone in her laments. Janis almost seemed to cry, "Isn't it wonderfully horrible? I'm so successful that I have to put up with all of this!"

The band spent ten days in Los Angeles, June 16–26, to record a new album. They arrived in Hollywood and dropped into a party at the home of Tom Wolfe, who was wearing all white—a latter-day Mark Twain, Sam Andrew said. Hollywood was not their kind of town. It oozed what Sam called a soft evil, a preoccupation with the image, the surface, the meaningless look of things, and ignored the substance. The general malaise of society at that time compounded their subconscious anxiety about life—bombing was intensified in Vietnam; Senator Edward Kennedy accidentally drove his car off a bridge, causing the drowning death of his companion, Mary Jo Kopechne. Even the stock market was down.

The band stayed at the Landmark Hotel in Los Angeles. Janis called Sam Andrew to her room and they shared some dope together. Afterward, with both of them chemically relaxed, she told Sam his services would no longer be needed. He didn't react, so she said, "Well, aren't you going to ask me why?" Sam replied that it didn't make much difference since he was going anyway. She just mumbled, "I guess you're right." A week later she asked him to stay on until she could find another guitar player, and he was glad to have the opportunity to be generous by agreeing.

The album they were wrestling with in the studio would be called *I Got Dem Ol' Kozmic Blues Again Mama!* The phrase *kozmic blues* was a true Joplinesque missile. It combined the real angst of worrying about death with the sophisticated twist of misspelling *cosmic*. The result laughed at itself because it was laughing.

Gabriel Mekler, who produced the album, was a professional taken with who was important and who wasn't, adding a divisive element to an already bumpy band relationship. He ignored the suggestions of the experienced musicians, making them bristle and curse under their breath, and spent most of his energy dealing with Janis, the star. This created a greater rift in the group, between Janis, who couldn't quite assume her position as leader, and a group of more experienced individuals who had little cohesiveness other than a common source of a paycheck.

In July, touring in the East again, Janis called the group the Band from Beyond. Later, that group was referred to as the Kozmic Blues Band, after the album title. That album never received the acclaim that some of her other work did, but it is a particularly grand collection of Janis's performances.

The group changed members frequently, a symptom of Janis's confusion about what direction to move in musically. John Cooke described the band's transitions in *Rolling Stone* on November 12, 1970:

> The only two musicians who were with the Kozmic Blues band throughout the year of existence are Brad Campbell [bass] and Terry Clements [alto sax]. Bill King was the original organ player but the Army started chasing him after two gigs and he was replaced by Richard Kermode, who stayed for the duration. Roy Markowitz was the drummer for about half of the year, followed for a week [during some of the recording sessions] by Lonnie Castille and then by Maury Baker. After Sam Andrew left, John Till brought his guitar to the group and has been with Janis ever since. Marcus Doubleday played trumpet briefly and decided the road was not for him anymore. He was followed first by Terry Hensley and then by Luis Gasca, who was with the band for more than eight months. . . . In the last few weeks Luis was followed by Dave Woodward. Snooky Flowers [baritone sax] was added to the band early along, and was in it to the end.

In 1969 Janis was truly in the big time. She had recorded her second *Dick Cavett Show* on July 18, a sign of her acceptance by the intelligentsia. She appeared in a pinkish-red satin V-necked blouse over matching bell-bottom pants, topped with an open-weave gold vest and the trademark strands of beads, hundreds of bangles, and multiple rings. She proudly wore gold-heeled sandals with red stockings that matched her outfit. She was happy and relaxed, in fine form that night. She opened with "To Love Somebody" and later in the show sang "Try."

She talked about characteristic topics: why she seemed different from other female singers; her feelings about touring; whether or not Cavett had "soul." Janis said, "You do, everybody does." She joked that when her career ebbed, she would "learn how to bake organic bread and have babies." Janis spoke repeatedly about reviewers. One had asked, "Can a rock star making hundreds of thousands of dollars sing the blues?" Janis fumed at the idea and explained that "when you get up there and play, it doesn't have anything to do with money.

Playing is about feeling. . . . It's about letting yourself feel all those things you have inside of you." Later in the show she interjected a note about excesses in reviews: "I've read pages upon pages comparing—'I noticed the Shelenberg influence in this particular riff'—when the guy was just going 'suubey-doobey.' " She also commented that writers are often saying more about themselves than about what they are ostensibly describing. She noted that this was particularly obvious to a reader if he or she had been to the event the guy was covering.

During the show, Janis also appeared with the Committee, the improvisational theater group that then numbered twenty-five people and had three locations—in San Francisco, Los Angeles, and New York. They provided a "Soul Lesson," with a black man teaching a white man how to walk and talk. Their final number was a "Symphony of Emotions," in which all the actors and guests on the show played an emotion. Cavett was love and Janis played frustration. It was a fun event, with a conductor guiding the overall tone of ten people or so emoting vigorously in unison.

She also taped the *Music Scene* television show on September 8. The Committee hosted the show, with Pat Paulsen and Janis among the guests. Janis was included in the group of privileged stars invited to Tommy Smothers's house the night of the broadcast for a party kicking off Donovan's tour. After listening to the man sing while he was perched atop a pillow on the diving board, the group gathered to watch themselves on TV. Also at the party were Andy Williams, Mama Cass, Peter Fonda, Mason Williams, Stephen Stills, and Graham Nash. That was in her off time! To think that she could relax in this kind of company was ludicrous. She was stuck in the all-capitals JANIS JOPLIN mode.

The veneer of fame was beginning to wear thin. A year earlier, she had sometimes behaved like a groupie. By 1969 she was explaining, "When I first met Dylan, I didn't recognize him, or George Harrison. People look different in person. They're always littler than you think." She realized that it had affected her personal life differently than expected. "Success gets in your way," she told *Newsweek*. "You have something that's bigger and more important than just being with people. I can't just hang out anymore on the street. Now, whenever I see people—except my own friends—there's an artificial atmosphere, people talking to you for the wrong reasons."

When the *Kozmic Blues* album was released, CBS gave Janis a stack of albums for her personal distribution. She piled the copies in her home, getting ready to give them to friends. She and Pat Nichols invited two Hell's Angels over to celebrate a birthday. In through the window stormed fellow Angels, who found the two-foot-high pile of albums enticing. As they helped themselves to the records, Janis screamed, "Get out!" She expected her invited friends to support her, especially when one of the uninvited hit her and knocked her back. "When you ask one of us, you ask all of us," they said. Helpless, Janis and Pat watched the party disappear, and most of her albums as well.

The most celebrated event of rock and roll, love, and community flowered on August 15 and 16, 1969, at Max Yasgur's dairy farm near Woodstock, New York. "The human onslaught created emergency conditions—food and water shortages, overflowing toilets, medical crises," wrote John Morthland in *The Rolling Stone Illustrated History of Rock & Roll*. "Rain turned the festival into a huge mud puddle. The talent lineup was the greatest ever assembled, but hardly anybody heard the music, and hardly anybody cared." More than 100,000 of the people attending had no tickets, adding to the already burdened logistical preparations. With help from the rock stars and donations from the promoters, the crowd made do, solving their own problems. Morthland wrote, "Woodstock became the symbol of youth solidarity."

"A whole new minority group," *Newsweek* quoted Janis as saying in her enthusiastic description of the event. "There's lots and lots and lots of us, more than anybody ever thought before. We used to think of ourselves as little clumps of weirdos." Not anymore. Woodstock announced the taking of America by the youth. The rebellion was no longer based in California; it had swept the nation.

The site was an easy drive to Albert Grossman's house, and invitations to his place to stay or eat were the credentials of elitism. Janis and other musicians bought food and brought it to the festival to give away, she told me later. Still, it felt pitifully inadequate to the challenge of enduring the hardships of rain, wind, mud, insufficient toilets, and the generalized mayhem of populating a medium-sized city in a couple of days.

The press called Woodstock the crowning achievement of the love culture, yet love hadn't changed Janis's mind about letting Sam

★

Andrew go. He had quietly packed his guitar and exited the band merely three gigs before the event. Sam thought Janis had wanted a musical change, but perhaps it was more. He was the last connection to her rock origins in Big Brother, and probably her best friend in the group. He had always told Janis there were better guitar players and was never sure why she kept him on that long. Perhaps letting go of Sam was another step in her commitment to long-term professional success. It was undoubtedly hard for her to fire Sam, no matter how sound she felt the reasons. Though romantic rumors had linked them together, the only time they slept together was shortly after she fired him. She was always unwilling to make clean breaks in her relationships. Was having sex with him after she'd severed his professional responsibilities a way of asking forgiveness? Were either of them testing whether Sam's leaving the band was what they wanted?

Janis played the Texas International Pop Festival on August 30, 31, and September 1. A lot of people were trying to copy the success of Woodstock. Promoters who had put on the Atlanta Pop Festival on July 4 scheduled one in Lewisville, Texas, at the Dallas International Motor Speedway, for Labor Day weekend. Heavy blues was the dominant music, and Janis received several standing ovations. The *Dallas Morning News* reported, "An unexplainable feeling of generosity and rapport developed over the 3-day period that exemplified the true meaning of brotherhood."

Stopping in Port Arthur for a brief family visit, Janis tried to explain the impact of these events. She expected us to realize that the hippies were now a horde of believers. The revolution had come! We smiled and said, "Wow, that must have been great," but for us, Woodstock was just another article in *Time*.

She brought Snooky Flowers, the baritone saxophone player in her new band. He was the first black man entertained in our house—a milestone of sorts, though it just felt like a friend coming over. He was gracious and affable. His warmth and protectiveness toward Janis was comforting to our parents, especially when he took her down to Houston Avenue to enjoy the local black clubs. Janis returned full of stories of meeting the African-American population of the city, which had been denied to her as a young white girl. She elatedly confided to me, "We talked to this really together old black lady who's seen it all, and she said I'm 'really down,' man, 'down'! I can't believe it!" Janis needed acceptance from black society, from those whom her high school friends had defined as the heroes of the underbelly of America, the guideposts of her life. When Otis Redding died, Janis and Sam Andrew sat up all night listening to his music. Janis said that she just wanted him to hear her sing and say that she was good.

Janis crowed about her Russian lynx coat. It wasn't enough for her that the coat was beautiful and that it fit her image perfectly; it also had a walloping good story behind it. She pranced about, telling us the tale she had told *The New York Times Magazine.* "I had the chick in my manager's office photostat every goddamn clipping that ever had me mentioning Southern Comfort, and I sent them to the company, and they sent me a whole lotta money. How could anybody in their right mind want me for their image? Oh, man, that was the best hustle I ever pulled—can you imagine getting paid for passing out for two years?" They offered to buy Janis a coat of her choosing. She went to a fur warehouse in New York when it was closed to the public and wandered through the racks of coats. She could pick any one of them. From a South Texas perspective, she had surely hit the big time. The climate was so temperate in Port Arthur, no one wore a fur coat unless they wanted to show off. For Janis, the gift of a fur was clearly a high honor.

The next time I saw Janis was on *This Is Tom Jones.* Taped on September 21, the show was telecast on December 6, 1969. She sang her favorite song, "Little Girl Blue," and a duet with Tom Jones, "Raise Your Hand." More than a year later, after Janis died, Mom received a lengthy letter from a Louisiana girl who said she had met Janis while working as a gofer on the *Tom Jones* show. She had run away from home with the dream of being an actress. She went to Los Angeles and, a few days before starvation, landed a job on that show. She was assigned to help Janis with whatever she wanted. The letter implied that she had found herself pregnant and didn't know what to do. Evidently, Janis took the girl under her wing, brought her to a party, introduced her to everyone, and then put her on a bus back to the Gulf Coast. "But I haven't talked to my family since I ran away," she had worried. "No matter," Janis told her, "they're your family and they'll love you and want you back." Janis could tell her that from experience. Enclosed with the letter sent to Mom was a photo of a woman with a baby she had named Janice. I wonder if Janis had held a fleeting wish to get on the bus alongside that girl.

Janis's career continued its skyrocketing climb. Hippies were becoming as common as the girl-next-door. The *Monterey Pop* film was released to acclaim in May 1969, and Janis's picture was on the cover of *Newsweek* that same month. *Easy Rider* opened in July, another in the series of alternative movies that included *Alice's Restaurant* and *if . . .* In spite of what looked like a trend, the top-grossing movie of 1969 was *The Love Bug,* far from a counterculture model. From the inside, the decay in the movement was more obvious. Thirty-six store-fronts stood empty in the Haight. The eighteen that remained open had added metal grates over their fronts, reported Charles Perry in *The Haight-Ashbury.* Dave Moriaty said, "That spring there were seventeen murders in one month." Compared with the dynamism of 1966–67, rock and roll and the social movement were directionless. Ever-increasing commercialization changed even the rock bands that emerged from the movement.

The ugliness underlying peace and love burst to the surface in Altamont, California. The Rolling Stones scheduled a free concert for the end of their 1969 United States tour. About 300,000 people gathered at the Altamont Speedway. Again, the facilities were woefully inadequate and crowds overwhelmed the intended excitement of the music. *The Rolling Stone Illustrated History of Rock & Roll* said, "Altamont turned into a nightmare of drug casualties, stench from toilets and fires and food and vomit, faulty sound, and, finally, the brutal violence visited on the audience by pool-cue- and knife-wielding Hell's Angels who said they had been hired (by the Stones and cosponsors Grateful Dead, for $500 worth of beer) as security guards." Late in the day a young black man pulled a gun and was knifed by Angels, reportedly in full view of the audience. Three other people died at Altamont as well. What had begun at Monterey and climaxed at Woodstock crashed and burned at Altamont.

If that wasn't enough, public opinion violently censured the communal-family ideal because of the distortions and insanity of the Charles Manson cult. His group had brutally murdered pregnant actress Sharon Tate and four others in her home. The unleashed emotions and unfettered behavior of the movement was backfiring all around.

The pithy, jocular, cocky Janis had already given way to the disillusioned, fed-up-with-their-ignorance Janis. "I've said it all fifty times," she complained to a reporter seeking an interview. The reporter said, "But I've got some really good new questions. Tell me about your past." Janis often made a stab at distancing herself from the heart of the very movement that had crowned her with such glory. She wrestled with whether or not to believe. She often said, "I'm a beatnik. They reject society and the world disappoints them. Beatniks believe things won't get better—so they say to hell with it and just stay stoned." Once she said, "Look, I'm not a spokesman for my generation. I don't even use acid. I drink." But on *The Dick Cavett Show* she defended hippies, saying, "I believe in the youth."

A more thoughtful Janis arose. "Usually, [interviewers] don't talk about my singing as much as about my life style," the *Port Arthur News* quoted her as saying. "The only reasons I can see is that maybe a lot of artists have one way of art and another way of life. In me, they're the same. It just came as a natural thing out of the way I love, the freedom needed and sought. I wanted the same thing that happened in music and I just happened to have a voice. The kids are interested because it is like a graphic representation of what it is like to really let go and be whatever you are."

Janis played the Hollywood Bowl on September 23. It was a rousing good time, highlighted by Aunt Barbara's attendance. Barbara went to the event intentionally dressed to kill in her mink stole. She sat proudly in the first row. Janis stopped her patter to the audience at one point, looked down at Barbara, laughing lovingly, and said, "You're going to ruin my image if they find out your my aunt."

On October 19 she arrived in Austin, Texas, looking "magnificently frowsy in a silk embroidered shawl, white imitation fur hat and lavender tinted sunglasses," wrote the *Austin American-Statesman*. She sang for seven thousand "frantically enthusiastic" people at Gregory Gym. It was a cathartic experience for fans and star alike. Janis said, "I used to go to school here and they never treated me like this." Finally, she had that sense of triumphant homecoming she needed.

But all was not well. Later that fall, John Cooke gave in to his reservations about the scene and retired as road manager with two months of the tour to go, saying, "It just isn't fun anymore." That year Janis's drinking had visibly affected her performing. Anyone with

★

knowledge of alcoholism could have seen signs of the disease in her behavior. She would wake the morning after an evening out and ask Linda, "How'd we get home last night?" Memory blackouts were one sign that she'd gone past any reasonable level of drinking. Janis said she drank before performing just to loosen up a bit. Like musicians tuning their instruments, Janis drank to get her emotions and adrenaline flowing.

But her abuse of alcohol also showed when she drank and did outlandish things. One time, she drove to a bus station with Snooky, stopped her Porsche, and called out for anyone who wanted to party a bit: "Two to go!" Snooky laughed about it, citing the story as Janis being "totally free." In New York, she went to Max's Kansas City, where Andy Warhol and friends held court. She ended up getting kicked all the way under the table by one of them during a verbal and physical fight.

On October 5, Janis and the band played Winterland in San Francisco, and Ralph Gleason blasted them. It was John Cooke's last gig with her, and he thought it marked her conclusion that the brassy black blues sound wasn't going to be publicly accepted.

Snooky reacted angrily when discussing those days. He felt that because of Ralph Gleason and the bad press, the Kozmic Blues Band got little credit for helping Janis to develop as a singer. They were the band that toured Europe, yet all the acclaim over there proved worthless back in the States. He summarized Janis's decision to disband the group, saying, "Kozmic Blues was a little too powerful for Janis. She never felt totally comfortable because she knew the band was better than she was, musically beyond her."

Janis had an encounter with the Houston fire marshal during a concert at the Houston Coliseum on October 26. At many concerts on that tour she had cautioned her audience about overreacting. She sometimes warned kids about dancing because there were cops in the wings waiting to put a bum rap on everyone. In Houston, the fire marshal walked onstage during her vocal absorption in "Ball and Chain," saying, "Miss Joplin, we'd like you to ask the crowd to move back and cool off." Janis stopped singing, the band ground to a halt, and she stared uncomprehendingly at Paul Carr of the Houston Fire Department. She put the microphone down, covered it with her hand,

and told Carr what she thought of his action. Janis finished the song and left the stage, grumbling to herself.

The police and firemen were cracking down at all concerts across the country. They were anxious about the potential problems that could result from thousands of kids standing on chairs and getting wild in a huge hall. People could get trampled. The Houston scene almost repeated itself for Janis in Tampa, Florida. There the cops pulled out a bullhorn to interrupt "Try." Janis stopped and replied, "I know there won't be any trouble if you'll just leave!" Refusing to exit the stage, the cops returned to using the bullhorn and Janis flipped out. Rather than holding the mike down and cursing at the policemen, as she had done in Houston, Janis rent the air in Florida with her expletives and was promptly arrested, hauled offstage, and taken to jail for using profanity. Her response to reporters was, "I say anything I want onstage. I don't mind getting arrested because I've turned a lot of kids on."

Her arrest made *Time* magazine on November 28. I read it and a lump formed in my stomach. What was happening to my sister? What did she think she was doing?

Her behavioral changes were noticed by people who followed the scene. Robert Somma wrote about Janis in the fall of 1969's *Drama Review* covering "Rock Theatricality." Somma wrote, "At first, Janis relied on her range and volume; then, as she ascended the scale of popularity, she loosened a bit, added a few stagey components (booze, skittish body English) and, with the inevitable fatigue and posturing, her once raw but compelling style became hardened, cynical, and neurotic. She seemed to lose touch with herself in the overwhelming contact she faced."

Perhaps in her search for her music after Big Brother, Janis was trying to jump beyond her "white girl blues." She was still emulating those she had idolized and thus was caught in a transitional period of musical expression. In 1969 she was being challenged to craft a new authentic white sound that also had soul.

That fall, Albert sent Janis to a physician, Dr. Edmund Rothschild, an internist who had often seen Albert's clients. Dr. Rothschild found Janis to be a bouncy, vibrant, and exciting young woman. She pranced into his office wearing a translucent blouse with feather boas

★

in her hair. She told him she wanted to quit using heroin but that she didn't think of herself as a heavy narcotics user. He took a thorough oral history and did a physical exam, finding nothing unusual. He found her heroin use to be intermittent and episodic.

Many heroin users take the drug to escape psychological pain. The practice Janis described to Dr. Rothschild was quite the opposite. She used heroin after a concert, a thrilling success. Perhaps she was using heroin the same way a speed freak does, to avoid the depression of the speed wearing off, as a way to ease back into life. Perhaps Janis used heroin to help come off of the adrenaline high that she roused herself to during performing, to get some peace from the intensity of being onstage.

Janis felt her alcohol use was a problem, and her doctor agreed. She used alcohol excessively and daily. Though the results of the tests he ran on her liver were normal, he counseled her about the complications that could arise if she continued drinking at her present rate. At the time she was very thin and described an atrocious diet to Dr. Rothschild. She ate a lot of junk food and sweets. Alcoholics often live in a state of hypoglycemic reaction to eating sugar, craving and being energized by sweets and then crashing when the sugar rush is gone, and starting the cycle again. Alcoholics often have poor diets, replacing healthy food calories with unhealthy alcoholic ones. Janis wasn't ready to deal with her drinking, bravely saying that the healthy lab results proved that she was okay.

They focused on her desire to quit heroin. Dr. Rothschild emphasized the dangers in what she was doing, that she could never know the strength or purity of the drugs she was injecting straight into her body. He didn't feel she was really physically addicted to heroin at that point but suggested methadone as a safe way to get her off of the drug. He prescribed enough methadone to last for one week.

Methadone prevents heroin from having its pleasurable effect and stops the craving addicts feel. But it isn't the high of heroin that hooks addicts; it is the side effects on their basic system. Clean addicts who relapse into using heroin again say, "It makes me feel normal again."

Successfully recovered addicts have found that dropping the drug isn't enough; you must also change your friends and social activities. Rather than partying in a group that reinforces the desire to use this or that drug, someone in recovery needs a social system that supports abstention. Without knowing it, Janis seemed to be trying just that. She and Pat Nichols made a pact with each other. They had both decided to quit using heroin. They felt that their mutual weakness for it fed on each other. They would not see each other until they were both clean. It was a beginning.

Quitting something as addictive as heroin is often a multi-staged process. Janis was trying, but she was just approaching the crux of the issue. She still invented reasons why dope was okay for her. As Janis saw it, physicians equated psychological health with social conformity. She saw her choice as either abandoning the life-style that had brought her such acclaim and behaving like a schoolteacher in our hometown, or continuing the habits that she was seeking to quit. The way she framed the choice itself almost obligated her to deny recovery as a viable option. She needed to drift back in time to the days when she wrote the lyrics, "I got no reason for living / Got no cause to die / Got to find a middle road." The question was, was she willing to give up something in order to see a middle road?

When Janis got back to California on brief visits, she felt the loss of her longtime roommate, Linda Gravenites. Linda was still in Europe, not eager to reenter Janis's drug-based way of life. Janis wrote to Linda and persuaded her to return to Marin. She plied her with stories of forgoing drugs and living her life the "other" way. According to one of Janis's letters that Myra Friedman had, she planned walks in the woods, yoga, and learning piano and possibly horseback riding. Her romantic version of clean living was merely a denial of the tasks she truly needed to do, as was her continuing consumption of alcohol.

The biggest constructive change she made was buying a house. Janis contacted Aunt Barbara's friend Ed and sent him to comb the area for a special retreat. He found a perfect home in Larkspur, a small community in Marin County, just across the Golden Gate Bridge from San Francisco. It was a mountain community consisting of many narrow roads snaking in and around the hills. Located at the end of a cul-de-sac in a hilly, treed area, the lot on which the house stood backed up to an open-space woodland. It was the quintessential rock-star home of the time: lots of decks with redwood trees growing up through them, and lots of glass. "It was in the West Baltimore area near a street called Shady Lane, which thrilled Janis to no end," said Bob Gordon. "She always said she wanted to live on Shady Lane."

Janis's musical taste was softening. She spontaneously debuted Kris Kristofferson's "Me and Bobby McGee" while playing Nashville in November. The reception was enthusiastic. It helped to give her a new sense of direction.

The Kozmic Blues Band played its final performance in Madison Square Garden on December 19, 1969. It was a triumph. She knocked the audience out and got them jumping in the way that she loved to do. Clive Davis threw a celebration for Janis after the gig. "She seemed in bad shape," John Cooke recalled about that party. He thought, "Gee, am I glad I left the tour when I did. I didn't want to watch this happen to her." Change was hard, especially when the part of her that was demanding the change was corralled by such lethal barbed wire as heroin, alcohol, and superstar status.

All her life Janis had craved freedom. It was her banner, her sword, her proudest description, and her most misunderstood goal. She thought being free meant doing what others didn't do. But it also means free *not* to act. By 1969 Janis couldn't choose whether to do her wild-woman, do-anything routine. She had to do it.

In 1969 Janis had learned many lessons. She had avoided responsibility for her career, left the decisions to too many experts, and lost touch with her very essence. Her touring schedule consumed her personal life. She had little time to develop or maintain relationships. She had lost control of her self-image, and believed the press stories about her uniqueness. She had courted the excesses that brought her meaningless strokes of approval. Janis was beginning to see that she had to make some changes. The year 1969 was a turning point.

CHAPTER FOURTEEN

REST, ROMANCE, AND REGROUP

★

I don't want much out of life
I never wanted a mansion in the South
I just wanted to find someone sincere
Who treated me like he talks
One good man . . .

—Janis Joplin, "One Good Man"

*I*N THE FIRST four months of 1970, Janis finally had time away from the hectic days of touring. She could sort out her life, plan her next professional moves, and relax. She inaugurated the era with a smashing housewarming party at the tail end of December 1969. This was no down-home party. She produced the counterculture equivalent of a country-club gala. The event was catered and a white-jacketed bartender stood ready to mix anything anyone requested. There was another, less elegant aspect to the party: The rock-and-roll crowd could not resist the tendency to party in excess. A few guests climbed woozily off into the pine woods to make mind-fogged love under the forest canopy. Others threw up and passed out under a redwood deck. The party was, at least, her attempt at a little grandeur.

Janis's Larkspur house felt cozy. The interior was all redwood. Sliding glass doors highlighted the walls. They brought the outside vistas into the room and framed the view like so many paintings. Janis's home did not fit the ostentatious, wild image that her press stories loved to portray. There was no neon there.

★

Janis decorated this new symbol of her arrival with Victorian furniture and Oriental carpets. She chose warm colors and soft textures that blended with the hippie folk-art style of the times. The house was full of knickknacks—things bought on impulse just because she liked them.

1-23-70

Dear Family . . .

I managed to pass my—gasp—27th birthday without really feeling it. Not doing much now—just enjoying the house. I'm one month into a supposedly 3 month long vacation which looks like it will end up a month & a half vacation. Sigh. Ah, such a funny game . . . when you're nobody & poor, you don't care—you can just drift but when you get a little position & a little money, you start really hustling to get more & then when you're numero uno, you've gotta really break ass so nobody catches you! Catches you?! Two years ago I didn't even want to be it! No, that's not true. I've been looking around & I've noticed something. After you reach a certain level of talent (& quite a few have that talent) the deciding factor is ambition, or as I see it, how much you really need. Need to be loved & need to be proud of yourself . . . . . & I guess that's what ambition is—it's not all a depraved quest for position, Mike, or money, maybe it's for love. Lots of love! Ha . . . . .

Having some beautiful work done on the house—the guys are half artists & half carpenters—turning a plain unused & unexciting wall into a sunburst of redwood planks w/a bar & a set of shelves flowing organically out of both ends—all rich wood & flowing shapes. Really defies description—I'll send a picture when I'm through.

Linda & I are going to Rio for Carnival in Feb. Did you see Black Orpheus? It took place there—the forefathers of Mardi Gras. The whole city parties for a week—dancing in the streets! So we're going to go. . . .

Got a new little white dog—George's daughter. If you ever decide to breed Lady, I'd like one of the puppies, we want lots of dogs! & Linda has asked specifically for a borzoi.

My piano teacher just arrived, got to go.

> *All my love & thanks for calling!!*
> *Love,*
>
> *Janis*

High on her list of new acquisitions was dogs. Janis's wonderful mutt George was the mainstay of her life in California. Loyal and loving, he was there whenever she came home. But one day in late 1969, she took him to town in her Porsche, and he jumped out to go for a stroll. Janis went on the local radio station asking for help in finding him, but the best she got was vague rumors. Sometimes she felt that a fan had taken George and was showing him off as a present she had given him. Janis gave up hope of ever seeing George again. Like many people faced with a loss they couldn't accept, Janis took steps to limit her vulnerability. Instead of replacing George with one dog, she got a pack of mutts from the pound as well as purebreds selected from dog shows.

"Her house was nice, tasteful," Nick Gravenites said, "not over- or underdone. I was always welcome there. She would have parties, not all night debaucheries, but an afternoon vodka and orange juice thing. She loved her home and her dogs."

Janis's roommate, Linda Gravenites, had returned from her extended stay in Europe. With her help Janis was trying to get back to the middle road. She had started trying to kick heroin in December, and the effort continued. There were trips to different physicians and the use of Dolophine to suppress the need for the drug. Some days were clean, others were not.

Janis and Linda schemed up the idea of going to Brazil for Carnival. "Going to Rio was to be without dope," explained Linda, "to have a crazy enough time without it." Linda never let Janis forget what she thought about dope—she hated it! It had gotten so that every time Janis went into her bedroom and shut the door, Linda held her breath until she reappeared. Janis knew she had to quit, but she wasn't sure how. Indeed, most of the people she knew who did the drug were also trying to quit. The heroin epidemic of 1968 and 1969 was turning into a battle to quit in 1970. As early as 1968, 60 percent of the drug busts in the Haight had been for speed or heroin, not marijuana. The years of use were showing. People were desperate to get clean.

Clearly the times were changing. In 1970, the mid-calf-length midiskirt replaced the mini. President Nixon was withdrawing troops from Vietnam. Unemployment was up to 6 percent, and eighteen-year-olds got the right to vote. The United Farm Workers gained recognition from the grape growers in California. The Beatles introduced the songs "The Long and Winding Road" and "Let It Be."

Janis telephoned home about her exciting plans to see the Rio Carnival. The folks tried to act supportive, hoping she would have fun. But on reflection, talking with Karleen in a grocery store, Pop said, "I don't know why she's going to all the trouble to get to Brazil. All she's going to do is get drunk, and she can do that as easily at home."

Officially, Carnival in Brazil started on Friday evening, February 6, and ran until the morning of Ash Wednesday, February 11. In reality, events last for two weeks. It is a pre-Lentan ritual, in preparation for a time of fasting and penance. During that time, all normal activity ceases throughout the country, but particularly in Rio. Daily parades, from midafternoon until dawn, link strangers dancing mindless sambas through the streets. Some are in wild costumes, though many wear as little as possible due to the hot Brazilian summers. Women often flaunt their sexuality in erotic dress. Timidity is the only thing that is frowned upon during Carnival. It is a time of banishing inhibitions and releasing desire. Carnival is not just a series of events. It is a state of mind, trying to force rebirth by the sheer intensity of personal abandon.

In the evenings there are many balls for the middle and upper classes. Janis and Linda attended the Municipal Ball, where every invitation must be sponsored. Janis had managed to be invited by a silver-haired aristocrat, Mr. Mayo. His invitation even gave her entry to the presidential box. Unbelievable! Here she was in a foreign country, and her success entitled her to such honors. But once she was in the presidential box, it became obvious that she was on a different social level. Someone asked her to leave. With typical Joplin aplomb—a glass of champagne supposedly thrown in the bouncer's face—Janis exited. Once among the everyday folk, Janis and Linda had a great time, dancing and laughing the night away.

On the beach, Janis wore a bikini that had dark-colored handprints on a white background. They were strategically placed on the panties and bra, as though gripping her body where it mattered. A slender fellow stood looking at Janis and her bathing suit. He had just come from a year and a half of canoeing and exploring the Amazon River in the Brazilian jungle. He looked rough, wild, and experienced.

"Hi, you cute thing," Janis said, in her jovial way of having fun with strangers. But this fellow started a conversation, and soon Janis and Linda were hanging out with David Niehaus and his traveling buddy, Ben Beall.

Janis always wanted a man who would love her for her soul. She wanted someone who could see past the veneer, whether it be the famous singer or the beatnik artist. In David Niehaus, she found that: "David was a real person," Linda said. "One of the few in the later part of her life." Amid a sea of one-night stands, she began a true love affair.

David and Ben were college friends reconnoitering after four years of intense living following graduation. David was an upper-middle-class Cincinnati kid who had studied communications at Notre Dame. He was an athletic six feet one and a half inches tall, two hundred pounds, with brown hair and green eyes. David had joined the Peace Corps after college and worked in a small village in Turkey. He saw traveling as a way to break out of the conditioning of American culture, to become free of prejudgments. He tried law school, but when he met Janis he was taking time off. He'd been to Woodstock, from there to Peru, and then down the Amazon River to meet Ben Beall in Rio. Ben had majored in international studies at Notre Dame and then joined the marines. He'd recently gotten out of a VA hospital, recuperating from multiple injuries from a grenade explosion.

Two days after meeting Janis, David said, "You know, you look like that rock star, Janis Joplin." She paused and turned, saying, "I am Janis Joplin." Could anything tell her better that David loved the person Janis and not her image? He hadn't even realized who she was when he fell for her! David was a kind man, but too intense to be soft. His voice never wavered, reflecting the kind of charged ferocity that could send him around the world and make him captain of the New York Yacht Club Boat of the Year.

The fellows soon moved into a large suite of rooms at a beachside hotel with the girls. Then they set out to have a good time. David and Ben had been in Rio awhile so they knew the sights. They were pretty disappointed with Carnival, finding it too commercial to be fun. So the group partied around its fringe, strolling around the nightly parades, dressing in costume, and frequenting the bars.

Janis kicked heroin when she was in Brazil, and David helped.

★

He held her through the symptoms of withdrawal—the weakness, insomnia, chills, and waves of gooseflesh that give the process its name: cold turkey. It was one day of hell surrounded by two days only slightly better. But it worked. She was clean. "I really did love her. She was a great girl, she's in my heart, I can tell you that," he said. "Janis chose to do heroin because she couldn't escape feeling all the emotions of her fans." He said that Janis was supersensitive to those around her and couldn't turn their emotions off, even when she was offstage.

"Albert wrote her a few telegrams saying, 'Get back here, get to work.' " David was proud that Janis wired back, "No. And don't lay that guilt trip on me." She was going back when she was ready. She was in charge of her life.

"We went into the jungle," he continued, "with nothing except stacks of money to buy antiques for her house. She went right with me." Hopping a jungle-bound flatbed, the breeze casting loose her billowing chestnut hair, Janis sang "Me and Bobby McGee" just for David. "Just two beatniks on the road," she described the experience later.

But still she couldn't escape her role. The first village they came to after weeks in the Brazilian jungle had its jukebox cranked up when they walked past the bus station. It was Janis's voice penetrating the South American air, singing a tune from her *Kozmic Blues* album, as though to shock her back to reality after her idyllic journey.

Janis did concede one professional gesture while she was in Brazil: She learned there had never been a rock-and-roll concert in Brazil, so she decided to put on the first one. Everything was ready when she climbed aboard David's motorcycle, dressed in a bikini and wrapped in a sleeping bag to keep warm on the drive to the site. It was scheduled at a beach five hours north of Rio. She lay her head on David's back and slept as they rode. Coming up over a hill, he swerved to miss a cement traffic island in the middle of the road. He hit the brakes, the bike skidded out from under them, and they rolled over and over and over. Janis hit her head on the curb and lay completely still. Someone came along in a Volkswagen and took them to a hospital. She had a concussion and couldn't do the concert.

Janis and David spent hours talking in Brazil, telling each other the stories of their lives. Janis talked about the importance of breaking into the music business and how she had first felt success in Austin at Ken Threadgill's bar. She told him that earlier in her life she had been really fat. She ate and ate because she was afraid she wasn't going to get anymore. Then she fasted down to nothing, and that helped her have the strength to finally make it. She tested her fear and rose above it. She saw the cycles of her life for what they were.

The lovers planned to return to California together, but the airport passport check uncovered an irregularity with David's papers—he had overstayed his visa. Janis's incensed attitude didn't help, irrationally yelling, "You're a cunt and this is a cunt country!" That was all the officials needed to hear to want to show her who had the power. They detained David for two days. Janis wasn't allowed to remain with him, either. They packed her off onto her scheduled flight to California. For someone with as tenuous a hold on reason as Janis, that was as good an excuse as any to score some heroin during plane changes in Los Angeles. Arriving back in San Francisco, she was already stoned.

What could David have said when he arrived two days later and was greeted by a gray ghost of a woman? Not to mention the chaos of the San Francisco rock scene. That was enough to confound anyone, but David seemed to know who he was. Janis was the one who seemed lost.

Watching Janis shoot heroin was hard for David, but he tried to see past it. He could accept alcohol, which, he felt, allowed people to face the things they weren't strong enough to face. He thought heroin was like alcohol, but much stronger. Once it was in your body, nothing mattered anymore, your whole body relaxed. He was totally against it, but he could understand why Janis used it. However, the drugs made him say, "Honey, I don't know how long I can do this."

Everyone oscillates emotionally. Sometimes life seems clear and easy, and other times it's almost overwhelming. But Janis also had to confront the crazy hours and schedule demanded of a musician. She could be intensely busy and out of touch with all her friends for several months and then be totally free for weeks. Her mood swings were always exacerbated by her use of alcohol and other drugs. Clearly her life had many moments of exquisite success. When she was on top, she loved it. Other times she felt small, and it terrified her.

★

But Janis tried to maintain an intimate relationship with David. She cooked him breakfast, rubbed his back when he was taking a bath, and talked with him for long hours about anything. Here was a man who confided, "Some of my best friends are books." David knew the soft Janis: "She made me happy. Nobody'd ever cared for me before. . . . I never really had somebody who loved me before except my ma."

They had fun together. Out riding around in Janis's Porsche, they passed Muddy Waters on the road. Janis hailed him, calling out, "Hey, come on over." They spent a couple of days together burning joints, drinking, and partying. There were always people around, good people.

"One night we wake up," David related, "and four or five Hell's Angels with guns in their belts and stoned on acid have eaten everything out of the refrigerator. 'Honey,' Janis said, 'get those boys out of here.' I got up, put my pants on, and walked into the living room, to be greeted with looks saying, 'Who is this asshole?' Returning to her side, I said, 'Oh, baby, you don't want me to do that. There's five of them.' So Janis opened the door and declared, 'You guys are assholes, 'cause you ate all my food and should have more sense than that. What are you doing here at this time in the morning, keeping me and my boyfriend up?' " Instantly, Janis turned those big, burly men into cowering third-graders, embarrassed about their indiscretions. Later, five grocery sacks were found in the kitchen, their contents neatly placed in the fridge.

Janis and David went to L.A. and wound up in a recording studio, curled up in a soundproof booth. They shared a bottle of tequila while Janis sang eight or nine songs in her beautiful voice, just for David.

David wrestled with the idea of staying with Janis as he tried to find a sense of his own life. Then, returning to Larkspur from a two-day solo skiing trip to Heavenly Valley, he discovered Janis in bed with a female lover, Peggy Caserta. Two days? Couldn't she be true for two days? But no, David had no claims on Janis, and this was the era of free sex. Peggy made it clear that she felt she had a prior claim on Janis. Their relationship went back for years. David thought Peggy tried to make him feel like the interloper. This proved to be more life than David cared to accept. He wanted a wife, a partner.

David declared, "Honey, I can't stay here." Janis proposed that he become her road manager on a planned tour with a new band that later became known as the Full Tilt Boogie Band. He considered it, but having a job wasn't the only problem. "I'll stop doing this shit [heroin] if you stay," Janis pleaded. But David didn't want Janis to blame him for her stopping drugs the next time she felt the craving. He wanted her to make the decision herself.

"It was too radical," David explained. "I'm sort of an ego person like she was, and every time we went out of the house she had five hundred people screaming around her car, that hand-painted Porsche. It just wasn't fun. I would have taken her with me in a hot second, but she wanted to go on this tour. . . . She almost came with me, but she had worked so long for all that. I called her a couple of times from Turkey, and sent her some radical antique things that the women used to wear. She wanted to be there, but it would have required her giving up everything. She wasn't ready to give it up. She'd worked a long time to get there. I was so young and so on fire. I wanted her to come with me. I didn't want to just go on her trip. I wanted to go on our trip." The best Janis could say was, "Maybe I'll see you later."

In December 1969, just four months before Janis parted with David, she had sat up all night with a woman she met at the Chelsea Hotel in New York. Janis advised her about whether she should marry her boyfriend or not. With the emphatic earnestness of one who was laying out the truth, Janis exclaimed, "If I ever meet a man who really loves me, I'll never let him go. I'll do anything to make it work." Only she didn't. By all accounts, David was the best thing that had ever happened to Janis. Yet when it came to choosing between love and her career, Janis stuck with the latter. That was hard. Many of her friends felt that she wasn't a feminist, that what she really wanted was a husband, kids, and a cozy home. But they were wrong; what she wanted was a career and a man who could fit into it. Did she just worry that the romance wouldn't last? Did she think David might prove as false as John Smith had? Was she forced to choose between her career self and her romantic self?

• • •

★

Janis's career questions were now endless. What kind of singer was she going to be? What kind of songs? What kind of band? Who to be in the band? Those are big questions for someone who always said her chief strength as a singer was her ability to communicate emotion. At least Janis wasn't alone. Albert Grossman provided the professional guidance and support that she needed. Realizing that the Kozmic Blues Band suffered from a lack of direction from Janis as band leader, she participated directly in selecting the next group. Albert and Janis listened to tapes of prospective musicians, visited shows to see them in action, and discussed and discussed.

"He doesn't direct me," she said of Albert. "He just finds out where I want to go, then he helps me get there. And he's there to comfort me when I need it. Man, that's important. I don't like to admit I need help, but I do, I do."

Janis had finished the blues-band fantasy, realizing it wouldn't be accepted by the public. She was a folk/blues singer who turned to rock and roll and then went to soul rock. The next step came through experimenting. Janis crafted a more individualized white-blues sound. She had risen to fame on the novelty of being a white female blues singer. Now she realized that it didn't mean acting and sounding black, it meant being the unique version of blues that could speak most directly to her audience.

Janis had asked both John Till, her guitarist, and Brad Campbell, her bass player, to continue from the Kozmic Blues Band to the new group. For the four months before the new tour, they received $123.40 per week, on retainer. She found her pianist, Richard Bell, while he was playing for Ronnie Hawkins's band. Listening to a Jesse Winchester album, she chose her organ player, Ken Pearson.

All she needed was a drummer. Janis heard him when she went to see John and Brad playing a gig with Snooky Flowers at a San Francisco topless club, the Galaxie. When Albert was in town, the two of them went. It must have been quite a sight to see Janis and Albert as a couple in a topless club—Albert with his paunch, gray corduroy jacket, and light sweater, with long gray hair in a ponytail; Janis with her saucy gait, bedecked in chattering bells and topped with mounds of wavy hair. Snooky turned the spotlight on them, saying, "Ladies and gentlemen, in this club tonight we have one of the finest singers . . ." They just sat there smiling.

After the set, Janis talked with Albert about Clark Pierson, the drummer playing with Snooky's band. She sent Brad over to see if he wanted to audition at Janis's house the next day. Clark hadn't even known who she was until Snooky introduced her. He laughed, "Well, I ain't got nothing else to do." He went over and the group played a couple of tunes in her makeshift studio in the garage. Standing beside Albert, Janis asked Clark if he wanted to join. She was happy when he said yes.

Clark was the last member to join the band. His week of drumming with Brad and John had already proven he could fit in. This band was a younger group than she had been working with in Kozmic Blues. Most important, explained John Cooke, "these guys were looking for a band that was their home. They knew that Janis was the boss, and they all liked each other right away. I think the fact that four out of five were Canadian helped."

April 1970

Hello!

Really rushing through rehearsals, have a new (2 of the same guys, 3 new) smaller band & it's really going fantastic! Great new songs—really needed new songs—so we'll do an album while on the next tour. Albert is lightening up my schedule a little because of my old age & because I put my foot Down! 2 mos on the road then 2 off, 2 on, 2 off, etc. So I can have a little personal life, I hope. I met a really fine man in Rio but I had to get back to work so he's off finding the rest of the world—Africa or Morocco now I think, but he really did love me & was so good to me & he wants to come back & marry me! I thought I'd die without someone besides fans asking me. But he meant it & who knows—I may get tired of the music biz, but I'm really gettin it on now! & doing much & fantastic & expensive work on the house. It's turning into a palace—all fur & wood & stained glass & velvet couches & chaise lounges & even a chandelier hanging in the middle of an eye-full of redwoods. FANTASTIC! Have a new puppy—a Great Pyrenees all white, one of the biggest dogs around—grows to be 180 lbs. all lumbering & loving, rare & expensive—from the Pyrenees mtns, long ago a cross between a St. Bernard & a Mastiff—named him Thurber, thanks for the books when I was young, Dad. It does make a difference.

LOVE,
Janis

★

277

By 1970, Janis had wide emotional swings, the highest of highs and the lowest of lows. She might change moment to moment, or stick in one frame of mind for days. "It was just that she was on fire. She had the power," David Niehaus said. "She was aware, and where that power comes from is from seeing the truth. She didn't always, but she had the power to see the truth. There was nothing that could stand up to her when she was clear. The only reason her career caused her problems," he explained, "was her personality oscillated to such extremes. So, when she was small, her career was overwhelming to her. You have to understand"—he paused—"it wasn't the career that was overwhelming to her, it was the state of mind. When she was in the big state of mind, her career wasn't overwhelming at all."

She sometimes lapsed into a needy-child routine, trying to force people to give her strokes. "Why don't people support me?" she wailed to Nick Gravenites. "People go out of their way to help others!" He replied, "Maybe you haven't asked them." "You do it," Janis urged Nick, because she was uncomfortable requesting help. "You ask for me." So Nick called friends and they suggested some songs for Janis to sing. That tough image Janis had chosen could be difficult to penetrate. She seemed more likely to chew someone out than to ask for help.

Janis needed what drug counselors call an intervention. An intervention should confront the user with the reality of what others see, of the changes that she may not notice in herself. Without knowing it, Linda Gravenites provided that experience for Janis.

When Linda saw David Niehaus leave, she decided that Janis would never quit dope. Linda couldn't live around heroin anymore. She was so close to Janis that she could tell her the truth. Sometimes Janis let herself hear it. Linda kept after her, talking about the heroin as the problem that it was. "Linda, you're being like a Jewish mother! Just don't talk about it," Janis yelled at her. "If you can't be quiet, just leave." Linda said, "Okay, I'll be gone tomorrow." She moved out of the house the next day.

Linda's declaration that she was moving out because Janis was incapable of quitting dope was enough to get Janis to make the decision. Linda had challenged her, and Janis never let anyone say she couldn't do something! She was still using heroin only on and off, so quitting at that point wasn't as hard as it could have been later. She was able to stop.

She took what help she could find, but found it hard to embrace the full psychiatric routine. Janis realized that heroin was an imposition on her life, and she wanted to quit. Did she pretend to herself that it was merely a bad drug that was the problem? The hippie belief in chemically based consciousness-raising was still in vogue. Did Janis buy that? The counselors she saw seemed to offer a remedy that denied the entire foundation and spirit of the sixties. Social-planner types with too little empathy is how John Cooke described her helpers.

And yet a new strength was guiding Janis's life, the power of a free mind. The nature of her artistry was changing. Her experience with Big Brother as a family band had made it difficult for her to adjust to the attitude of her second band as musicians for hire. With the third and newest group, Janis realized once again that the good vibes among them as people were essential. "Janis needed to love the people she worked with," John Cooke explained. Knowing that, she had been able to choose appropriate people. They became her boys.

Janis was becoming the vocalist that she had been telling people she could be. Throughout 1969 she gave interviews saying that she was learning to use her voice more, laying back and not pushing as much, yet getting the same effect. She used her power for emphasis. Janis also studied music, taking piano lessons to learn the theory behind what she knew only on an intuitive level. Nick Gravenites exclaimed, "Janis could sing a chord, three notes at once. How did she do that?" In his book *The Story of Rock,* Carl Belz wrote, "Unlike Big Brother, Full Tilt Boogie [her third band's eventual name] did not compete with Joplin's voice; instead, they let it range spontaneously, enriching it with a folk dignity that was its natural counterpart."

Equally vital was Janis's growing awareness of the difference between her personal and professional selves. She was thinking about the life and career she had crafted for herself. She and Bobby Neuwirth, among others, had lengthy discussions about the "need to have a certain stage persona, as a mask, not a phony, just a distancing of your most intimate self. . . . You don't have to give them all of you, just selected parts as appropriate."

In the converted garage studio in Janis's home, the new band rehearsed. One day, as John Cooke explained to me, Janis had a whim to acquire a nickname. Tossing a few around, the guys settled on "Pearl." Janis was trying to find a symbol for herself, to remember the "real" Janis. Her own name had become synonymous with her stage persona. "Pearl" was part of her attempt to be more of a singer and less of an entertainer.

Pat Nichols said that Janis's public and private selves were very different. "It wasn't that she was more subdued, but her laughter was free, not forced. Her sense of humor was more subtle. She sounded more like a little girl than a hooker," Pat finally exclaimed. She sighed and firmly explained that "Janis would have done as well without the persona of a loud-mouthed blatant hooker type."

Pat Nichols found Janis "a very spiritual person." She said that Janis was "afraid to let others see that." She didn't just throw the *I Ching,* she read the whole book. Pat said that Janis also read Rosicrucian pamphlets. Ken Thompson, a spokesperson for the Rosicrucian study complex in San Francisco, explained that they aren't a religion but a fraternity-type institution devoted to spiritual education. "Hippies were members," he explained, "because they believed education was good for people. Rosicrucians believe in mind expansion through education. We talk about the God of our heart. . . ." Their main teaching organ is a correspondence course, with weekly meditations, exercises, and suggested readings. A fundamental belief is the equality of all sexes and races.

A spiritual sense of personal responsibility tugged at Janis's continued drug use. Pat said that quitting heroin was part of Janis's inner recognition that she would have to get her karma together to achieve spiritual grace. Of course, Janis didn't jump on the resolution. She said she was going to clean her act up later, putting it on hold, so to speak.

One reason hippies came to rock concerts was to find themselves. Janis's generation was more strongly moved by rock concerts than by *any* social or civic gathering. When the hippies collectively started their search for meaning, they turned to lesser known religions. They chose spiritual practices from other societies, drug induced states, musical experiences, and an amalgamation of beliefs that constituted another way of viewing life.

Beyond her respect for the soul of humanity, Janis questioned formalized religion. The cynicism of her high school days and the built-in cultural conditioning of science led Janis to complain about some religion-oriented people: "Arrgh! They're believers!" Even when her former roommate had started meditating every day, Janis announced, "Linda, don't get too holy on me."

Janis needed religion without the judgment, an affirmation of her validity as a feeling person. She needed a way to discover her true nature, not an institution that enforced guilt and fear of hell. She needed a place where people freely admitted their failure at being the people they wanted to be. She needed honesty and openness.

Janis was ready to admit to the flaws in her life and be proud of her strength as well. She was forming a relationship with a new roommate, Lyndall Erb, who was trying to fill Linda Gravenites's shoes. But she was more easygoing and malleable than Linda. The new band was coming together, and it felt good. Perhaps that made it possible for her to return to the past a bit. On April 4, 1970, Janis appeared onstage with Big Brother and the Holding Company. She sang backup on "Mr. Natural," a song Sam Andrew wrote. She was still friends with the fellows in Big Brother, but there was a rift that had come from breaking the professional relationship. Their careers had not been doing as well as hers. It was strange that while the five of them were together, Janis got all the good reviews and the band got only negative press. When they put out an album without Janis, the reviews were great, but nobody cared. Their record didn't sell. Sam Andrew recalled Janis musing in 1969, "Back in 1968, would Big Brother have considered giving me more money and bringing horn players into the band?" He told her that the band probably would have, but she hadn't asked.

In 1970, questions about the advisability of having left Big Brother were still playing in her mind. In April she was getting ready for the Full Tilt band to try its wings in public in May. Her anxiety over the uncertainty of the public's response was very difficult to handle. Bobby Neuwirth, with his pal Kris Kristofferson, rose to the occasion. Kris had the charm and good looks that spelled Southern seduction. He was a Rhodes scholar with a gift for poetic lyrics, and was making a name for himself in the country-music scene.

★

Bobby and Kris brought the perfect escape, a roaring alcoholic romp that became known as "The Great Tequila Boogie." The partying started with Bobby and Kris in Greenwich Village. There was a whole night with Odetta, and then they carried it on out to the West Coast, landing at Janis's house. Perhaps Kris reminded Janis of David Niehaus. He was strong, rugged, and extremely attractive, as well as intelligent and well educated. He could be soft and gentle, but also liked to bellow in alcoholic abandon, just as Janis was prone to do. The main difference was that the music scene wasn't foreign to him. He was already working in it. While David couldn't find a place for himself within her professional world, Kris envisioned his future along a similar path.

They listened to Kris's albums, one with his picture as a young man at the Newport Folk Festival. He looked like a scared young kid onstage. It actually was the first time he had played in front of an audience. Janis mused, "Boy, am I glad you didn't look like this when I met you. I'd of never gone out with you." Shocked, Kris replied, "That's such a shallow way of looking at somebody, Janis."

Their first day of alcoholic revelry grew into three weeks of steadily downing tequila. "Janis drank them both under the table," laughed Nick Gravenites. She banged on his door early one morning, bottle in hand, saying she'd brought some friends over to meet him. Nick asked, "Where are they?" She pointed to some distant spots down the road, which were walking laboriously and hanging on to each other. They were barely able to make the trek to the house. Janis was bright and chipper.

Janis invited everyone to join the partying. She called Jerry Ragovoy, the composer of many of her most famous hits. She woke him up in the middle of the night with a telephone call, urging, "Come right over, we're having a party." He laughed to himself, responding, "It might take a few days. I live in New York, you know, Janis." "That's all right. The party will still be going on."

The Tequila Boogie culminated with a party at Janis's house, fondly called the Lyle Tuttle Tattoo Party. Tuttle, with his tattooed torso, set up shop and provided body artwork as a party favor. There was more than one person who woke the next morning wondering how he had allowed himself to be so adorned. The partying was grand

and Janis and Kris were close, but it was not a romance made to last. They were each drawn to the demands of their careers.

It was debut time for the band. The group was tight and the music was good, but something was missing. "If only John Cooke were here," Janis said to Bobby. "You want John Cooke? I'll get you John Cooke," Bobby chivalrously exclaimed as he headed for the telephone.

It took some explaining. After all, the last time John had seen Janis she was excusing herself to go to the bathroom to shoot heroin. Her drug use had turned touring into a drag. Bobby just kept enthusing, "Hey, man, Janis is in great shape. You got to do this, and you got to see this new band!" John arrived five days before the tour started, and three days before the Tequila Boogie ended.

Janis was ready to tour, but the weeks of tequila merriment had made an impression. She needed to reduce the drinking. The doctor she asked for help said that it was either all or nothing. Reducing one's drinking wasn't the prescribed treatment for a problem with liquor— the only proven remedy was total abstinence. She was in a quandary. She wanted to *be* clean, but not to go through the steps that would *get* her clean, such as not drinking at all. Going on tour was hardly an ideal alcohol-treatment method. She wasn't ready to quit, so she decided to try to manage it alone. If she could do nothing else, she would abstain from drinking for a few hours before going onstage.

Kicking off the tour was her engagement by the Hell's Angels for a private party at Pepperland in San Rafael, California. It was a double bill with Big Brother and the Holding Company. The office hadn't booked the date, Bennett Glotzer said. Janis had called Albert and told him she wanted to play there and he had concurred. "Albert, you're nuts!" Bennett exclaimed.

The Hell's Angels seemed to be a good group for the debut of her new band because she could count on them to be an enthusiastic audience. After all, Janis always seemed to care more about whether the audience got off on the music than whether the band performed precisely. She wanted the local crowd to tell her the group was good. She also enjoyed playing a double bill with Big Brother.

The Angels were a mind-blowing audience. A special kind of intensity seemed to hang in the darkened, smoke-filled room. It was reflected in the exhaustion Nick Gravenites felt when he stepped offstage, having sung with Big Brother for the opening act. He was barely able to walk, he was so drained. There was a surreal demand on the artists that night.

Bennett, Albert, and others were there for the debut. Pepperland was full of drunk people in biker clothes. When it was Janis's turn to go to the stage, her entourage walked up together. Bennett explained, "The band went to the stage first, and then I went, and then Janis. There was some woman who was the lady of a biker, and she asked Janis for her bottle. When Janis refused to share the liquor, the girl screamed, 'When a Hell's Angel asks you for something, you give it to them!' They went down on the floor slugging, until Sweet William, who was chairman of the Oakland chapter of the Hell's Angels, came over and stopped it. In a matter of minutes they pulled all the lunatics off and she went onstage. Janis said, 'See, I told you it would be all right.'"

The Angels took a special pride in caring for their musicians. As Clark Pierson was drumming intensely, an Angel said, "You look like you're getting warm. Why don't you take your shirt off?" Clark declined and kept on playing. A few minutes later, Clark realized the guy wasn't asking him, he was telling him. He stopped playing and took his shirt off. The Angel carefully folded the shirt and placed it on a chair. The rest of the night, Clark's private Angel protectively wiped the drummer's brow as he played.

The night was just plain bizarre. Some stories tell of a nude couple dancing, others about a couple making love onstage. When Janis finished playing, she understood the exhaustion that Nick had felt when he'd finished singing earlier. It was some way to start a tour.

CHAPTER FIFTEEN

FULL TILT TRIUMPH

★

You know that I need a man
You know that I need a man
But when I ask you to, you just tell me
That maybe you can

—Janis Joplin, "Move Over"

"THE SUMMER WAS a dream. She had more fun being straight," related John Cooke. Janis initially planned an eight-week limit on the Full Tilt tour, based on her plan with Albert for two months on the road and two months off. The eight weeks began creeping out on both ends of the tour, until the total package was twelve weeks. She opened on May 29 in Gainesville, Florida.

Her former Austin lover, Bill Killeen, lived in Gainesville. He had moved there to run a student humor magazine and later opened a head shop. Janis telephoned and together they planned a getaway at his Thoroughbred horse farm in the country. Then business intervened. The New York office booked concerts for Jacksonville on May 30 and Miami on May 31. A private life was so difficult to maintain while she was on the road. Janis had a hard time turning down money, and the concerts meant income.

The tour was a joyous departure from former ones. Janis was full of energy and enthusiasm. She had fun with the guys. In Maryland on June 19-20, waiting for the performance, she brought out a box of

★

beads that she had brought from California. The whole band sat around stringing beads and talking, being friends.

Maryland was a memorable concert for Janis because she started feeling ill toward the end of the show and couldn't do an encore. The promoter brought a car around so that an ambulance wouldn't cause a scene, and off they whisked her to the emergency room, with John Cooke following them at high speed. Janis lay on a gurney waiting patiently for help for forty-five minutes before a young intern diagnosed her problem. She had a pulled muscle.

She made the most of the incident later on the June 1970 *Dick Cavett Show*. He asked her about tearing a muscle, and she replied, "Yeah, I sure did, somewhere down around Maryland." The audience roared, catching her insinuation to a spot on her body and not the state. Janis knew how to play her image for all it was worth, but in private, she was changing in small but important ways. When someone who latched on to her group at some social gathering was grumbling angrily about the "pigs" abusing their power, Janis cut him short. "They're cops, just people doing their job, honey. Don't call them pigs, it just makes it worse." When she first started touring with Big Brother, if a waitress was rude to them because of their attire and style, they often left without tipping. On the Full Tilt tour, a rude waitress might be left a $100 bill, as a way to change her attitude about hippies. Most important, her casual attitude toward sex was markedly different. No longer did Janis feel that having sex with a guy was a good way to get to know him. Now she told people she never slept with people she worked with.

After five weeks of touring the East, Janis was off on a chartered-train trip across Canada, with no one on board but musicians who played concerts at stops along the way. It could hardly be better, especially since she received seventy-five thousand dollars for the three concerts and got to participate in a five-day party.

Janis had a fresh look in her stage clothes to go with the new act. Perhaps it was Kristofferson's country influence that led her to have a few outfits made by the famous country-and-western costume designer Nudie. Her favorite was a pair of tight bell-bottom pants and a long open-front vest in royal purple. Swirls of gold braid and white and red stones cascaded down and around the garments. They were the perfect accent for a flashing figure onstage.

"Going across the border into Canada," laughed John Cooke, "was the first time she crossed the border without having anything to hide. They could search everything and they weren't going to find anything. . . . This little French-Canadian immigration customs guy started going through Janis's stuff. She went wild, and by that time it was the feather boa. . . . She was egging him on. He found a powdered substance in her toilet kit. She said, 'Don't you want to know what that is, honey?' And he said, *'Qu'est-ce que c'est?'* And she said, 'It's douche powder, man.' And he turned beet red. It just took forever, she was having such fun with the inspection!"

"The train across Canada was the high point that summer," explained John Cooke. "It was a rolling festival, a combination of people who never got such an opportunity to play together, to jam together, to be together around music, perform, practice, and talk." The chartered train included Ian and Sylvia, Delaney and Bonnie, Buddy Guy, the Grateful Dead, the Band, and more. John Cooke wandered through the eighteen cars with a shoe box, saying, "Money for the people's bar." He got $350 in ten minutes, all of which was spent in Saskatoon, buying bottles for on-train consumption.

The musicians designated one lounge car for acoustic musicians and the other for electric. "It really was like a vacation," explained John. "Other people were doing the driving and there was this beautiful scenery outside. It became very celebratory. And people, including myself, drank a good deal of the day instead of just the evening."

In this environment, there was little suggestion that Janis should worry about alcohol. The entire crowd reveled in its intoxicating delights. When people drink, they want music. When they have music, they want a drink, right? John said, "I sort of remember Janis and me saying, 'Hey, man, you got to try this, stay drunk all day, it's wild!' If you do it on the right level, you aren't getting all bleary and stupid, you're just sort of maintaining." Janis may have been on the bandwagon, preaching against drugs, but she put alcohol in another category. She liked to mix it with sweet juices to make it slide down ever so easily. By experimenting with the amount she took, she hoped to get rid of alcohol's frustrating tendency to get one sloppy and fuzzy.

Speaking with a reporter from *Circus* in Toronto, Janis shared her elation with the band, the tour, and the new sound. "I always used

★

to get drunk onstage," she said, "but now I don't need it. Sometimes I drink, sometimes I don't. I can get high just on the music!"

Janis was infatuated with her new band. They were the group she had always wanted. They were musicians, friends, and fellow artists who clicked together. In the solo of "Tell Mama" or "Move Over," John Till said, "she'd come boogeying up to me and our faces would come right together like that, and then she'd give me a great big kiss. And I wouldn't remember nothing except big asterisks and fucking exclamation marks over my head. I'd be trying to take a solo and this—woooo! It was an experience, taking a guitar solo in front of forty thousand people and getting this beautiful (*sigh*) kiss from Janis."

There was a shadow of 1966 on the train when someone laced the tequila with acid. By 1970 people were generally against that kind of thing. Luckily, someone intervened before too many people had sampled the surprise.

After the train, Janis's schedule took the band to Hawaii. After the concert there, the band got a chance to relax, but Janis had another engagement. She was off to Austin, a surprise guest at Ken Threadgill's jubilee birthday party on July 10, 1970. Old friend Juli Paul had called and invited Janis. "Can't you make it another day? I work weekends," Janis asked. She went anyway, direct from Hawaii to the party barn at Oak Hill in Austin.

Eight thousand people attended and all were in a mood of celebration. Many people performed, playing some of the folk standards the audience expected. Then they asked Janis to sing and the audience began to erupt. Janis hollered, "Are you ready for some rock and roll?" The reply was emphatic. Fumbling, asking for the loan of a "gitar," and adjusting the microphones, Janis wailed, "I can't tune worth a shit, will someone tune this thing?" She joked with the audience about why she played acoustic guitar. She explained that if she screwed up the chords, no one could hear. At the worst they would think the band was out of tune!

Ken Threadgill's support had been one of the turning points in her life. He had helped her when it mattered the most. She went to Austin to honor him, and so refrained from hogging the eager eyes of the press or dominating the stage. She sang "Me and Bobby McGee," telling the crowd that Kris Kristofferson was going to be famous real soon because he wrote such good songs. At the crowd's insistence, she also sang another of Kris's tunes, "Sunday Mornin' Comin' Down."

There were eight thousand voices cheering in unison that they loved Austin, Ken Threadgill, the music he sponsored, and Janis. She saw people she used to know in the crowd. One asked her, "Do you like what you're doing?" Her quick reply was, "I wrote the part."

The next day she went back on tour. The band played San Diego on July 11, a double bill with Big Brother and the Holding Company. Sam said the drinking was beginning to show in Janis's body and she was gaining weight again. Sam also recalled the puffy red skin that she had, a clear sign of excessive alcohol consumption.

The emotional roller coaster was still going fast for Janis. High and then low, she struggled to maintain an equilibrium. The presence of old friends in San Diego had energized her for the airplane journey back to San Francisco. She bought drinks for everyone. James Gurley found her too exuberant, as though desperately trying to be the life of the party. But Sam Andrew didn't even notice that Janis was on the airplane. He was too absorbed in listening to Michael Bloomfield, guitar virtuoso, tell about his sexual experiments. Janis asked James to join her on the rest of the tour, but he declined.

Most of the time, life on the road was boring. Janis kept trying to make it more palatable, carrying little things from home to make the endless motel rooms seem more personalized. She draped silk scarves over the lamps to give the light a soft glow. She often turned on the color television set, and using the fine-tuning knob, she blurred the picture so that a continuous light show played in the background.

"When Janis was on the road, she spent a lot of time reading, as opposed to what most people think," explained Bobby Neuwirth. "She was by herself, not loaded but reading. There were a lot of quiet conversations, because there was a lot of time."

In 1970 *Zelda,* by Nancy Milford, was published. Janis bought it immediately. She loved biographies, and F. Scott and Zelda Fitzgerald were guiding influences in her life. Scott and Zelda led the Jazz Age, famous for their elegant escapades as much as his writing, some of which was borrowed from Zelda.

On the June 1970 *Dick Cavett Show,* Cavett asked Janis if she wanted to hear any stories about Fitzgerald, because another guest,

Douglas Fairbanks, Jr., had known him. Janis pursed her mouth and very earnestly said, "No, only the truth." Janis recommended the book on camera and commented, "The impression I got from all the Fitzgerald biographies was that he sort of destroyed her. But he wrote her a letter [reprinted in *Zelda*] that said, 'They keep saying we destroyed each other, I don't think that's true. I think we destroyed ourselves.'"

During the tour, Janis confronted questions about the record the band would be making. Who should be the producer? How will it work? Gabriel Mekler, the producer of her *Kozmic Blues* album, had created a rift between Janis and the previous band. She knew she didn't want that, but she only had a vague sense of what she did want.

Slowly came the recollection that Paul Rothchild had liked her singing. Long before fame had colored people's perceptions of Janis, Paul had made his respect for her known. It just so happened that Paul was an old friend of John Cooke's. John called Paul and went through the same song and dance that Bobby had to do to get John to join the tour. "I don't know," Paul stated. "The last time I saw Janis she was a junkie. She couldn't focus on her art." Cooke exclaimed in his emphatic fashion, "No, it's all better now. She's off junk and hardly drinking and got a new band. They're green, wide awake, and innocent! Janis wants you to come on tour with them for a while, to see what's going on." Paul told me, "It was a joyous reunion and Janis's eyes were bright and clear, and her spirit up."

Paul Rothchild was a moderate five feet eight inches tall, with bushy blondish-brown hair and blue eyes. His face had what he calls a "quirky" look, but women found it cute and handsome, in spite of his dominating Roman nose. His lithe build looked perfect in black jeans, black shirts, and cowboy boots, set off by one good Indian turquoise bracelet. He was often seen under a dark green Borsalino hat, the kind gentlemen ranchers wore, not cowboys on the open range.

Rothchild was a man of humor who liked to have fun. Trained as a classical conductor, he was drawn to produce folk, blues, and bluegrass in the fifties and sixties. He was the recording director for Prestige Records and then Elektra Records until 1968. Then he became an independent producer. He produced all of the Doors' albums and also did the Paul Butterfield Blues Band. His connection to an obscure folk-blues group from the Minneapolis folk scene—Koerner, Ray and Glover—earned him Janis's special respect.

Rothchild accompanied her on the last few gigs of the tour, from July 11 in San Diego to August 12 at Harvard. Wandering around backstage, he could occasionally be seen peering deeply into the amplifiers, pondering the mix, and checking other details of the band's sound. In San Diego, Janis gave him a stopwatch, saying, "Look, I've only got thirty-five good minutes in me. You stand behind the amps and I'll look over, you flash me how much time I have left." Paul thought it was a good sign that she was pacing herself like a runner.

One of his questions in working with Janis had been about her voice. When Paul heard the Kozmic Blues Band, he worried that she had killed it. Standing backstage in San Diego, within the first ten seconds he realized the voice was all there again. "She was singing and I was enraptured because I was listening to one of the most brilliant vocalists I ever heard in classical, pop, or jazz music. What a voice! I went, 'Oh! My God!' All of the woman was revealed. The vessel of Janis vanished. For somebody like me who was always talking about the inner beauty and all that stuff, it got me big. So, I was totally hooked from that moment on, on every single possible level."

Paul was a marked contrast to other producers she had worked with. He was a sixties guy who thought the musicians should be the central focus. Paul believed that a producer should create an atmosphere in which musicians were comfortable and could bring forth their best. He understood that though the focus of recording was always on the music, the musicians couldn't bring forth their best unless the ambience and feelings were right.

He became her champion in a fight over the CBS restriction that required their artists to record in a CBS studio with CBS engineers. "Wait a minute," Paul exclaimed. "CBS engineers all come from the age of Noah. The studios are out of date, and they're geared to making the Johnny Mathis sound." Presenting his case to Clive Davis, Paul continued, "We want to do this right, in an environment that will be rock and roll." No matter the arguments, the corporate attorneys could say only that the engineers would strike.

Finally, a compromise was reached. The executives were sensitive to the argument that if CBS were not responsive to the new music, they couldn't sign new acts. Paul would do two demonstration recordings with Janis. One would be in a CBS studio with CBS engineers; the other would be at the independent studio, Sunset Sound. Clive Davis agreed, with the stipulation that the work at Sunset Sound would include a CBS engineer sitting in the room, feather-bedding.

They made the two recordings, and played them in a blind test for all involved. Everyone chose the Sunset Sound recording, and so Clive Davis allowed the record to be made there. He stated emphatically that if there were any complaints from the union, he was closing the studios in L.A., where 176 engineers worked. The engineers complained, and the CBS studios in L.A. were closed and remain closed.

Between making the demos and starting work on the record, Paul came to Larkspur with John Cooke. "She didn't realize it at the time," he said, "but I was very carefully studying her. Drugs weren't there, at all." He asked Janis, "What do you want to be when you're forty-five, or fifty-five?" "I want to be the greatest blues singer in the world," she shouted. Nodding his head with a smile on his face, he replied, "That's available to you, but not if you blow your voice out."

Paul then commenced to prove his point. In her sunlit redwood living room, they each sang in the church-choir voices they had used when they were ten. He explained, "What we want to do is work that part of your voice into songs and develop it into the full passionate one, so the effect is more dramatic." "Yes, yes, yes! Great, let's do it," was how he remembered Janis's reply.

Janis had been struggling with this issue ever since she became prominent. She told a *Playboy* interviewer that the reason she was working so hard was "sure as hell not the money. At first it was to get love from the audience. Now it's to reach my fullest potential, to go as far as I can go. I've got the chance. It's a great opportunity!"

What a boon for Janis to find Paul, someone who knew how to help. Janis's friends often said that she liked people who didn't have self-doubts and knew what they were talking about. She thrived on their conviction, knowledge, and power. Part of it was that she valued competence on its own merits. Part of it was her own insecurity, feeling she needed someone to tell her what to do. She didn't understand her rise to fame and was unable to talk clearly to musicians due to her lack of training. She sought help whenever she found someone who knew. In recording, Paul Rothchild was someone to lean on and learn from.

People were always important to Janis. In spite of her penchant for angry outbursts, mostly in 1968 and 1969, she was loyal to a fault. Backstage at an Elton John concert, Jack Nicholson was "verbally abusing Albert's office for not following through in getting her the part of Helena in *Five Easy Pieces*," Bennett Glotzer said. Janis coolly replied to Nicholson, "My managers are terrific. Whatever they wanted to do, they had a reason." Bennett smiled. Janis and he both knew the office had screwed up, but Janis's standing by them anyway touched him.

"Janis always made me welcome in her home," Bennett continued. People often dropped in, for dinner, for a drink, or just to talk. Backstage at a concert she declared to the entourage, "Everyone cool it. There's a kid in the room." Bennett Glotzer thought that was a considerate gesture due to the presence of his eight-year-old daughter. Consideration for people was a growing part of her life in 1970.

"Janis said if she wasn't doing what she was doing, she would be interested in being a sociologist," Linda Gravenites explained. That's what she last studied in college. People were her motivating force. "My whole purpose is to communicate," Janis once said. "What I sing is my own reality. But just the fact that people come up to me and say, 'Hey, that's my reality, too,' proves to me that it's not just mine." Janis intended to own a bar called Pearl's after her singing career ended. Pat Nichols would bartend, Linda Gravenites would design it, and there would be good food, like Barney's Beanery had. Janis wanted a spot away from the city where she could cultivate a steady clientele.

Her life was still going up and down, though. Dave Moriaty, a Port Arthur friend turned San Franciscan, saw her at an art-gallery opening for the comic-book art he printed at his company, Rip Off Press. "She seemed disillusioned," he said. Sitting atop her Porsche, "Janis was drinking from a bottle of Southern Comfort and complaining to me about how all this fame and everything had backfired. The people she really valued no longer came around and talked to her. She never saw them because she was too busy," Dave recalled. "Then she'd belt out a yodel once in a while, just to draw some of the crowd that was hanging out around the Porsche."

I think she began to realize that she had strayed. Far from challenging the world and changing it, she had become one of its pawns. The revolution set to usher in a world of love had imploded. It was then bottled, packaged, and co-opted by the establishment. Janis thought her role as a rocker was really to guide her audience into feeling their innermost emotions. Stripped of her righteousness, she sometimes felt like a prostitute, selling her heart, rather than her body, to people who couldn't touch their own feelings and so sucked off hers.

Life is like that. It could look as promising as a shiny red apple one moment, but turn out to be a mealy bummer the next. As wonderful as life is, each person also must face her death. It seemed so unfair to Janis; no loving God could do that to people. Yet in 1970 she seemed to move through even that. She got a tattoo on her wrist as a "celebration of accepting life," she said. "I had the kozmic blues real bad once. You've got to realize that you'll never have as much as you want and that when you die, you'll be alone—everyone is. Once you've really accepted this, then it doesn't hurt so much. Get it while you can . . . 'cause it may not be there tomorrow."

How opportune that the mail brought an invitation to her tenth-annual high school reunion, to be held on August 15, 1970. I've often wondered why she decided to go. On The Dick Cavett Show aired on June 25, she sang "Move Over" and "Get It While You Can." In that vein she discussed her high school reunion, saying, "They laughed me out of class, out of town, and out of the state—so I'm going home." She smiled with such satisfaction that her audience of sophisticated others, who could agree that the world had not treated them fairly, roared with empathy. They wished they could return triumphantly as well. She must have winced when she realized what she had said on network television. Port Arthur wasn't so backward that we didn't get that channel.

Janis also appeared on Dick Cavett on August 3, 1970, less than two weeks before the scheduled high school reunion. Was it an attempt to make amends, to correct the record? She was hardly in the same high-flying form that night as she had been in June. The August discussion with Cavett shows an inebriated woman whose slurred speech and rambling comments were interesting but not up to par. The most Joplinesque truth that night came in response to what appeared to be a scheduled question by Cavett about her relations with the press and feelings about interviews. Janis said, "Other than having to do them, and other than having to talk to someone who doesn't seem to understand what you're saying a lot of the time, I don't mind them."

Cavett also asked Janis about the bad press due to riots at a few rock concerts. Janis felt the problem was a logistical one. The increasing popularity of the events meant larger numbers of people, and it took top organizers to run a rock concert well. She equated the problem to the scene in Haight-Ashbury when the hordes descended on the movement. The scene just wasn't equipped to deal with the overflow of bodies, and consequently it degenerated.

On August 12 the Full Tilt Boogie Band played at Harvard Stadium. After the rousing finale of the concert, Janis added a note of caution to the audience: "If you have energy to work off, go home and do it together with somebody you love." She was asking them not to run riot in the neighborhood. There had been an increasing number of criminal incidents after rock concerts. The only entry in Janis's FBI file concerns an earlier warning that there might be an attempt to disrupt Janis's concert in Illinois and cause violence. Two hundred police officers patroled the Ravinia Park, Illinois, concert to prevent problems.

The Boston police were also ready. They cruised the area in cars after the Harvard concert, stopping any suspicious characters. They chanced upon John Cooke and some of the guys in the band who were walking to their parked car to drive to a restaurant. "It's okay, we live here," they told the police, showing them their hotel keys. It didn't matter, they had to turn and *run* back to their hotel to keep from getting in trouble. Even then, the car circled the block five times while John Cooke was on the telephone to the police station asking them to call off the hounds. He was just hungry. The officer said, "Yeah, well, I heard from my officers down there that she incited to riot." Cooke kept his cool and said "in very literate English, 'This is precisely *not* correct.'" After much talking, the police said they'd had a lot of problems in the area after several rock concerts. The next day it came to light that this was the first concert that had *not* been followed by vandalism.

The next day Janis flew to Texas. We stood on the airport tarmac with other folks, waiting for the little twin-engine commuter plane that was flying Janis to the Golden Triangle Airport. When she stepped off the plane and hugged us, we realized that the people around us were from the press. She mussed my hair, asking, "How you doing, frizzy?" By this time in life, I had let my hair grow, adopting the hippie style of parting it in the middle and letting it fall naturally. As Janis walked on, a woman rushed up to me, notebook and pencil in hand. "Is that her nickname for you, 'Frizzy'?" "What? No, it isn't, just an offhand comment," I quickly replied.

In spite of the emotional groundwork she had laid on the *Cavett Show,* we felt little of it from her. She was coming home, ready to visit and have a good time. Full of stories, she told how she preferred shopping at Paraphernalia, where they knew her on sight, setting things aside, saying, "I know you'll like this, Miss Joplin." Other stores, Janis explained, snubbed her because of her attire, in spite of her paying with an American Express card! Realizing that meant nothing to us, she added, "You have to make fifty thousand dollars to even get one!" She was trotting out the trappings of success to impress the locals.

"Please come," she kept asking me. "Please come to the reunion committee meeting with me. I don't want to go by myself." I finally relented, and was glad for the opportunity to visit with Janis alone. Our relationship needed time to catch up with our evolving selves. By 1970 I was adopting hippie dress and ideas as much as was possible in Port Arthur. Driving in my car at night, Janis asked, "Getting enough sex?" I grumbled angrily, "Enough for me, though not for you, I gather." Her whole countenance changed, to one of shock and innocence. "You mean, you're not a . . ." she exclaimed softly. I glared, saying, "You're not the only one who grows up, you know, Janis!" While we were at it, I said, "I resent your comments about me to the press. Think about it, Janis. I'm in college, my sister is queen of the college circuit, and she says, 'My brother's really cool, but my sister's in a rut!' Thanks a lot." Her words had flown like barbs straight to my heart. I loved her and she was denying me in public. Not many college students get the benefit of nationally aired, individualized social judgments by one so awesome as Janis! She sighed. I fumed, asking, "How the hell do you think that makes me feel?" She just sat with her head bowed. Thoughts ran through my mind: Should I be surprised? Did she ever think how her actions might affect others? Not in my experience. "You can be awfully frustrating, Janis." She looked up. "Yeah, I'm sorry." At least it was out in the open. Venting my anger and seeing that she was sorry mended my ruffled feathers a bit. The conversation cleared the air for the rest of our visit.

Arriving at a former classmate's house, we sat in the living room and I listened to Janis reply to their anxious questions about the reunion. "What do you want, Janis?" "Nothing special," she explained. "I just came to see everyone." Who was she kidding? Nothing special? Why, she wanted them to plan a lengthy toast, hold a receiving line, and ask her to say something to the crowd. She wanted them to publicly recognize her success! But they took her at her word. Sam Monroe, a member of the committee, asked, "We've had several requests for interviews, Janis. How should we handle that?" She nodded. "Yes, I guess a special place for interviews and a set time would be good." After her comments on *Dick Cavett*, the reunion steering committee was afraid the event was going to become a three-ring circus. They wanted reassurance, and she gave it to them. Together they planned a method of handling the press. Before departing, Glenda South asked Janis the hard question, the one that burned everyone's ears in Port Arthur. "Janis, why did you think some of us didn't like you?" Gasp, she was going to have to explain it to one of them! She tried, with a parade of stories punctuated by language that was uncommon in Port Arthur's social circles. She said that people had called her names in the halls and spit at her. Unmoved, all Glenda could reply was, "I didn't know any of that, and wasn't part of it." They felt unjustly vilified in the national press. Most hadn't hated her. They didn't realize that their worst crime, in her eyes, was not recognizing the correctness of her views and the wrongness of their own!

Several people had been crude and rude to Janis in high school, but she had not been alone in receiving their attention. However, Janis had let their taunts grind deeper and deeper into her psyche, until the events were elaborately woven into her personal mythology.

It affected even as good a friend as Karleen. Karleen had been in the beauty shop and overheard Glenda South share her excitement about seeing Janis. Karleen thought, "Why are you glad to see her now? You never were before." Karleen decided to put Janis's friendship on the line. Karleen thought, "If Janis wants to see me, she'll call. I don't want to add to the Glenda calls." Karleen found out later that when Janis asked Mom about Karleen, Mom said she had moved to Houston. Janis did not call, and Karleen didn't go to the reunion. Janis's best friend in the class was not there to run excitedly through the crowd and give her the bear hug that she so desperately wanted.

★

Turning onto our street and approaching the house, we realized we would not have another undisturbed moment. It forced Janis to ask the question that was choking her. "Are Mama and Daddy proud of me?" I breathed deeply, grasping the significance of that question. "Yes, Janis, they are fairly bursting with pride!" I answered. "But you don't make it easy on them, you know. Janis, you told the national press that they kicked you out of the house at age fourteen! That's not true! How can you say that? What are they supposed to do around town? Laugh lightly and say, 'Oh, she didn't mean it.' " Janis sucked in her breath and then sighed deep and long, saying, "Oh," and slumping back into her bucket seat, too aware of the whole mess. The caricature of the woman who was known as Janis Joplin had even affected her relationships in the family. Janis was very clever in getting press attention and slinging out one-liners that cried, "Headline." But the quotes had changed people's views of her.

On the morning of the reunion, Janis rose, eager to play hostess to the entourage who had arrived to attend the events with her. She had them come for show, but also for the very practical need of security. A public person making a public appearance needs some muscle around. Janis had wanted to bring Tary Owens, a San Francisco musician and also a classmate. She had offered to pay his way, but he declined, too absorbed in his drugs at the time to deal with the rest of the world. Janis entertained gaily by making eggs Benedict for everyone. Mom and Pop made their excuses, saying they had a prior obligation to attend a friend's daughter's wedding. Janis was miffed that they would leave while she was at home, but the folks resented the way she had come home. They weren't going to give up their commitments for her sporadic visits. She was only one of five people in the family. After they left, the rest of us hung out in the kitchen, talking and watching Janis stir the sauce and tell stories.

I stopped her cold in the midst of the brouhaha and asked the obvious: "But are you happy?" Pausing, she reflected and then caught herself, all in a split second. "I'm on top of the world!" she shouted. "I know," I said, "but are you happy?" Turning aside, all she could do was mumble some sounds that meant she wasn't going to answer a dumb question like that.

Janis excused herself to dress for the afternoon and evening events. The next I saw of her was when we walked out to the waiting rented luxury auto. She had on San Francisco rock clothes—complete with beads, bangles, and feathers in her hair. It was the feathers that bothered me. I turned and asked, "Why are you wearing those? This isn't a concert, you know." She replied curtly, "This isn't your business." I didn't let up. "Janis, this is a group of people coming to see people, not stars. Just be yourself!" Her eyes flashed daggers. "Stay out of other people's business." I began to dread the event, a party that wasn't a celebration but a contest of one-upmanship.

Arriving at the Goodhue Hotel, we walked up the street. Following was Janis's entourage of John Cooke, Bobby Neuwirth, and a New York chauffeur, John Fisher, brought along to drive her through the town in style. Regrettably, he had been unable to rent a limousine for the event.

Janis strolled over to the room set aside for the press. The *Port Arthur News* wrote, "Drink in hand, she approaches a long table filled with reporters. 'Looks like the Last Supper, doesn't it?' she asks." Janis was in a playful mood, trying to be honest but having fun with the press. Someone asked, "What do you think about Port Arthur now?" She replied, "Well, it seems to have loosened up a little bit since I left. There's a lot of long hair and rock, which also means drug use, you know. Looks like it's doing just about what the rest of the country's doing: getting loose, getting together." The follow-up was, "Does it surprise you to see Port Arthur that way?" "Yeah, quite a bit," she replied.

Microphones were grouped on a cloth-covered table. Janis sat, tossing her hair, smoking a cigarette, and smiling at the cameras. I looked at the scene, framed by the picture window's view of the downtown streets of Port Arthur. John Cooke smiled and then grabbed me. He shoved me into the limelight, saying, "Go sit with Janis." "No," I kept repeating, until Janis and the press noticed. She called, "Hey, Laura, come sit beside me." I smiled and sat beside her as the questions continued.

Question: "What do you think young people are looking for today?" Answer: "Sincerity and a good time." Question: "Did you entertain in high school?" Answer: "Only when I walked down the aisles. No, I didn't. I was a painter, sort of a recluse, in high school. I've

★

changed." Question: "What happened?" Answer: "I got liberated. No, I don't know. I just started to sing and singing makes you want to come out, whereas painting, I feel, really keeps you inside. When I started singing it just sort of made you want to talk to people more and go out more."

The reporters asked several questions about her unhappy times in high school, feelings about the hometown since, etc. She answered them in many different ways. To a query on how she was different, she said, "Why don't you ask them?" Asked if she was an eccentric in high school, she quipped, "I think I thought of myself as being eccentric. I wasn't even old enough to be an eccentric." Asked about whether she had attended her high school prom, Janis said seriously, "No, I don't think they wanted to take me." Then she laughed and added, "And I've been suffering ever since. It's enough to make you want to sing the blues."

They asked about her new band, the new record, special songs on it, her producer, etc. They wanted to know if she would do a concert in Port Arthur or Austin and she said, "Yes, if they pay me."

The only time she got upset was at a question about her nickname, which the reporter thought was "Pearl Barley." Janis was flustered, replying, "That name was not supposed to reach the press. I was telling that to my mother. I didn't realize I was surrounded by reporters. That name's a private name for my friends to call me so they won't have to call me Janis Joplin. It's just for my friends to say, 'Hey, Pearl, fix me another drink.' It's actually not a new name. It's just a nickname."

The questions then fell on me. "Do you listen to her records much?" I panicked, groping among several answers in my mind. Nodding yes, I said, "We had three of them, but we lost two. Yes, we listen to Janis's music." "You do?" was her feigned shocked and laughing reply.

The final question to Janis was, "What do you think you've got in common with your classmates of 1960 besides the fact that you were classmates?" Janis roamed among replies, settling on, "There's always a point of communication for people. You just get down to human level and discard the accent or the dress or whatever. We've still got things to talk about. We've just got different kinds of experiences.

They've got kids, I ain't got kids, you know. I wear feathers, they don't wear feathers. See, we have a lot of common ground. We can talk about birds." On that note, Janis asked about the time. The reporters took the hint and drifted away.

Janis turned to me. "You have to learn to smile, Laura," she explained quietly after the press had completed their barrage of questions. "Like this," she said, "with your lips parted and your teeth open. Try it, it's not hard," she coaxed. She kept pushing until I flashed the pearly grin but also said, "Janis, no one wants to talk to me. I'm not famous!"

Later, we milled around the cocktail party. She greeted folks and recalled teachers and special times. She sat on a couch with Glenda South and Clarence Bray, the class president. They tried to remember the school song. We joined Kristen Bowen downstairs in the bar. Janis played pool and had a few drinks before the group assembled for dinner.

Sam Monroe was the master of ceremonies for the evening, and he prudently put a formal tone on his remarks. Summarizing the class, he listed the number of children born to members, and the various numbers of doctors, lawyers, and other occupations. Wilting in her seat beside me, Janis heard him finish with an offhand "Is there anything I've missed?" Sigh—Sam's somber sense of humor hardly created the jovial uproar I felt he was seeking. "Janis Joplin," someone said in a matter-of-fact tone. "Oh, yes, and Janis Joplin!" They applauded, a few whistled, and Janis rose in place, politely nodding her head. "In honor of having come the greatest distance to this reunion, the committee wanted to give Janis a tire." Ahhhh, Janis smiled. It was less than the ovation Ken Threadgill had received at his jubilee, and somehow she seemed crushed. Janis had really wanted more.

"It's just Sam, Janis. He's trying to be funny, and he's not very good at it. He didn't know what to do," I whispered at the table. She looked quizzically at me, and then her face registered agreement, the tensed muscles eased.

No one with Janis wanted to stay for the dance. We piled into the rented car and headed to the Pelican Club, having heard that Jerry Lee Lewis was in town. It wasn't the first time Janis had met him. In Louisville on June 12, she'd gone to his concert and tried to visit backstage. He had refused to talk with her, and so had his group of beefy, country bodyguards. Janis and her friends had left, but not before she almost crowned a security cop with a whiskey bottle. Why, I wonder, did she expect him to be different here? Was she attempting to offer him local hospitality, or did she want to commiserate about what a second-rate burg Port Arthur was? Perhaps after the less than laudatory reunion program, she just wanted to touch the other reality of her life, the glitter and special bond of one performer to another. After all, which of her classmates could even dream of approaching Jerry Lee?

Sitting on the hard chairs in the open lounge, Janis commented with John and Bobby about Jerry Lee's antics playing that outlaw piano. He put on a show, and the locals loved it.

Janis pulled me along to say hello backstage and I stood at the door. Walking up to him, she chortled, "This is my hometown, and I'd like you to meet my sister." He looked up at her gruffly. Then his scowling eyes moved across the room to me. "You wouldn't be bad-looking," he snarled, "if you weren't trying to look like your sister!" A flash must have jumped in her mind, because she sent a reflexive fist to his face. Just as quickly, he hit her back!

The boys rushed to her defense, leading her out of the room. Whimpering amid the circle of our bodies walking out of the club, she kept repeating, "How could he do that?" Surprised at the whole event, I said, "Who cares, Janis? We're the ones who love you. We're the opinions that matter. Who is he anyway?" Bobby picked it up. "Yeah, yeah, he's nothing, Janis." "Okay"—she straightened her shoulders— "okay."

Back home, our family was already asleep. No matter, the whole group came in and sat around the dining table. "Janis," I asked, "do you remember that song you wrote a long time ago, 'Come away with me and we'll build a dream?' " Her head shot up, and she left the room, mumbling, "No, no, I don't know what you're talking about." Bobby's eyes had lit up, eager to make some caustically cynical remark about believing in dreams. Her exit was all that cut him off.

The next day Mom and Pop were furious to find that Bobby was asleep in the car with the motor running and John Fisher was on the couch. Neither had bothered to drive back to the motel. The guys left sheepishly, and Janis tried to explain that it wasn't important, but it created tension in the house.

Jimmy Pryor came over to ask Janis if he could quote her in the newspaper he and Michael published, *Agape*. They had an international circulation since someone from Panama had subscribed. It was youth writing to youth, about Christianity as universal love. "I believe in that," Janis stated in that deep, emphatic voice that had a tinge of humor in it. In flowing script, one half-page of the next issue said, "Don't Compromise Yourself, It's All You Got," with Janis Joplin the signatory.

Janis told me about a girlfriend who had fallen in love with a fellow who had lots of money and lived out in Montana. "He asked her to marry him, and he flew to California in a helicopter and took her away," Janis said wistfully. "I wish someone would take me away," she continued, sighing.

Janis asked me, "Why don't you come visit?" I was pleased by the invitation and replied, "Okay, I'd like that, but I won't have any time until Christmas break." So we made plans for me to spend the holidays with her in Larkspur.

In 1990, I talked with Bobby Neuwirth about the reunion. He said, "After the reunion, she had mixed feelings. It was sort of a letdown, but also gave her a sense of completion at the same time. Like, she didn't really have to play with it anymore . . . didn't have to regret the original experiences anymore."

I think the whole experience was a good one for her, for her growth as a human being. Mom had written in a round-robin letter to the family earlier, "It's a strange scene to read of one's eldest as 'the Queen,' 'the Goddess,' 'the Superstar.' She calls now and then, but never writes anymore. Perhaps the home folks bring this halo down to polishing distance."

Back in California, she told people about her experiences at home. She was putting perspective on the mortally wounded outcast role she had presented to the press. She had told the *Port Arthur News* during the reunion interview, "Well, to tell you the truth, it [high school] made me very unhappy. It may have been a problem of my own, but problems aren't all one-sided. It just made me very unhappy. I didn't have anyone to talk to. . . . Now I can talk to anybody in Port

Arthur because I'm older and I can go on their trip. I can relate to them on their trip whether they can relate to me or not. But then I was very young and I didn't have any experience in relating to people and every time one of my overtures would be refused, it would hurt."

Bob Gordon realized that her attitude toward her family had changed, and suggested that she rewrite her will. Janis agreed, and he drafted a new document. The former will had left everything to Michael, because in the mind of the star Janis, he was the only one who loved her. Coming back home, she had realized that was not true. Everyone in the family loved her, as much as she would let them. She was giving up the feeling of being wronged by the world.

She was trying to make things right, to have the kind of life that she'd always wanted. Part of that meant a good love relationship. Back in California, she began a romance with Seth Morgan, a fellow she had met in May at the Lyle Tuttle Tattoo Party. Janis had been on tour in the East, based in New York, for most of the intervening months. After August 12 she was on vacation and living back at her home in Larkspur. Their romance bloomed with the unique blending of their personal brands of outrageousness.

Seth had large, sexy lips and thick, dark, wavy hair that curled seductively around his face. He was a student at Berkeley who'd grown up in a house frequented by many of the literary greats of the day because his father edited a literary journal. He was a member of *the* Morgan family, the descendants of J. P. Morgan. He was slender, muscular, and a few years younger than Janis. He was also intelligent, interesting, fun, and spontaneous. He could carry his own, and was not afraid or put off by the rock-and-roll scene.

Seth was wonderful to be seen with in public because he was good-looking, punky, and brash. He rode a motorcycle and had a cocky, haughty air. Janis could be as outrageous as she wanted to be with Seth. In fact, he liked to be seen with Janis in the Porsche, out about town. It was Janis who had put the kibosh on that, preferring to stay at home, having a glass of wine and watching television together. Whereas David Niehaus had disliked his visibility with Janis, Seth thrived on it. Nevertheless, they lived a quiet life. John Cooke remembered those evenings with amazement, emphatic in his description of the relationship as a positive one for her. She was slowing down her partying.

Seth had a modest income from family trust funds and it gave him an independence that was needed for a relationship with Janis. He wasn't overwhelmed by her personality or her career, though he took pains to continue pursuing his college studies and his own career goals as a way of preserving his sense of self.

Seth offered Janis the perfect balance. She didn't need to choose between a career and a mate. He could handle both. They talked about their future together. Janis wanted to retire soon, even though the recording sessions and Full Tilt tour had convinced her the new band was great. She wanted to have a child and change her life. Seth was all for it, though he was quick to add that theirs would be an "open" marriage. Janis must have felt that what he offered was enough, because she focused on their future together.

But Seth was also something of a con—a "silver-tongued devil." Several years after Janis died, he served time at Vacaville on a five-to-life sentence for armed robbery. While incarcerated, he wrote an article about his relationship with Janis. He said he had met her when he was dealing cocaine (not a drug commonly associated with Janis). Even later, after he wrote a successful novel, he talked to the press about her on his book-promotion trips. "If she was any old body, I wouldn't have looked at her. . . . No, that's *not* true. Janis and I had a real genuine flame. If she hadn't been Janis Joplin, we just would have been rip-roaring friends."

None of the tortured insanity that marked much of Seth's later days was evident yet. He was still a neophyte. That's why later he could truly say, "Who knows what would have happened if she hadn't died?" It wasn't until after her death that he first did heroin. I would think that seeing Janis die would have stopped him from doing the same drug that killed her. But for Seth, it was a reason to start.

Janis was tired of waiting for a good man who could handle the life she was leading. In 1969 she told a *Playboy* interviewer, "Oh hell, all any girl really wants is just love and a man. But what man can put up with a rock and roll star?" Seth looked like he might, but later evidence says that he was no strength to lean on.

They made big plans—a wedding at sea on a Caribbean cruise ship. Janis's attorney, Bob Gordon, drew up a prenuptial agreement at her request. They hadn't announced it to friends yet. They were waiting for the proper moment.

★

Who knows if they would have gotten married. The twenty years of his life after her death were a roller coaster of drugs and alcohol, fast motorcycles, and a constant stream of women. He said he had a fatal attraction to self-destructive women, whom he liked to help along their self-chosen paths. He died in 1990, high on alcohol, cocaine, and Percodan, in a motorcycle crash that also took the life of a lover. Minutes before the bike went out of control, she was seen beating desperately on his back, yelling, "Slow down!"

In September 1970, Janis stayed in L.A., recording her next album. Seth stayed at Larkspur and flew in for visits. He didn't much like the scene in L.A., since there was nothing for him to do except hang around the recording studio.

Janis was making history of sorts, the first CBS act allowed to record in an independent studio. Sunset Sound was in a converted garage, the perfect atmosphere for a rock band, Paul Rothchild explained. She had the studio, the producer, a band she loved, and good material. Work was great.

Recording could be especially hard for a performer like Janis, who was tuned to the audience. Hers was not an independent sound; it relied on audience feedback. She liked the fans to get up, clap, stomp, sing, and show that the music moved them. That was missing from the studio. Yet Paul could make it work without the audience.

Paul helped her to develop as a singer. She learned to use the subtle nuances of her voice instead of sheer power alone. "She demanded greatness from herself and delivered it," he said. "The band had come up and grown so spectacularly in such a short time. And they were committed, just welded to Janis. They would do anything for her and so would I. . . . She trusted me and I trusted her. We relied on each other being faithful and honest."

There was plenty of boredom in recording. The singer had to wait for the instrumental tracks to be laid down before the vocals could begin. Janis spent the time hunting for the right tunes and the best arrangements. They were crafting a piece of art.

Entertaining the gang during a break, Janis sang a novelty song, "Mercedes Benz," which she had penned in a bar along with Bobby Neuwirth. They took Michael McClure's poetic zinger of a line—"Oh, Lord, won't you buy me a Mercedes Benz?"—and turned it into a song.

Janis had never intended for it to be part of the record. The song was, however, placed on tape during the process.

"It wasn't a sad and tragic time," Paul said, smiling. "Fun was the underlying thing. We were joyous explorers. We were exploring land that was forbidden by our forebears and it was all about dress-up and it had the same kind of innocence. It was all about smiles and fun and laughter and then talking about it the next day because secrets didn't exist.

"How can I say this without it sounding sexist? Janis was one of the guys. When I was with her, there was no sense of she's female, I'm male," Paul Rothchild explained. Walking to the band car after recording in Los Angeles, Janis turned and surveyed the group of guys, wondering who should drive. She asked, "Who's got the biggest balls?" Then she answered, "I do." "Her humor frequently came from almost a male orientation," Paul explained. "Like her male balance was as strong as my female balance. We both acknowledged that place, the other side of our sexual whole."

Janis told Seth that she was using heroin again. She explained it away to Seth, saying, "I started since I couldn't get to work for being so goddamned drunk all the time. When the album's over I'll kick like before." She kept the drug use to herself, hitting up only late at night, after she finished recording. There was no one around like Linda Gravenites, who would have yelled, "No, you can't go back to that stuff, not after what you went through in quitting!" Seth wasn't the one to take a stand, in spite of her calling him and asking, "Please make me stop." He wouldn't even try, telling her, "It's something you have to do for yourself." Instead Lyndall Erb was Janis's roommate, a woman Seth felt was taken with the Joplin fame. He said she was never one to say no to Janis. He felt she was fawning and her relationship to Janis was "pernicious." In Los Angeles, Peggy Caserta was around, a woman who was heavily into heroin at the time.

Several people knew or guessed that Janis was using heroin, because her behavior would change. The strange truth was that when she did heroin, she turned into a hazy little girl. She lost the vibrant energy that was the persona of Janis Joplin. She became passive and oh-so-quiet. When she was straight, her intellect bloomed; she knew what she wanted and she knew ahead of time what the people around her wanted. One of the times she did heroin during the L.A. stay, she wandered in to band member John Till's room. She seldom came to visit, but she was feeling lonely. John and Dorcas wanted to reach out to her, but didn't know how to say, "Heroin is the problem, not the answer." People weren't that clear about such things then.

Overall, Los Angeles was a fun time for Janis. She worked with people who thrived on enacting the ideas that jumped into their minds. "We both had Porsches," Paul Rothchild said. "We'd race along Sunset Boulevard to Laurel Canyon. She was a lot crazier than I was—and I was nuts. She'd go against traffic on blind curves, with the top down, laughing, 'Nothing can knock me down.' "

She flew out to Santa Fe to meet Albert for a photo session for what would be her first job as a commercial representative. Albert had her booked to represent a cigar company. The photos were taken on the Rio Grande gorge bridge in New Mexico. It wasn't a time of visiting and reflecting with Albert. Instead photographer Lisa Law introduced her to a fellow Janis called "her mountain man," and she went off with him for the evening. One day in, the next day out. Janis returned to Los Angeles.

She called Pat Nichols, who lived in L.A. They hadn't seen each other since 1969, when they agreed to get together again only when they were both off heroin. Talking on the telephone, they made a date for October 5 to see a Toshiro Mifune Japanese samurai movie.

Janis had been in touch with Jerry Ragovoy in New York. "Haven't you got a new tune for my new album?" she asked. He wrote her one called "I'm Going to Rock and Roll Heaven." She didn't want to wait for the demo to arrive, so she had him sing it to her over the telephone. She loved it! He went out to get a demo made so the band could learn it.

In the studio, Janis telephoned Nick Gravenites, asking him too for a new tune for the album. He was producing a record for Brewer and Shipley, but took time to fly down to L.A. He sat in the corner of Sunset Sound, absorbing the music and the jive. He wrote "Buried Alive in the Blues," a tune that thrilled everyone.

Walking across the street with Bennett Glotzer, Janis ordered hamburgers for everyone. Waiting for them, "she spilled the beans," Bennett said. "She talked about Seth, how she felt about him, her trepidation, her doubts about it being the right relationship for her, and whether he really loved her."

Saturday, October 3, 1970, the band laid down the instrumental tracks for "Buried Alive." Everything was ready for Janis to record the vocals the next day. It looked good and the group was pleased. They finished around eleven P.M. As usual, Janis stopped for a drink at Barney's Beanery before heading to the Landmark Hotel. She had two drinks at the bar, on top of the liquor she had consumed at the studio. She drove to the hotel with Ken Pearson, her organ player, and they headed to their separate rooms.

Janis frequently went for a swim after work, but not that night. She only went to the lobby to buy cigarettes about one A.M. The last person who talked with her was Jack Hagy, at the desk. He gave her change for five dollars so she could use the cigarette machine.

After closing the door to her room, Janis sat on the bed clad in a blouse and panties. She put the cigarettes on the bedside table, and still holding the change in her hand, she fell forward. Her lip was bloodied as she struck the bedside table. Her body became wedged between the table and the bed. Sometime after returning to the hotel, she had injected herself with heroin. Janis skin-popped the drug instead of putting it into a vein. An intravenous injection gives the strongest impact immediately. Skin-popping gives a delayed maximal impact, up to ninety minutes.

The heroin Janis used that night she had purchased around four P.M. that afternoon from George, her supplier for as long as she used the drug. She was careful to use only one supplier, and he was careful about what he sold. Usually, he had a chemist check the drug before he sold it. For that batch, his chemist had been out of town. He had sold the dope without checking it. The dope Janis had bought that Saturday was four to ten times stronger than normal street heroin. It was 40 to 50 percent pure.

No one found Janis, lying crumpled on the floor, until the following evening around seven-thirty. Seth had refused to fly down the night before because he was playing strip pool with some waitresses from the Trident Restaurant, but he arrived Sunday afternoon. He called John Cooke before he left San Francisco, because he couldn't find Janis to tell her when to pick him up. John checked with Paul

Rothchild to see if Janis was at the studio, but Paul said she was uncharacteristically late for recording. John was at the hotel, so he grabbed a desk key (he had done that before) and went to her room.

When John saw Janis lying on the floor, he approached her, holding out a hand as though to shake her awake. One touch of her cold, firm flesh was all he needed to realize that he would not need to call her name again. He telephoned Bob Gordon, her attorney. Bob called a doctor friend and the police. As John waited for them to arrive, he sent someone to the airport to meet Seth and break the news to him.

Later John drove to the studio. He couldn't bear to give the band the news over the telephone. He wanted to do it in person. He pulled Paul outside and told him. Then they asked the engineers to leave. There was no way to say it but quick, so John just said, "Janis died." You could watch the effect sink into people, visibly changing their bodies. It continued to sink in for days.

The coroner and police searched the room the next day at eleven A.M. They found Janis's hype kit in the top dresser drawer of her room. They found a towel, some gauze, and a ball of cotton with blood on them. Later, they also found a red balloon containing a powder in the wastebasket. Tests determined it was heroin. The time lapse between finding the syringe and then the heroin seems to have been due to a friend's impulsive act. Someone had thought to remove the heroin from the room after her death, hoping to keep drugs out of the press. Later it was obvious that that wasn't a good idea, so the balloon was returned.

They called Janis's death an accidental overdose, though the coroner did a psychological autopsy, interviewing friends, checking her activities and establishing a state of mind. He needed to be sure it wasn't suicide. Strange, that a person known for dedication to the verve and excitement of life should immediately be considered potentially suicidal.

Questions and rumors about the details of her death circulated in the gossip circuit for years. People speculated on Janis's death as a CIA job, a contract killing, or some other fantasy. No such theory can surmount the facts. Some of Janis's friends knew that she had been using heroin for a few weeks. In addition to one fresh needle mark, there were several marks on her arms that showed enough healing to have been from the last week or so. The drug Janis used was extremely pure, though it may not have caused her to die on its own. Janis was also legally drunk. A death labeled "heroin overdose" is often the result of the interaction of different drugs, particularly heroin and alcohol. That weekend, several other people who had been customers of George, the heroin supplier, died. Their deaths were also called heroin overdoses.

Janis's friends still remember the shock of hearing she was dead. Even twenty years later, the feelings of the day rushed back as they described commiserating among themselves. Janis's death affected them, like me, in ways different from her life. Juli Paul had talked with Janis the Friday before she died. "She wanted me to come out to L.A. As soon as I heard that she died, I felt like, if I'd gone, maybe she wouldn't have, so there was guilt, too." Pat Nichols, who had been waiting for their movie date, vowed to stay away from heroin forever. She listened to Janis's death like she had listened to nothing before. Twenty years after Janis died, Pat is still clean.

"I lost six friends in six months from drugs," said Paul Roth-child. "The world changed radically. Janis's death was the most devastating thing in my life. We'd threatened to work together for years, and when we did, we decided we'd be together forever. It was the most fun we'd ever had in the studio. She was always one hundred ten percent there. I miss her tremendously, still." Sam Andrew, however, went out and scored some more dope, to help ease the pain of losing yet another friend.

Our hearts ached, those of us who loved her, but life went on. Paul and the band had to finish the album. They gave 100 percent, just like they did when Janis was in the room with them. A surreal quality entered the studio as they recorded new instrumental tracks to go under the vocal tracks they had cut for the original battle of the studio sounds. A strange feeling came over them, that anything they did had to be perfect this time. There would be no second chance. Janis's voice dominated their senses as they listened to the vocal and played their hearts onto the tape.

They also found the fun song "Mercedes Benz," recorded on a lark. During the band's summer tour, Janis had been sending messages through friends to have Michael McClure call her. He had written a song for a group he played with called Freewheeling McClure Montana. Michael McClure's friends Emmett Grogan and Rip Torn sang it

★

to Janis over a game of pool when they were all in New York. Janis finally called Michael, saying, "I'm singing a song with your 'Mercedes Benz' line in it." He said, "Will you sing it for me?" So she sang it over the telephone. He said, "I like my song better." "Do you mind if I use it?" she asked. "No, go ahead," he said, ignoring any discussions of money or credit. So they agreed they would both sing their own versions. Michael never thought of it as a business arrangement. He was just sharing art, as he was prone to do. Days later she died. Much later, he found she had shared the writer's royalty with him.

Finishing the recording took a few weeks. By October 18 they had completed a masterful album, *Pearl*. Critics often cite it as the best recording of Janis's work, the only time the musicians in the studio worked with her and not against her. *Popular Music,* an annotated guide to recordings, called *Pearl* "probably one of the best albums overall in the rock genre."

The day after Janis died, Paul ran into Bobby Neuwirth. Each commented on the haggard look of the other. "What's wrong?" "The telephone keeps ringing, and it's Janis. She says, 'It's okay, man. This is a good place. I'm in good shape. Don't worry about a thing.' " "Wow! I don't believe it! The same thing's been happening to me."

Bob Gordon had a similar experience. His life had been consumed by the mob scene of questioning people and legal details after her death. For weeks he did nothing but deal with the coroner's office, the investigation, the press, and our family. One Sunday afternoon, when the chaos was subsiding, he remembered, "I just kind of collapsed and was taking a nap and had a vision. It was very vivid, not like a dream that disappears. It was very forceful. She and I were sitting on the couch that was in the *Pearl* album cover, talking to each other. She said that she was just fine, that she had never felt as calm as she did then, and that it was time to go."

John Cooke had his own vision. "Some months after Janis died, I had a dream. It was at the end of a concert. Janis came offstage and I was waiting for her. She said, 'Was I okay?' with that little-girl uncertainty of hers, and I said, 'You were great.' I hugged her. It was incredibly vivid. I woke up with this ball of emotion inside me, and I felt that Janis had visited me from the grave. She wasn't just asking if she did all right in the concert. She was asking about her life. And I was so glad to have a chance to reassure her. 'You were great, Janis.' "

CHAPTER SIXTEEN

THE MEMORIAL
CELEBRATION

★

Come back and believe in my love
Come back and believe in my love
Come back and believe in the magic of love!

—Mark Spoelstra, "Magic of Love"

"GO BACK TO Port Arthur?" I asked incredulously. "I haven't been there in eighteen years!" My mother prevailed upon my brother and me to represent the family in a memorial ceremony for our sister, Janis. Sam Monroe, the head of the local historical society, had called her with the request. As the son of her former boss, Sam always had Mother's ear. He wanted help in developing an exhibit honoring Janis.

Sam was working with John Palmer, a Port Arthuran whom Janis vaguely knew in school. One of life's cruel ironies brought the successful businessman, John, a run-in with local society when he testified against a prominent family in an oil-siphoning scam. Smarting from the sting of a tarnished personal image, he developed a renewed empathy with outcasts. What more obvious totem was there to hoist in our town than Janis, a high school classmate of his, a woman applauded by the nation but whose name still evoked seething resentment in some proper hometown citizens? It was time, he declared earnestly, to welcome Janis back home, with full honor and love. Underwriting the cost of creating a bronze statue of her was his way of doing that.

★

John Palmer's symbolic effort was all it took to bring forth the fans in our hometown area—those dedicated to her and her music, those who shared her resentment of social rules, and those who wanted to make peace with the past. The press caught it, and the ideas kept rolling. On January 19, 1988, which would have been her forty-fifth birthday, Port Arthur held a dedication ceremony for the museum exhibit and unveiled a statue of Janis Joplin.

More than five thousand people crammed into a hall that was designed to hold only three thousand. Refinery workers, college students, and housewives stood alongside toddlers and adolescents. Most came from in and around our hometown of Port Arthur, Texas. Chartered busloads of people traveled from nearby Houston, and some came from places as distant as Iowa and Canada.

They came to honor a hometown girl who had made good in the distant and seemingly foreign world of San Francisco and 1960s rock and roll. Janis had publicly scorned our hometown during many press interviews. The kindest thing she had said about it was that it was a good place to leave. Twenty years after her death, the local town fathers felt it was acceptable to bury the hatchet that she had lofted. They ignored her role as rock-and-roll knight jousting with our culture's innate hypocrisy. Instead, they grasped her more acceptable achievement of making great music that sold many records and earned her an enduring spot in many music lovers' hearts.

Whether fans or friends, their ideas of Janis were determined in part by the hoopla of fame in our culture. In *The Frenzy of Renown*, Leo Braudy said there were four elements to fame: the person, her accomplishment, the immediate publicity, and what posterity thought about her ever since. In *Intimate Strangers: The Culture of Celebrity*, Richard Schickel wrote, "After death, stars become cartoon characters, owned by fans, with the true elements that didn't fit allowed to disappear, and the other aspects embellished." People came to the ceremony with their own viewpoints, but all were ready to pay their respects.

The nature of Janis's death, from a heroin overdose, seems to have overshadowed her image in life. The press seldom writes about her fun-loving character, her concentration on art, or her social attitudes, which were so familiar to those of us who knew her. In many people's minds, the Janis Joplin story is mostly about the steps she took that led to her overdosing on drugs.

When Janis died in 1970, we never expected her image to grow, evolve, and gel into one of the preeminent symbols of the times. We were waiting for the public interest to fade, for her life and image to return to those who knew her for longer than the four years she was in the spotlight. Instead, we shared her love with the public.

Mother put her heart into finding items to send for the exhibit. True to her character, she decided that if they were going to do a Janis Joplin presentation, then they were going to do it right. She did her best to send all the trivia of Janis's early life, the commonplace things that she touched or used. Pulled from the bottoms of bureau drawers and boxes long packed away, Mom sent the mementos and her love.

How odd the things seemed in glass-and-wood display cases as historical evidence of the particulars of my sister's existence. Her slide rule, the one we all shared, was still kept safe in its dark green hard-leather case, with only a few teenage scribbles on it. The curator placed it next to her black cloth-covered Bible, the one she got when she joined the First Christian Church downtown. The book showed the wear of curious young hands turning the fine paper pages and pondering the colorful pictures within it. A big green book grabbed my heart. In large type the cover announced, *The Letters of F. Scott Fitzgerald.* Reading was the backbone of the Joplin family, and nothing represented Janis better than that book.

Mother included the *Port Arthur News* piece about Janis during the summer of 1957, when she worked at Gates Memorial Library. The yellowing newsprint photo captured the adolescent Janis with neatly curled hair and a beaming, proud, innocent smile next to an illustration she did of L. Frank Baum's *Oz* characters. People in town donated the original sketches, which they had purchased from Janis long ago. Her carefree Patchwork Girl of Oz danced merrily alongside her jaunty Scarecrow.

What Michael and I didn't know ahead of time, but probably should have surmised, was our responsibility to talk to the press. There is an art to giving interviews that Janis knew. Being new to the game, I found it awkward. The press people were genuine, honest folk, but many were fresh out of college. They had been in grade school when Janis was singing. They assumed too much from what little research they did. That inadequacy made their questions strange to us. One woman asked, "What was the first odd thing you noticed about Janis?"

★

Michael and I looked at each other and laughed! How can we tell someone that our sister was never weird to us?

The press had a heyday, crafting such headlines as TOWN THAT SCORNED JANIS, NOW APPLAUDING HER. One reporter asked about Janis's hideaway, a retreat that she purportedly had fixed up in our garage. She told us it was a place Janis had gone when life in Port Arthur became too frustrating. Where did these stories come from? Michael and I could only murmur that we hadn't noticed Janis retreating to anywhere. Instead, Janis had stood in the center of things. We explained that she did sometimes paint in the garage when the weather was good or when she wanted the extra room. We couldn't figure out how to get across that artistic expression was the norm in our family. We told the reporter that most of those Port Arthur stories were a bit overstated. "It's just a town, you know, nothing particularly special one way or the other." Michael added, "Janis was a great showman, that was part of her line. It had a great effect and made a point."

Janis's image and quotes have been so distilled and twisted over the years that their relevance has faded. Explaining her and her statements about Port Arthur was impossible without talking about the sixties and how they evolved. I couldn't get that across in one quick phrase, the kind that newsfolk like to quote.

After a while their questions sounded the same, as though the news corps had gathered over a cup of strong Texas coffee and arrived at a consensus about what was important in the event. A staple query was, "What do you think Janis would say about this ceremony?" That question more than any other evoked clear memories of Janis at home. I felt safe saying that she would have liked the ceremony. I could imagine her chuckling and saying, "Well, it's about time," with a smile showing a twinge of ironic amusement.

After we completed our obligatory public-relations job, our attention returned to the event that was unfolding around us. We were taken with the slow-moving, densely packed crowd of strangers who stared at Michael and me as though we were also on view inside a glass-and-wood display case.

Among the hordes of unfamiliar bodies, long-forgotten faces began appearing, older but still recognizable as our former neighbors. Their presence immediately made the event into a true homecoming.

Bodie Pryor, who still lived directly behind our old house, hugged us and said that he came to honor Janis. He was solid and caring, a person who never wavered from his inner sense of faith. "Janis was a wonderful, happy girl. Whatever is written, I don't care about. I knew her as a wonderful person."

Bodie and the other familiar faces took seats in the center of the large gymnasiumlike room. There was a stage, with little metal chairs at one end, and a line of dark-suited gentlemen who filled them. They were the local dignitaries who gave the ceremony its civic legitimacy. There were rows of metal chairs in front of the stage and bleachers along both sides of the room, which the growing crowd had long since filled. Those who merely came on time stood, if they could get into the room at all. From time to time a body pushed its way near enough to the stage to yell, "Laura, Laura, do you remember me?" The air was charged with emotional expectancy.

The obvious love displayed for Janis helped me form the words I was planning to speak to the crowd. The rising din of their talking developed into an acoustical roar that was hardly dented by the speaker's insistent pounding with the gavel. The call to order slowly rippled from the stage as people shushed those around them.

The ceremony began. It could have been a convention of the Kiwanis Club or the Rotarians, I thought, with the dry comments of literal-minded citizens called to stand at the podium. The audience listened politely, waiting. The mayor of Port Arthur, Malcolm Clark, surprised us all by bellowing, "Happy Birthday, Janis!" He tripped the spring that had held the crowd's bottled-up emotions. The happiness was compelling, overwhelming my mental retreat into reflection, encouraging a feeling of euphoria.

The noise dimmed as the tone returned to proper comments about the ceremony. Sam Monroe announced his pleasure in opening the permanent Janis Joplin exhibit in the Lamar University Library. He was honest in saying that Mayor Malcolm Clark, the chamber of commerce, and the museum hoped that the exhibit would be a success.

Though the fans came because they loved Janis, the local businessmen supported the event to draw visitors to the town. Port Arthur was hurting economically, and they wanted tourist dollars. The mayor

★

got the necessary local support by explaining that Elvis Presley did a lot for Memphis, and so Janis Joplin could do a lot for Port Arthur.

I overheard a local dignitary explain, "God tells us to forgive, and I can forgive Janis." I think that part of his frustration with Janis was due to her condemnation of a town that he liked. People remembered her derogatory press comments, and they aroused emotion, even in 1988. But much of his anger seemed due to Janis's press statements about using drugs. It took him twenty years, but he managed to forgive Janis for encouraging others to use drugs by her public conduct. Janis was surely the biggest loser on that score. Drugs killed her, with her youthful folly of thinking she was tough enough to handle them. I have often wondered if Janis and her crowd believed, like Timothy Leary, that drugs were a shortcut to discovering a greater reality. Was it her search for truth, honesty, and self? No matter, they forgave Janis.

Others, however, haven't forgiven *them* for their disdain for her kind. Dave Moriaty railed about it to me. "The opinion that irritates me," he exclaimed, "is that Janis was some kind of singer from hell, that she had a terribly sordid life-style, while society was rewarding the ability to lie and how well someone conformed. Port Arthurans weren't sexually pure. They had their gays and fornicators! I don't think Janis was any more orgiastic or amoral or drugged than any of the rest of society at that time. Housewives had speed, Benzedrine, and Seconal so they could go to sleep! Drinking alcohol was the way boys were supposed to prove they were men. My friends nearly killed themselves trying to be men!

"What the hell was Janis doing that was so bad on the West Coast? She wasn't ripping people off. She wasn't stealing their money, exploiting her workers, or engaging in a giant con game where she got everybody's bread and split. . . . Janis just rubbed society's own prejudices in its face. . . . Janis had a more stringent moral code than normal, because she didn't engage in the normal polite lies that society requires of us!"

Some people have seen Janis as the embodiment of wrong. The rock-and-rollers who followed her generation built on the shocking behavior of their forebears. To catch up to the new norm, Janis stories became increasingly embellished in order to maintain her reputation for being outrageous. I have been told in serious tones that Janis performed naked at the Texas International Pop Festival. The young man who spoke so authoritatively was not old enough to have attended the event. He knew only by hearsay, and he believed every word of it.

Some people took a superficial meaning from phrases like the song lyric "Get it while you can." They thought in terms of getting sex, getting money, getting experience, etc. Some, like John Cooke, understood that it had to do with total concentration, a willingness to give *all* of yourself to the art, to not hold back, to not wait. At any one moment, there is nothing going on but one thing. What someone produces or gets out of that moment depends on how much he or she can concentrate and commit to it. Singing enabled Janis to give all of herself to her performing. Janis often said that she "lived for that half hour onstage," because it was so real to her.

People heard Janis say, "Get off your butt and feel," and some felt scared of what they might feel. And Janis could empathize with them too. She said, "Oh, yeah, I'm scared. I think, Oh, it's so close, can I make it? If I fail, I'll fail in front of the whole world. If I miss, I'll never have a second chance on nothing. But I gotta risk it. I never hold back, man. I'm always on the outer edge of probability."

So the Port Arthur ceremony embodied a local compromise about her. Many citizens didn't want to honor Janis and wrote angry letters to the editor of the *Port Arthur News*. To appease that sensitivity, the ceremony grew to encompass all local musicians who were successful in the entertainment industry. The list amazed me. In the exhibit hall, alongside the cabinets holding Janis's slide rule and high school yearbook, were displays covering the other musicians. There were numerous gold albums and rhinestone-encrusted performing costumes with summary notes beside them.

The son of the Big Bopper was there, accepting the honors for his father, who had been a local disk jockey before he wrote "Chantilly Lace." Later he toured with Buddy Holly and Ritchie Valens, and the three died in a plane crash together. The list of local stars was long, and included Johnny and Edgar Winter, Tex Ritter, Ivory Joe Hunter, Harry James, Clarence "Gatemouth" Brown, J. P. "Big Bopper" Richardson, Glen Wells, ZZ Top, and George Jones.

When the announcer called each name, a representative

mounted the stage to stand in a line before the crowd. I increasingly wondered what it was about this area that produced such talent. I often thought that few people understood Janis's album *Kozmic Blues* because they couldn't relate to its base in Port Arthur. I think it was her rendition of the Louisiana music she had heard in the Big Oak Club, where underage Texans went to dance and drink.

They saved Janis for last, as the chief honoree of the evening. Michael and I were her stand-ins. Even the two of us didn't give fans what they wanted. We were just the best available. I was asked to speak to the crowd for a moment.

"It's good to be here tonight," I began, "back in Texas, back in Port Arthur, back home." The crowd applauded and whistled on "home."

"There is just something about home, where all the familiar sights and sounds remind you of pleasant memories of a wonderful time growing up.

"There is just something about being a Texan that sticks in your blood, so that no matter where you live or what you do, you'll always be a Texan." The crowd erupted again, and I felt like I had struck a chord with them.

"In many ways I think that Janis was like the quintessential Texan, the oil wildcatter, determined to do whatever was necessary to succeed at her chosen profession." The developing roar from the crowd forced me to pause.

"In one of her many letters home, Janis wrote of her career. She said that when she was first starting out, she had to work hard to get any success. When she had some success, she found she had to work even harder to maintain it." The crowd quieted, listening to actual words from Janis: " 'Then, when you're number one, why, you have to knock yourself out to stay on top.' " The crowd was then dead silent.

"Certainly, Janis had a way with the press that garnered her much useful publicity. Perhaps it is because of that that I am so pleased to be among friends and neighbors, among those who can, with me, remember the child, the adolescent, the young woman, apart from the flash and glitter that so dominated her time in the spotlight.

"I have mixed emotions about being here tonight. I don't want to be here. I would prefer being at home, in my kitchen, baking a birthday cake, drinking coffee, and talking with my sister."

A resounding "Amen" came from the audience, from the cold metal chairs near the stage. I was so grateful. Someone was with me.

"But I can't be there, and it does give me particular pleasure to be here with you tonight, the people of Port Arthur, remembering the woman, my sister, Janis Joplin."

The audience roared and stood. As I sat back down, a blue-suited gentleman tapped me on the shoulder and said, "That was wonderful!" I had surprised him. I had intended to say something meaningful, but it was only then that I realized all they had wanted from me was to show up and say, "Thank you." Oh, well, I had done what I wanted to do.

I continued to reflect until I noticed that everyone onstage was moving aside to watch a twenty-minute clip from the documentary *Janis*. The excerpts included a wonderful interview with her in Stockholm. She was so young then, hardly twenty-six years old, while I would be forty just a few months after the ceremony. Yet Janis will always be my older sister, and so I felt younger than her.

The movie showed her onstage, singing and looking radiantly happy. On the screen, a reporter asked about her musical influences, and I smiled, knowing the first two: Mom and Pop. Pop, who couldn't hold a tune, had a musical soul, though. Several times he called us kids to the living room. He sat us on the couch in the living room and said, "Now, just listen." He carefully selected his favorite record of cello music, Pablo Casals playing "Kol Nidrei," and placed it on the turntable. As the needle settled into the record's grooves, our father settled into his chair, transfixed, with tears in his eyes. "Can you kids hear that? The sadness? Just listen," he pleaded. So, his firstborn child sang her heart out, with her father's tears woven into her melodies.

The crowd loved the music on the film. I didn't think the screaming and thundering could get much louder, but it did. We almost felt like a living and breathing animal as we swayed and sang with the music.

Next was the unveiling of the statue. The sculptor, Doug Clark, and his benefactor stood near the drape-covered piece. Though John Palmer liked to explain his reasons to the press, Clark seemed to be a man who preferred to let his art speak for him. Michael and I pulled a cord and revealed the statue. I raised my eyes to get a good view of it. Suddenly, the newsfolk were back. Light bulbs were flashing everywhere. Hands were on me, and someone said, "Stand in front of the statue," and flash went the cameras. Another person pushed a dozen roses into my hands. I wanted to hold the roses gracefully, like a beauty queen, but the flowers were in a vase full of water. I could hardly hold them upright and get my head over the top. "Smile and look up at the statue. Stand to the side," the photographers directed. They posed Michael and me repeatedly, but we took it calmly. After all, we had said we would come. We couldn't say, "Forget it," just because we hadn't known how greatly the event would intrigue the press.

The lights were still flashing as the ever-eager reporters were asking, "What do you think of the statue, Laura?" I wanted to give them some glowing and inspiring comment, but I couldn't even see it because of the blinding flashbulbs! Rush, rush, rush.

The crowd broke up the press action. The stands were emptying and people were trying to get a better glimpse of the statue. Old friends were tugging at our sleeves, trying to get a chance to say hello. It was a great feeling.

Two press people were insistent. They hadn't gotten an interview, and so they interrupted me as I was talking to one of Janis's old high school gang, Jim Langdon. His deep voice and piercing eyes challenged me to prove I could recall the girl beyond all of this. I wanted to escape the hubbub around us and find a convivial drinking hole in which to absorb his recollections. I wanted to know what he thought of Janis saying she was a "loner" in high school. All I remembered as a child was Janis continually being with friends.

Then the reality of the event hit me. The fans were loose. Most people milled around in the intensely packed crowd, looking at the exhibits and casting curious glances our way. Their eyes showed calmness, that the ceremony had given them the outlet they had needed. Occasionally someone came close to say, "It's about time they honored her," or, "I'm a real fan of Janis's. Just wanted you to know how much I loved her." Their voices were somber and at times I felt as though they were reciting a litany and I was an icon.

There were several requests for us to sign a poster from this event. One girl wanted her blue-jean jacket signed, high on the back of the shoulder. People were sweet, loving, and moved, and they were sharing that with us. The mood was joyous and jubilant. No one could have attended this event without feeling the warmth and excitement.

There was also something else, which hit me full force when a fan ran from the crowd and grabbed me from behind with an unwanted bear hug. "I just had to do that," she said. She grasped my shoulders and stared into my eyes. "Wow!" She could only repeat that word. I tried to pull clear, feeling that she was using my body to hug something in herself, and I wasn't sure I wanted the job. Later I heard her say, "Why can't I be Janis Joplin's sister?" I wondered why that was her wish. If she were going to wish at all, why didn't she just wish to be Janis?

Perhaps the audience also held someone like the fellow who introduced himself to Mother years ago while she was tending her flowers in the front yard. "I want you to know," he said, "that the day your daughter died, I quit using drugs. I figured if she wasn't strong enough to handle it, then I wasn't either." Wherever I looked in the faces around me, I relived experiences like those I had heard from others. Pop had told me that the fans didn't want anything from them, even the ones who wrote years after Janis died. They just wanted Mother and him to know them.

The crowd at the ceremony besieged us, and we felt overwhelmed. I understood why famous people have bodyguards. It was the hands. People reached out from every direction, like elephant trunks searching for peanuts. Michael and I needed to leave.

We stepped outside into the balmy South Texas air. We relaxed as its cool buoyancy pulled us from the intensity of the building. The true magnitude of the event then confronted us. There were loudspeakers on the lawn, which had conveyed our words to hundreds of people unable to fit into the Jefferson County Civic Center. The speakers vibrated with music from the continuing celebration as we stared at the packed parking lot. Automobiles were everywhere—on the grass, on the interstate, and even on the access road.

As we piled into my car, I looked back at the auditorium. Through the open doors I could see the crowd looking at the exhibit.

Above them on the wall I saw the display of Janis's artwork. My eyes clung to the portrait she did of me as an eleven-year-old. I remembered sitting in the bedroom, being still and very bored. I had hoped Janis would paint me as I felt myself. I had fantasized she would give me the image of a beautiful Southern belle in a fancy ball gown standing elegantly beside a fireplace mantel. Instead, she painted me as I was: a bored eleven-year-old looking over her shoulder to see what her big sister was doing.

Janis saw me as I was and loved me as I was. I didn't need to be a Southern belle to be worthy of her unlimited affection. Throughout her career she gave to her fans in the same way. In her own stumbling, determined fashion, she let them know that all were worthy of total acceptance and love just because of who they were.

She sang songs that helped people find themselves. One woman told the story of her constant vigilance to maintain her sobriety. One morning she had been sorely tempted to drink, until she heard Janis singing "Me and Bobby McGee" on the radio. The line about *freedom* meaning there's nothing left to lose released her from her desire to drink. She knew she had something to lose—she had her sobriety.

Because Janis died from drugs, her life can never be separated from the growth of the love generation's use of alcohol and other drugs. Some people see the sixties generation turning their backs on the standards their parents held, and on moderation in all things. It may be equally true that they merely took the subliminal messages of the culture that raised them and put them into practice. If billboards and advertisements showed men and women romancing with cigarettes and alcohol, the kids inextricably linked them. If sporting events and concerts were promoted by beer companies, then kids equated alcohol with physical health and good, clean fun. If all adult parties and celebrations started with an alcoholic toast, then the kids learned that good times require drink.

Janis's death was labeled a heroin overdose, allowing people who don't use heroin to feel safe from such a fate. Yet her death was probably due to the interaction of heroin with alcohol. If so, she died an alcohol-related death. Also, she didn't start her "drug use" with heroin. She started with tobacco, then went on to alcohol, marijuana, speed, and a smattering of other readily available social drugs.

Janis's drinking started like most people's, socially before the age of twenty-one. She was on the accepted path to maturity. She bought the medical profession's belief in drugs as panaceas. She accepted the culture's faith in chemical substances solving feeling problems. She agreed with the writers and cultural leaders of her day that the illegal drugs used by her group were little different from the legal ones used by the older generation.

Janis was brave enough to face the inequities of life head-on. She spoke out against racial discrimination when it wasn't popular to do so. She pursued a life bent on appeasing her gut-level desire to know the soul. She rejected any compromises like settling down into a suburban routine. Janis turned her back on her intellect as a means to awaken her emotional self, believing that what eluded her mentally, she might find in feelings. She zeroed in on the cultural weakness of her day—how to handle emotions. Our ordered society is so incredibly great with the mind and so inept in dealing with emotional discomfort.

She tried to find a new way of living. She was appropriately named after the Roman god Janus, who ruled over endings and beginnings. Janus is depicted in profile, with two identical faces looking in opposite directions. January, my sister's birth month, was named for Janus. Her whole life was intertwined with the mission of change and becoming.

Janis tried valiantly to change herself, and so she helped many who sought emotional change in themselves. She was never one to let the old ways die silent, undisturbed deaths. She drove them over cliffs and hurled torrents of anger after them. Before her death, a new, calmer self was just visible in the thicket of her voluminous cynical diatribes. Her rebirth was still in labor when her death cut it short.

The truth that she found was in her music. She gave up everything for it because she found nothing else like it. She found a new reality for herself while she was singing, and when she was tuned in to that power, she gave pure love to her audience.

Her rapport with her audience taught her that love wasn't about *getting* something from other people. The good feeling comes from *giving*—giving love. She struggled to apply that lesson to the rest of her life.

She tried valiantly to relate to others past the veils of cultural conditioning. It was as if she followed the traditional Hindu greeting ritual where two people, upon meeting, place their hands on their chests, palms together, with fingertips pointing to their chins. In this way they signify, "The God in me greets the God in you." Janis sang to the world from inside a tidal wave that swept her along and called itself a social revolution. Janis was one of the movement's standard-bearers, crying against the "You just can't do that!" rules.

Janis sang: "There's a fire inside of every one of us / You're gonna need it now." We can't hold on to the ideas of past days; the 1960s blew them apart for us. We are changed. And still Janis's songs encourage us. What we'll find, we don't know, but the urge to seek is ever compelling. We know, like Janis, that if we don't seek, we'll merely stagnate in empty social roles.

Janis and the love generation showed us the importance of love as a guide. Janis and Big Brother called, "Come back and believe in my love/Come back and believe in the magic of love." Janis's music always seemed to go straight to the heart.

She even answered the questions about how she would be described by future writers looking back on the 1960s. "What are they going to say about me," Janis repeated the interviewer's question, "a silly kid up there? I think it's going to be that my music was when the black and white thing broke down, and black could dig what white sang, and white could dig what black sang . . . and it was all music, and get down to where it is supposed to be."

Because of Janis, Michael and I get together at least twice a year to deal with her business. It's a funny reason for getting together. It's much different, say, from joining for Thanksgiving dinner (which we also do). The work of wrestling with decisions has spilled over and brought us closer than I think we would have been otherwise. Family is an ongoing commitment in our lives.

Once, we were in Tucson, at Michael's house. With the aromas of bacon and coffee wafting through his adobe home, we were enjoying the morning quiet. *Honk, honk,* went a car horn, disturbing the silence. Later, another person repeated the maneuver, yelling loudly, "Janis was the greatest!"

"It's the Day of the Dead," Michael explained to my quizzical expression. "*Día de los muertos.* It's a day Mexicans remember their deceased loved ones. Fans of Janis's have been driving by my house this day every year, since someone found out I lived here," he continued.

The celebration is so much more exuberant than those of Anglo-Saxon culture. This most Mexican of events is a time of respect, love, and enjoyment. Relatives honoring their dead do so actively, not just in quiet recollections. They might serve the honored person's favorite meal, set a place for him or her at the table, or do a favorite activity of that person—for instance, tending a special tree in the yard.

Like many Mexican holidays, special folk art developed to signify the Day of the Dead. Artists carve tiny little figures of people and paint them to look like skeletons. They place them in a scene that is expressive of the pleasures that the person found special during his or her life. The whole piece is often no bigger than six inches long.

A setting for Janis would include a tiny human figure, painted white with black bones, dressed in her favorite clothes. Janis's artist might put rose-colored glasses on her eyes and a sequined performing costume on her frame. There would be a skeleton rock band behind Janis, complete with tiny carved guitars and drums, and a crowd of skeleton fans dancing in front of the stage. I would put dozens of roses on the stage, a light show on the stage wall, and her lost dog, George, waiting in the wings. Surely that would be Janis's favorite scene, to be savored on this most special of days, the day for remembering.

The cars kept coming by Michael's house, slowing significantly as they passed. Their shouted words warmed me with their blessings. She was not forgotten.

A few months later, I was at home, working on a new boxed-set collection of Janis's music. I was listening to each of her albums, one after the other, in a new sequence. Tunes from different time periods were mixed together.

I listened intently to "Try" and "Piece of My Heart," and thought back on the Day of the Dead, Janis's fans, and the fun of a Janis concert. I listened on through "Work Me, Lord" and "Mercedes Benz," drawn to sing along, defying her stereophonic voice to overshadow my real-life volume. My daughter and a friend ran in to check out this unmotherly behavior, two gleeful five-year-olds chanting,

"Aunt Janis, rock and roll." I raised my eyebrows, never missing a word of the melody, and started to dance, encouraging them to join the music.

Jumping up and down, swaying, shaking our hair, twisting, strutting with our arms, we danced. We screamed along on "Summertime" and "Maybe," and swayed and caught our breath on "A Woman Left Lonely." We grooved together, watching each others' eyes, smiling at the replies within on "Nobody Knows You When You're Down and Out." On and on we went, tune after tune, until our feelings were exhausted. "Little Girl Blue" called us to each other, in one big kissing cuddle, with Janis the most hugged. We lay on the floor and listened to "I Need a Man to Love" and "Blindman," and started to cry with "Me and Bobby McGee."

My beloved sister is remembered.

ACKNOWLEDGMENTS
AND SOURCES

★

I AM ETERNALLY indebted to the many wonderful people who gave me their time and shared their hearts, memories, and insights. Both my work and my life have benefited from their willing gifts. Acknowledging and thanking individuals is inherently inadequate because of the intangible ideas and the feelings that can never be fully expressed.

Feelings were a large part of writing this book—hearing about others', uncovering my own, and resolving many of them. The Sedona Institute's "Release" technique was instrumental in helping me deal with the emotional ups and downs that come with writing a book like this. I am sure that I could not have completed this manuscript without taking the Phoenix-based workshop and video course.

In the following pages I want to acknowledge the individuals who provided information and my major written references for the appropriate chapters. Though many interviews and texts provided information useful in many chapters, I have listed names by area of primary contribution. I do so with the expectation that the reader will realize that information was often used generally, not just in a specific chapter.

There are some people whose contributions were so broad that I want to acknowledge them here.

First, I want to thank my mother, Dorothy Joplin, for her faith, trust, and help in my years of working on this project.

Second, I want to thank my brother, Michael Joplin, for his constant support and continual help in putting the book together. In particular, Michael researched and helped select the photographs in the book.

Third, I want to express my gratitude for my husband, Richard,

★

and his support over the years it took me to put this book together. He also served as my computer expert, keeping our system functional and training me in how to use it.

Fourth, I want to thank Robert Gordon, Janis's attorney, for his quality, caring advice throughout the past twenty-two years.

Fifth, I am grateful to Manny Fox for his steady attention and input as I wrote the book, especially in the early stages when the task seemed so daunting.

Sixth, I am indebted to my many friends who have read through early drafts and given me much-needed feedback: Marilyn Green, Carolyn Koplin, Liz Kreider, Carolyn Manly, Rod and Marilyn Mitchell, Barbara Pollack, and Nancy Sparks. Special thanks to those who helped edit early drafts: Mae Chu, Laura Museo, and Marie Rallis.

Seventh, I want to thank my editor, Doug Stumpf, and my production editor, Beth Pearson, at Villard Books. Doug's attention, ideas, and faith, along with Beth's prodding questions and focus on detail, helped immeasurably in turning a rough manuscript into the book I wanted it to be.

Eighth, I want to acknowledge the special support and contribution of several of Janis's friends:

Jim Langdon and Dave Moriaty, who both encouraged me to write the book, feeling that a more complete story of Janis's life needed to be told. I especially want to thank Dave for fact-checking the manuscript.

John Cooke, who provided support, access to his files documenting the times, his brilliant memory, and a friendly willingness to talk whenever needed. Special thanks for his editorial comments on an early draft.

Pat Nichols, whose sincerity and caring in providing information helped me understand many things.

The members of Big Brother and the Holding Company—Sam Andrew, Peter Albin, Dave Getz, and James Gurley—who provided information and permission to use the lyrics published by their Cheap Thrills Music Company. Thanks also to Sam for his help in fact-checking the book.

I want to apologize in advance for any oversights in acknowledging the time, information, and attention of anyone that I may have neglected to mention. No slight was intended.

CHAPTER 1: OCTOBER 1970

Peggy Caserta, Dr. Henry Chu, John Cooke, Bob Gordon, Mimi Krohn, Pat Nichols. "Rock and Roll Woman," by Michael Thomas, in *The Age of Rock,* Jonathan Eisen, ed., Vintage, New York, 1969.

CHAPTER 2: OUR ANCESTORS

Ima Jo Bryant, Gerald East, Vern and Eva East, Bob and Eleanor Hanson, Grace Hanson, Lorena Hempell, J. Mike Joplin, Marjorie Joplin, Ellen Jopling, Mimi Krohn, Donna MacBride, Kate McDonald, Violet Merryman, Wilma Parnell, Pauline Webb.

"The Ancestors of Henry Sherman Hanson," a paper by James Hanson, 1991.

"The English Ancestry of Hezekiah Hoar of Taunton, Massachusetts," by Lyon J. Hoard; New England Historical and Genealogical Register, Boston, January 1987.

Generations: The History of America's Future 1584-2069, by William Strauss and Neil Howe, Morrow, New York, 1991.

A History of Women in America, by Carol Hymowitz and Michaele Weissman, Bantam Books, New York, 1978.

"The Jopling-Joplin Family," by Dorothy Eason, Fricks and Adams.

Lone Star: A History of Texas and the Texans, by T. R. Fehrenbach, Collier, New York, 1985.

"Memoirs of the Robert Ury Porter Home and Family," a paper by Eleanor Porter McSpadden, 1970.

The Oxford History of the American People, volumes I and II, by Samuel Eliot Morison, New American Library, New York, 1972.

The Reformation, by Edith Simon and the editors of Time-Life Books, Time Inc., New York, 1966.

A Religious History of the American People, by Sydney E. Ahlstrom, Yale University Press, New Haven, 1972.

Slavery and Freedom, by James Oakes, Alfred A. Knopf, New York, 1990.

Texas: An Album of History, by James L. Haley, Doubleday, New York, 1985.

Trial by Fire: A People's History of the Civil War and Reconstruction, by Page Smith, Penguin, New York, 1982.

CHAPTER 3: JANIS'S CHILDHOOD

Karleen Bennett, Kristen Bowen, Dorothy Joplin, Michael Joplin, Mimi Krohn, Roger and Jimmy Pryor, Dorothy Robyn, Jack Smith, Marilyn and Carolyn Thompson.

Great Expectations: America and the Baby Boom Generation, by Landon Y. Jones, Ballantine, New York, 1981.

Lone Star: A History of Texas and the Texans, by T. R. Fehrenbach, Collier, New York, 1985.

The Oxford History of the American People, volume I, by Samuel Eliot Morison, New American Library, New York, 1972.

Port Arthur, sponsored by the writer's program of the WPA in Texas, Anson Jones Press, 1940.

Texas: An Album of History, by James L. Haley, Doubleday, New York, 1985.

★

CHAPTER 4: ADOLESCENCE

Karleen Bennett, Kristen Bowen, Adrian Haston, Jim Langdon, Grant Lyons, Sam Monroe, Dave Moriaty, Tary Owens, Jack Smith, Randy Tennant.

Great Expectations: America and the Baby Boom Generation, by Landon Y. Jones, Ballantine, New York, 1981.

In a Different Voice: Psychological Theory and Women's Development, by Carol Gilligan, Harvard University Press, Cambridge, Mass., 1982.

In the New World: Growing Up with America 1960-1984, by Lawrence Wright, Alfred A. Knopf, New York, 1988.

South to Louisiana: The Music of the Cajun Bayous, by John Broven, Pelican Publishing Co., Gretna, La., 1987.

CHAPTER 5: COLLEGE AND THE VENICE BEAT SCENE

All of the people and references in Chapter 4, plus: Gloria Haston, Rae Logan, John Maynard, Dave McQueen, Patti Mock, Lionel Rolfe.

In Search of Literary L.A., by Lionel Rolfe, California Classics Books, Los Angeles, 1991.

Modigliani, the Pure Bohemian, by June Rose, St. Martin's Press, New York, 1990.

Venice West: The Beat Generation in Southern California, by John Arthur Maynard, Rutgers University Press, New Brunswick, N.J., 1991.

CHAPTER 6: AUSTIN, TEXAS

Pat Brown, John Clay, Bill Helmer, Jack Jackson, Bill Killeen, Ted Klein, Jim Langdon, Rod and Marilyn Mitchell, Dave Moriaty, Gilbert Shelton, Powell St. John, and many of Janis's friends from high school and college mentioned earlier.

Special thanks to Dave Harman for researching the Austin music scene; Claude Matthews's video on Kenneth Threadgill, *Singing the Yodeling Blues*; John Wheat and John Slate at the Barker Texas History Library at the University of Texas; and Texas Student Publications in Austin, Texas, for allowing us to use articles, photographs, and cartoons from the *Ranger* and *The Summer Texan.*

A History of Underground Comics, by Mark James Estren, Ronin Publishing, Berkeley, 1989.

In the New World: Growing Up with America 1960-1984, by Lawrence Wright, Alfred A. Knopf, New York, 1988.

Screening the Blues: Aspects of the Blues Tradition, by Paul Oliver, Da Capo Press, New York, 1968.

CHAPTER 7: THE SAN FRANCISCO BEAT SCENE

Peter Albin, Pat Brown, Nick Gravenites, Adrian and Gloria Haston, Chet Helms, Seth Joplin, Kenai, Jim Langdon, Rae Logan, Pat Nichols, Gilbert Shelton, Linda (Gottfried) Wauldron.

The Female Hero in American and British Literature, by Carol Pearson and Katherine Pope, R. R. Bowker Co., New York, 1981.

Ferlinghetti, by Barry Silesky, Warner Books, New York, 1990.

Ginsberg, by Barry Miles, Harper Perennial, New York, 1989.

Jack Kerouac, by Tom Clark, Paragon House, New York, 1984.

CHAPTER 8: HOME AGAIN

Karleen Bennett, Adrian and Gloria Haston, Chet Helms, Patti Mock, Tary Owens, Jack Smith, Linda (Gottfried) Wauldron.

Buried Alive, by Myra Friedman, William Morrow & Co., New York, 1973.

The Story of Rock, by Carl Belz, Harper Colophon Books, New York, 1969.

CHAPTERS 9-15

The remainder of the book deals with Janis's life in the San Francisco rock-and-roll scene. Many people provided important information from this time period. I include their names here to note their contribution to the rest of the book. Peter Albin, Sam Andrew, Peggy Caserta, John Cooke, Dave Getz, Bob Gordon, Linda Gravenites, Nick Gravenites, James Gurley, Pat Nichols, Tary Owens, Richard Ryan. The following texts were resources for the period 1966 through 1970.

The Age of Rock, Jonathan Eisen, ed., Vintage Books, New York, 1969.

Buried Alive, by Myra Friedman, William Morrow & Co, New York, 1973.

The Haight-Ashbury: A History, by Charles Perry, Vintage Books, New York, 1985.

A History of Underground Comics, by Mark James Estren, Ronin Publishing, Inc., Berkeley, 1974.

Hit Men: Power Brokers and Fast Money Inside the Music Business, by Fredric Dannen, Times Books, New York, 1990.

Intoxication, by Ronald K. Siegel, Pocket Books, New York, 1989.

Licit and Illicit Drugs, by Edward M. Brecher and the editors of Consumer Reports, Little, Brown and Co., Boston, 1972.

One More Saturday Night, by Sandy Troy, St. Martin's Press, New York, 1991.

The Pharmer's Almanac: A Training Manual on the Pharmacology of Psychoactive Drugs, by Anthony B. Radcliffe, Carol F. Sites, Peter A. Rush, and Joe Cruse, MAC Publishing, Denver, 1985.

Rock Folk, by Michael Lydon, Citadel Press, New York, 1990.

Rock of Ages: The Rolling Stone History of Rock and Roll, by Ed Ward, Geoffrey Stokes, and Ken Tucker, Rolling Stone Press, New York, 1986.

The Rolling Stone Illustrated History of Rock & Roll, by Jim Miller, ed., Random House, New York, 1980.

Storming Heaven: LSD and the American Dream, by Jay Stevens, Harper Perennial Library, New York, 1988.

Uncovering the Sixties: The Life and Times of the Underground Press, by Abe Peck, Citadel Press, New York, 1991.

CHAPTER 9: THE SAN FRANCISCO HIPPIE MOVEMENT
through
CHAPTER 12: BREAKING UP WITH BIG BROTHER

Primary contributors: Fred Catero, Nancy Getz, Sharry Gomez, Jay Good, Bruce Harah-Konforth, Chet Helms, Richard Hundgen, Julius Karpen, Joe McDonald, "Bear" Owsley, D. A. Pennebaker, Dan Weiner, Baron Wolman.

★

LAURA JOPLIN

CHAPTER 13: THE BAND FROM BEYOND
Sam Andrew, John Cooke, Cornelius "Snooky" Flowers, Linda Gravenites, Nick Gravenites, Bobby Neuwirth, John Till.

CHAPTER 14: REST, ROMANCE, AND REGROUP
THROUGH CHAPTER 15: FULL TILT TRIUMPH
Sam Andrew, Ben Beall, Peggy Caserta, Dr. Henry Chu, John Cooke, Bennett Glotzer, Linda Gravenites, Nick Gravenites, James Gurley, Michael McClure, Sam Monroe, Seth Morgan, Bobby Neuwirth, Pat Nichols, David Niehaus, Tary Owens, Clark Pierson, Jimmy Pryor, Paul Rothchild, Dr. Ed Rothschild, Glenda South, John and Dorcas Till.

CHAPTER 16: THE MEMORIAL CELEBRATION
The Frenzy of Renown: Fame and Its History, Oxford University Press, New York, 1986.
Intimate Strangers: The Culture of Celebrity, by Richard Schickel, Doubleday, Garden City, N.Y., 1985.
Several articles in the *Port Arthur News* in 1987 and 1988.

PERMISSION
ACKNOWLEDGMENTS

★

Grateful acknowledgment is made to the following for permission to reprint previously published material:

AUSTIN AMERICAN-STATESMAN: Excerpts from Jim Langdon's 1965 "Nightbeat" column.

CHEAP THRILLS MUSIC: Excerpts from the lyrics of the following songs: "Catch Me, Daddy" by Janis Joplin; "Turtle Blues" by Janis Joplin; "Last Time" by Janis Joplin; "Magic of Love" by Mark Spoelstra; "Down On Me," arranged by Janis Joplin; "Caterpillar" by Peter Albin; "Blindman" by Peter Albin. All lyrics © Cheap Thrills Music. All rights reserved. Used by permission.

FOLKWAYS MUSIC PUBLISHERS, INC.: Excerpt from the lyrics of "Bourgeois Blues," words and music by Huddie Ledbetter, edited with new additional material by Alan Lomax. TRO—Copyright © 1959 (renewed) Folkways Music Publishers, Inc., New York, NY. Used by permission.

MAINSPRING WATCHWORKS MUSIC: Excerpts from "Bye Bye Baby" by Powell St. John. Copyright © Mainspring Watchworks Music, ASCAP, R. P. St. John, Jr. All rights reserved. Used by permission.

STRONG ARM MUSIC: Excerpts from the lyrics of "What Good Can Drinking Do?" by Janis Joplin; "Move Over" by Janis Joplin; "No Reason for Livin' " by Janis Joplin; "Come Away with Me" by Janis Joplin; "Mercedes Benz" by Janis Joplin; "One Good Man" by Janis Joplin. © Strong Arm Music. Used by permission. All rights reserved.

STRONG ARM MUSIC AND MCA MUSIC PUBLISHING: Excerpt from the lyrics of "Kozmic Blues," words and music by Janis Joplin and Gabriel Mekler. Copyright © 1969 by Strong Arm Music and MCA Music Publishing, a division of MCA Inc. Used by permission. All rights reserved.

WARNER/CHAPPELL MUSIC, INC.: Excerpts from the lyrics of "Work Me, Lord" by Nick Gravenites. © 1969 Fourth Floor Music, Inc. All rights administered by WB Music Corp.; "Try" by Jerry Ragovoy and Chip Taylor. © 1968 Unichappell Music Inc.; "Piece of My Heart" by Bert Berns and Jerry Ragovoy. © 1967 Unichappell Music Inc. and WEB IV Music Inc. All rights reserved. Used by permission.

★

INDEX

★

Adams, Don, 236
Adkins, Lieuen, 94, 111-12
Adler, Lou, 195
Albin, Cindy, 159-61
Albin, Lisa, 159-61
Albin, Peter, 119, 147-48, 159-61, 164,
    166, 169, 176-77, 184, 187, 190,
    201, 205, 220, 236, 247
Alexander, George, 85
Alexander, Stan, 110
Allen, Mike, 140
Allen, Steve, 54
Andrew, Sam, 119, 147, 159, 172, 185,
    195, 201, 223, 225, 228-29, 233,
    236-37, 246-47, 249, 251-55, 257-59,
    281, 289, 311
Animals, 202

Baez, Joan, 101
Bailey, G. W., 78
Bailey, Pearl, 221-22
Baker, Maury, 255
Ball, William, 12
Band, the, 287
Beall, Ben, 271
Beatles, 192, 194, 211, 238, 252, 270
Behan, Brendan, 219
Bell, Richard, 276
Belz, Carl, 153, 279
Bennett, Karleen, 40-43, 49-50, 52-53,
    56-57, 60, 62-69, 71, 75, 134, 191,
    245, 270, 297
Berg, Beatrice, 229
Big Bopper (Jay P. Richardson), 55, 62,
    319
Big Brother and the Holding Company,
    6, 142, 146-49, 152-97, 201-14,
    217-44, 246-47, 249, 251, 258, 279,
    281, 283-84, 286, 289, 326
Big Daddy (Harry Hilmuth Pastor),
    83-84

Bill Haley and the Comets, 55
Bland, Bobby "Blue," 62
Bloomfield, Michael, 207, 243, 289
Bonaparte, Berkeley, 191
Bowen, Kristen, 49, 70, 301
Brand, Stewart, 151-52
Braque, Georges, 75
Braudy, Leo, 234, 314
Bray, Clarence, 301
Brewer and Shipley, 308
Brown, Clarence "Gatemouth," 85, 319
Brown, Joe E., 93, 121-22
Brown, Pat, 123
Brown, Sidneh Rosine, 13
Brubeck, Dave, 61
Bruce, Lenny, 187
Bukowski, Charles, 81
Butterfield, Paul, 207, 290

Caen, Herb, 210-11
Campbell, Brad, 246, 255, 276-77
Canned Heat, 161
Captain Beefheart & His Magic Band,
    146
Carr, Paul, 262-63
Carter, Phillip, 67, 75, 77-78, 85
Casals, Pablo, 321
Caserta, Peggy, 155, 274, 307
Castille, Lonnie, 255
Catero, Fred, 224, 228
Cato, Bob, 228
Cavallon, Carol, 223
Cavett, Dick, 255-56, 286, 289-90,
    294-97
Chamberlain, Richard, 186
Chantels, 250
Charlatans, 173
Cher, 146
Cherry, Keith, 246
Chocolate George, 6
Chopin, Frédéric, 27

★

Christie, Julie, 186
Ciccone, Stanley, 186
Clark, Bob, 88
Clark, Doug, 321-22
Clark, Guy, 139
Clark, Malcolm, 317-18
Clark, Tom, 118
Clay, John, 91, 94, 99, 109, 112
Clements, Terry, 246-47, 255
Cohen, Allen, 155
Coleman, Ornette, 147
Colon, Jeanne, 210
Coltrane, John, 147
Cooke, John, 7, 179, 209-10, 218, 220, 247, 251, 255, 261-62, 266, 277, 279-80, 283, 285-87, 290, 295, 299, 302, 304, 309-10, 312, 319
Country Joe and the Fish, 186-87, 193
Crumb, R., 228, 230

Dalí, Salvador, 250
Dameron, Allan, 140
Davidson, John, 231
Davis, Adelle, 151
Davis, Clive, 197, 218-19, 235, 244, 266, 291-92
Davis, Judy, 190
Delaney and Bonnie, 287
Denson, Ed, 171-72
Dirty Shames, 176
Donovan, 256
Doors, 290
Doubleday, Marcus, 255
Du Bois, W. E. B., 17
Duckett, Leonard, 213
Dylan, Bob, 103-4, 124, 158, 193, 207, 224, 256

East, Cecil (grandfather), 18-19, 23-24
East, Donna (cousin), 80, 174, 181, 183
East, Harry (uncle), 80
East, Laura Hanson (grandmother), 18-19, 23-26, 57-58
East, Mimi (aunt), 25-26, 79-80, 84, 181, 183, 250
East, Ulysses Sampson Grant, 16
Eden, Barbara, 236
Eisenhower, Dwight D., 55-56
Elliott, Cass, 195-96, 220, 256
Elster, Arlene, 49-50, 66, 191

Elwood, Philip, 190-91, 195
Erb, Lyndall, 6-7, 281, 307

Fairbanks, Douglas, Jr., 290
Faubus, Orval, 55-56
Ferlinghetti, Lawrence, 59-60, 83-84, 116-17, 182
Fisher, John, 299, 302-3
Fitzgerald, F. Scott, 64, 289-90, 315
Fitzgerald, Zelda, 289
Flatt & Scruggs, 101
Fleming, George, 13
Flowers, Cornelius "Snooky," 249, 253, 255, 258-59, 262, 276-77
Fonda, Peter, 256
Franklin, Aretha, 218, 243
Franklin, Erma, 218
Fredeman, Mary Carmen, 71
Freewheeling McClure Montana, 311
Friedman, Myra, 110, 122, 217-18, 220, 253, 265
Frosch, William, 200
Full Tilt Boogie Band, 275, 279-81, 283-93, 295, 305

Gasca, Luis, 255
Gates, John "Bet-a-Million," 25
Gauthier, Dale, 68
Getz, Dave, 147-48, 159-60, 180, 195, 205, 228, 231, 233, 236, 239-40, 247
Giarratano, Bernard, 134-35, 164
Gibb, Barry, 250
Gibb, Robin, 250
Gillespie, Dizzy, 184
Ginsberg, Allen, 60, 83, 116, 118, 121, 150, 184, 191
Gladstones, 154
Gleason, Ralph, 194-95, 205, 262
Glotzer, Bennett, 231, 233, 253, 283-84, 293, 308
Gomez, Sharrie, 186
Gordon, Robert, 4-7, 190, 197, 266, 304-5, 310, 312
Gordon, Sam, 208
Graham, Bill, 156, 206, 228
Grass Roots, 149, 157
Grateful Dead, 6, 149, 152, 156, 159, 170, 173, 183-84, 260, 287
Gravenites, Linda, 185-87, 191, 201, 209, 214, 219, 226-27, 232-35, 237,

249, 251–52, 262, 265, 268–71, 278, 281, 293, 307
Gravenites, Nick, 115, 124, 145, 163, 185–86, 236, 243, 246, 269, 278, 282, 284, 308
Grogan, Emmett, 311–12
Grossman, Albert, 196, 206–10, 220, 223, 231, 233, 235–36, 244, 246, 253, 257, 263, 272, 276–77, 283–84, 293, 308
Grossman, Stefan, 161
Gurley, James, 118–19, 147–48, 155, 159–61, 163, 189, 201, 203, 224–25, 232–33, 247, 252, 289
Gurley, Nancy, 147, 155, 159–61, 177, 186, 252
Gustaitis, Rasa, 232, 234
Guthrie, Woody, 61, 85
Guy, Buddy, 287

Hanks, Larry, 119
Hanson, Henry W., 16
Hanson, Herbert, 16–17
Hanson, John Milton, 14–15
Hanson, Lauretta, 14–15
Hanson, Stella Mae Sherman, 17
Harrison, George, 192, 252, 256
Harry, Debbie, 250
Hart, Lorenz, 250
Haston, Adrian, 46, 53, 59, 61, 74–75, 78–79, 88, 134, 212, 244
Haston, Gloria Lloreda, 74, 76, 78–79, 121, 135, 139, 212, 244
Havens, Richie, 207
Hawkins, Ronnie, 276
Heinlein, Robert, 151
Helmer, Bill, 104, 113
Helms, Chet, 113, 115, 117, 120, 142, 145–49, 156, 158, 166–67, 204
Hensley, Terry, 246
Hentoff, Nat, 221, 223–26
Hoar, Shadrach, 13
Hoar, William, 14
Hofmann, Albert, 150
Holiday, Billie, 125–26, 233
Hollister, Leo, 150
Holly, Buddy, 55, 319
Holtzman, Scott, 196
Hopkins, Lightnin', 147
Hore, Hezekiah, 11–12
Howe, Neil, 19–20

Hunter, Ivory Joe, 319
Huxley, Aldous, 150–51

Ian and Sylvia, 287
Irwin, Barbara (aunt), 4, 79–81, 83–84, 174, 176–77, 181–83, 202–3, 227, 261, 265
Irwin, Jean (cousin), 80–81, 181, 202–3
Iverson, Roger, 53

Jackson, Jack, 99, 230
Jackson, Teodar, 140
Jahn, Mike, 219–20
James, Harry, 319
Jefferson Airplane, 149, 157, 183–84, 214
Jerry LeCroix and the Counts, 65
John, Elton, 293
Jones, George, 319
Jones, James, 60
"Jones, Tom," 128–29, 259
Jones, Tom (singer), 259
Joplin, Charles Alexander, 17
Joplin, Dorothy East (mother), 4–5, 8, 19, 21–29, 32–42, 47–48, 54, 57–58, 61–63, 66–70, 72, 77, 86, 91–92, 132–34, 138–39, 142–43, 196, 203, 239–41, 250, 298, 302–4, 313, 315, 321, 323
Joplin, Florence Porter (grandmother), 17–18, 23
Joplin, Laura Lee (sister), 3–9, 27, 30–39, 42–43, 63, 66, 86, 92, 94, 122–23, 132–33, 136, 143, 158–59, 176, 183, 203–5, 212, 227, 240–41, 244–45, 250, 258–59, 295–304, 313, 315–24, 326–28
Joplin, Michael Ross (brother), 4, 8–9, 27, 31, 36, 42, 63, 66, 86–87, 133, 139, 158, 176, 183, 203–4, 212, 214–15, 227, 231, 238, 240–41, 244, 268, 303–4, 313, 315–16, 320, 322, 326–27
Joplin, Seeb Winston (grandfather), 17–18, 22–23
Joplin, Seth Ward (father), 4–5, 8, 18, 22–36, 38–42, 51, 56–58, 61–63, 66–70, 72, 86, 91–92, 123, 125, 132–33, 136, 163–64, 183, 203, 227, 240–41, 270, 277, 298, 302–4, 321, 323

★

Jopling, Benjamin, 14
Jopling, Thomas, 12–13

Kaprow, Alan, 153
Karpen, Julius, 187, 190, 195–97, 205–6, 220
Kenai, 117–18, 127
Kennedy, John F., 120
Kermode, Richard, 246, 255
Kerouac, Jack, 52, 54, 56, 61, 64, 116, 118, 124, 127
Kesey, Ken, 150–52, 184, 211
Killarney, Jim, 175
Killeen, Bill, 107–9, 112, 285
King, B. B., 205, 217, 225
King, Bill, 255
King, Martin Luther, Jr., 225
Kingston Trio, 103
Kinney, Albert, 81
Kirkland, Karen Kay, 108–9
Klein, Ted, 97, 100, 109
Knoll, Linda, 122
Koerner, Ray and Glover, 290
Kozmic Blues Band, 243–44, 246–55, 258, 261–63, 266, 272, 276–77, 279, 290–91
Krainis Consort, 219
Kristofferson, Kris, 239, 266, 281–83, 286, 288–89
Kunkin, Art, 154–55

Langdon, Jim, 46–47, 53, 55, 57, 59, 61–62, 65, 68, 74–76, 78–79, 84–89, 92, 120, 137–43, 159, 196, 245, 322
Langdon, Rae Logan, 78–79, 89, 121, 139, 245
Law, Lisa, 308
Lawrence, D. H., 60
Leadbelly (Huddie Ledbetter), 61, 91, 97, 138
Leary, Timothy, 121, 150–51, 184, 211, 318
Leaves, 149
Lewis, Jerry Lee, 54, 301–2
Lipscomb, Mance, 140
Lipton, Lawrence, 81–82
Lolita, 100–101
Love, 149
Lovin' Spoonful, 157
Lyons, Grant, 45–46, 53, 61, 79, 87–88

McCartney, Paul, 192, 195, 203
McClure, Michael, 117, 199, 306, 311–12
McDonald, Country Joe, 186–87, 193
McGowsky, George, 163
MacPhee, Chester, 116
McQueen, Dave, 75, 78, 85, 87–89, 134, 139, 240
McQueen, Patti Mock, 75–78, 85, 87–88, 134, 136, 139–40, 240
Malone, Bill, 102
Mamas and the Papas, 195
Mann, Steve, 119
Manson, Charles, 260
Marinello, Frank, 195
Markowitz, Roy, 246, 255
May, Roy, 62
Mazer, Elliot, 223–24, 228, 235–36, 244
Mekler, Gabriel, 73, 254, 290
Miles, Barry, 121
Miles, Buddy, 207
Miller, Henry, 82, 143
Miller, Stanley "Mouse," 148, 160, 175, 183
Modigliani, Amedeo, 75
Monroe, Sam, 297, 301, 313, 317
Morgan, Seth, 7, 304–10
Moriaty, Dave, 46, 53, 59, 61, 79, 88, 110–11, 142, 229–30, 260, 293, 318
Morrison, Jim, 231
Morthland, John, 257
Moyer, Johnny, 110–11
Muldaur, Maria, 101

Nash, Graham, 256
Nelson, Paul, 246, 248
Neuwirth, Bobby, 179, 199, 223, 231–33, 250–51, 253, 279, 281–83, 289, 299, 302–3, 306, 312
Nichols, Pat "Sunshine," 126–27, 170, 177, 179, 235, 242, 253, 257, 265, 280, 293, 308, 311
Nicholson, Jack, 293
Niehaus, David, 271–75, 278, 282, 304
Nixon, Richard M., 269
Normand, Hal, 94
Nudie, 286

Odetta, 61–62, 135, 207, 282
O'Donohue, Steve, 62
Oldenburg, Claes, 153

Outfit, 173
Owens, Tary, 59, 67, 75, 96, 99, 110-11, 140, 159, 191, 298

Paine, Thomas, 14
Palmer, John, 313-14, 321-22
Pasea, Elton, 67
Paul, Juli, 109-11, 239, 288, 311
Paul Butterfield Blues Band, 290
Paulsen, Pat, 256
Pearson, Ken, 276, 309
Peck, Abe, 154-55, 230
Pennebaker, D. A., 224
Perkins, Roger, 119
Perkoff, Stu, 81-82
Perry, Charles, 260
Peter, Paul and Mary, 120, 207-8
Phillips, John, 195
P.H. Phactor Jugband, 173
Picasso, Pablo, 75
Pierson, Clark, 277, 284
Pollard, Michael J., 227
Polte, Ron, 187
Porter, Beverly, 15
Porter, John W., 12-13, 15
Porter, Robert Ury, 15-17
Pound, Ezra, 125
Pratt, Wynn, 108, 110-11
Presley, Elvis, 55, 318
Pryor, Bodie, 317
Pryor, Jimmy, 212, 231, 303
Pryor, Roger, 30, 36-37, 70-71

Quicksilver Messenger Service, 149, 154, 173, 183-84, 187

Ragovoy, Jerry, 243, 282, 308
Rainey, Ma, 171
Ray Solis group, 85
Redding, Otis, 259
Rexroth, Kenneth, 82, 116-17
Richards, Dave, 241
Ritchie, Jean, 61
Ritter, Tex, 319
Rivers, Larry, 250
Rivers, Travis, 110-11, 142, 145-46
Robert, John, 62
Roberts, Billy, 119
Robinson, Smokey, 195
Robyn, Dorothy, 40

Rodgers, Jimmie, 102
Rodgers, Richard, 250
Roky and the 13th Floor Elevators, 140
Rolling Stones, 202, 222, 260
Rooney, Paul, 49-50
Rothchild, Paul, 161-63, 166, 172, 223, 231, 290-92, 306-12
Rothschild, Edmund, 263-64
Rubinstein, Arthur, 27

St. John, Powell, Jr., 45, 96, 98-100, 107, 112, 140
Schickel, Richard, 314
Sedgwick, Edie, 250
Shad, Bob, 166-67, 171, 176, 218
Sharpe, Pat, 97-99
Shaw, Robert, 140-41
Shelton, Gilbert, 93, 101, 105, 108-9, 111-12, 121-22, 230
Shelton, Robert, 218
Sherman, Jacob, 14
Sherman, Phillip, 12-13
Shirley & Lee, 171
Sigmund and the Freudian Slips, 176
Simmons, Jimmy, 84
Simon, John, 223, 228
Simon, Paul, 195
Slick, Grace, 214, 220
Smith, Bessie, 77, 125-26, 135, 171, 174
Smith, Jack, 41-43, 56, 59, 67, 75, 78, 84, 86, 88-89, 91, 105-7, 135, 137
"Smith, John," 127-29, 132-34, 138-39, 146, 165, 193
Smothers, Tommy, 256
Somma, Robert, 263
South, Glenda, 297, 301
Spanky, 220
Spillane, Mickey, 60
Spock, Benjamin, 29
Spoelstra, Mark, 313
Stanley Brothers, 101
Stills, Stephen, 256
Stilwell, Arthur, 24-25
Stopher, Tommy, 75, 99, 112
Stopher, Wally, 75, 93, 110-11
Strauss, William, 19-20
Sullivan, Ed, 250
Sweet William, 284
Swinging Saints, 176

★

Taj Mahal, 161
Tate, Sharon, 260
Taylor, Chip, 243
Teele, Kit, 146
Teele, Margo, 146
Tennant, Randy, 46, 53, 79, 88
13th Floor Elevators, 140
Thomas, Dylan, 219
Thomas, Michael, 6
Thompson, Ken, 280
Thornton, Big Mama, 217
Thornton, Willie Mae, 61-62
Threadgill, Kenneth, 101-4, 111, 140, 239, 273, 288-89, 301
Till, John, 255, 276, 288, 308
Tiny Tim, 250
Todd, Fred, 230
Tolkien, J. R. R., 159
Tork, Peter, 214
Torn, Rip, 250, 311-12
Trocchi, Alexander, 81
Turner, Lana, 53
Tuttle, Lyle, 7, 282, 304

Uris, Leon, 60

Valens, Ritchie, 319
van Gogh, Vincent, 60, 75
Vickers, Miss, 56
Virginia Woolves, 176

Wade, Clyde, 68
Walker, T-Bone, 205
Wallace, Mike, 246
Waller Creek Boys, 98, 100-101
Warhol, Andy, 250, 262
Washington, George, 12
Waters, Muddy, 274
Watts, Alan, 151
Wauldron, Linda Gottfried, 119, 121-22, 124-26, 128-29, 133, 141, 146, 169, 174, 189, 235, 238
Wauldron, Malcolm, 129, 174, 238
Wauldron, Sabrina, 174, 235, 238
Wein, George, 208
Wells, Glen, 319
Whyte, William, 116
Wiggins, Lanny, 98-100
Wilde, Oscar, 191, 244
Williams, Andy, 256
Williams, Mason, 256
Williams, Roger, 12
Wilson, Al, 161
Wilson, Sloan, 116
Winchester, Jesse, 276
Winter, Edgar, 85, 319
Winter, Johnny, 85, 319
Wolfe, Tom, 254
Woodward, Dave, 255

ZZ Top, 319

ABOUT THE AUTHOR

★

LAURA JOPLIN was born six years after her sister, Janis, in Port Arthur, Texas. She has a Ph.D. in higher education and has established and conducted several motivational programs and workshops. She is currently developing a play about Janis's life and a CD boxed set of her sister's music for Sony. She lives in Denver.

A retrospective compilation of Janis Joplin's recorded music will be available soon in a three-CD/three-cassette boxed set from Columbia/Legacy (C3K/C3T 48845).